Energy Security

Energy Security

Dharmendra Kumar

RANDOM PUBLICATIONS
NEW DELHI (INDIA)

Energy Security

ISBN 978-93-5111-635-6

Published in 2015 in India by

RANDOM PUBLICATIONS

4376-A/4B, Gali Murari Lal, Ansari Road
New Delhi-110 002
Phone : +9111-43580356, 011-23289044, 011-43142548
e-mail: sales@randompublications.com,
info@randompublications.com, randomexports@gmail.com

Reprinted 2025

Type Setting by : Friends Media, Delhi-110089
Digitally Printed at : Replika Press Pvt. Ltd.

Preface

Energy is fundamental to the economic development of a society. Ensuring energy security is critical to the security, sovereignty, and well being of any country.

Everyone needs energy in different forms to bad life luxuriously. The existing energy sources, except, some forms of renewable energy, may not last for a long time. Energy security, hence, has become a part of all human activities.

The modern world relies on a vast energy supply to fuel everything from transportation to communication, to security and health delivery systems. Perhaps most alarmingly,peak oil expert Mike Ruppert has claimed that for every calorie of food produced in the industrial world, ten calories of oil and gas energy are invested in the forms of fertilizer, pesticide, packaging, transportation, and running farm equipment. Energy plays an important role in the national security of any given country as a fuel to power the economic engine. Some sectors rely on energy more heavily than others; for example, the Department of Defense relies on petroleum for approximately 77% of its energy needs.Threats to energy security include the political instability of several energy producing countries, the manipulation of energy supplies, the competition over energy sources, attacks on supply infrastructure, as well as accidents, natural disasters, terrorism, and reliance on foreign countries for oil.

The IEA defines energy security as "the uninterrupted availability of energy sources at an affordable price". Energy security has many dimensions: long-term energy security mainly deals with timely investments to supply energy in line with economic developments and sustainable environmental needs. Short-term energy security focuses on the ability of the energy system to react promptly to sudden changes within the supply-demand balance. Lack of energy security is thus linked to the negative economic and social impacts of either physical unavailability of energy, or prices that are not competitive or are overly volatile.

This book would be an indispensable source of knowledge on the issue of energy security and extremely helpful for policy makers academicians as well as researchers.

I would like to thank my team for standing beside me throughout my career and writing this book. My special thanks go to "Random Publications" who have published the book.

– Dharmendra Kumar

Contents

1

Introduction to Energy Security

ENERGY SECURITY

Energy security is the association between national security and the availability of natural resources for energy consumption. Access to cheap energy has become essential to the functioning of modern economies. However. the uneven distribution of energy supplies among countries has led to significant vulnerabilities.

Renewable energy resources and significant opportunities for energy efficiency exist over wide geographical areas. in contrast to other energy sources. which are concentrated in a limited number of countries. Rapid deployment of renewable energy and energy efficiency. and technological diversification of energy sources. would result in significant energy security and economic benefits.

ENERGY SECURITY THREATS

The modern world relies on a vast energy supply to fuel everything from transportation to communication. to security and health delivery systems. Perhaps most alarmingly.peak oil expert Mike Ruppert has claimed that for every calorie of food produced in the industrial world. ten calories of oil and gas energy are invested in the forms of fertilizer. pesticide. packaging. transportation. and running farm equipment. Energy plays an important role in the national security of any given country as a fuel to power the economic engine. Some sectors rely on energy more heavily than others; for example. the Department of Defence relies on petroleum for approximately 77% of its energy needs.Threats to energy security include the political instability of several energy producing countries. the manipulation of energy supplies. the competition over energy sources. attacks on supply infrastructure. as well as accidents. natural disasters. terrorism. and reliance on foreign countries for oil.

Foreign oil supplies are vulnerable to unnatural disruptions from in-state conflict. exporters' interests. and non-state actors targeting the supply and transportation of oil resources. The political and economic instability caused by war or other factors such as strike action can also prevent the proper functioning of the energy industry in a supplier country. For example. the nationalization of oil in Venezuela has triggered strikes and protests in which Venezuela's oil production rates have yet to recover. Exporters may have political or economic incentive to limit their foreign sales or cause disruptions in the supply chain. Since Venezuela's nationalization of oil. anti-American Hugo Chávezthreatened to cut off supplies to the United States more than once. The 1973 oil embargo against the United States is a historical example in which oil supplies were cut off to the United States due to U.S. support of Israel during the Yom Kippur War. This has been done to apply pressure during economic negotiations—such as during the Russia-Belarus energy dispute. Terrorist attacks targeting oil facilities. pipelines. tankers. refineries. and oil fields are so common they are referred to as "industry risks". Infrastructure for producing the resource is extremely vulnerable to sabotage. One of the worst risks to oil transportation is the exposure of the five ocean chokepoints. like the Iranian-controlled Strait of Hormuz. Anthony H. Cordesman. a scholar at the Centre for Strategic and International Studies in Washington. D.C.. warns. "It may take only one asymmetric or conventional attack on a Ghawar Saudi oil field or tankers in the Strait of Hormuz to throw the market into a spiral."

New threats to energy security have emerged in the form of the increased world competition for energy resources due to the increased pace of industrialization in countries such as India and China. Although still a minority concern. the possibility of price rises resulting from the peaking of world oil production is also starting to attract the attention of at least the French government. Increased competition over energy resources may also lead to the formation of security compacts to enable an equitable distribution of oil and gas between major powers. However. this may happen at the expense of less developed economies. The Group of Five. precursors to the G8. first met in 1975 to coordinate economic and energy policies in the wake of the 1973 Arab oil embargo. a rise in inflation and a global economic slowdown. NATO leaders meeting in Bucharest. Romania. in April 2008 may discuss the possibility of using the military alliance "as an instrument of energy security". One of the possibilities include placing troops in the Caucasus region to police oil and gas pipelines.

LONG-TERM SECURITY

Long-term measures to increase energy security centre on reducing dependence on any one source of imported energy. increasing the number of suppliers. exploiting nativefossil fuel or renewable energy resources. and reducing overall demand through energy conservation measures. It can also involve entering into international agreements to underpin international energy trading relationships. such as the Energy Charter Treaty in Europe. All the concern coming from security threats on oil sources long term security measures will help reduce the future cost of importing and exporting fuel into and out of countries without having to worry about harm coming to the goods being transported.The impact of the 1973 oil crisis and the emergence of the OPEC cartel was a particular milestone that prompted some countries to increase their energy security. Japan. almost totally dependent on imported oil. steadily introduced the use of natural gas. nuclear power. high-speed mass transit systems. and implemented energy conservationmeasures. The United Kingdom began exploiting North Sea oil and gas reserves. and became a net exporter of energy into the 2000s.In other countries energy security has historically been a lower priority. The United States. for example. has continued to increase its dependency on imported oil although. following the oil price increases since 2003. the development of biofuels has been suggested as a means of addressing this.

Increasing energy security is also one of the reasons behind a block on the development of natural gas imports in Sweden. Greater investment in native renewable energy technologies and energy conservation is envisaged instead. India is carrying out a major hunt for domestic oil to decrease its dependency on OPEC. while Iceland is well advanced in its plans to become energy independent by 2050 through deploying 100% renewable energy.

SHORT-TERM SECURITY

Petroleum

Petroleum or otherwise known as "crude oil" has become the resource most used by countries all around the world including Russia. China and the United States of America. With all the oil wells located around the world energy security has become a main issue to ensure the safety of the petroleum that is being harvested. In the middle east oil fields become main targets for sabotage because of how heavily countries rely on oil. Many countries hold strategic petroleum reserves as a buffer against the economic and political impacts of an energy crisis. All 28 members of the International Energy Agency hold a minimum of 90 days of their oil imports. for example.The value of such reserves was demonstrated by the relative lack of disruption caused by the 2007 Russia-Belarus energy dispute. when Russia indirectly cut exports to several countries in the European Union. Due to the theories in peak oil and need to curb demand. the United States military and Department of Defence had made significant cuts. and have been making a number of attempts to come up with more efficient ways to use oil.

Natural gas

Compared to petroleum. reliance on imported natural gas creates significant short-term vulnerabilities. Many European countries saw an immediate drop in supply when Russian gas supplies were halted during the Russia-Ukraine gas dispute in 2006. Natural gas has been a viable source of energy in the world. Consisting of mostly methane. natural gas is produced using two methods: biogenic and thermogenic. Biogenic gas comes from methanogenic organisms located in marshes and landfills. whereas thermogenic gas comes from the anaerobic decay of organic matter deep under the Earth's surface. Russia is the current leading country in production of natural gas.

One of the biggest problems currently facing natural gas providers is the ability to store and transport it. With its low density. it is difficult to build enough pipelines in North America to transport sufficient natural gas to match demand. These pipelines are reaching near capacity and even at full capacity do not produce the amount of gas needed.

Nuclear power

Uranium for nuclear power is mined and enriched in diverse and "stable" countries. These include Canada (23% of the world's total in 2007). Australia (21%). Kazakhstan (16%) and more than 10 other countries. Uranium is mined and fuel is manufactured significantly in advance of need. Nuclear fuel is considered by some to be a relatively reliable power source. being more common in the Earth's crust than tin. mercury or silver. though a debate over the timing of peak uranium does exist.

Nuclear power reduces carbon emissions. Although a very viable resource. nuclear power can be a controversial solution because of the dangers associated with it. Another big factor in the debate with nuclear power is that many people or companies simply do not want any nuclear energy plant or radioactive waste near them.

Currently. nuclear power provides 13% of the world's total electricity. The most notable use of nuclear power within the United States is in U.S. Navy aircraft carriers. cruisers. and submarines. which have been exclusively nuclear-powered for several decades. These classes of ship provide the core of the Navy's power. and as such are the single most noteworthy application of nuclear power in that country.

Renewable energy

The deployment of renewable technologies usually increases the diversity of electricity sources and. through local generation. contributes to the flexibility of the system and its resistance to central shocks. For those countries where growing dependence on imported gas is a significant energy security issue. renewable technologies can provide alternative sources of electric power as well as displacing electricity demand through direct heat production. Renewable biofuels for transport represent a key source of diversification from petroleum products. As the resources that have been so crucial to survival in the world to this day start declining in numbers. countries will begin to realize that the need for renewable fuel sources will be as vital as ever. With the production of new types of energy. including solar. geothermal. hydro-electric. biofuel and wind power. With the amount of sun that hits the world in one hour there is enough energy to power the world for one year. With the addition of solar panels all around the world a little less pressure is taken off the need to produce more oil.

Geothermal can potentially lead to other sources of fuel. if companies would take the heat from the inner core of the earth to heat up water sources we could essentially use the steam creating from the heated water to power machines. this option is one of the cleanest and efficient options. Hydro-electric which has been incorporated into many of the dams around the world produces a lot of energy and is very easy to produce the energy as the dams control the water that is allowed through seams which power turbines located inside of the dam. Biofuels have been researched using many different sources including ethanol and algae. these options are substantially cleaner than the consumption of petroleum. "Most LCA results for perennial and ligno-cellulosic crops conclude that biofuels can supplement anthropogenic energy demands and mitigate GHG emissions to the atmosphere".

WHAT IS ENERGY SECURITY?

The IEA defines energy security as "the uninterrupted availability of energy sources at an affordable price". Energy security has many dimensions: long-term energy security mainly deals with timely investments to supply energy in line with economic developments and sustainable environmental needs. Short-term energy security focuses on the ability of the energy system to react promptly to sudden changes within the supply-demand balance. Lack of energy security is thus linked to the negative economic and social impacts of either physical unavailability of energy. or prices that are not competitive or are overly volatile.

In cases such as the international oil market. where prices are allowed to adjust in response to changes in supply and demand. the risk of physical unavailability is limited to extreme events. Supply security concerns are primarily related to the economic damage caused by extreme price spikes. The concern for physical unavailability of supply is more prevalent in energy markets where transmission systems must be kept in constant balance. such as electricity and. to some extent. natural gas. This is particularly the case in instances where there are capacity constraints or where prices are not able to work as an adjustment mechanism to balance supply and demand in the short term. Ensuring energy security has been at the centre of the mission of the IEA since its inception.

The ability to respond collectively in the case of a serious oil supply disruption with short-term emergency response measures remains one of the core activities of the IEA. The long-term aspect of energy security was also included in the Agency's founding objectives. which called for promoting alternative energy sources in order to reduce oil import dependency. The IEA continues to work to improve energy security over the longer term by promoting energy policies that encourage diversification. both of energy types and supply sources. and that facilitate better functioning and more integrated energy markets.

QUANTIFYING ENERGY SECURITY

Historically. energy security was primarily associated with oil supply. Whilst oil supply remains a key issue. the increasing complexity of energy systems requires systematic and rigorous understanding of a wider range of vulnerabilities. Disruptions can affect other fuel sources. infrastructure or end-use sectors. Thus. analysis of oil supply security alone is no longer sufficient for understanding a country's energy security situation as a whole.

One of the ways in which the IEA is responding to this challenge is by developing a comprehensive tool to measure energy security. The IEA Model of Short-term Energy Security (MOSES) examines both risks and resilience factors associated with short-term physical disruptions of energy supply that can last for days or weeks. MOSES extends beyond oil to monitor and analyse several important energy sources. as well as the non-energy components (such as infrastructure) that comprise an energy system. Analysis of vulnerability for fossil fuel disruptions. for example. is based on risk factors such as net-import dependence and the political stability of suppliers. Resilience factors include the number of entry points for a country (*e.g.* ports and pipelines). the level of stocks and the diversity of suppliers.

ENERGY SECURITY OF THE PEOPLE'S REPUBLIC OF CHINA

Energy security of the People's Republic of China concerns the need for the People's Republic of China to guarantee itself and its industries long- term access to sufficient energy and raw materials. China has been endeavoring to sign international agreements and secure such supplies; its energy security involves the internal and foreign energy policy of China. Currently. China's energy portfolio consists mainly of domestic coal. oil and gas from domestic and foreign sources. and small quantities of uranium. China has also created a strategic petroleum reserve. to secure emergency supplies of oil for temporary price and supply disruptions. Chinese policy focuses on diversification to reduce oil imports. which rely almost exclusively on producers in the Middle East.

According to Professor Zha. China's dependence on foreign sources of energy is not a threat to China's energy security. since the world energy market is not opposed to China's pursuit of growth and prosperity. The key issue is actually internal: growing internal consumption without energy efficiency threatens both China's growth and world oil markets. Chinese imports are a new determinant encouraging oil price rises on the world market. a concern to developed countries. The international community advocates a move Towards energy efficiency and more transparency in China's quest for energy worldwide. to confirm China's responsibility as a member of the international community. Energy efficiency is the only way to avoid excessive Chinese demands on oil at the expense of industrialized and industrializing countries. International projects and technology transfers are ongoing. improving China's energy consumption and benefit the whole energy-importing world; this will also calm Western-Chinese diplomatic tensions. China is trying to establish long-term energy security by investment in oil and gas fields abroad and by diversifying its providers.

BACKGROUND

Thanks to the transfer of Soviet oil extraction technologies prior to July 1960 and domestic reserves such as the Daqing oil field. the PRC became oil self-sufficient in 1963. A US-led embargo isolated the Chinese oil industry from 1950 to 1970. preventing it from selling on the world oil market. After the embargo was lifted. China reactivated its links with Japan and other industrialized nations thanks to its oil exports. which helped bring in foreign currencies and fund key industrial plants and technologies for developing its own export-oriented economy. Chinese oil exports peaked in 1985 at 30 million tons. Rapid reforms. in turn. increased domestic oil demand and led China to become a net oil importer in 1993. and net crude oil importer in 1996.

Since 1996 Chinese oil production has slowly and continuously decreased. while demand and imports have steadily increased. Future Chinese oil reserves (such as the Tarim basin) are difficult to extract. requiring specific technologies as well as the construction of pipelines thousands of kilometers long. As a result such reserves would be very difficult to develop and not cost-effective. given current market prices.

ISSUES THAT CHINA FACES

China's demand for oil

China accounts for 40% of the 2004 oil-consumption increase. and thus is a key part of the cycle which had led to the oil price increase worldwide. China's import dependence remains at 60% as of 2014. In 2005. a campaign to increase energy efficiency was launched without official Ministry of Energy approval;

since the campaign was sporadic. this objective seems hard to meet. Zha Daojiong encouraged increased management of oil and energy in China. noting that "It is fair to say that the threat from ineffective energy industry governance is probably as great as that from the international energy market.". A projection that China would reach South Korean levels of per-capita oil consumption in 30 years. combined with the current average global decline in production. could mean that up to 44 Mbbl/d (7.000.000 m^3/d) (barrels per day) in production would have to be found in the next decade to keep up with increased demand and production declines. That would be the equivalent of roughly five times Saudi Arabia's production. Superimpose a production plateau of 100 Mbbl/d (16.000.000 m^3/d). and significant real-price increases would be necessary to balance supply and demand. Such increases might have severe effects on the growth of emerging market economies such as China's.

Nuclear and coal

Nuclear power in China accounts for approximately 1.4% of China's electricity. which is considered relatively low compared to other developing nations. China still mainly relies on coal for electricity. China is first in the world in both coal production and consumption. which has sparked environmental concerns. In order to achieve environmental targets in combating pollution and global warming. China must ultimately improve its coal efficiency and switch to alternative energy sources.

Limitations of pipelines and stocks

China's eastern and southern regions have chronic energy shortages. causing blackouts and limiting economic growth. For supplying these regions. liquefied natural gas from Australia and Indonesia is more feasible and cheaper to import than the Tarim basin pipeline.However. the first West–East Gas Pipeline from Xinjiang to Shanghai was commissioned in 2004. and construction of the second pipeline from Xinjiang to Guangzhou in Guangdong began in 2008.

Sinopec accounts for 80% of Chinese oil imports. Refinery capacity is continuously strained. and perennially lags behind fast domestic-demand growth. China has had to rely on entrepôt refineries located in Singapore. Japan and Korea. Oil and gas exploration in the Tarim Basin is ongoing. However. developing this potential reserve is currently not cost-effective due to technological limitations coupled with fluctuations in world oil prices. Therefore. this is considered by some as a last-resort option.

In China. the gas price is not market-driven. which causes uncertainty in the production process.

Energy efficiency

A key point for China's energy-security goal of reducing oil imports is to improve the efficiency of its domestic energy markets by accelerating pricing. regulatory and other reforms. China is actively looking for smart-energy technology.

FOREIGN RELATIONS

Chinese oil imports by region of origin

	1990	2000	2004
Mdl East	39.4%	53.5%	45.4%
Africa	0%	23%	28.7%
Asia Pacific	60.6%	15.1%	11.5%
other	0%	7.2%	14.3%

Middle East

On the issue of energy security. China relies mainly on Persian Gulf exports. In contrast with the USA. China is not associated with the Arab-Israeli conflicts and may focus simply on oil supply from an economic standpoint. The increase in Chinese dependence on Persian Gulf oil also means an associated increasing economic dependence on Arabian exporters. who will probably not join hands to block exports to China.Chinese dependence on the Middle East is also a cause of concern for the US. In 2004. when the Bush administration actively discouraged oil companies from investing in Iran. the Chinese company Sinopec did not comply with its call.

Recently. China has changed its anti-Western diplomatic stance to a softer. global. more efficient diplomacy with a focus on energy and raw-materials security. In post-2003 Iraq. China does its best to comply with UN sanctions.

Japan and Korea

When China became an oil importer during the 1990s. its relations with neighboring countries (as exporter to East Asia and importer of Korean and Japanese oil) changed. Its main oil provider changed in a few years from domestic production. to East Asian production. and then to Mideast production. On the other hand. despite insufficient domestic oil output China does its best to stabilize exports to Japan and Korea. China endeavors to continue energy relationships it has created with developed nations. since they contribute to China's energy security with investment and technology. More Chinese oil output is in Japanese. Korean. Chinese. and world interests. Since China lacks strategic entrepôt refineries. it relies heavily on refineries in Singapore. Japan. and Korea.

Taiwan

China's dependence on foreign oil weakens its ability to pressure Taiwan.

since a conflict may trigger a US oil embargo as a consequence. Since Sudan is pro-Chinese andChad was pro-Taiwan (and an oil producer since 2003). China had an interest in replacing Chad's president Idriss Déby with a pro-Chinese leader. The FUC Chad rebellion. based in Sudan and aiming to overthrow the pro-Taiwanese Déby. seems to have received Chinese diplomatic support as well as weapons and Sudanese oil. The 2006 Chadian coup d'état attempt failed after French Air Force intervention. but Déby then switched his friendship to Beijing; the field defeat became a Chinese strategic victory.

Russia

In February 2009. Russia and China signed an agreement in which a spur of the Eastern Siberia–Pacific Ocean oil pipeline to China would be built and Russia would supply China with 15 million tonnes of oil (300.000 barrels (48.000 m^3) per day) each year for 20 years. in exchange for a loan worth US$25 billion to Russian companies Transneft andRosneft for pipeline and oilfield development.

Australia

On August 19. 2009. Chinese petroleum company PetroChina signed an A$50 billion deal with American multinational petroleum company ExxonMobil to purchase liquefied natural gas from the Gorgon field in Western Australia; this was believed to be the largest contract ever signed between China and America – ensuring China a steady supply of LPG fuel for 20 years. and comprising China's largest supply of relatively clean energy. This agreement has been formalised despite relations between Australia and China being at their lowest point in years following the Rio Tinto espionage case and the granting of a visa to Rebiya Kadeer to visit Australia.

Central Asia

China has constructed an oil pipeline from Kazakhstan and started construction of a Central Asia–China gas pipeline.

Sea lanes

Ratification of the Law of the Sea Treaty is linked to China's need to secure its oil and raw materials shipping from the Middle East. Africa. and Europe. since those materials have to pass through the Strait of Malacca and the Red Sea.

Oil diplomacy

The appearance of China on the world energy scene is somewhat disturbing for developed nations. China's relative energy inexperience also raises diplomatic difficulties. Strengthening ties with oil producers such as Iran. Sudan.

Uzbekistan. Angola and Venezuela also raised concerns for U.S. and other Western diplomacy. since several of these countries are known to be anti-American and/or known for human rights abuses. political censorship. and widespread corruption. These moves seem to challenge Western powers. by strengthening anti-Western countries. But this is unlikely; as a developing consumer economy. China does not have much of a choice in its sources of supply.

Poor communication

It is claimed that Chinese oil companies are unaccustomed to political risks and avoiding diplomatic conflict. In any case. the Chinese government will still be seen as ultimately responsible for conflict resolution. Communication has also been a weak point for Chinese companies. Lack of transparency in cases such as Chinese involvement in Sudan have raised concern in the US. until it was revealed that most of the oil produced was sold on international markets. Lack of cooperation with other major oil companies has led to business clashes. spilling into the diplomatic arena when both sides call their respective governments to support their interests (CNOOC versus Chevron-Texaco forUnocal. for example).

ENERGY IN AFGHANISTAN

Fig. Inside the power station at the Kajaki Dam in the southern Helmand Province of Afghanistan.

Energy in Afghanistan describes energy and electricity production. consumption. import and export in Afghanistan. Energy policy of Afghanistan describes the politics of Afghanistan related to energy more in detail.

Energy in Afghanistan is primarily provided by hydropower. Two decades of warfare have left the country's power grid badly damaged. As of 2012. approximately 33% of Afghan population has access to electricity and in the capital Kabul. 70% have access to reliable 24hr electricity. Afghanistan generates around 600 megawatts (MW) of electricity mainly from hydropower followed by fossil fuel and solar. Officials from Da Afghanistan Breshna Sherkat (DABS) estimate that the country will need around 3.000 MW to meet its needs by 2020. The Afghan National Development Strategy has identified alternative energy. such as wind and solar energy. as a high value power source to develop. Alternative energy projects are already being tested across the country. from wind turbines in Panjshir Province to micro hydro dams in Badakhshan. to family-size biogas digesters throughout the country.

HYDROELECTRICITY

Fig. The Sarobi hydroelectric power plant. built in the 1950s.

Hydroelectric plants were built between the 1950s and the mid-1970s. which included the Sarbobi hydroelectric power plant in Kabul Province. the Naghlu in the eastern Nangarhar Province. the Kajaki in Helmand Province and a number of others. Other hydroelectric facilities that were operational as of 2002 included plants at Puli Khumri. Darunta in Nangarhar Province. Dahla in Kandahar Province. and one in Mazar-i-Sharif. Also in operation was the Breshna-Kot Dam in Nangarhar. which had a generating capacity of 11.5 MW. Construction of two more power stations. with a combined capacity of 600 kW. was planned in Charikar City.

The southern region of Afghanistan is lacking adequate electricity due to problems with the Kajaki power plant in Helmand. which has been destroyed and neglected for many years. A third generating turbine is being added with the assistance of the United States Agency for International Development (USAID). This will add 16.5 MW to its generating capacity and eventually provide the southern Afghan cities of Kandahar and Lashkar Gah with 24-hour electricity once the Kajaki project is completed. A number of other water mega dams are being built in different parts of the country. which are mainly for irrigation purposes. Two new dams are under construction inKunar Province. one of which has the capacity of 1500 MW in Surtak area of the subjected province.

NATURAL GAS AND OIL

Natural gas was Afghanistan's only economically significant export in 1995. going mainly to Uzbekistan via pipeline de marde. Natural gas reserves were once estimated at 140 billion cubic metres. Production started in 1967 with 342 million cu m but had risen to 2.6 billion cubic metres by 1995. In 1991. a new gas field was discovered in Chekhcha.Jowzjan Province. Natural gas was also produced at Sheberghan and Sar-e Pol. As of 2002. other operational gas fields were located at Djarquduk. Khowaja Gogerdak. andYatimtaq. all in Jowzjan Province. In 2002. natural gas production was 1.77 billion cubic feet.

In August 1996. a multinational consortium agreed to construct a 1.430 km pipeline through Afghanistan to carry natural gas from Turkmenistan to Pakistan. at a cost of about $2 billion. However. US air strikes led to cancellation of the project in 1998. and financing of such a project has remained an issue because of high political risk and security concerns. As of 2012. the leaders of four countries had signed an agreement to build the Turkmenistan-Afghanistan-Pakistan-India (TAPI) pipeline.

A very small amount of crude oil is produced at the Angot field in the northern Sar-e Pol Province. Another small oilfield at Zomrad Sai near Sheberghan was reportedly undergoing repairs in mid-2001. Petroleum products such as diesel. gasoline. and jet fuel are imported. mainly from Pakistan and Central Asia nations. A small storage and distribution facility exists in Jalalabad on the highway between Kabul and Peshawar. Pakistan.

Afghanistan is reported to have oil reserves totaling 2.9 billion barrels.

ELECTRICITY IMPORT

Uzbekistan

Discussions on electricity supplies began back in 2006. the Construction of a 442-kilometre (275 mi) high voltage transmission line from Uzbekistan to Afghanistan was completed by October 2008. It runs from Kabul through five Afghan provinces towards the country's border with Uzbekistan. and connects to the Uzbek electricity transmission system. It is expected the project will cost $198 million [USD] the transmission lines were jointly funded by India and the Asian Development Bank. As a result by early April 2009. all of Kabul all of the capital city of kabul had 24-hour electricity. the increase in power has already made a difference to many ordinary Afghans. By 2011. the 220 kV line form Uzbekistan had a capacity of nearly 300 MW.

COAL

Afghanistan is reported to have coal reserves totalling 100-400 million tons. These mines are located from Badakhshan and extend up to Herat Province. Afghanistan has more than 11 coal reserves which include

Bamyan province

1. Ashposhta and Sarasia coal reserves - 150 million tons
2. Sarjungel and Sar Asia coal reserves

Baghlan province

1. Karkar coal reserves
2. Dodkash coal reserves

Samangan province

1. Dara e sof-Shabashak reserves (Very High Quality) 74 million tons
2. Darae e sof- Gola badri - Keshine Mabayen Village and Balkhab District coal reserves

Badakhshan province

1. Kotal khaki - Barf District coal reserves

Parwan province

1. Farakort Gorband Province and Gawoparan Surkhparsa District coal reserves

Herat province

1. Karukh coal reserves - 15 million tons

Daikundi province

1. Lagharjoe - Kacharan District coal reserves

Uruzgan province

1. Kandalan Village Mudakhil District coal reserves

SOLAR

In 1991. a new 72-collector solar installation was completed in Kabul at a cost of $364 million. The installation heated 40.000 liters of water to an average temperature of 60°C around the clock. The use of solar power is becoming widespread in Afghanistan.Solar-powered street lights are seen in several Afghan cities and towns. including the capital Kabul. Many villagers in rural parts of the country are also buying solar panels and using them.

GEOTHERMAL

An area of vast untapped potential lies in the heat energy locked inside the earth in the form of magma or dry. hot rocks. Geothermal energy for electricity generation has been used worldwide for nearly 100 years. The technology currently exists to provide low-cost electricity from Afghanistan's geothermal resources. which are located in the main axis areas of the Hindu Kush. These run along the Herat fault system. all the way from Herat to the Wakhan corridor in the North.

With efficient use of the natural resources already abundantly available in Afghanistan. alternative energy sources could be directed into industrial use. supply the energy needs of the nation and build economic self-sufficiency.

URANIUM

The Helmand Province in southern Afghanistan has got uranium reserves. confirmed by Afghan Ministry of Mines. Although. no report has been given for its use in energy sector yet.

BIOGAS

Besides wind and sun. potential alternative energy sources for Afghanistan include biogas and geothermal energy. Biogas plants are fuelled by animal dung. and produce a clean. odourless and smokeless fuel. The digestion process also creates a high-quality fertilizer which can benefit the family farm.

Family-sized biogas plants require 50 kilograms of manure per day to support the average family. Four to six cows are required to produce this amount of manure. or eight to nine camels. or 50 sheep/goats. Theoretically. Afghanistan has the potential to produce about 1.400 million cubic meters of biogas annually. A quarter of this amount could meet half of Afghanistan's energy needs. according to a January 2011 report from the United States National Renewable Energy Laboratory.

WIND

At least one wind farm was successfully completed in Panjshir Province in 2008. which has the potential to produce 100 kW of energy.United States Agency for International Development has teamed up with the United States National Renewable Energy Laboratory to develop a wind map of Herat province. They have identified approximately 158.000 megawatts of untapped potential wind energy. Installing wind turbine farms in Herat could provide electricity to much of western Afghanistan. Smaller projects are wind pumps that already have been attached to water wells in several Herat villages. along with reservoirs for storing up to 15 cubic meters of water.

ENERGY SECURITY THROUGH DIVERSITY

South Korea is forced to import 97% of its primary energy demand due to minimal natural energy reserves and a slow starting renewable energy industry. In 2013 this meant the East Asian country was the second-largest importer of liquefied natural gas (LNG). the fourth-largest importer of coal. and the fifth-largest net importer of total petroleum and other liquids. according to the US

Energy Information Administration (EIA). Keen to diversify its supply to secure energy for its 50 million plus inhabitants and its $1 trillion trade industry. the country has relied significantly on nuclear power. refined oil products. LNG and coal to boost its energy mix.

Uniquely. despite its lack of domestic oil reserves. the country is one of the largest petroleum product exporters with three of the ten largest crude oil refineries in the world. The government has actively encouraged its state-owned and private oil companies to aggressively invest in overseas energy exploration and production in a bid to secure back-up supply.

In the long-term the ministry is seeking to reduce the country's use of nuclear and dirty coal. and instead benefit from cleaner fossil fuel from America's shale gas boom and from increasing the deployment of renewables. But it has a long way to go to meet these ambitious targets and it won't be able to reach them without nuclear and coal.

NULCEAR OUT. SAFETY IN

As reported by Platts. latest figures reveal that currently LNG meets about 25% of South Korea's total electricity consumption. while coal and nuclear reactors account for 40% and 30% respectively and oil for only 3%.

In mid-January. South Korea's Cabinet. headed-up by President Park Geun-hye. released the 'Second Basic Energy Plan'. an energy policy framework covering the period 2014-2035. The forward-planning document outlined the government's plan to cut down its reliance on nuclear power after a safety scandal saw some of the country's reactors close down. The plan is to reduce South Korea's reliance on nuclear to 29% of total power supply by 2035. down from a previously planned 41% by 2030.

Currently. South Korea has the highest density of nuclear reactors in the world - 23 - which makes up 26% of the country's power mix. according to the UK Trade and Investment department.

The country's new stand on nuclear doesn't mean. however. that planned construction of eleven more nuclear power reactors. five of which are already under construction. will stop. According to a Reuters article published in January. the ministry will still need 43.000 megawatts (MW) of nuclear power capacity by 2035. up from 36.000 MW by 2024.

This increase in supply is fuelled by the country's continued growth. In 2013. South Korea's gross domestic product (GDP) grew by 2.8%. up from 2% in 2012. according to the EIA. Even higher GDP growth of 3.8% is expected in 2014 due to rising exports and recovering economic growth in other developed countries.

LNG - partnering with America

"most of South Korea's installed generation capacity is fossil fuel-based."

Platts reported in May that South Korea is seeking to import more LNG and shale gas from America to adhere to new. tighter environmental laws. "Natural gas as a source of power generation needs to be increased to reduce consumption of coal that is blamed for greenhouse gas emissions." Kim Jun-Dong. deputy minister of energy and resources policy told Platts.

He highlighted the cost of LNG. which is higher than coal-based electricity production. "Import costs from the US are likely to be lower than those of LNG from the Middle East." he added.The deputy energy minister said state-run energy firms have been investing in the US shale gas development but these projects are currently at exploration stage so it would take some time before "they bear fruit".South Korea has four LNG regasification facilities. with a total capacity of 4.5 trillion cubic feet per year. according to IHS Global Insight - more than two-thirds of the country's 2013. LNG imports came from Qatar. Indonesia. Malaysia and Oman. with the rest coming from Australia. The government predicts overall natural gas demand to grow about 1.7% annually until 2035. as the fuel is a cleaner energy than coal.

To meet some of this demand. state-owned Korea Gas Corporation plans to import 3.5 million metric tons of LNG a year from the Sabine Pass project over 20 years. starting in 2017. On the domestic front. the country possessed discovered proven reserves of 203 billion cubic feet. as of January 2014. Currently. according to Oil and Gas Journal. domestic gas production accounts for less than 2% of total consumption in South Korea.

From July 2014. the South Korean government will lower consumption taxes on LNG and raise the tax on coal used for power generation.

COAL STILL PART OF SOUTH KOREA'S ENERGY FUTURE

Jun-Dong has said that South Korea cannot abandon coal just yet and that the commodity will be a part of the country's strategy for decades to come.

The country is trying to increase its stake in renewable energies but costs have proven a barrier. therefore coal won't be ruled out for some time. Director general for Energy Industry Policy Seung Il Cheong said last year the government will invest in technologies such as integrated gasification combined cycle with carbon capture and storage to minimise greenhouse gases and environmental pollution.

"For the present. South Korea's energy supply is diverse and fairly robust."

In relation to installed capacity. coal plants consist of about 24.5 GW. or about 30% of total capacity. In the new electricity plan released in January. South Korea laid out plans to raise coal capacity to 44.9 GW by 2027 and by the end of 2017. the government plans to install 15 more coal-fired facilities with 12.5 GW of capacity. In regards to South Korea's other fossil fuel source - oil - dependency on petroleum and other liquids is anticipated to fall from earlier predictions. According to the Korea Energy Economics Institute. petroleum and other liquids will account for about 34% of total primary energy consumption by 2017. down from EIA's estimate of 41% in 2012. because of an expected increase in the use of coal. natural gas and nuclear power. The state-owned Korea National Oil Corporation has a modest 3.2 million barrels of ultra-light crude (condensates) in domestic reserves. However. most of the company's oil comes from acquisitions of overseas companies - in 2012 it produced 231.000 barrels per day and held 1.3 billion barrels of equivalent of oil and gas reserves from overseas assets - but the company's aggressive overseas investment strategy has been scaled back due to high levels of debt.

Future investments - new sources hoping to enter the mix

Although South Korea's bid for energy diversity has seen the country rely heavily on fossil fuels - most of South Korea's installed generation capacity is fossil fuel-based - the country is investing in research and development for other forms of energy. such as deposits of methane hydrates in the Sea of Japan. According to the EIA. the government is currently spending around $30m per year on methane hydrates research and development. While the government's goal of developing gas hydrates is potentially decades away from being reached. increasing renewable energy is more achievable. Il Cheong. writing for Siemens. said South Korea's government hopes renewables will one day serve as the country's main energy supply. Currently only 8% of the country's energy mix comes from hydroelectricity and 3% from other renewables. such as solar. wind power and fuel cell power plants. "South Korea is trying to increase the portion of renewable sources in power generation. but it is not easy because it requires massive investments and long time." Jun-Dong told Platts. To demonstrate its commitment to increasing renewables. the International Renewable Energy Agency was launched in South Korea in May. For the present. South Korea's energy supply is diverse and fairly robust. However. by relying primarily on imports. the country is only ever a geopolitical dispute away from potential disruption. True energy security relies on rapid development of South Korea's renewables sector. which will take huge investment. increased overseas oil and gas exploration and production investment and a restoration of faith in the safety of the country's many nuclear reactors.

INDIA'S CAPABILITY AND COMPETENCE IN ENERGY SECTOR R&D

Energy requirement of Indian economy is enormous and growing fast. Per capita consumption however. is very low and is expected to grow both because of rising population and raised standards of living. Growth of industry implied growing requirement of energy much of what comes from petroleum and products and electricity. Coal. oil. and natural gas are the three primary commercial energy sources. A huge part of this demand for energy is met through imports of direct energy resources. Vulnerability of the country to global supply shocks is increasing. Other than the traditional or conventional sources. the non-conventional renewable and new energy sources. namely solar. bio-energy. gas hydrates. hydrogen. wind and nuclear energy offer viable potential options to address the energy security concerns of a country. Added to the country's increasing dependence on energy imports are the conditionalities and imperatives of climate related direct and indirect instruments that has made it near obligatory for us to have sufficient energy resources. additional and secure capacity and the capability to harness. The recent energy policy. and before that the Prime Minister's statement. has laid out the broad policy framework on energy. Givcn such a framework and global vicissitudes. the country's capability to identify. cultivate. develop and harness novel energy resources based on novel applications of S&T.

DEMAND AND SUPPLY SCENARIO

Coal

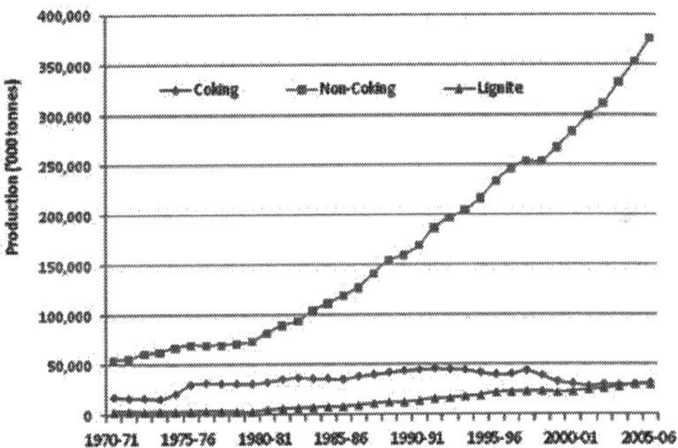

Fig. Production of Coal and Lignite in India

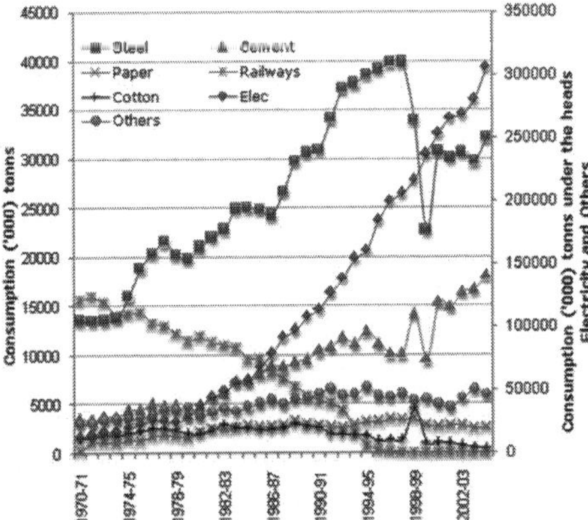

Fig. Consumption of Raw Coal by different industries in India

Coal dominates the energy mix in India. contributing to 55% of the total primary energy production. In terms of peta joules. coal and lignite were the major sources of energy. accounting for about 49.8% of the total production from all the primary sources of conventional energy during 2006-07. The consumption of raw coal by industry has increased in the period 1970-71 to 2006-07. Till the mid 70's railways were the major consumer of coal followed by steel. electricity generation and cement industries.

Gradually railways upgraded their technology and reduced their share of direct consumption. Today electricity generation is the biggest consumer followed by steel. This figure foretells the ever-increasing demand for electricity. As per ministry of commerce and industry the wholesale prices of coal. coke and lignite in India are also on an increasing trend. Keeping the wholesale price indices for the year 1993-94 as 100. the prices have risen to 239. 364 and 184 for coking coal. coke and lignite respectively.

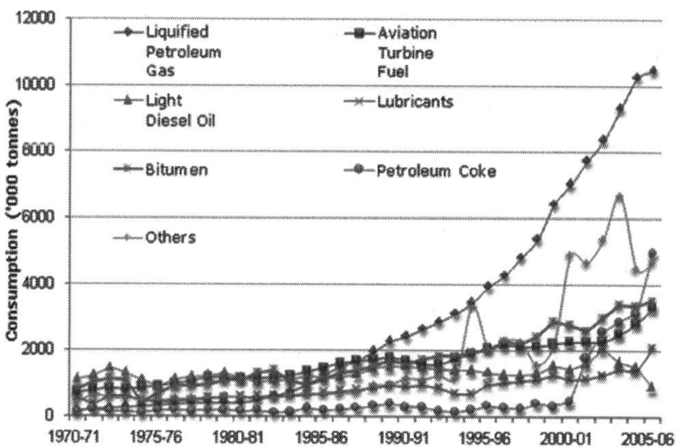

Fig. Consumption of Domestic-petroleum products in India

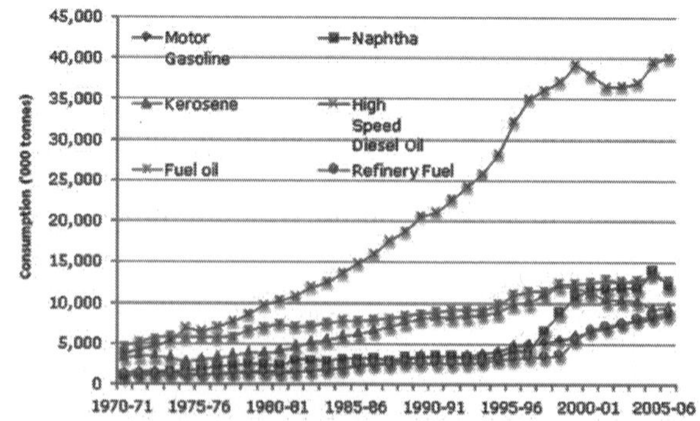

Fig. Consumption of Domestic-petroleum products in India

Crude oil

India's crude oil reserves tend to be light and sweet. with specific gravity varying from 38° API in the offshore Mumbai (Bombay) High field to 32° API at other onshore basins. Much of India's crude oil reserves are located off the western coast (Mumbai High) and in the northeast of the country. although substantial undeveloped reserves are located in the offshore Bay of Bengal and in Rajasthan state.Of the total world production of 3.914 million tonnes of crude oil in 2006. India's share is about 1.0% whereas in consumption. its share is 3.1% of the total world consumption of 3.889.8 million tonnes. Out of the total domestic production of 135.3 million tonnes of all types of petroleum products in 2006-07. high speed diesel oil accounted for the maximum share (39.5%) followed by naphtha (12.3%). fuel oil (11.6%). motor gasoline (9.3%) and kerosene (6.3%). High speed diesel oil accounted for 32.9% of total consumption of all types of petroleum products in 2006-07. This was followed by naphtha (9.8%). fuel oil (9.5%). refinery fuel (8.4%) and liquefied petroleum gas (8.3%). The wholesale price indices of petroleum products are also on the rise. Keeping the year 1993-94 equal to 100. the maximum rise was seen in light diesel oil followed by high-speed diesel oil and furnace oil. Transport sector accounts for the lion's share (50.4%) of the total consumption of high-speed diesel oil in India.

Natural gas

Natural gas has emerged as the most preferred fuel due to its inherent environmentally benign character. Production of natural gas. which was almost negligible at the time of independence. is at present at the level of around 87 million metric standard cubic meters per day (MMSCMD). The main producers of natural gas are Oil and Natural Gas Corporation Ltd. (ONGC). Oil India Limited (OIL) and JVs of Tapti. Panna-Mukta and Ravva. Under the Production Sharing Contracts. private parties from some of the fields are also producing gas. Government have also offered blocks under New Exploration Licensing Policy (NELP) to private and public sector companies with the right to market gas at market determined prices.

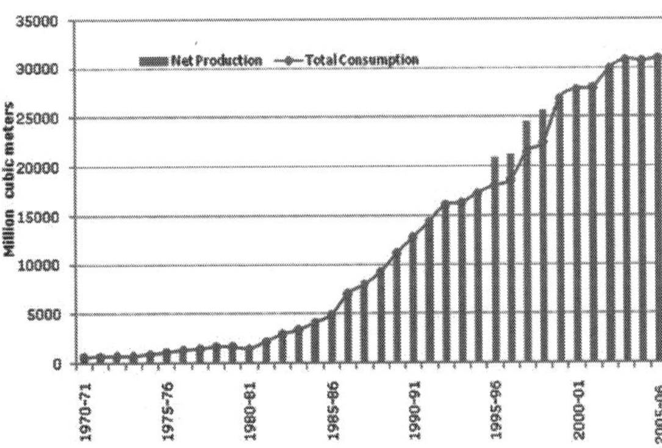

Fig. Production and consumption of natural gas in India

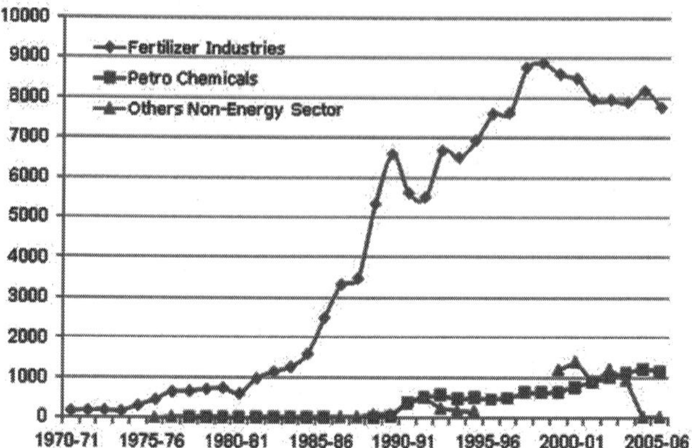

Fig. Industry-wise Off-take of Natural Gas for non-energy purposes in India

In case of production and consumption of natural gas. India's share is to the tune of 1.1% and 1.4% respectively. Out of the total production of around 87 MMSCMD. after internal consumption. extraction of LPG and unavoidable flaring. around 74 MMSCMD is available for sale to various consumers. Production of natural gas increased from 1.445 million cubic metres in 1970-71 to 31.747 million cubic metres in 2006-07. Of the total quantity of natural gas off-take in India in 2006-07. the largest share was by power generation (38.1%). followed by fertilizer industry (27.1%).

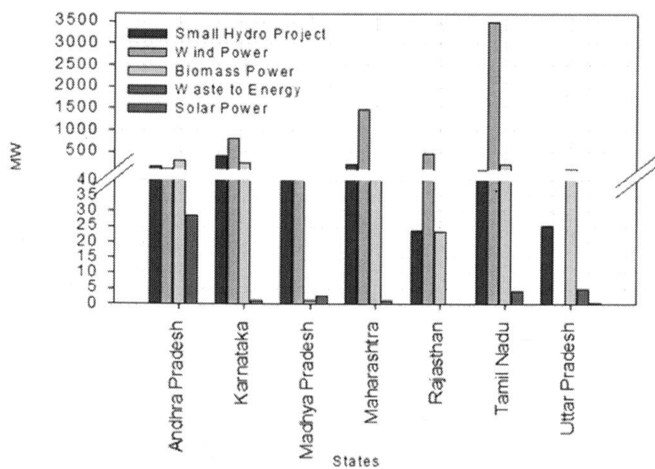

Fig: Grid-connected Renewable Power (State wise details of schemes/programmes being implemented and cumulative achievements)

Renewable resources

India is blessed with an abundance of sunlight. water and biomass. There have been vigorous efforts in exploiting them as energy sources as these resources will not only provide sustainable alternative to fossil fuels but also result in mitigating global warming. Renewable energy growth in India has been significant. The various non-conventional energy resources are solar. biomass. wind and water. The total installed capacity for grid connected renewable power is more than 10 thousand Megawatts as on March 2007. Tamil Nadu is the leading state with 3.802 MW capacity followed by the state of Maharashtra with 1.774 MW capacity and Karnataka with 1.493 MW capacity. Contribution of Wind power is maximum at 70% to the total installed capacity followed by small Hydropower (19%) and Biomass power (11%).

Electricity

Total installed capacity (utilities only) for electricity generation. has increased from 14.709 MW in 1970-71 to 1.32.329 MW in 2006-07. Among the utilities. the largest share was on account of 'Thermal' electricity followed by 'Hydro' and 'Nuclear'. Average generation of electricity per Kilowatt of the installed capacity in India is found to be the highest for Thermal (5.711 KWH) followed by Nuclear (4.771 KWH) and Hydro (3.271KWH).

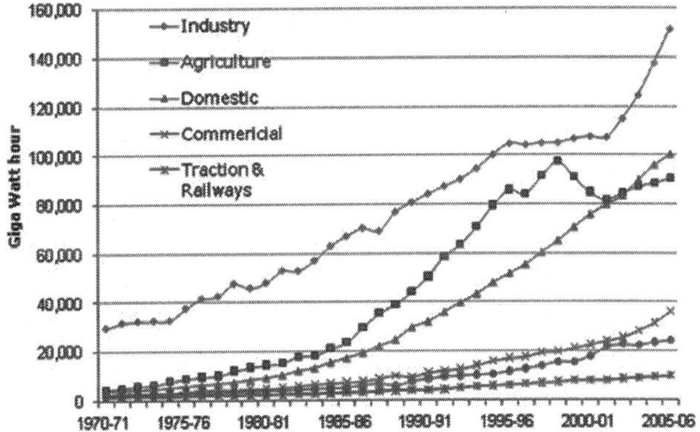

Fig. Consumption of electricity (from utilities) by sectors in India

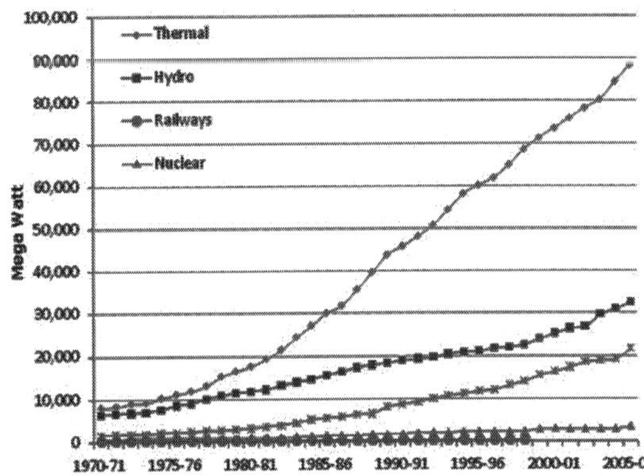

Fig. Installed Generating Capacity of Electricity in Utilities and Non-utilities in India

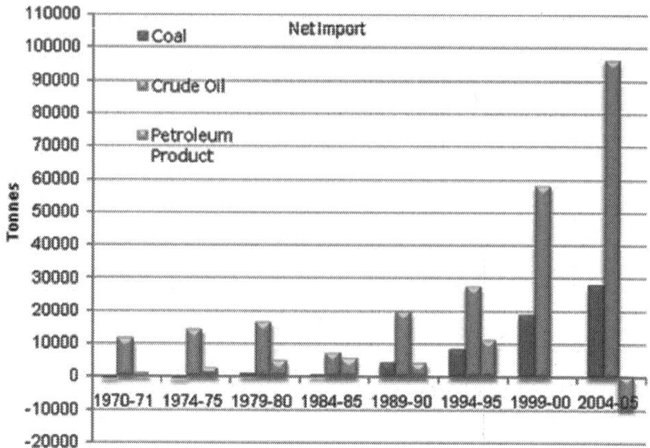

Fig. Foreign Trade in Coal. Crude Oil and Petroleum Products in India

Of the total electricity consumed in 2006-07. industry sector accounted for the largest share followed by domestic. agriculture and commercial sector. However. electricity consumption in domestic sector and agriculture sector has increased at a much faster pace compared to other sectors during 1970-71 to 2006-07. It is a cause of concern that transmission losses have increased from about 17% in 1970-71 to about 30% in 2006-07.

OVERALL

If we look at the pattern of consumption of these sources of energy. it is seen that there is a huge gap in production and consumption of crude petrol as well as in electricity generated from hydro and nuclear sources.

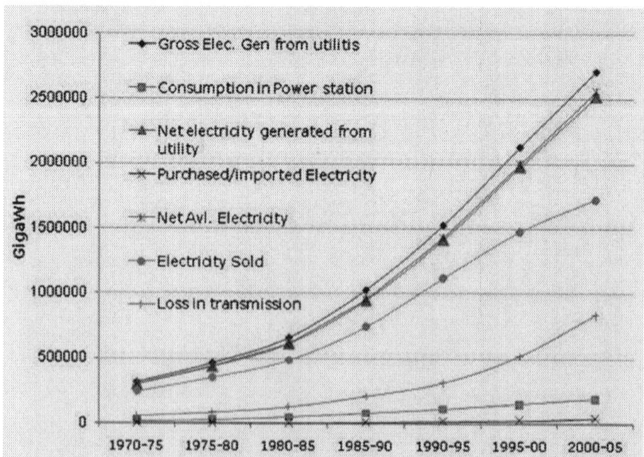

Fig. Electricity Generated. Distributed. Sold and Lost in India

Total production of four primary sources of conventional energy namely coal and lignite. crude petroleum. natural gas and electricity (hydro and nuclear). shows an increase during last thirty years. Production of natural gas increased from 1.445 million cubic metres in 1970-71 to 31.747 million cubic metres in 2006-07. Total production of crude petroleum and coal and lignite has increased about 5 and 6 times respectively during the same period. Production of electricity has. however. gone up by about 4.7 times during 1970-71 to 2006-07. implying a smaller growth rate compared to others. The wholesale price indices of coal. LPG and electricity have increased dramatically in the last decade. The maximum rise was seen in LPG (334.8) followed by electricity (271.7) and coking coal (239).

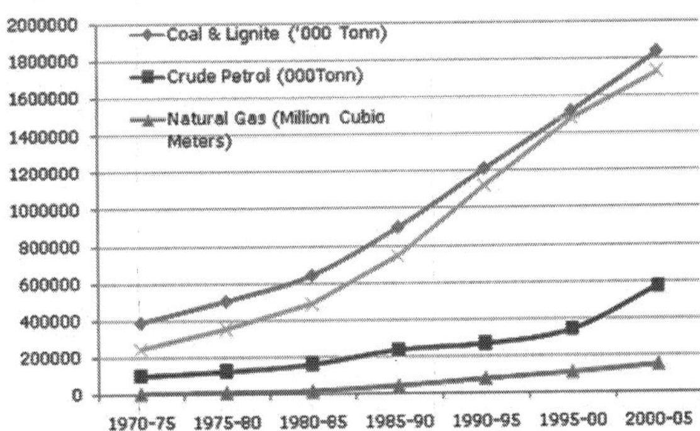

Fig. Source wise Consumption of Conventional Energy in India

The combination of rising oil consumption and fairly stable production levels leaves India increasingly dependent on imports to meet consumption needs. In 2006. the country produced an average of 846.000 barrels per day (bbl/d) of total oil liquids. of which 77 percent. or 648.000 bbl/d. was crude oil. During 2006. India consumed an estimated 2.63 million bbl/d of oil. As per EIA estimates.

India registered an oil demand growth of 100.000 bbl/d during 2006. This huge shortage of energy sources has led India to import energy to satisfy its demands. India has become a net importer of coal and crude oil. It's last three decades data shows that the net import of crude oil is increasing at a very fast pace as compared to import of coal. However. for petroleum products. India has become a net exporter since 2001-02.

India ranks fifth in terms of primary energy consumption (16.205 x 1015 Btu) while the net electricity generation is only 661.64 billion kWh. The demand exceeds the supply. Though India currently has a capacity of 137.578 million kWh of total electricity and 3.958 million kW of renewable energy but still the demand is way ahead to be satisfied by domestic conventional energy production.

Petroleum (thousand barrels/day)	664.66	2438
Natural gas (cubic feet)	1.05trillion	1269 trillion
Coal (million short tons)	473.17	507.315
Hydroelectric power(billion kWh)	99	99
Renewable electric power (geothermal. solar. wind. wood and waste electric power) (billion kWh)	7.68	7.68

With increasing demand of energy. India continues to face serious energy shortages. This has led to increased reliance on imports to meet the energy demand. India's crude oil import bill has jumped over 40 per cent to $68 billion in 2007-08 on relentless rise in international prices. The nation imported 121.672 million tons of crude oil for $67.988 billion in 2007-08 as opposed to 111.502 million tons imported for $48.389 billion previous year. according to the data released by the Ministry of Petroleum and Natural Gas. This imposes a heavy burden on our fast growing economy and raises serious concerns on our energy security.

In his speech on climate change PM Manmohan Singh has reiterated "the requirement of a new paradigm of energy security to address our developmental needs focusing on issues like a less-energy intensive path of development. increasing use of non-conventional and renewable energy sources. also aimed at reducing carbon emissions. and improving efficiency in production and consumption. Such a strategy would have to be based on coordinated development and judicious use of domestic and global resources. This will require exploring new technological options. new financing means. identifying new sources and building new bridges with new partners. We need to develop all our energy resources keeping in mind environmental concerns."

So. how can India become self reliant in energy? Increasing the supply of energy is one way of dealing with energy shortage in our country. A second way is to improve energy efficiency or reduce energy requirement. The challenge therefore before the nation is to focus R&D on technologies that seek to achieve progressively higher levels of efficiency covering all the different stages and forms of energy conversion. as well as those that seek to improve the efficiency at the end-use stage. As a result. R&D in the energy sector is quite critical for India's energy prospects. Partners in the development of country's capacity and capability would be the public sector R&D and the university/IIT systems. the public sector and the private sector. as well as the non-profit social development agencies.

This current discussion would remain limited. however. to a mapping of the country's current competence in new energy research. We attempt to map India's capability and competence in energy research by analyzing the research outputs. for example. number of publications in research institutes and universities; patents and innovation index in listed companies dealing in energy sector. All the major areas of energy research *i.e.* coal. petroleum. solar. water. bio-energy. gas hydrates. hydrogen. battery technology and fuel cells are taken into account. We identify current capacity. institutions. respective capabilities. areas in need of improvement and we limit this study to non-nuclear.

Our data is drawn from Web of Science database which covers a total of 23.285 journals. Data for listed companies is drawn from Centre for Monitoring Indian Economy (CMIE). for the period 1995-2005. The data includes innovation in terms of sales turnover. total forex spending in terms of import of raw material. finished goods. capital goods and royalty/technical knowhow and forex earnings in terms of export of goods. services and others.

ROLE OF PRIVATE SECTOR IN ENERGY SECTOR R&D

Industry consumes more energy and produces perhaps more emissions than any other sector of the economy. as depicted earlier. The industries consuming energy are manufacturing. mining. and construction industries—and for a wide range of activities. such as process and assembly uses. space conditioning. and lighting. The rising cost of energy and the growing concern over climate change and global warming has led industries to carry out research and development (R&D) for new technologies aimed among other things. at reducing the environmental impact of energy production and consumption. Thrust is on achieving energy efficiency. Energy consumption per unit of gross output or per value add is an important indicator of the industry's investment in reduction of energy consumption and this dimension has been examined in detail elsewhere. The other dimension of research effort by industry is on securing alternate modes of energy. smart systems including smart grid. cogeneration through utilization of byproducts etc.. and in novel research.

In year 2005. there were around 188 listed Indian industries dealing in energy sector in areas of coal and lignite. electricity generation. crude oil. dry cell. storage battery. refinery and solar energy. Out of these 33 companies were involved in R&D while 38 were paying royalty or technical knowhow for securing/licensing knowledge on energy or R&D assets. The number of listed companies has doubled in the last decade while the foreign exchange earnings from providing services are on a declining mode as compared to year 1995.

Within the last ten years the expenditure on R&D has remained nearly constant. If we look at the power consumption of the industries with respect to their sales. it shows that it has decreased considerably. During late 1990's companies were more into paying royalty for technical know-how as compared to the millennium era. and this payment trend has presently become stable. Now if we compare the total forex earnings and expenditure with respect to sales. the ratio of forex expenditure to sales is very high. It also depicts that both are a rising trend but the rate of increase of earning is more than the forex expenditure since last year.

This shows that there has been considerable amount of technological innovation regarding enhancing energy efficiency in the industries which is reflected from the data showing lowered power consumption. It also seems that at present this innovation is largely dependent on the technical know-how from outside rather than from in-house R&D. But with the increase in rate of forex earning than expenditure. a time is not far when the earning will surpass expenditure and India will be the hub of R&D.

PUBLIC SECTOR R&D/S&T

As it is felt that R&D in the energy sector is critical to augment our energy resources. to promote energy efficiency. to secure India's energy security and to deliver energy independence; the role of the public secdtor R&D/S&T in energy R&D is therefore important. An analysis of publication data has been undertaken to assess the performance of research under broad areas of energy as well as under major institutions. India's overall growth in publication output and publication trends in areas of coal. petroleum. battery. fuel cell. gas hydrates. hydrogen. bio-energy. solar has been assessed on the basis of publications. citations. number of authors and collaboration data.

COAL R&D CAPACITY AND CAPABILITY

Coal is an abundant. and the most important fossil fuel in India. It accounts for 55% of the country's energy needs. The proven mineable reserves of coal in India are estimated at 96.0 billion tonnes. The geological reserves are estimated to be about 253 billion tonnes. The coal reserves are roughly 8.6% of the world total and the geological reserves are approximately 0.8% of total gcological rcscrvcs in thc world. Thcrc is a large difference between total coal production and consumption *i.e.* nearly about 35 million tons short. As our country is more dependent on thermal energy. this gap is leading us into a crisis. This sector therefore needs reforms urgently.

In India the scientific research on coal related areas is being conducted by both universities as well as institutes. Among institutes CSIR holds the maximum number of research papers in coal area followed by Indian Institutes of Technology. while in academic sector BHU holds the maximum number of research papers. Moreover CSIR and IIT are far ahead in paper publishing as compared to other institutes and universities. It can be perceived from Tables 3&4 that research institutes are more active in coal research as compared to academic institutions in India.

Majority of papers being published are coauthored followed by papers having three. single and four authors. The main collaborating countries in coal research output are USA. Canada and France. This shows good research linkages and co-development of knowledge in coal research.

PETROLEUM R&D CAPACITY AND CAPABILITY

This sector has played a crucial role in economic development of our country since independence. The share of petroleum products in the total primary energy components has been increasing over the years. The crude oil production is estimated at around 664.66 thousand barrels/day while the petroleum consumption is 2.438 thousand barrels/day. India has to rely on imports heavily. The trend in number of research paper published in petroleum sector has remained stable by and large though an increase was seen during

2007. However a large increase was seen in the involvement of authors in publishing those papers. This shows that the scope of research is high in this area. The quality of papers published has declined as measured in terms of number of citations. CSIR holds the maximum number of papers publications followed by IITs and other oil companies. And. in university system. Jadavpur University has maximum number of research papers followed by BHU.

Here also number of 2-authored papers is higher than 3 or 4 authored papers. USA is the major foreign collaborator in petroleum research followed by Germany and Korea.

NEW AND RENEWABLE ENERGY R&D CAPACITY AND CAPABILITY

Solar Energy

India being located in a belt which receives abundant sunshine makes solar energy a viable source of energy generation. The country receives around 5.000 trillion kWh/year equivalent energy through solar radiation. The average solar radiation incident over India is about5.5 kWh/m2 per day. Just 1 per cent of India's land area can meet India's entire electricity requirement till 2030. Solar energy is starting to make its mark even though the installed PV remains low. The installed solar energy capacity in 2007 was 2.1 MV for solar PV and 2.15 mm2 for solar thermal water heating. The Indian government introduced a new policy for manufacturers of all semiconductors. storage devices. solar cells and photovoltaics.which has already seen investment flowing in.

An increasing trend was seen till 2004 but after that a negative growth in number of research papers output in solar energy as well as in number of authors involved was seen. Even the citations are abysmally low. IITs hold maximum number of papers in solar energy research and are way ahead. followed by DRDO and CSIR. Among the universities. Shivaji University tops the list with 50 publications.

In solar energy research 2-authored papers had maximum occurrence followed by 3 and 4 authored papers. With regard to foreign collaboration Japan tops the list followed by USA and China.

Wind Energy

India is endowed with a large. viable and economically exploitable wind power potential. According to the Ministry of New and Renewable Energy (MNRE). India's potential is conservatively estimated at 45.195 MW. The use of wind power in India ranks fourth by worldwide comparison with an installed capacity of 7.092 MW. India is third in the world in terms of new construction and this corresponds to an overall increase of over 40% in new wind power stations.There has hardly been any significant increase in publication output in wind energy research since last ten years and the citation number has also gone down from 48 to 8 showing that the papers are not good quality. The silver lining in wind energy research is that. researchers have started taking interest and are entering this area.

Among institutes. IITs top the list and are far ahead of other institutes and universities. in wind field. Multiple co-authored papers having three and two authors are seen to have maximum occurrence in wind research. USA is the major collaborator followed by Germany and Japan.

Bio-Energy

Bio-energy includes energy from bio-fuels as well as from biomass. Around the world demand for bio-fuels is growing rapidly. India aims to replace 5% to 20% of fossil based liquid petroleum fuel consumption with ethanol and bio-diesel. The period 2000 to 2006 has seen a growth rate of 6.37 per cent in bio-ethanol production.

The trend in number of research papers published during the last 10 years pertaining to Bio-Energy research has more or less remained stable. with the exception in 2007 where it showed significant increase. In the beginning of this millennium both number of papers and authors decreased but after that there has been a significant increase in number of researchers and papers till date. Citations of papers published in bio-energy sector. is a decreasing inclination.

Among institutions CSIR tops the list in publishing papers followed by the IITs and IISc while in academic sector Jadavpur University has published 10 research paper followed by BHU and Delhi University (DU). In Bio-energy India holds 8 patents.

In bio-energy maximum numbers of papers are 2-authored or 3-authored. Major foreign collaborators in bio-energy research are USA and Thailand.

Gas Hydrates

Gas hydrates are an important source of large quantity of methane gas and available within the Clathrate structures at a shallow sediment depth of about 6.000 ft. The total gas resource from the gas hydrates in the country is estimated to be around 1.894 TCM. The work being done world over is in research stage.

In India scientific work on gas hydrates was initiated during 1997 and is still in its nascent stage. Since 2004 there has been a slight increase in Gas Hydrate research in India. Similarly the authors involved in publishing their research are on an increase that too significantly from 2005 onwards. This reflects the scope of further research in this area. Here too CSIR has taken over in maximum number of research paper output followed by IITs and oil companies. But till date none of the Indian universities have tried to venture inside gas hydrates.

Multiple co-authored papers having three and five authors are seen to have maximum occurrence in gas hydrates. Only three countries are collaborating as seen from publications output: namely USA. England and South Korea.

Hydrogen

Hydrogen is a new area. It has significant potential as a clean energy source for broad range of applications including power production and transportation.

In hydrogen energy area. the trend of number of published articles shows that it is increasing at a very slow pace with an exception in 2007 when it leaped. Similar is the case with the number of authors involved which also increased slightly during the years but showed a quantum jump in 2007. Though in recent years publication output and researchers involved in hydrogen field has increased but a sharp fall is seen in the paper citations especially after 2001 that too going below the initial years. IITs hold maximum numbers of research papers in Hydrogen energy and are quite well ahead of other institutes. followed by CSIR.

Battery

It is estimated that India could eliminate its oil dependence over the next 40-50 years by developing cheap batteries with high storage density. Therefore research on battery technology finds its significance as a storage option for solar PV based electrical energy.

The number of publications has increased double fold in battery research during the last 10 years while the number of authors involved has tripled thereby showing an increase in interest in this area. The papers citation shows a reverse trend with a sharp drop in year 2007 indicating that though newer researchers are entering this field their scientific output is still dismissal. In battery research India holds 11 patents.Here also CSIR holds the maximum number of research papers (127) published in battery research in India followed by IITs which hold 53 papers. In academic system. Alagappa University holds maximum number of research papers followed by BHU.

Scientific papers having three authors are a majority as compared to papers with two or four authors. The main collaborating countries in battery research related publications are USA. South Korea. Japan. and Australia.

Fuel Cell

India stood nowhere in scientific output in fuel cell field. But gradually India entered this area. with number of publications increasing though at a very slow rate. The authors involved in fuel cell research publications have shown an incremental leap from 2005 to 2007. With reference to the trends of citations of published paper. it is seen that between 2004 and 2005 it reached a peak and since then is declining and is now nearing what it was way back in 1995.

OVERALL PICTURE OF PUBLIC SECTOR R&D

On examining the complete picture of Indian energy R&D scenario both by the private and the public sector it seems that R&D is progressing in all fields.

In public sector the number of publications emanating from both university system and research based institutions is increasing at a fast rate depictive of advances in R&D.

The field of coal research being the most preferred one by the institutes followed by solar and petroleum. while research on storage systems like hydrogen.

Battery and fuel cell all stand at par. But the citations received are appallingly very low indicating that the standard of research being pursued is either retrograde or not up to international standards. Therefore the criterion of energy research has to be relooked into and brought at par of ongoing international research.

Inferences

According to various projections. in near future. India's demand of energy would rise so sharply. that it would be quite difficult for India to sustain itself in this competitive world. So. how can India become self reliant or achieve security in energy? For achieving this. India should aim at two goals namely

- Increase the supply of energy and
- Improve energy efficiency or reduce energy requirements.

As these goals can be achieved through research and development only. R&D in the energy sector is therefore quite critical for India's energy prospects.

The broad concern of energy R&D should be:

- Develop technologies that seek to achieve progressively higher levels of efficiency covering all the different stages and forms of energy conversion. as well as those that seek to improve the efficiency at the end-use stage.
- To identify new and novel resources/methods of energy generation (render economic. known but uneconomic)
- Improve technology to tap known but uneconomic and novel energy resources
- Develop energy conversion systems with higher efficiency
- Develop standards for new energy sources etc.

Put together the country needs to develop critical capacities and capabilities in new energy research and this has to be achieved by a set of policies already enshrined in the framework enunciated by the Prime Minister and by the Energy Policy.

The main challenge facing India's energy sector would be to increase its efficiency in an environmentally and socially acceptable manner. It needs to augment its domestic energy resources. It is a long term imperative that renewable resources are exploited optimally as India's sustained economic development is vitally dependent on its energy security and on the promotion of sustainable and environment friendly energy technologies. The underlying assumption therefore is that novel S&T capability and capacity would endow the country with required energy resources.

2

Energy Security and Renewable Technology

The environmental benefits of renewable energy technologies are widely recognised. but the contribution that they can make to energy security is less well known. Renewable technologies can enhance energy security in electricity generation. heat supply. and transportation.

ENERGY SECURITY

Access to cheap energy has become essential to the functioning of modern economies. However. the uneven distribution of fossil fuel supplies among countries. and the critical need to widely access energy resources. has led to significant vulnerabilities. Threats to global energy security include political instability of energy producing countries. manipulation of energy supplies. competition over energy sources. attacks on supply infrastructure. as well as accidents and natural disasters.

The Fukushima I nuclear accidents in Japan have brought new attention to how national energy systems are vulnerable to natural disasters. with climate change already bringing more weather and climate extremes. These threats to our old energy systems provide a rationale for investing in renewable energy. Shifting to renewable energy "can help us to meet the dual goals of reducing greenhouse gas emissions. thereby limiting future extreme weather and climate impacts. and ensuring reliable. timely. and cost-efficient delivery of energy". Investing in renewable energy can have significant dividends for our energy security.

TRANSPORTATION

The International Energy Agency's *World Energy Outlook 2006* concludes that rising petroleum demand. if left unchecked. would accentuate vulnerability to a severe supply disruption and resulting sudden price increases. in consuming countries. Renewable biofuels for transport represent a key source of diversification from petroleum products. Biofuels from grain and beet in temperate regions have a role. but they are relatively expensive and their energy efficiency and carbon dioxide savings. vary. Biofuels from sugar cane and other highly productive tropical crops are much more competitive and beneficial. But all first generation biofuels ultimately compete with the production of food for land. water. and other resources.

More effort is required to develop and commercialize second generation biofuel technologies. such as biorefineries and cellulosic ethanol. enabling the flexible production of biofuels and related products from non-edible parts of the plant.

According to the International Energy Agency (IEA). cellulosic ethanol commercialization could allow ethanol fuels to play a much larger role in the future than previously thought. Cellulosic ethanol can be made from plant matter composed primarily of inedible cellulose fibers that form the stems and branches of most plants.

Dedicated energy crops. such as switchgrass. are also promising cellulose sources that can be produced in many regions of the United States.

HEATING

In those countries where growing dependence on imported gas is a pressing energy security issue. renewable energy technologies can provide alternative sources of electric power production as well as displacing electricity demand through production of direct heat.

The IEA suggests that the direct contribution that renewable energy can make to domestic or commercial space heating and industrial process heat should be examined more closely. Heat from solar. geothermal sources. and heat pumps. is increasingly economic but is often overlooked in government programmes that promote public acceptance and provide incentives for renewable electricity and energy efficiency.

Solar heating systems are a well known technology and generally consist of solar thermal collectors. a fluid system to move the heat from the collector to its point of usage. and a reservoir or tank for heat storage.

The systems may be used to heat domestic hot water. swimming pools. or homes and businesses.

The heat can also be used for industrial process applications or as an energy input for other uses such as cooling equipment. In many warmer climates. a solar heating system can provide a very high percentage (50 to 75%) of domestic hot water energy.

ELECTRICITY GENERATION

As the electricity grid becomes increasingly vulnerable to faults from equipment failure. willful attack or even sunspot activity. the risk of a major national scale grid failure is rising.

The deployment of renewable technologies usually increases the diversity of electricity sources and. through local generation. contributes to the flexibility of the system and its resistance to central shocks. The IEA suggests that attention in this area has focused too much on the issue of the variability of renewable electricity production.However. this only applies to certain renewable technologies. mainly wind power and solar photovoltaics. and its significance depends on a range of factors which include the market penetration of the renewables concerned. the balance of plant and the wider connectivity of the system. as well as the demand side flexibility. Variability will rarely be a barrier to increased renewable energy deployment. But at high levels of market penetration it requires careful analysis and management. and additional costs may be required for back-up or system modification. Renewable electricity supply in the 20-50+per cent penetration range has already been implemented in several European systems. albeit in the context of an integrated European grid system:

In 2010. four German states. totaling 10 million people. relied on wind power for 43-52% of their annual electricity needs. Denmark isn't far behind. supplying 22% of its power from wind in 2010 (26% in an average wind year). The Extremadura region of Spain is getting up to 25% of its electricity from solar. while the whole country meets 16% of its demand from wind. Just during 2005-2010. Portugal vaulted from 17% to 45% renewable electricity.

Minnkota Power Cooperative. the leading U.S. wind utility in 2009. supplied 38% of its retail sales from the wind.

Physicist Amory Lovins has said that following hundreds of blackouts in 2005. Cuba reorganized its electricity transmission system into networked microgrids and cut the occurrence of blackouts to zero within two years. limiting damage even after two hurricanes.

Networked island-able microgrids describes Lovins' vision where energy is generated locally from solar power. wind power and other resources and used by super-efficient buildings. When each building. or neighborhood. is generating its own power. with links to other "islands" of power. the security of the entire network is greatly enhanced.

COMBINED POWER PLANT

The Combined Power Plant. a project linking 36 wind. solar. biomass. and hydroelectric installations throughout Germany. has demonstrated that a combination of renewable sources and more-effective control can balance out short-term power fluctuations and provide reliable electricity with 100 percent renewable energy.

IMPACT OF FOREIGN INVESTOR DISPUTE RIGHTS

It has been argued that investor-state dispute settlement rights may grant investors in carbon-intensive industries a mechanism to inhibit government policies promoting renewable energy technologies.

RENEWABLE ENERGY

Fig. Wind. solar. and biomass are three emerging renewable sources of energy.

Renewable energy is generally defined as energy that comes from resources which are naturally replenished on a human timescale such as sunlight. wind. rain. tides. waves and geothermal heat. Renewable energy replaces conventional fuels in four distinct areas: electricity generation. hot water/space heating. motor fuels. and rural (off-grid) energy services.

Based on REN21's 2014 report. renewables contributed 19 percent to our energy consumption and 22 percent to our electricity generation in 2012 and 2013. respectively. Both. modern renewables. such as hydro. wind. solar and biofuels. as well as traditional biomass. contributed in about equal parts to the global energy supply. Worldwide investments in renewable technologies amounted to more than US$ 214 billion in 2013. with countries like China and the United Statesheavily investing in wind. hydro. solar and biofuels.

Renewable energy resources exist over wide geographical areas. in contrast to other energy sources. which are concentrated in a limited number of countries. Rapid deployment of renewable energy and energy efficiency is resulting in significant energy security. climate change mitigation. and economic benefits. In international public opinion surveys there is strong support for promoting renewable sources such as solar power and wind power. At the national level. at least 30 nations around the world already have renewable energy contributing more than 20 percent of energy supply. National renewable energy markets are projected to continue to grow strongly in the coming decade and beyond.

While many renewable energy projects are large-scale. renewable technologies are also suited to rural and remote areas and developing countries. where energy is often crucial in human development. United Nations' Secretary-General Ban Ki-moon has said that renewable energy has the ability to lift the poorest nations to new levels of prosperity.

OVERVIEW

Renewable energy flows involve natural phenomena such as sunlight. wind. tides. plant growth. and geothermal heat. as theInternational Energy Agency explains:

Renewable energy is derived from natural processes that are replenished constantly. In its various forms. it derives directly from the sun. or from heat generated deep within the earth. Included in the definition is electricity and heat generated from solar. wind. ocean. hydropower. biomass. geothermal resources. and biofuels and hydrogen derived from renewable resources.

Wind power is growing at the rate of 30% annually. with a worldwide installed capacity of 282.482 megawatts (MW) at the end of 2012. and is widely used in Europe. Asia. and the United States. At the end of 2012 the photovoltaic (PV) capacity worldwide was 100.000 MW. and PV power stations are popular in Germany and Italy. Solar thermal power stations operate in the USA and Spain. and the largest of these is the 354 MW SEGS power plant in the Mojave Desert. The world's largest geothermal power installation isThe Geysers in California. with a rated capacity of 750 MW. Brazil has one of the largest renewable energy programmes in the world. involving production of ethanol fuel from sugar cane. and ethanol now provides 18% of the country's automotive fuel. Ethanol fuel is also widely available in the USA.

Renewable energy resources and significant opportunities for energy efficiency exist over wide geographical areas. in contrast to other energy sources. which are concentrated in a limited number of countries. Rapid deployment of renewable energy and energy efficiency. and technological diversification of energy sources. would result in significant energy security and economic benefits.

Renewable energy replaces conventional fuels in four distinct areas: electricity generation. hot water/space heating. motor fuels. and rural (off-grid) energy services:

- *Power generation:* Renewable energy provides 21.7% of electricity generation worldwide as of 2013. Renewable power generators are spread across many countries. and wind power alone already provides a significant share of electricity in some areas: for example. 14% in the U.S. state of Iowa. 40% in the northern German state of Schleswig-Holstein. and 49% in Denmark. Some countries get most of their power from renewables. including Iceland (100%). Norway (98%). Brazil (86%). Austria (62%). New Zealand (65%). and Sweden (54%).
- *Heating:* Solar hot water makes an important contribution to renewable heat in many countries. most notably in China. which now has 70% of the global total (180 GWth). Most of these systems are installed on multi-family apartment buildings and meet a portion of

the hot water needs of an estimated 50–60 million households in China. Worldwide. total installed solar water heating systems meet a portion of the water heating needs of over 70 million households. The use of biomass for heating continues to grow as well. In Sweden. national use of biomass energy has surpassed that of oil. Direct geothermal for heating is also growing rapidly.

- *Transport fuels:* Renewable biofuels have contributed to a significant decline in oil consumption in the United States since 2006. The 93 billion liters of biofuels produced worldwide in 2009 displaced the equivalent of an estimated 68 billion liters of gasoline. equal to about 5% of world gasoline production.

As of 2011. small solar PV systems provide electricity to a few million households. and micro-hydro configured into mini-grids serves many more. Over 44 million households usebiogas made in household-scale digesters for lighting and/or cooking. and more than 166 million households rely on a new generation of more-efficient biomass cookstoves.United Nations' Secretary-General Ban Ki-moon has said that renewable energy has the ability to lift the poorest nations to new levels of prosperity.

At the national level. at least 30 nations around the world already have renewable energy contributing more than 20% of energy supply. National renewable energy markets are projected to continue to grow strongly in the coming decade and beyond. and some 120 countries have various policy targets for longer-term shares of renewable energy. including a 20% target of all electricity generated for the European Union by 2020. Some countries have much higher long-term policy targets of up to 100% renewables. Outside Europe. a diverse group of 20 or more other countries target renewable energy shares in the 2020–2030 time frame that range from 10% to 50%.

Climate change and global warming concerns. coupled with high oil prices. peak oil. and increasing government support. are driving increasing renewable energy legislation. incentives and commercialization. New government spending. regulation and policies helped the industry weather the global financial crisis better than many other sectors.According to a 2011 projection by the International Energy Agency. solar power generators may produce most of the world's electricity within 50 years. reducing the emissions of greenhouse gases that harm the environment. Renewable energy sources. that derive their energy from the sun. either directly or indirectly. such as hydro and wind. are expected to be capable of supplying humanity energy for almost another 1 billion years. at which point the predicted increase in heat from the sun is expected to make the surface of the earth too hot for liquid water to exist.

HISTORY

Prior to the development of coal in the mid 19th century. nearly all energy used was renewable. Almost without a doubt the oldest known use of renewable energy. in the form of traditional biomass to fuel fires. dates from 790.000 years ago. Use of biomass for fire did not become commonplace until many hundreds of thousands of years later. sometime between 200.000 and 400.000 years ago.

Probably the second oldest usage of renewable energy is harnessing the wind in order to drive ships over water. This practice can be traced back some 7000 years. to ships on the Nile.

Moving into the time of recorded history. the primary sources of traditional renewable energy were human labour. animal power. water power. wind. in grain crushing windmills. and firewood. a traditional biomass. A graph of energy use in the United States up until 1900 shows oil and natural gas with about the same importance in 1900 as wind and solar played in 2010.

By 1873. concerns of running out of coal prompted experiments with using solar energy. Development of solar engines continued until the outbreak of World War I. The importance of solar energy was recognised in a 1911 *Scientific American* article: "in the far distant future. natural fuels having been exhausted [solar power] will remain as the only means of existence of the human race".

The theory of peak oil was published in 1956. In the 1970s environmentalists promoted the development of renewable energy both as a replacement for the eventualdepletion of oil. as well as for an escape from dependence on oil. and the first electricity generating wind turbines appeared. Solar had long been used for heating and cooling. but solar panels were too costly to build solar farms until 1980.

MAINSTREAM TECHNOLOGIES

Wind power

Fig. The 845 MW Shepherds Flat Wind Farm near Arlington. Oregon. USA.

Airflows can be used to run wind turbines. Modern utility-scale wind turbines range from around 600 kW to 5 MW of rated power. although turbines with rated output of 1.5–3 MW have become the most common for commercial use; the power available from the wind is a function of the cube of the wind speed. so as wind speed increases. power output increases up to the maximum output for the particular turbine.

Areas where winds are stronger and more constant. such as offshore and high altitude sites. are preferred locations for wind farms. Typical capacity factors are 20-40%. with values at the upper end of the range in particularly favourable sites.

Globally. the long-term technical potential of wind energy is believed to be five times total current global energy production. or 40 times current electricity demand. assuming all practical barriers needed were overcome. This would require wind turbines to be installed over large areas. particularly in areas of higher wind resources. such as offshore.

As offshore wind speeds average ~90% greater than that of land. so offshore resources can contribute substantially more energy than land stationed turbines.

Hydropower

Energy in water can be harnessed and used. Since water is about 800 times denser than air. even a slow flowing stream of water. or moderate sea swell. can yield considerable amounts of energy. There are many forms of water energy:

- Hydroelectric energy is a term usually reserved for large-scale hydroelectric dams. The largest of which is the Three Gorges Dam inChina and a smaller example is the Akosombo Dam in Ghana.
- Micro hydro systems are hydroelectric power installations that typically produce up to 100 kW of power. They are often used in water rich areas as a remote-area power supply (RAPS).
- Run-of-the-river hydroelectricity systems derive kinetic energy from rivers and oceans without the creation of a large reservoir.

Hydropower is produced in 150 countries. with the Asia-Pacific region generating 32 percent of global hydropower in 2010. China is the largest hydroelectricity producer.

with 721 terawatt-hours of production in 2010. representing around 17 percent of domestic electricity use. There are now three hydroelectricity stations larger than 10 GW: the Three Gorges Dam in China. Itaipu Dam across the Brazil/Paraguay border. and Guri Dam in Venezuela.

Wave power. that captures the energy of ocean surface waves. and tidal power. converting the energy of tides. are two forms of hydropower with future potential. however. not yet widely employed commercially. while ocean thermal energy conversion. that uses the temperature difference between cooler deep and warmer surface waters. has currently no economic feasibility.

SOLAR ENERGY

Solar energy. radiant light and heat from the sun. is harnessed using a range of ever-evolving technologies such as solar heating.photovoltaics. concentrated solar power. solar architecture and artificial photosynthesis.

Solar technologies are broadly characterised as either passive solar or active solar depending on the way they capture. convert and distribute solar energy. Passive solar techniques include orienting a building to the Sun. selecting materials with favorable thermal massor light dispersing properties. and designing spaces that naturally circulate air.

Active solar technologies encompass solar thermal energy. using solar collectors for heating. and solar power. converting sunlight intoelectricity either directly using photovoltaics (PV). or indirectly using concentrated solar power (CSP).

A photovoltaic system converts light into electrical direct current (DC) by taking advantage of the photoelectric effect. Solar PV has turned into a multi-billion. fast-growing industry. continues to improve its cost-effectiveness. and has the most potential of any renewable technology. Concentrated solar power systems use lenses or mirrors and tracking systems to focus a large area of sunlight into a small beam. Commercial concentrated solar power plants were first developed in the 1980s.

In 2011. the International Energy Agency said that "the development of affordable. inexhaustible and clean solar energy technologies will have huge longer-term benefits. It will increase countries' energy security through reliance on an indigenous. inexhaustible and mostly import-independent resource. enhance sustainability. reduce pollution. lower the costs of mitigating climate change. and keep fossil fuel prices lower than otherwise. These advantages are global. Hence the additional costs of the incentives for early deployment should be considered learning investments; they must be wisely spent and need to be widely shared".

BIOMASS

Fig. A combined heat and power plant inMetz. France. The station uses wood and supplies 30.000 households.

Biomass is biological material derived from living. or recently living organisms. It most often refers to plants or plant-derived materials which are specifically called lignocellulosic biomass. As an energy source. biomass can either be used directly via combustion to produce heat. or indirectly after converting it to various forms of biofuel. Conversion of biomass to biofuel can be achieved by different methods which are broadly classified into: *thermal. chemical.* and *biochemical* methods.

Wood remains the largest biomass energy source today; examples include forest residues (such as dead trees. branches and tree stumps). yard clippings. wood chips and even municipal solid waste. In the second sense. biomass includes plant or animal matter that can be converted into fibers or other industrial chemicals. including biofuels. Industrial biomass can be grown from numerous types of plants. including miscanthus. switchgrass. hemp. corn. poplar. willow. sorghum. sugarcane. bamboo. and a variety of tree species. ranging from eucalyptus to oil palm (palm oil).

Plant energy is produced by crops specifically grown for use as fuel that offer high biomass output per hectare with low input energy. Some examples of these plants are wheat. which typically yield 7.5–8 tonnes of grain per hectare. and straw. which typically yield 3.5–5 tonnes per hectare in the UK. The grain can be used for liquid transportation fuels while the straw can be burned to produce heat or electricity. Plant biomass can also be degraded from cellulose to glucose through a series of chemical treatments. and the resulting sugar can then be used as a first generation biofuel. Biomass can be converted to other usable forms of energy like methane gas or transportation fuels like ethanol and biodiesel. Rotting garbage. and agricultural and human waste. all release methane gas – also called “landfill gas” or “biogas”. Crops. such as corn and sugar cane. can be fermented to produce the transportation fuel. ethanol. Biodiesel. another transportation fuel. can be produced from left-over food products like vegetable oils and animal fats. Also. biomass to liquids (BTLs) and cellulosic ethanol are still under research.

There is a great deal of research involving algal. or algae-derived. biomass due to the fact that it’s a non-food resource and can be produced at rates 5 to 10 times those of other types of land-based agriculture. such as corn and soy. Once harvested. it can be fermented to produce biofuels such as ethanol. butanol. and methane. as well asbiodiesel and hydrogen.

The biomass used for electricity generation varies by region. Forest by-products. such as wood residues. are common in the United States. Agricultural waste is common inMauritius (sugar cane residue) and Southeast Asia (rice husks). Animal husbandry residues. such as poultry littre. are common in the UK.

BIOFUEL

Fig. Sugarcane plantation to produceethanol in the state of São Paulo. Brazil.

Biofuels include a wide range of fuels which are derived from biomass. The term covers solid biofuels. liquid biofuels. and gaseous biofuels. Liquid biofuels include bioalcohols. such as bioethanol. and oils. such as biodiesel. Gaseous biofuels include biogas. landfill gas and synthetic gas.

Bioethanol is an alcohol made by fermenting the sugar components of plant materials and it is made mostly from sugar and starch crops. These include maize. sugar cane and. more recently. sweet sorghum. The latter crop is particularly suitable for growing in dryland conditions. and is being investigated by ICRISAT for its potential to provide fuel. along with food and animal feed. in arid parts of Asia and Africa. With advanced technology being developed. cellulosic biomass. such as trees and grasses. are also used as feedstocks for ethanol production. Ethanol can be used as a fuel for vehicles in its pure form. but it is usually used as a gasoline additive to increase octane and improve vehicle emissions. Bioethanol is widely used in the USA and in Brazil. The energy costs for producing bio-ethanol are almost equal to. the energy yields from bio-ethanol. However. according to the European Environment Agency. biofuels do not address global warming concerns.

Biodiesel is made from vegetable oils. animal fats or recycled greases. Biodiesel can be used as a fuel for vehicles in its pure form. but it is usually used as a diesel additive to reduce levels of particulates. carbon monoxide. and hydrocarbons from diesel-powered vehicles. Biodiesel is produced from oils or fats using transesterification and is the most common biofuel in Europe.

Biofuels provided 2.7% of the world's transport fuel in 2010.

GEOTHERMAL ENERGY

Fig. Steam rising from the Nesjavellir Geothermal Power Station in Iceland.

Geothermal energy is from thermal energy generated and stored in the Earth. Thermal energy is the energy that determines thetemperature of matter. Earth's geothermal energy originates from the original formation of the planet (20%) and from radioactive decayof minerals (80%). The geothermal gradient. which is the difference in temperature between the core of the planet and its surface. drives a continuous conduction of thermal energy in the form of heat from the core to the surface. The adjective *geothermal* originates from the Greek roots *geo*. meaning earth. and *thermos*. meaning heat.

The heat that is used for geothermal energy can be from deep within the Earth. all the way down to Earth's core – 4.000 miles (6.400 km) down. At the core. temperatures may reach over 9.000 °F (5.000 °C). Heat conducts from the core to surrounding rock. Extremely high temperature and pressure cause some rock to melt. which is commonly known as magma. Magma convects upward since it is lighter than the solid rock. This magma then heats rock and water in the crust. sometimes up to 700 °F (371 °C).

From hot springs. geothermal energy has been used for bathing since Paleolithic times and for space heating since ancient Roman times. but it is now better known forelectricity generation.

COMMERCIALIZATION

Growth of renewables

From the end of 2004. worldwide renewable energy capacity grew at rates of 10–60% annually for many technologies. For wind power and many other renewable technologies. growth accelerated in 2009 relative to the previous four years. More wind power capacity was added during 2009 than any other renewable technology. However. grid-connected PV increased the fastest of all renewables technologies. with a 60% annual average growth rate. In 2010. renewable power constituted about a third of the newly built power generation capacities.

Projections vary. but scientists have advanced a plan to power 100% of the world's energy with wind. hydroelectric. and solar power by the year 2030.

According to a 2011 projection by the International Energy Agency. solar power generators may produce most of the world's electricity within 50 years. reducing the emissions of greenhouse gases that harm the environment. Cedric Philibert. senior analyst in the renewable energy division at the IEA said: "Photovoltaic and solar-thermal plants may meet most of the world's demand for electricity by 2060 – and half of all energy needs – with wind. hydropower and biomass plants supplying much of the remaining generation". "Photovoltaic and concentrated solar power together can become the major source of electricity". Philibert said.

Selected renewable energy global indicators	2008	2009	2010	2011	2012	2013
Investment in new renewable capacity (annual) (10^9 USD)	130	160	211	257	244	214
Renewables power capacity (existing) (GWe)	1.140	1.230	1.320	1.360	1.470	1.560
Hydropower capacity (existing) (GWe)	885	915	945	970	990	1.000
Wind power capacity (existing) (GWe)	121	159	198	238	283	318
Solar PV capacity (grid-connected) (GWe)	16	23	40	70	100	139
Solar hot water capacity (existing) (GWth)	130	160	185	232	255	326
Ethanol production (annual) (10^9 litres)	67	76	86	86	83	87
Biodiesel production (annual) (10^9 litres)	12	17.8	18.5	21.4	22.5	26
Countries with policy targets for renewable energy use	79	89	98	118	138	144®

Economic trends

Renewable energy technologies are getting cheaper. through technological change and through the benefits of mass production and market competition. A 2011 IEA report said: "A portfolio of renewable energy technologies is becoming cost-competitive in an increasingly broad range of circumstances. in some cases providing investment opportunities without the need for specific economic support." and added that "cost reductions in critical technologies. such as wind and solar. are set to continue." Hydro-electricity and geothermal electricity produced at favourable sites are now the cheapest way to generate electricity. Renewable energy costs continue to drop. and the levelised cost of electricity (LCOE) is declining for wind power. solar photovoltaic (PV). concentrated solar power (CSP) and some biomass technologies.

Renewable energy is also the most economic solution for new grid-connected capacity in areas with good resources. As the cost of renewable power falls. the scope of economically viable applications increases. Renewable technologies are now often the most economic solution for new generating capacity. Where "oil-fired generation is the predominant power generation source (*e.g.* on islands. off-grid and in some countries) a lower-cost renewable solution almost always exists today".

A series of studies by the US National Renewable Energy Laboratory modeled the "grid in the Western US under a number of different scenarios where intermittent renewables accounted for 33 percent of the total power." In the models. inefficiencies in cycling the fossil fuel plants to compensate for the variation in solar and wind energy resulted in an additional cost of "between $0.47 and $1.28 to each MegaWatt hour generated"; however. the savings in the cost of the fuels saved "adds up to $7 billion. meaning the added costs are. at most. two percent of the savings."

Hydroelectricity

The Three Gorges Dam in Hubei. China. has the world's largest instantaneous generating capacity (22.500 MW). with the Itaipu Dam in Brazil/ Paraguay in second place (14.000 MW). The Three Gorges Dam is operated jointly with the much smaller Gezhouba Dam (3.115 MW). As of 2012. the total generating capacity of this two-dam complex is 25.615 MW. In 2008. this complex generated 98 TWh of electricity (81 TWh from the Three Gorges Dam and 17 TWh from the Gezhouba Dam). which is 3% more power in one year than the 95 TWh generated by Itaipu in 2008.

Wind power development

Wind power is growing at over 20% annually. with a worldwide installed capacity of 238.000 MW at the end of 2011. and is widely used in Europe. Asia. and the United States. Several countries have achieved relatively high levels of wind power penetration. such as 21% of stationary electricity production in Denmark. 18% in Portugal. 16% in Spain. 14% in Ireland and 9% in Germany in 2010. As of 2011. 83 countries around the world are using wind power on a commercial basis. As of 2012. the Alta Wind Energy Centre (California. 1.020 MW) is the world's largest wind farm. The London Array (630 MW) is the largest offshore wind farm in the world. The United Kingdom is the world's leading generator of offshore wind power. followed by Denmark. There are many large wind farms under construction and these include Anholt Offshore Wind Farm (400 MW). BARD Offshore 1 (400 MW). Clyde Wind Farm (548 MW). Fântânele-Cogealac Wind Farm (600 MW). Greater Gabbard wind farm (500 MW). Lincs Wind Farm(270 MW). London Array (1000 MW). Lower Snake River Wind Project (343 MW). Macarthur Wind Farm (420 MW). Shepherds Flat Wind Farm (845 MW). and the Sheringham Shoal (317 MW).

Top 10 windpower countries of 2012

Country	capacity (MW)	per cent of total
China	75.564	26.8
United States	60.007	21.2
Germany	31.332	11.1
Spain	22.796	8.1
India	18.421	6.5
United Kingdom	8.845	3.0
Italy	8.144	2.9
France	7.196	2.5
Canada	6.200	2.2
Portugal	4.525	1.6
(rest of world)	39.853	14.1
World total	282.482	100%

nameplate capacity is shown. figures by year-end.

SOLAR THERMAL

Fig. Solar Towers of the PS10 and PS20solar thermal plants in Spain.

The United States conducted much early research in photovoltaics and concentrated solar power. The U.S. is among the top countries in the world in electricity generated by the Sun and several of the world's largest utility-scale installations are located in the desert Southwest.The oldest solar thermal power plant in the world is the 354 megawatt (MW) SEGS thermal power plant. in

California. The Ivanpah Solar Electric Generating System is a solar thermal power project in the California Mojave Desert. 40 miles (64 km) southwest of Las Vegas. with a gross capacity of 377 MW. The 280 MW Solana Generating Station is a solar power plant near Gila Bend. Arizona. about 70 miles (110 km) southwest of Phoenix. completed in 2013. When commissioned it was the largest parabolic trough plant in the world and the first U.S. solar plant with molten salt thermal energy storage.

The solar thermal power industry is growing rapidly with 1.3 GW under construction in 2012 and more planned. Spain is the epicenter of solar thermal power development with 873 MW under construction. and a further 271 MW under development. In the United Statcs. 5.600 MW of solar thermal power projects have been announced. Several power plants have been constructed in the Mojave Desert. Southwestern United States. The Ivanpah Solar Power Facility being the most recent. In developing countries. three World Bank projects for integrated solar thermal/combined-cycle gas-turbine power plants in Egypt. Mexico. and Morocco have been approved.

Photovoltaic development

Photovoltaics (PV) uses solar cells assembled into solar panels to convert sunlight into electricity. It's a fast-growing technology doubling its worldwide installed capacity every couple of years. PV systems range from small. residential and commercial rooftop or building integrated installations. to large utility-scale solar plants. The predominant PV technology is crystalline silicon. while thin-film solar celltechnology accounts for about 10 percent of global photovoltaic deployment. In recent years. PV technology has improved its electricity generating efficiency. reduced the installation cost per watt as well as its energy payback time (EPBT). and has reached grid parity in at least 19 different markets by 2014. Financial institutions are predicting a second solar "gold rush" in the near future.

At the end of 2013. worldwide PV capacity reached 139.000 megawatts. Photovoltaics grew fastcst in China (+11.8 GW). followed byJapan (+6.9 GW) and the United States (+4.75 GW). while Germany remains the world's largest overall producer of photovoltaic power with a total capacity of 35.5 GW. contributing almost 6 percent to the overall electricity generation. Italy meets 7 percent of its electricity demands with photovoltaic power—the highest share worldwide.For 2014. global photovoltaic capacity is estimated to increase by another 45 gigawatts (GW). By 2018. worldwide capacity is projected to reach as much as 430 gigawatts. This corresponds to a tripling within five years. Solar power is expected to become the world's largest source of electricity by 2050. with solar photovoltaics (PV) and solar thermal (CSP) contributing 16% and 11% respectively. This will require an increase of installed PV capacity from 139 GW to 4.600 GW. of which more than half will be deployed in China and India.

Photovoltaic power stations

Fig. Nellis Solar Power Plant. 14 MW power plant installed 2007 in Nevada. USA.

Many solar photovoltaic power stations have been built. mainly in Europe. As of May 2012. the largest photovoltaic (PV) power plants in the world are the Agua Caliente Solar Project (USA. 247 MW). Charanka Solar Park (India. 214 MW). Golmud Solar Park (China. 200 MW). Perovo Solar Park (Ukraine. 100 MW). Sarnia Photovoltaic Power Plant (Canada. 97 MW). Brandenburg-Briest Solarpark(Germany. 91 MW). Solarpark Finow Tower (Germany. 84.7 MW). Montalto di Castro Photovoltaic Power Station (Italy. 84.2 MW). and the Eggebek Solar Park (Germany. 83.6 MW).

There are also many large plants under construction. The Desert Sunlight Solar Farm is a 550 MW solar power plant under construction in Riverside County. California. that will use thin-film solar photovoltaic modules made by First Solar. The Topaz Solar Farm is a 550 MW photovoltaic power plant. being built in San Luis Obispo County. California. The Blythe Solar Power Project is a 500 MW photovoltaic station under construction in Riverside County. California.

The California Valley Solar Ranch (CVSR) is a 250 MW solar photovoltaic power plant. which is being built by SunPower in the Carrizo Plain. northeast of California Valley. The 230 MW Antelope Valley Solar Ranch is a First Solar photovoltaic project which is under construction in the Antelope Valley area of the Western Mojave Desert. and due to be completed in 2013.

Many of these plants are integrated with agriculture and some use tracking systems that follow the sun's daily path across the sky to generate more electricity than fixed-mounted systems. There are no fuel costs or emissions during operation of the power stations.

However. when it comes to renewable energy systems and PV. it is not just large systems that matter. Building-integrated photovoltaics or "onsite" PV systems use existing land and structures and generate power close to where it is consumed.

Carbon-neutral and negative fuels

Carbon-neutral fuels are synthetic fuels (including methane. gasoline. diesel fuel. jet fuel or ammonia) produced by hydrogenating waste carbon dioxide recycled from power plant flue-gas emissions. recovered from automotive exhaust gas. or derived from carbonic acid in seawater. Such fuels are considered carbon-neutral because they do not result in a net increase in atmospheric greenhouse gases. To the extent that synthetic fuels displace fossil fuels. or if they are produced from waste carbon or seawater carbonic acid. and their combustion is subject to carbon capture at the flue or exhaust pipe. they result in negative carbon dioxide emission and net carbon dioxide removalfrom the atmosphere. and thus constitute a form of greenhouse gas remediation.

Such renewable fuels alleviate the costs and dependency issues of imported fossil fuels without requiring either electrification of the vehicle fleet or conversion to hydrogen or other fuels. enabling continued compatible and affordable vehicles. Carbon-neutral fuels offer relatively low cost energy storage. alleviating the problems of wind and solarintermittency. and they enable distribution of wind. water. and solar power through existing natural gas pipelines. Nighttime wind power is considered the most economical form of electrical power with which to synthesize fuel. because the load curve for electricity peaks sharply during the warmest hours of the day. but wind tends to blow slightly more at night than during the day. so. the price of nighttime wind power is often much less expensive than any alternative. Germany has built a 250 kilowatt synthetic methane plant which they are scaling up to 10 megawatts.

The George Olah carbon dioxide recycling plant in Grindavík. Iceland has been producing 2 million liters of methanol transportation fuel per year from flue exhaust of theSvartsengi Power Station since 2011. It has the capacity to produce 5 million liters per year.

Biofuel development

Biofuels provided 3% of the world's transport fuel in 2010. Mandates for blending biofuels exist in 31 countries at the national level and in 29 states/ provinces. According to the International Energy Agency. biofuels have the potential to meet more than a quarter of world demand for transportation fuels by 2050.

Since the 1970s. Brazil has had an ethanol fuel programme which has allowed the country to become the world's second largest producer ofethanol (after the United States) and the world's largest exporter. Brazil's ethanol fuel programme uses modern equipment and cheapsugarcane as feedstock. and the residual cane-waste (bagasse) is used to produce heat and power. There are no longer light vehicles in Brazil running on pure gasoline. By the end of 2008 there were 35.000 filling stations throughout Brazil with at least one ethanol pump.

Nearly all the gasoline sold in the United States today is mixed with 10% ethanol. a mix known as E10. and motor vehicle manufacturers already produce vehicles designed to run on much higher ethanol blends. Ford. Daimler AG. and GM are among the automobile companies that sell “flexible-fuel” cars. trucks. and minivans that can use gasoline and ethanol blends ranging from pure gasoline up to 85% ethanol (E85). By mid-2006. there were approximately 6 million E85-compatible vehicles on U.S. roads. The challenge is to expand the market for biofuels beyond the farm states where they have been most popular to date. Flex-fuel vehicles are assisting in this transition because they allow drivers to choose different fuels based on price and availability. The *Energy Policy Act of 2005*. which calls for 7.5 billion US gallons (28.000.000 m^3) of biofuels to be used annually by 2012. will also help to expand the market.

Geothermal development

Fig. Geothermal plant at The Geysers. California. USA.

Geothermal power is cost effective. reliable. sustainable. and environmentally friendly. but has historically been limited to areas neartectonic plate boundaries. Recent technological advances have expanded the range and size of viable resources. especially for applications such as home heating. opening a potential for widespread exploitation. Geothermal wells release greenhouse gases trapped deep within the earth. but these emissions are much lower per energy unit than those of fossil fuels. As a result. geothermal power has the potential to help mitigate global warming if widely deployed in place of fossil fuels. The International Geothermal Association (IGA) has reported that 10.715 MW of geothermal power in 24 countries is online. which is expected to generate 67.246 GWh of electricity in 2010. This represents a 20% increase in geothermal power online capacity since 2005. IGA projects this will grow to 18.500 MW by 2015. due to the large number of projects presently under consideration. often in areas previously assumed to have little exploitable resource.

In 2010. the United States led the world in geothermal electricity production with 3.086 MW of installed capacity from 77 power plants; the largest group of geothermal power plants in the world is located at The Geysers. a geothermal field in California. The Philippines follows the US as the second highest producer of geothermal power in the world. with 1.904 MW of capacity online; geothermal power makes up approximately 18% of the country's electricity generation.

Developing countries

Renewable energy can be particularly suitable for developing countries. In rural and remote areas. transmission and distribution of energy generated from fossil fuels can be difficult and expensive. Producing renewable energy locally can offer a viable alternative.

Technology advances are opening up a huge new market for solar power: the approximately 1.3 billion people around the world who don't have access to grid electricity. Even though they are typically very poor. these people have to pay far more for lighting than people in rich countries because they use inefficient kerosene lamps. Solar power costs half as much as lighting with kerosene. An estimated 3 million households get power from small solar PV systems. Kenya is the world leader in the number of solar power systems installed per capita. More than 30.000 very small solar panels. each producing 12 to 30 watts. are sold in Kenya annually. Some Small Island Developing States (SIDS) are also turning to solar power to reduce their costs and increase their sustainability.

Micro-hydro configured into mini-grids also provide power. Over 44 million households use biogas made in household-scale digesters for lighting and/or cooking. and more than 166 million households rely on a new generation of more-efficient biomass cookstoves. Clean liquid fuel sourced from renewable feedstocks are used for cooking and lighting in energy-poor areas of the developing world. Alcohol fuels (ethanol and methanol) can be produced sustainably from non-food sugary. starchy. and cellulostic feedstocks. Project Gaia. Inc. and CleanStar Mozambique are implementing clean cooking programmes with liquid ethanol stoves in Ethiopia. Kenya. Nigeria and Mozambique. Renewable energy projects in many developing countries have demonstrated that renewable energy can directly contribute to poverty reduction by providing the energy needed for creating businesses and employment. Renewable energy technologies can also make indirect contributions to alleviating poverty by providing energy for cooking. space heating. and lighting. Renewable energy can also contribute to education. by providing electricity to schools.

Industry and policy trends

U.S. President Barack Obama's American Recovery and Reinvestment Act of 2009 includes more than $70 billion in direct spending and tax credits for clean energy and associated transportation programmes. Clean Edge suggests that the commercialization of clean energy will help countries around the world pull out of the current economic malaise. Leading renewable energy companies include First Solar.Gamesa. GE Energy. Q-Cells. Sharp Solar. Siemens. SunOpta. Suntech Power. and Vestas.

The military has also focused on the use of renewable fuels for military vehicles. Unlike fossil fuels. renewable fuels can be produced in any country. creating a strategic advantage. The US military has already committed itself to have 50% of its energy consumption come from alternative sources.

The International Renewable Energy Agency (IRENA) is an intergovernmental organization for promoting the adoption of renewable energy worldwide. It aims to provide concrete policy advice and facilitate capacity building and technology transfer. IRENA was formed on January 26. 2009. by 75 countries signing the charter of IRENA. As of March 2010. IRENA has 143 member states who all are considered as founding members. of which 14 have also ratified the statute.

As of 2011. 119 countries have some form of national renewable energy policy target or renewable support policy. National targets now exist in at least 98 countries. There is also a wide range of policies at state/provincial and local levels.

United Nations' Secretary-General Ban Ki-moon has said that renewable energy has the ability to lift the poorest nations to new levels of prosperity. In October 2011. he "announced the creation of a high-level group to drum up support for energy access. energy efficiency and greater use of renewable energy. The group is to be co-chaired by Kandeh Yumkella. the chair of UN Energy and director general of the UN Industrial Development Organisation. and Charles Holliday. chairman of Bank of America".

100% Renewable Energy

The incentive to use 100% renewable energy. for electricity. transport. or even total primary energy supply globally. has been motivated by global warming and other ecological as well as economic concerns. The Intergovernmental Panel on Climate Change has said that there are few fundamental technological limits to integrating a portfolio of renewable energy technologies to meet most of total global energy demand. Renewable energy use has grown much faster than even advocates anticipated. At the national level. at least 30 nations around the world already have renewable energy contributing more than 20% of energy supply. Also. Professors S. Pacala and Robert H. Socolow have developed a series of "stabilization wedges" that can allow us to maintain our quality of life while avoiding catastrophic climate change. and "renewable energy sources." in aggregate. constitute the largest number of their "wedges."

Mark Z. Jacobson. professor of civil and environmental engineering at Stanford University and director of its Atmosphere and Energy Programme says producing all new energy with wind power. solar power. and hydropower by 2030 is feasible and existing energy supply arrangements could be replaced by 2050. Barriers to implementing the renewable energy plan are seen to be "primarily social and political. not technological or economic". Jacobson says that energy costs with a wind. solar. water system should be similar to today's energy costs.

Similarly. in the United States. the independent National Research Council has noted that "sufficient domestic renewable resources exist to allow renewable electricity to play a significant role in future electricity generation and thus help confront issues related to climate change. energy security. and the escalation of energy costs ... Renewable energy is an attractive option because renewable resources available in the United States. taken collectively. can supply significantly greater amounts of electricity than the total current or projected domestic demand.".

The most significant barriers to the widespread implementation of large-scale renewable energy and low carbon energy strategies are primarily political and not technological. According to the 2013 *Post Carbon Pathways* report. which reviewed many international studies. the key roadblocks are: climate change denial. the fossil fuels lobby. political inaction. unsustainable energy consumption. outdated energy infrastructure. and financial constraints.

EMERGING TECHNOLOGIES

Other renewable energy technologies are still under development. and include cellulosic ethanol. hot-dry-rock geothermal power. and ocean energy. These technologies are not yet widely demonstrated or have limited commercialization. Many are on the horizon and may have potential comparable to other renewable energy technologies. but still depend on attracting sufficient attention and research. development and demonstration (RD&D) funding.

There are numerous organizations within the academic. federal. and commercial sectors conducting large scale advanced research in the field of renewable energy. This research spans several areas of focus across the renewable energy spectrum. Most of the research is targeted at improving efficiency and increasing overall energy yields.Multiple federally supported research organizations have focused on renewable energy in recent years. Two of the most prominent of these labs are Sandia National Laboratories and the National Renewable Energy Laboratory (NREL). both of which are funded by the United States Department of Energy and supported by various corporate partners. Sandia has a total budget of $2.4 billion while NREL has a budget of $375 million.

CELLULOSIC ETHANOL

Companies such as Iogen. POET. and Abengoa are building refineries that can process biomass and turn it into ethanol. while companies such as the Verenium Corporation.Novozymes. and Dyadic International are producing enzymes which could enable a cellulosic ethanol future. The shift from food crop feedstocks to waste residues and native grasses offers significant opportunities for a range of players. from farmers to biotechnology firms. and from project developers to investors.

Selected Commercial Cellulosic Ethanol Plants in the U.S. (Operational or under construction)

Company	Location	Feedstock
Abengoa Bioenergy	Hugoton. KS	Wheat straw
BlueFire Renewables	Irvine. CA	Multiple sources
Gulf Coast Energy	Mossy Head. FL	Wood waste
Mascoma	Lansing. MI	Wood
POET	Emmetsburg. IA	Corn cobs
SunOpta	Little Falls. MN	Wood chips
Xethanol	Auburndale. FL	Citrus peels

MARINE ENERGY

Marine energy (also sometimes referred to as ocean energy) refers to the energy carried by ocean waves. tides. salinity. and ocean temperature differences. The movement of water in the world's oceans creates a vast store of kinetic energy. or energy in motion. This energy can be harnessed to generate electricity to power homes. transport and industries.

The term marine energy encompasses both wave power – power from surface waves. and tidal power – obtained from the kinetic energy of large bodies of moving water. Offshore wind power is not a form of marine energy. as wind power is derived from the wind. even if thewind turbines are placed over water.

The oceans have a tremendous amount of energy and are close to many if not most concentrated populations. Ocean energy has the potential of providing a substantial amount of new renewable energy around the world.

ENHANCED GEOTHERMAL SYSTEMS

Enhanced geothermal systems are a new type of geothermal power technologies that do not require natural convective hydrothermal resources. The vast majority of geothermal energy within drilling reach is in dry and non-porous rock. EGS technologies "enhance" and/or create geothermal resources in this "hot dry rock (HDR)" through hydraulic stimulation.

EGS/ HDR technologies. like hydrothermal geothermal. are expected to be baseload resources which produce power 24 hours a day like a fossil plant. Distinct from hydrothermal. HDR/ EGS may be feasible anywhere in the world. depending on the economic limits of drill depth. Good locations are over deep granite covered by a thick (3–5 km) layer of insulating sediments which slow heat loss. There are HDR and EGS systems currently being developed and tested in France. Australia. Japan. Germany. the U.S. and Switzerland. The largest EGS project in the world is a 25 megawatt demonstration plant currently being developed in the Cooper Basin. Australia. The Cooper Basin has the potential to generate 5.000–10.000 MW.

EXPERIMENTAL SOLAR POWER

Fig. Concentrating photovoltaics in Catalonia. Spain

Concentrated photovoltaics (CPV) systems employ sunlight concentrated onto photovoltaic surfaces for the purpose of electricity generation. Thermoelectric. or "thermovoltaic" devices convert a temperature difference between dissimilar materials into an electric current.

ARTIFICIAL PHOTOSYNTHESIS

Artificial photosynthesis uses techniques including nanotechnology to store solar electromagnetic energy in chemical bonds by splitting water to produce hydrogen and then using carbon dioxide to make methanol. Researchers in this field are striving to design molecular mimics of photosynthesis that utilize a wider region of the solar spectrum. employ catalytic systems made from abundant. inexpensive materials that are robust. readily repaired. non-toxic. stable in a variety of environmental conditions and perform more efficiently allowing a greater proportion of photon energy to end up in the storage compounds. *i.e.*. carbohydrates (rather than building and sustaining living cells). However. prominent research faces hurdles. Sun Catalytix a MIT spin-off stopped scaling up their prototype fuel-cell in 2012. because it offers few savings over other ways to make hydrogen from sunlight.

DEBATE

Renewable electricity production. from sources such as wind power and solar power. is sometimes criticized for being variable orintermittent. However. the International Energy Agency has stated that deployment of renewable technologies usually increases the diversity of electricity sources and. through local generation. contributes to the flexibility of the system and its resistance to central shocks.

There have been "not in my back yard" (NIMBY) concerns relating to the visual and other impacts of some wind farms. with local residents sometimes fighting or blocking construction. In the USA. the Massachusetts Cape Wind project was delayed for years partly because of aesthetic concerns. However. residents in other areas have been more positive. According to a town councilor. the overwhelming majority of locals believe that the Ardrossan Wind Farm in Scotland has enhanced the area.

A recent UK Government document states that "projects are generally more likely to succeed if they have broad public support and the consent of local communities. This means giving communities both a say and a stake". In countries such as Germany and Denmark many renewable projects are owned by communities. particularly throughcooperative structures. and contribute significantly to overall levels of renewable energy deployment.

The market for renewable energy technologies has continued to grow. Climate change concerns. coupled with high oil prices. peak oil. and increasing government support. are driving increasing renewable energy legislation. incentives and commercialization. New government spending. regulation and policies helped the industry weather the 2009 economic crisis better than many other sectors.

MANUFACTURE RENEWABLES TO BUILD ENERGY SECURITY

China's rise to become the world's largest power producer and source of carbon emissions through burning coal is well recognised. But the nation's renewable-energy systems are expanding even faster than its fossil-fuel and nuclear power. China leads the world in the production and use of wind turbines. solar-photovoltaic cells and smart-grid technologies. generating almost as much water. wind and solar energy as all of France and Germany's power plants combined. Production of solar cells in China has expanded 100-fold since 2005. As the scale of Chinese manufacturing has grown. the costs of renewable-energy devices have plummeted. Innovation has played a part. But the main driver of cost reduction has been market expansion. Germany and South Korea are following similar paths. In short: industrialization can go hand in hand with decarbonization.Too many countries have yet to take notice. The United States and European Union are pursuing counterproductive policies. such as increasing trade tariffs on imported Chinese photovoltaic panels. Restricting global trade in renewable devices will only slow the rate at which costs decrease and will decelerate the world's retreat from fossil fuels.

As a result. uptake of renewable energies globally has been too sluggish to seriously reduce greenhouse gases and tackle climate change. For 15 years. countries have failed to deliver their carbon-reduction commitments under the Kyoto Protocol. hindered by the vested interests of the fossil-fuel industry and fears that the alternatives are costly.

The narrative around renewable energies needs to change. As in China. renewables must be seen as a source of energy security. not just of reduced carbon emissions. Today's discussions about energy security focus almost exclusively on maintaining access to fossil fuels. But unlike oil. coal and gas. the supplies of which are limited and subject to geopolitical tensions. renewable-energy devices can be built anywhere and implemented wherever there is sufficient water. wind and sun.

GREEN GROWTH

As the scale of manufacture and use of renewables rises. market forces will make them more accessible. affordable and efficient. Energy policies should therefore focus on promoting manufacturing. trade and competition in low-carbon technologies. rather than supporting ever more expensive. dangerous and inaccessible fossil fuels. Emissions reductions will follow.China generates more than 5 trillion kilowatt-hours (kWh) of electricity. about 1 trillion kWh more than the United States. China's rapid economic expansion since it joined the World Trade Organization (WTO) in 2001 has been based on fossil fuels: it consumes around 23% of the world's coal production for electricity. But fossil fuels alone cannot power the industrial growth the country needs to keep up with the West.

Since the mid-2000s. China has also pursued a low-carbon energy strategy. Investment in hydroelectric. wind. solar and nuclear-power generating facilities increased by 40% between 2008 and 2012 — from 138 billion renminbi (US$22 billion) to about 200 billion renminbi. The share of investment in fossil-fuel power facilities in China. meanwhile. fell from around 50% to 25% over the same period. In 2013. China also hit its target — two years early — to generate almost 30% of electricity from renewables. The Chinese government aims for renewables capacity to reach 550 gigawatts (GW) by 2017. or 48% above the 2013 level. No other country is investing so much money or generating so much renewable energy.

ECONOMIES OF SCALE

China is upgrading its power grid to accommodate power fluctuations and distributed generation for intermittent sources. In one demonstration project. the State Grid Corporation of China (SGCC) is investing 9.4 billion renminbi to integrate wind and solar-photovoltaic generation and storage devices into the main grid. The SGCC is helping to set international product standards for smart-grid elements that will underpin the export of these technologies to countries such as Brazil.

How has China's energy security improved? China became a net importer of oil in 1993. of natural gas in 2007. and of coal in 2011. Hitting its 2017 wind. water and solar power targets. we calculate. would translate into a saving of 45% on current imports of oil. coal and natural gas.

There are two keys to China's success in renewables. Focused policies drive investment in selected sectors and encourage domestic take-up by measures such as feed-in tariffs. And industrial dynamics. including economies of scale and efficiencies gained through learning. drive down unit costs as the global market expands.

Renewable-energy generation requires the manufacture of many components. such as wind turbines. solar-photovoltaic cells. mirrors. lenses. batteries and energy-storage systems. From 2010 to 2013. while total global photovoltaic installation more than tripled from 40 GW to 140 GW. China's installation expanded 22-fold. from 0.8 GW to 18 GW. Supplying the international market. as well as the domestic one. has helped to drive down costs of photovoltaic panels by 80% since 2008. Solar-power users around the world have benefited from lower prices.

A few other countries are following a similar strategy. South Korea. for example. is committed to 'green growth' — expanding its smart grid and focusing its production on emerging clean sectors such as zero-emission vehicles.

And Germany has been expanding its manufacture and use of solar and wind power (under its *Energiewende* energy-transition programme) since the early 2000s. with the aim of replacing its nuclear power with renewables.

The same principle of industrial-scale production established US supremacy in the automotive industry a century ago. Between 1909 and 1916. Henry Ford reduced the cost of his Ford Model T by 62%. from $950 to $360. Each year. sales doubled — from fewer than 6.000 in 1908 to more than 800.000 in 1917.

Yet US energy policy emphasizes exploiting domestic coal seam gas and shale oil. through innovations such as hydraulic fracture (fracking) and horizontal drilling. The problems of diminishing returns and environmental costs of fossil fuels remain. The United Kingdom. too. is inclined to build up its supplies of coal seam gas by fracking. and to expand its fleet of nuclear reactors. a portfolio approach that will leave the country importing others' technology.

CHANGING THE CONVERSATION

Reframing the emissions debate in terms of energy security has profound implications for international negotiations under the terms of the United Nations Framework Convention on Climate Change. In December. national representatives will gather in Lima for the preparatory meeting to the Paris conference in 2015. Their agenda remains negotiating voluntary national carbon-emissions reductions. rather than promoting renewable-energy industries. as the fastest route to decarbonization.

But governments that build strong renewables sectors can achieve those emissions reductions while enhancing their energy security and building their manufacturing industries. Another advantage of the market-oricntcd approach is that renewables are not burdened with the task of resolving the entire climate-change problem. Few countries will be able to rely on water. wind and solar power alone. and some fossil fuels will continue to be used.

"No other country is investing so much or generating so much renewable energy."

Our critics will counter that technology-based solutions raise concerns over the availability of industrial materials and land for building solar and wind devices and farms. But our calculations suggest that a global renewables push for an extra 10 terawatts of power-generation capacity could be achieved on current industrial scales over the next 20 years. by which time the world energy system would be well on the way to total conversion. Producing the extra 10 terawatts from renewables needed to transform global electric power would require more than 5 million square kilometres (about twice the size of Kazakhstan) filled with around 3 million wind turbines. 14.000 concentrated solar-power installations and 12.500 solar-photovoltaic farms. These technologies could perhaps be accommodated in the world's desert and semi-desert regions. The targets are large — but they are manageable compared with current world production levels of 1.75 billion mobile phones per year or 84 million vehicles per year.

TRADE SOLUTIONS

The main obstacles to expanding renewables uptake are failed policies and continuing subsidization of fossil fuels. All governments should enlarge the market for renewable power by encouraging manufacture and trade of devices. Countries should foster export and import of renewable electric power (from. say. North Africa to Europe under the DESERTEC project. or from Mongolia to China. Japan and South Korea under the east Asian super-grid proposal). Above all. the narrow agenda that the Kyoto process has enforced needs to be broadened. How? One way involves expanding free trade in renewable devices. Here. the WTO could complement the Kyoto process. A preliminary agreement to free up trade in renewables was adopted by Asia-Pacific Economic

Cooperation countries in 2012. and could be proposed to the WTO. A precedent exists with trade in personal computers and other information-technology products. It was expanded from a voluntary agreement to reduce tariffs. signed up to by most major industrial countries. and adopted by the WTO in 1997.

Private finance must also play a part. The Kyoto-process negotiators have so far considered that financing for climate-related initiatives should come from tax-based public finance rather than from private or even government-backed development banks. This emphasis needs to change. Green bonds lower the costs of capital and facilitate the scaling up of investments. One example is the $500-million bond issued by the Export-Import Bank of Korea last year allocated exclusively to finance green projects around the world.

China is leading the way. By placing the emphasis on production scale and market growth. it is contributing more than any other country to a climate-change solution. Its build-up of renewable-energy systems at serious scale is driving cost reductions that will make water. wind and solar power accessible to all.

THE COMMERCIAL RENEWABLE ENERGY TECHNOLOGIES

Fundamentally. the answer depends on why the question is being asked. and in which country the policy is being applied. There are. however. guidelines which may prove useful to policy strategists making this determination in any country. Essentially. form must follow function. In other words. it is essential that the policy strategist understand the nature of each of the renewable resources and the nature of the process by which each of those resources is developed.The resources are fundamentally different. Although any resource that relies on the heat or motion of the earth. the moon or the sun (or the sun's radiation) to produce power for human consumption is a renewable resource. the ways one harnesses the resources are sufficiently different that laws and regulations governing these resources usually deal with each resource on an individual basis - treating each resource as unique. At present. the major commercial grid-connected renewable resources are hydroelectric. geothermal. biomass. wind energy and solar. In the majority of legal regimes. hydroelectric and geothermal resources are identified as owned in common by the people of the country and husbanded by the government for their benefit.

- *Geothermal resources* require extraction (and reinjection). Drilling for geothermal resources involves many of the same discrete considerations involved with drilling for petroleum (hydrocarbons) and individual treatment is prudent.

GEOTHERMAL RESOURCES

- *Hydroelectric resources* are inextricably linked with surface water rights. including potable water. navigation. irrigation. navigation and recreational rights. The historical complexities of sorting out these juxtaposed rights usually dictate individual treatment of hydroelectric resource issues.

HYDROELECTRIC RESOURCES

- *Wind energy and solar* draw on resources: wind and sun energy - generally thought of as being free for the taking. The principal resource issue with both of these renewables is surface land. Therefore there is no general technical requirement for individual treatment.

WIND ENERGY AND SOLAR

- *Biomass* is a broadly inclusive term. often encompassing wood and wood waste. agricultural waste and residue. energy crops. and - sometimes - landfill gas resources. Resource availability and cost can be highly variable. and resources may require management of a type not frequently required for other renewables. Individual treatment is one method of addressing this complication.

BIOMASS

Renewable energy applications generally break down into two categories or applications. "on-grid" and "off-grid".

- A *"grid"* may be defined as an integrated generation. transmission. and distribution system serving numerous customers. Characteristically. a grid is a portfolio of generating units operating under the control of a central dispatch centre. Grids may be national. regional or local (in the latter case they are typically referred to as *"mini-grids"*).
- *"On-grid"* and *"off-grid"* are terms which describe how electricity is delivered. Technically. every one of the commercial renewable resources can be and have been installed both on-grid and off-grid. Furthermore. although larger megawatt installations tend to be on-grid. large renewable plants may profitably be built *"inside the fence"* - *a* term describing a self-generator. a plant built to supply a single customer such as a mine. a manufacturing plant or an agribusiness. Hydroelectric. biomass and geothermal facilities tend to be economical at capacity levels well in excess of one megawatt (1 MW) and. therefore. are typically - but not necessarily - developed and financed as *"base load"* electricity resources (*i.e.*. the normally operated generating facilities within a utility system) and connected to a grid. Solar arrays and "wind farms" also can be grid-connected.

- *"Off-grid"* applications. in general. serve only one load. such as a home or small business. Off-grid applications can take many forms. from photovoltaics for an individual village home to centralized windmills to power a village water pump or a commercial battery charging facility. These off-grid applications are most generally used in remote or rural settings.
- *"Mini-grids"* have begun to be developed by system engineers over the past few years. for isolated communities. These systems may integrate wind. solar energy and. in some cases. diesel generators and/or storage systems to provide power from a mix of resources to more than one customer. typically a village or cooperative.

On-Grid Uses	Hydro	Wind	PV	Geo-thermal	Bio-mass	Solar thermal
Bulk Power	•	•	•	•	•	•
Grid support	•	•	•	•	•	•
Demand-side management	•	•	•	•	•	•
Distributed generation	•	•	•	•	•	•
Cogeneration				•	•	•

ON-GRID USES

- In addition to generating bulk electricity. the renewable energy technologies can serve a number of other valuable on-grid roles.
  - For grid support. a power station is constructed somewhere along a transmission line to remedy high resistance in the line. This reduces transmission losses and prevents expensive substation equipment from being degraded by excessive heat (this application is a type of*"distributed generation"*).
  - In distributed generation. as opposed to central station generation. power plants are smaller and they exist at more locations on the grid. This reduces transmission costs. Distributed generation tends to yield the largest returns in locations where it averts the need to increase transmission capacity.
  - Biomass and geothermal are well-suited to regeneration.
- This table is not exhaustive. There are many other uses of each technology.

Off-Grid-Uses	Hydro	Wind	PV	Goo-thermal	Bid-mass	Solar thermal
Mini-grid power for village. island. industry military. tourism. etc.	•	•	•	•	•	•
Individual systems for housc. clinic school. store. more	•	•	•	•		•
Water pumping. water treatment	•	•	•	•		•

Unattended loads (*e.g.*. telecom)	•	•		•	•	•
Space heating. water heating	•	•	•	•	•	
Process heat. cogeneration				•	•	•

OFF-GRID USES

- This chart is not comprehensive. but lists some of the common off-grid applications for which renewable energy is best suited.
  - Power and heat for remote villages. islands. tourist facilities. industrial and military installations. houses. clinics. schools. and stores.
  - Water pumping. disinfection. and desalination.
  - Communication stations. navigational aids. and road signals.
- For most types of energy applications. on-and off-grid. one or more of the renewable energy technologies is cost-competitive.
- Worldwide. millions upon millions of dollars are wasted by utilities. governments. businesses. and individuals that ignore opportunities to improve cost-effectiveness through the use of renewable energy.
- Energy decision-makers can improve their energy costs and performance by giving full and informed consideration to the renewable energy sources every time they choose an energy technology.

POLICY BENEFITS OF RENEWABLE ENERGY FACILITIES

Cost-benefit analysis is a generally accepted method of evaluating the value of competing energy sources.

Although a complete list of the benefits of renewable technologies can be very extensive. they can be categorized under four headings: environment. diversification. sustainability and economics.

RENEWABLE RESOURCES ARE ENVIRONMENTALLY BENIGN

Renewable energy facilities generally have a very modest impact on their surrounding environment. The discharges of unwanted or unhealthy substances into the air. ground or water commonly associated with other forms of generation can be reduced significantly by deploying renewables. Clean technologies can also produce significant indirect economic benefits. For example. unlike fossil-fuel facilities. renewable facilities will not need to be fitted with scrubbing technology to mitigate air pollution. nor will a country need to expend resources in cleaning up polluted rivers or the earth around sites contaminated with fossil-fuel by-products. Furthermore. they provide greenhouse gas reduction benefits and should a worldwide market for air emission credits emerge as has been predicted. countries with a strong portfolio of renewable energy projects may be able to earn pollution credits which can be exchanged for hard currency. Finally. having a clean environmental profile enhances the attractiveness of renewable projects in the eyes of investors. especially the multilateral development agencies. many of whom operate under guidelines that require the promotion of non-polluting technologies.

RENEWABLE RESOURCES PROMOTE ENERGY DIVERSIFICATION

Development of a diverse portfolio of generation assets reduces both a country's dependence on any one particular form of technology or fuel and its vulnerability to supply disruption and price increases.

The primary long-term benefit of renewable technologies is that once a renewable project has been constructed. and fully depredated. it becomes a permanent. environmentally dean. and low cost component of a country's energy system. In effect. the construction of a renewable energy project provides future generations a low cost. energy facility that produces power with little or no environmental degradation.

RENEWABLE RESOURCES ARE SUSTAINABLE

Renewable technologies are designed to run on a virtually inexhaustible or replenishable supply of natural "fuels." Expanding a nation's electricity supply by attracting investment to renewable energy projects is. by defintion. a strategy for sustainable growth. since operation of the facilities does not deplete the earth's finite resources.

Renewable energy facilities enhance the value of the overall resource base of a country by using the country's indigenous resources for electricity generation. Moreover. since these facilities operate on "fuels" that are both indigenous and renewable (as distinguished from imported fossil fuels). they may reduce balance-of-payment problems. Reduced dependence on fuel imports reduces exposure to currency fluctuations and fuel price volatility. The construction and operation of renewable projects normally generate significant local economic activity. often in previously "resource poor" areas of a country. Renewable energy projects thus act as engines for regional economic development. In the case of large scale. on-grid projects. easements will need to be purchased and local workers hired to construct and operate the facility. Frequently. a local industry such as a sugar mill or a paper mill (when biomass technology is employed) will be associated with the development. enhancing the opportunities for joint ventures between local landowners and private investors who may supply technological expertise. Smaller scale facilities often attract local private sector involvement. Local involvement. in turn. stimulates new economic activity in a multiplier effect and adds value to the local tax base.

3

Energy Scenario in India

The decade of seventies has witnessed major world oil supply disruptions. During the 1970s the OPEC production was cut down by two and a half per cent causing severe oil supply distortions. From 1975 oil prices remained high but not as high as in 1973-74. But the Iranian revolution in 1979 worsened the situation and oil prices again rose sharply in 1979. generating the second oil shock. From the mid 1980s. there was again a resumption of the growth of demand for refined products. This demand upsurge led to an increase in oil prices from the late 1980s. From July to October 1990. following Iraq's invasion of Kuwait. there was a near doubling of oil prices. However. this 1990 oil price shock had substantially lesser impact on the world economy than the other two oil price shocks. The reason for this diminished effect was the short duration (only 4 months) of the 1990s oil price hike. the substitution of oil. to a large extent. by competing energy sources and an overall recession of economic activities that had already begun before the price hikes. India being an oil importing country witnessed significant changes in the energy consumption pattern due to the oil shocks. After then inflationary situation arose in India. Faced with rising inflation and a balance of payment crisis in mid 1991 the government of India introduced a fairly comprehensive policy reform package-comprising currency devaluation. deregulation. de-licensing. privatisation of the public sector. The government of India initiated these policy changes to overcome the critical situation. The rising oil import bill has been the focus of serious concerns due to the pressure it has placed on scarce foreign exchange resources.

The brief discussion about the commercial energy shows that the country is having potential in some cases but utilisation is not upto the desired level. From the oil front. it is apparent that country has to rely on import. Due to the volatility of the international market country's import bill is rising. On the other hand transmission and distribution losses are making the electricity sector critical. The industrial sector in India is a major energy user. accounting for about 65% of the commercial consumption. There are wide variations in energy consumption among different units within the same industry using comparable technology. The energy saving potential in this sector may be as high as 25% making this sector as having the maximum potential in the economy. Despite the large potential. energy efficiency investments having financially attractive returns. only a small fraction is being tapped actually.

Table. Growth of energy consumption in different sectors of the economy

Years	Energy consumed in agriculture	Energy consumed in industry	Energy consumed in transport	Energy consumed in services
1990-91	4.36	56.01	24.93	14.69
1991-92	4.75	55.89	24.85	14.50
1992-93	4.96	55.69	24.88	14.47
1993-94	5.31	55.43	24.67	14.60
1994-95	5.70	54.74	24.74	14.81
1995-96	5.19	53.53	27.87	13.41
1996-97	5.16	57.14	26.06	11.64
1997-98	5.40	48.01	29.49	17.10
1998-99	4.86	44.04	31.29	19.82
1999-2000	4.79	45.69	32.30	17.31
2000-1	3.53	47.26	32.64	17.56
2001-2	3.02	46.52	33.30	17.75
2002-3	3.33	49.52	31.93	15.27
2003-4	3.85	47.05	32.16	17.27

The growth pattern of the energy consumption in different sectors of the economy since the 1990s. Transport sector shows high energy consumption growth through out. Though the industrial sector records high growth in first half of the 1990s but it starts decline from later half of the 1990s.

Further we know that the energy consumption —fossil fuel based —always is responsible for environmental pollution. India is currently the fifth-largest carbon emitter in the world (behind only the United States. China. Russia. and Japan) and currently accounts for about 4.2% of the world's total fossil fuel-related carbon emissions. There is concern for climate change which has been induced by green house gases owing to use of fossil fuels in generation of energy and transportation. Increasing concern about environmental problems caused by the combustion of fossil fuels has generated a need for knowledge on energy production and consumption patterns.

With this background it is needed to analyse the sources of changes of the energy consumption in India during the reform period which will help to formulate or change policies if necessary.

Towards this end the objective of the current paper is to identify the sources of changes in energy consumption in India using input-output structural decomposition analysis (SDA) during reform period.

RENEWABLE ENERGY DEVELOPMENT IN INDIA

India has done a significant progress in the power generation in the country. The installed generation capacity was 1300 megawatt (MW) at the time of Independence *i.e.* about 60 year's back. The total generating capacity anticipated at the end of the Tenth Plan on 31-03-2007. is 1. 44.520 MW which includes the generation through various sectors like Hydro. Thermal and Nuclear. The power generation in the country is planned through funds provided by the Central Sector. State Sector and Private Sector. The power shortages noticed is of the order of 11%. In the opinion of the experts such short fall can be reduced through proper management and thus almost 40% energy can be saved. It has been noticed that one watt saved at the point of consumption is more than 1.5 watts generated. In terms of Investment it costs around Rs.40 million to generate one MW of new generation plant. but if the same Rs.40 million is spent on conservation of energy methods. it can provide up to 3 MW of avoidable generation capacity.

There are about 80.000 villages yet to be electrified for which provision has been made to electrify 62.000 villages from grid supply in the Tenth Plan. It is planned that participation of decentralized power producers shall be ensured. particularly for electrification of remote villages in which village level organizations shall play a crucial role for the rural electrification programme.

Emphasis is given to the renewable energy programme towards gradual commercialization. This programme is looked after by the Ministry of Non-Conventional Sources of energy. Simultaneously private sector investments in renewable energy sources are also increased to promote power generation. So far an excessive reliance was preferred on the use of fossil fuel resources like coal. oil and natural gas to meet the power requirement of the country which was not suitable in the long run due to limited availability of the fossil fuel as well as the adverse impact on the environment and ecology.

Since the availability of fossil fuel is on the decline therefore. in this backdrop the norms for conventional or renewable sources of energy (RSE) is given importance not only in India but has attracted the global attention.

The main items under RSE are as follows:

i. Hydro Power
ii. Solar Power
iii. Wind Power
iv. Bio-mass Power
v. Energy from waste
vi. Ocean energy
vii. Alternative fuel for surface transportation

HYDRO POWER

India is endowed with a large potential of hydro power. of which only 17% has been harnessed so far. The hydro electricity is a clean and renewable source of energy. It has been felt that there is a long gestation period in hydro projects due to delays in forest and environment clearance. rehabilitation of the project effected people besides inter-state disputes and construction holdups due to several reasons. Under RSE only small hydro projects are considered since they do not require large pondage and have the capacity to provide power to remote and hilly terrain where extension of the grid system is either uneconomic or not possible. It has been estimated that the potential available in the country under small hydropower schemes is of the order of 15000 MW in which the plans that are considered are up to 25 MW capacity individually which are classified as small hydro projects under the Ministry of Non-Conventional Sources of energy. The small hydro power stations are mostly located in hilly areas and are given priority for local benefits to the residents which provide them gainful employment through the energy potential.

SOLAR POWER

The climatic condition in India provides abundant potential of solar power due to large scale radiation available during a wider part of the year due to tropical condition in the country. The solar power can be developed for long term use through the application of solar photo- voltaic (SPV) Technology which provides a potential of 20MW per sq. Km. The other method for Utilization of solar energy is through the adoption of solar thermal Technology. The programmes are under way to utilize SPV by connecting to grid power systems.

It has come to notice from a report of Xinhva news agency that Shanghai. the business capital of China. is launching a 100000 rooftop solar photo voltaic (SPV) system which would generate 430 million KWH of electricity which would be enough to supply power to the entire city for two days.

The other popular use is by stand- alone applications which include solar powered street lights. domestic lights. water pumps etc. The cost of the photo SPV modules is quite expensive which is in the range of $ 3-4 per watt. in spite of best efforts. the price could not come down in India. China and other countries. The effort is to bring the price down to $ 1 per watt when it may be more popular for use. The efforts to use amorphous silicon technology were cheaper but its long terms use is not practicable. The SPV technology if cheep. would be useful for people living in far - flung areas as extending grid would involve high cost.

The solar thermal devices are widely used in the country for various purposes such as solar water heaters. solar cookers. solar dryers etc. There is wide scope for development of solar thermal application for which the research is in progress. The energy obtained through Solar Thermal route is 35 MW per sq. km.

WIND POWER

The wind power development in the country is largely of recent period which has been found to be quite impressive. As per available data. it is 5340

MW by March 31. 2006. through wind power. Earlier it was estimated that the potential for wind power in the country was 20.000 MW which has been revised to 45000MW after collecting the data on the potential available in the coastal and other areas of the country. At present India is fifth in the world after Germany. USA. Denmark and Spain in terms of wind power. It has been observed that the private sector is showing interest in setting of wind power projects. The unit size of wind turbine generators which were earlier in the range of 55-100 kw are now preferred in the range of 750-1000 kw. It has been observed that the productivity of the larger machine is higher as compared to the smaller machine. In respect of cost consideration. it has been noticed that the cost of such a projcct is about Rs.40 million to Rs.50 million per MW which includes all local civil. electrical works and erection also. The life of a wind power project is estimated to be about 20 years.

China has guaranteed all certified renewable energy producers in its service area that the grid will purchase their power and the price will be spread out to all the users across the grid. According to sources. such commitments can only spur further development in the renewable energy sector.

BIO-MASS POWER

There is quite a high energy potential available in the country in resources such as firewood. agroresidues and animal wastes. These resources are mainly utilized by the rural population of the country. It has been estimated that there is a potential to install 19500 MW capacity through biomass conservation technologies like combustion. gasification. incineration and also bagasse – based co- generation in sugar mills. So far only around 380 MW of this potential has been tapped and there is wide scope for expanding the size of their use for the benefit of the majority of the rural population to meet their energy needs.

ENERGY FROM WASTE

It has been estimated that there is about 30 million tones by solid waste and 4400 million cubic meters of liquid waste generated every year in urban areas through domestic as well as commercial establishment. The manufacturing sector also contributes high quantity of waste. It has been estimated that through garbage there is a potential to generate 1700 MW of electricity. However all these activities are still to be given a practical shape.

OCEAN ENERGY

The Ocean on the earth covers about 71% of the total surface which collects and store solar energy. If this energy is quantified in terms of Oil. it can be said that an amount of solar radiation equivalent in heat content to about 245 billion barrels of oil is absorbed by the sea. The energy available in the Ocean is clean. continuous and renewable. In future it would be possible to tap energy from the sea.

ALTERNATIVE FUEL FOR SURFACE TRANSPORTATION

Hydrocarbons used as fuels for transportation are to be replaced by other eco-friendly fuels for surface transport vehicles. Many options such as compressed natural gas (CNG). battery – powered vehicles and fuel cells are currently available.

The use of diesel in transportation in Delhi was causing pollution in the air. The Government has adopted CNG use for all vehicles using diesel fuel. which has improved the environment significantly

POLICY FOLLOWED IN CHINA

Renewable energy is very much promoted by the Chinese Government. Earlier the emphasis was quite low but of late it has been observed that a high priority is given to renewable sources of energy. The new law stipulates the responsibilities of government and society in developing and applying renewable energy. At the same time as the law was passed. the Chinese Government set a target for renewable energy to contribute 10% of the country's gross energy consumption by 2020. a huge increase from the current 1% Seeing this as a future stimulus of renewable energy development. many Chinese and international observers are very excited. expecting a tremendous growth in the renewable energy market in the next 15 years as the result of the implementation of this law.

The policy adopted also provides subsidies and tax credits. However. wind power development in China has lagged far behind the world leaders in the past 10 years The total installed capacity only hit 769 MWrecently. whereas. in India. the second largest developing country. the total capacity is 5340 MW. Between 1999 and 2002. only 211 MW was installed in China. while globally. 18.000 MW was added during the same period.

TRANSFORMER TECHNOLOGY

Transformers were first used in India in 1897 to light Darjeeling Municipal area. The commercial production of transformers commenced. in 1936 at Government Electrical factory. Bangalore. Later on new companies have started production and improvement in the Transformer Technology. When transformer factories were set up in 1960s there were no vendors in the country to supply processed raw materials and accessories.

Evolution of power transformer technology in the country during the past five decades is quite impressive. There are manufacturers in the country with full access to the latest technology at the global level. Some of the manufacturers have impressive R&D set up to support the technology.

AMORPHOUS METAL DISTRIBUTION TRANSFORMER

Huge amount of energy has been lost due to no-load loss of transformer core. Energy efficient transformer such as AMDT can effectively lower such energy wastage and at the same time reduce green house gases emission.

Reliability in distribution system can be brought about by incorporating following steps.

- Use transformers. which have minimum maintenance problems.
- Improve power factor of the system.
- Ensure proper protection to the system.
- Neutral grounding system should be effective.
- Introduce maintenance free equipment like Vacuum Circuit Breakers for all 11 KV feeders with auto re-closers.
- Undertake preventive maintenance and avoid emergencies.

GLOBAL WARMING AND CLIMATE CHANGE

It has been felt that there is rising demand for energy. food and raw materials by a population of 2.5 billion Chinese and Indians. Both these countries have large coal dominated energy systems in the world and the use of fossil fuels such as coal and oil releases carbon dioxide (Co_2) into the air which adds to the greenhouse gases which lead to global warming. At present US is the largest contributor of Co_2 emissions but the development in India and China is going to increase their share in emission of such a gas. According to Kyoto Protocol this has to be controlled. Climate change shall be a cause of extinction of many bird varieties and other animals on the earth. Renewable source of energy is the best solution for such a problem in the world. Both India and China are trying to develop their technology in this regard. India has the world's fourth largest wind power industry. while China is the global leader in harnessing solar energy for hot water.

Wind Power could generate almost 29 percent of the world's electricity by 2030 and was growing faster than any other clean energy source. a wind business group and environmental lobby Greenpeace said. 'At good locations wind can compete with the cost of both coal and gas-fired Power' the Global Wind Energy Council (GWEC) and Greenpeace said in a study. 'Global Wind Energy Outlook 2006'.The two said that wind. which now accounts for 0.8 percent of the world's electricity supply. was expanding faster than other renewable energies such as solar. geothermal or tidal power in a shift from fossil fuels.

There have been cases of farmers committing suicides due to poverty and failure of crop in some parts of India. A World Bank study released has found a correlation between climate change and farmer suicides. It says poor farmers who are unable to adapt to changing climates fall into debt and later. death traps. It can be surmised that energy development should be preferable by adopting measures which does not give rise to greenhouse gasses as it would effect change in climate leading to overall difficulties to the people who are accustomed to the climate as prevailing on the earth.

4

Potential and Conservation of Energy Security

In conservative systems. we can define another form of energy. based on the configuration of the parts of the system. which we call potential energy. This quantity is related to work. and thus kinetic energy. through a simple equation. Using this relation we can finally quantify all mechanical energy. and prove the conservation of mechanical energy in conservative systems.

POTENTIAL ENERGY

Since mechanical energy must be conserved under conservative forces. but the kinetic energy can fluctuate based on the speed of the particles in the system. there must be an additional quantity of energy that is a property of the structure of the system. This quantity. potential energy. is denoted by the symbol U and can be easily derived from our knowledge of conservative systems.

Consider a system under the action of a conservative force. When work is done on the system it must in some way change the velocity of its constituent parts (by the Work Energy Theorem). and thus change the configuration of the system. We define potential energy as the energy of configuration of a conservative system. and relate it to work in the following way:

$$\Delta U = -W$$

In other words. work applied by a conservative force reduces the energy of configuration of a system (potential energy). converting it to kinetic energy.

To see exactly how this conservation works. let's derive the expression for the potential energy of a system acted upon by gravity. Consider a ball of mass m dropped from a height h. The only force acting upon the ball is gravity. so we know the system is conservative. How much work is done during the fall? A constant gravitational force of mg acts over a distance of h. so $W = mgh$. Thus. over the course of the fall. the potential energy is reduced by a factor of - mgh. We may define the potential energy to be zero when the ball hits the ground and calculate the potential energy at height h:

$$\ddot{A}U = U \; \Delta U = U_{f-}U_0 = -mgh$$

Thus:

$$U_G = mgh$$

Since our choice of height h was arbitrary. this equation holds for all h relatively close to the centre of the earth. and the equation is a universal definition of the gravitational potential energy.An important property of energy is that it is a relative quantity. Just as observers moving with different velocities observe different values for the kinetic energy of a given particle. observers at a different height observe different values for gravitational potential energy. for example. When working problems we are free to choose whatever origin we like. to correspond to a convenient value for our potential energy.

Having defined potential energy. we can now see how it relates to kinetic energy. and generate our principle of conservation of mechanical energy.

WORK AND POTENTIAL ENERGY

Potential energy is closely linked with forces. If the work done by a force on a body that moves from *A* to *B* does not depend on the path between these points. then the work of this force measured from *A* assigns a scalar value to every other point in space and defines a scalar potential field. In this case. the force can be defined as the negative of thevector gradient of the potential field.

If the work for an applied force is independent of the path. then the work done by the force is evaluated at the start and end of the trajectory of the point of application. This means that there is a function *U* (x). called a "potential." that can be evaluated at the two points x_A and x_B to obtain the work over any trajectory between these two points. It is tradition to define this function with a negative sign so that positive work is a reduction in the potential. that is

$$W = \int_C \mathbf{F}\cdot d\mathbf{x} = U(\mathbf{x}_A) - U(\mathbf{x}_B)$$

where *C* is the trajectory taken from A to B. Because the work done is independent of the path taken. then this expression is true for any trajectory. *C*. from A to B.The function *U*(x) is called the potential energy associated with the applied force. Examples of forces that have potential energies are gravity and spring forces.

DERIVABLE FROM A POTENTIAL

The relationship between work and potential energy is presented in more detail. The line integral that defines work along curve *C* takes a special form if the force Fis related to a scalar field ö(x) so that

$$\mathbf{F} = \nabla\varphi = \left(\frac{\partial\varphi}{\partial x}, \frac{\partial\varphi}{\partial y}, \frac{\partial\varphi}{\partial z}\right).$$

In this case. work along the curve is given by

$$W=\int_C \mathbf{F}\cdot d\mathbf{x}=\int_C \nabla\varphi\cdot d\mathbf{x},$$

which can be evaluated using the gradient theorem to obtain,

$$W=\varphi(\mathbf{x}_B)-\varphi(\mathbf{x}_A).$$

This shows that when forces are derivable from a scalar field. the work of those forces along a curve *C* is computed by evaluating the scalar field at the start point *A* and the end point *B* of the curve. This means the work integral does not depend on the path between *A* and *B* and is said to be independent of the path.Potential energy *U*=-ö(x) is traditionally defined as the negative of this scalar field so that work by the force field decreases potential energy. that is,

$$W=U(\mathbf{x}_A)-U(\mathbf{x}_B).$$

In this case. the application of the del operator to the work function yields.

$$\nabla W=-\nabla U=-\left(\frac{\partial U}{\partial x},\frac{\partial U}{\partial y},\frac{\partial U}{\partial z}\right)=\mathbf{F},$$

and the force F is said to be "derivable from a potential." This also necessarily implies that F must be a conservative vector field. The potential *U* defines a force F at every point x in space. so the set of forces is called a force field.

COMPUTING POTENTIAL ENERGY

Given a force field F(x). evaluation of the work integral using the gradient theorem can be used to find the scalar function associated with potential energy. This is done by introducing a parameterized curve ã(t)=r(t) from ã(a)=A to ã(b)=B. and computing.

$$\begin{aligned}\int_\gamma \nabla\varphi(\mathbf{r})\cdot d\mathbf{r} &= \int_a^b \nabla\varphi(\mathbf{r}(t))\cdot\mathbf{r}'(t)dt,\\ &= \int_a^b \frac{d}{dt}\varphi(\mathbf{r}(t))dt=\varphi(\mathbf{r}(b))-\varphi(\mathbf{r}(a))=\varphi(\mathbf{x}_B)-\varphi(\mathbf{x}_A).\end{aligned}$$

For the force field F. let v= dr/dt. then the gradient theorem yields.

$$\begin{aligned}\int_\gamma \mathbf{F}\cdot d\mathbf{r} &= \int_a^b \mathbf{F}\cdot\mathbf{v}dt,\\ &= -\int_a^b \frac{d}{dt}U(\mathbf{r}(t))dt=U(\mathbf{x}_A)-U(\mathbf{x}_B).\end{aligned}$$

The power applied to a body by a force field is obtained from the gradient of the work. or potential. in the direction of the velocity v of the point of application. that is,

$$P(t) = -\nabla U \cdot \mathbf{v} = \mathbf{F} \cdot \mathbf{v}.$$

Examples of work that can be computed from potential functions are gravity and spring forces.

POTENTIAL ENERGY FOR NEAR EARTH GRAVITY

Fig. Trebuchet uses the gravitational potential energy of the counterweight to throw projectiles over two hundred meters

In classical physics. gravity exerts a constant downward force $F=(0.\ 0.\ F_z)$ on the centre of mass of a body moving near the surface of the Earth. The work of gravity on a body moving along a trajectory $r(t) = (x(t).\ y(t).\ z(t))$. such as the track of a roller coaster is calculated using its velocity. $v=(v_x.\ v_y.\ v_z)$. to obtain,

$$W = \int_{t_1}^{t_2} \mathbf{F} \cdot \mathbf{v} dt = \int_{t_1}^{t_2} F_z v_z dt = F_z \Delta z.$$

where the integral of the vertical component of velocity is the vertical distance. Notice that the work of gravity depends only on the vertical movement of the curve $r(t)$.

The function,

$$U(\mathbf{r}) = mgh,$$

is called the potential energy of a near earth gravity field.

POTENTIAL ENERGY FOR A LINEAR SPRING

A horizontal spring exerts a force F = (“kx. 0. 0) that is proportional to its deflection in the x direction. The work of this spring on a body moving along the space curve $s(t) = (x(t).\ y(t).\ z(t))$. is calculated using its velocity. $v = (v_x.\ v_y.\ v_z)$. to obtain,

$$W = \int_0^t \mathbf{F} \cdot \mathbf{v} dt = -\int_0^t kxv_x dt = -\frac{1}{2}kx^2.$$

For convenience. consider contact with the spring occurs at $t = 0$. then the integral of the product of the distance x and the x-velocity. xv_x. is $x^2/2$.

The function,

$$U(x) = \frac{1}{2}kx^2,$$

is called the potential energy of a linear spring.

Elastic potential energy is the potential energy of an elastic object (for example a bow or a catapult) that is deformed under tension or compression (or stressed in formal terminology). It arises as a consequence of a force that tries to restore the object to its original shape. which is most often the electromagnetic force between the atoms and molecules that constitute the object. If the stretch is released. the energy is transformed into kinetic energy.

POTENTIAL ENERGY FOR GRAVITATIONAL FORCES BETWEEN TWO BODIES

Gravitational potential energy between two bodies in space is obtained from the force exerted by a mass M on another mass m is given by,

$$\mathbf{F} = -\frac{GMm}{r^3}\mathbf{r},$$

where r is the position vector from M to m.

This can also be expressed as,

$$\mathbf{F} = -\frac{GMm}{r^2}\hat{\mathbf{r}},$$

where $\hat{\mathbf{r}}$ is a vector of length 1 pointing from M to m.

Let the mass m move at the velocity v then the work of gravity on this mass as it moves from position $r(t_1)$ to $r(t_2)$ is given by,

$$W = -\int_{r(t_1)}^{r(t_2)} \frac{GMm}{r^3}\mathbf{r}\cdot d\mathbf{r} = -\int_{t_1}^{t_2} \frac{GMm}{r^3}\mathbf{r}\cdot\mathbf{v}dt.$$

Notice that the position and velocity of the mass m are given by,

$$\mathbf{r} = r\mathbf{e}_r, \qquad \mathbf{v} = \dot{r}\mathbf{e}_r + r\dot{\theta}\mathbf{e}_t,$$

where e_r and e_t are the radial and tangential unit vectors directed relative to the vector from M to m. Use this to simplify the formula for work of gravity to.

$$W = -\int_{t_1}^{t_2} \frac{GmM}{r^3}(r\mathbf{e}_r)\cdot(\dot{r}\mathbf{e}_r + r\dot{\theta}\mathbf{e}_t)dt = -\int_{t_1}^{t_2} \frac{GmM}{r^3}r\dot{r}dt = \frac{GMm}{r(t_2)} - \frac{GMm}{r(t_1)}.$$

This calculation uses the fact that,

$$\frac{d}{dt}r^{-1} = -r^{-2}\dot{r} = -\frac{\dot{r}}{r^2}.$$

The function,

$$U = -\frac{GMm}{r},$$

is the gravitational potential function. also known as gravitational potential energy. The negative sign follows the convention that work is gained from a loss of potential energy.

POTENTIAL ENERGY FOR ELECTROSTATIC FORCES BETWEEN TWO BODIES

The electrostatic force exerted by a charge *Q* on another charge *q* is given by,

$$\mathbf{F} = \frac{1}{4\pi\varepsilon_0}\frac{Qq}{r^3}\mathbf{r},$$

where r is the position vector from *Q* to *q* and $\mathring{a}_0$ is the vacuum permittivity. This may also be written using Coulomb's constant $k_e = 1/4_{TT\varepsilon_0}$

The work *W* required to move *q* from *A* to any point *B* in the electrostatic force field is given by the potential function,

$$U(r) = \frac{1}{4\pi\varepsilon_0}\frac{Qq}{r}.$$

REFERENCE LEVEL

The potential energy is a function of the state a system is in. and is defined relative to that for a particular state. This reference state is not always a real state. it may also be a limit. such as with the distances between all bodies tending to infinity. provided that the energy involved in tending to that limit is finite. such as in the case of inverse-square lawforces. Any arbitrary reference state could be used. therefore it can be chosen based on convenience.

Typically the potential energy of a system depends on the *relative* positions of its components only. so the reference state can also be expressed in terms of relative positions.

GRAVITATIONAL POTENTIAL ENERGY

Gravitational energy is the potential energy associated with gravitational force. as work is required to elevate objects against Earth's gravity. The potential energy due to elevated positions is called gravitational potential energy. and is evidenced by water in an elevated reservoir or kept behind a dam. If an object falls from one point to another point inside a gravitational field. the force of gravity will do positive work on the object. and the gravitational potential energy will decrease by the same amount.

Consider a book placed on top of a table. As the book is raised from the floor. to the table. some external force works against the gravitational force. If the book falls back to the floor. the "falling" energy the book receives is provided by the gravitational force. Thus. if the book falls off the table. this potential energy goes to accelerate the mass of the book and is converted into kinetic energy. When the book hits the floor this kinetic energy is converted into heat. deformation and sound by the impact.

The factors that affect an object's gravitational potential energy are its height relative to some reference point. its mass. and the strength of the gravitational field it is in. Thus. a book lying on a table has less gravitational potential energy than the same book on top of a taller cupboard. and less gravitational potential energy than a heavier book lying on the same table. An object at a certain height above the Moon's surface has less gravitational potential energy than at the same height above the Earth's surface because the Moon's gravity is weaker. Note that "height" in the common sense of the term cannot be used for gravitational potential energy calculations when gravity is not assumed to be a constant.

LOCAL APPROXIMATION

The strength of a gravitational field varies with location. However. when the change of distance is small in relation to the distances from the centre of the source of the gravitational field. this variation in field strength is negligible and we can assume that the force of gravity on a particular object is constant. Near the surface of the Earth. for example. we assume that the acceleration due to gravity is a constant $g = 9.8$ m/s^2 ("standard gravity"). In this case. a simple expression for gravitational potential energy can be derived using the $W = Fd$ equation for work. and the equation

$$W_F = -\Delta U_F.$$

The amount of gravitational potential energy possessed by an elevated object is equal to the work done against gravity in lifting it. The work done equals the force required to move it upward multiplied with the vertical distance it is moved (remember $W = Fd$). The upward force required while moving at a constant velocity is equal to the weight. mg. of an object. so the work done in lifting it through a height h is the product mgh. Thus. when accounting only for mass. gravity. and altitude. the equation is:

$$U = mgh$$

where U is the potential energy of the object relative to its being on the Earth's surface. m is the mass of the object. g is the acceleration due to gravity. and h is the altitude of the object. If m is expressed in kilograms. g in m/s^2 and h in metres then U will be calculated in joules.

Hence. the potential difference is

$$\Delta U = mg\Delta h.$$

GENERAL FORMULA

However. over large variations in distance. the approximation that g is constant is no longer valid. and we have to use calculus and the general mathematical definition of work to determine gravitational potential energy. For the computation of the potential energy we can integrate the gravitational force. whose magnitude is given by Newton's law of gravitation. with respect to the distance r between the two bodies. Using that definition. the gravitational potential energy of a system of masses m_1 and M_2 at a distance r usinggravitational constant G is

$$U = -G\frac{m_1 M_2}{r} + K$$

where K is an arbitrary constant dependent on the choice of datum from which potential is measured. Choosing the convention that $K=0$ (*i.e.* in relation to a point at infinity) makes calculations simpler. albeit at the cost of making U negative; for why this is physically reasonable.

Given this formula for U. the total potential energy of a system of n bodies is found by summing. for all $\frac{n(n-1)}{2}$ pairs of two bodies. the potential energy of the system of those two bodies.

Considering the system of bodies as the combined set of small particles the bodies consist of. and applying the previous on the particle level we get the negative gravitational binding energy.

This potential energy is more strongly negative than the total potential energy of the system of bodies as such since it also includes the negative gravitational binding energy of each body.

The potential energy of the system of bodies as such is the negative of the energy needed to separate the bodies from each other to infinity. while the gravitational binding energy is the energy needed to separate all particles from each other to infinity.

$$U = -m\left(G\frac{M_1}{r_1} + G\frac{M_2}{r_2}\right)$$

therefore.

$$. U = -m \sum G \frac{M}{r}$$

WHY CHOOSE A CONVENTION WHERE GRAVITATIONAL ENERGY IS NEGATIVE

As with all potential energies. only differences in gravitational potential energy matter for most physical purposes. and the choice of zero point is arbitrary. Given that there is no reasonable criterion for preferring one particular finite r over another. there seem to be only two reasonable choices for the distance at which U becomes zero: $r = 0$ and $r = \infty$. The choice of $r = \infty$ at infinity may seem peculiar. and the consequence that gravitational energy is always negative may seem counterintuitive. but this choice allows gravitational potential energy values to be finite. albeit negative.

The singularity at $r = 0$ in the formula for gravitational potential energy means that the only other apparently reasonable alternative choice of convention. with $U = 0$ for $r = 0$. would result in potential energy being positive. but infinitely large for all nonzero values of r. and would make calculations involving sums or differences of potential energies beyond what is possible with the real number system. Since physicists abhor infinities in their calculations. and r is always non-zero in practice. the choice of $U = 0$ at infinity is by far the more preferable choice. even if the idea of negative energy in a gravity well appears to be peculiar at first.

The negative value for gravitational energy also has deeper implications that make it seem more reasonable in cosmological calculations where the total energy of the universe can meaningfully be considered; see inflation theory for more on this.

Uses

Gravitational potential energy has a number of practical uses. notably the generation of pumped-storage hydroelectricity. For example in Dinorwig. Wales. there are two lakes. one at a higher elevation than the other. At times when surplus electricity is not required (and so is comparatively cheap). water is pumped up to the higher lake. thus converting the electrical energy (running the pump) to gravitational potential energy. At times of peak demand for electricity. the water flows back down through electrical generator turbines. converting the potential energy into kinetic energy and then back into electricity. The process is not completely efficient and some of the original energy from the surplus electricity is in fact lost to friction.

Gravitational potential energy is also used to power clocks in which falling weights operate the mechanism.It's also used by counterweights for lifting up an elevator. crane. or sash window. Roller coasters are an entertaining way to utilize potential energy - chains are used to move a car up an incline (building up gravitational potential energy). to then have that energy converted into kinetic energy as it falls.

Another practical use is utilizing gravitational potential energy to descend (perhaps coast) downhill in transportation such as the descent of an automobile. truck. railroad train. bicycle. airplane. or fluid in a pipeline. In some cases the kinetic energy obtained from potential energy of descent may be used to start ascending the next grade such as what happens when a road is undulating and has frequent dips. The commercialization of stored energy (in the form of rail cars raised to higher elevations) that is then converted to electrical energy when needed by an electrical grid. is being undertaken in the United States in a system called Advanced Rail Energy Storage (ARES).

Further information: Gravitational potential energy storage

CHEMICAL POTENTIAL ENERGY

Chemical potential energy is a form of potential energy related to the structural arrangement of atoms or molecules. This arrangement may be the result of chemical bondswithin a molecule or otherwise. Chemical energy of a chemical substance can be transformed to other forms of energy by a chemical reaction. As an example. when a fuel is burned the chemical energy is converted to heat. same is the case with digestion of food metabolized in a biological organism. Green plants transform solar energy to chemical energy through the process known as photosynthesis. and electrical energy can be converted to chemical energy through electrochemical reactions.

The similar term chemical potential is used to indicate the potential of a substance to undergo a change of configuration. be it in the form of a chemical reaction. spatial transport. particle exchange with a reservoir. etc.

ELECTRIC POTENTIAL ENERGY

An object can have potential energy by virtue of its electric charge and several forces related to their presence. There are two main types of this kind of potential energy: electrostatic potential energy. electrodynamic potential energy (also sometimes called magnetic potential energy).

ELECTROSTATIC POTENTIAL ENERGY

Electrostatic potential energy between two bodies in space is obtained from the force exerted by a charge *Q* on another charge *q* which is given by

$$\mathbf{F} = -\frac{1}{4\pi\varepsilon_0}\frac{Qq}{r^3}\mathbf{r},$$

where r is the position vector from *Q* to *q* and $\mathring{a}_0$ is the vacuum permittivity.

This may also be written using Coulomb's constant $k_e = 1/4_{TT\varepsilon_0.}$

If the electric charge of an object can be assumed to be at rest. then it has potential energy due to its position relative to other charged objects. The electrostatic potential energy is the energy of an electrically charged particle (at rest) in an electric field. It is defined as thework that must be done to move it from an infinite distance away to its present location. adjusted for non-electrical forces on the object. This energy will generally be non-zero if there is another electrically charged object nearby.

The work W required to move q from A to any point B in the electrostatic force field is given by the potential function

$$U(\mathbf{r}) = \frac{1}{4\pi\varepsilon_0} \frac{Qq}{r}.$$

A related quantity called *electric potential* (commonly denoted with a V for voltage) is equal to the electric potential energy per unit charge.

MAGNETIC POTENTIAL ENERGY

The energy of a magnetic moment m in an externally produced magnetic B-field B has potential energy

$$U = -\mathbf{m}\cdot\mathbf{B}.$$

The magnetization M in a field is

$$U = -\frac{1}{2}\int \mathbf{M}\cdot\mathbf{B}dV,$$

where the integral can be over all space or. equivalently. where M is Non-zero. Magnetic potential energy is the form of energy related not only to the distance between magnetic materials. but also to the orientation. or alignment. of those materials within the field. For example. the needle of a compass has the lowest magnetic potential energy when it is aligned with the north and south poles of the Earth's magnetic field. If the needle is moved by an outside force. torque is exerted on the magnetic dipole of the needle by the Earth's magnetic field. causing it to move back into alignment. The magnetic potential energy of the needle is highest when its field is in the same direction as the Earth's magnetic field. Two magnets will have potential energy in relation to each other and the distance between them. but this also depends on their orientation. If the opposite poles are held apart. the potential energy will be the highest when they are near the edge of their attraction. and the lowest when they pull together. Conversely. like poles will have the highest potential energy when forced together. and the lowest when they spring apart.

NUCLEAR POTENTIAL ENERGY

Nuclear potential energy is the potential energy of the particles inside an atomic nucleus. The nuclear particles are bound together by the strong nuclear force. Weak nuclear forces provide the potential energy for certain kinds of radioactive decay. such as beta decay.Nuclear particles like protons and neutrons are not destroyed in fission and fusion processes. but collections of them have less mass than if they were individually free. and this mass difference is liberated as heat and radiation in nuclear reactions (the heat and radiation have the missing mass. but it often escapes from the system. where it is not measured). The energy from the Sun is an example of this form of energy conversion. In the Sun. the process of hydrogen fusion converts about 4 million tonnes of solar matter per second into electromagnetic energy. which is radiated into space.

FORCES. POTENTIAL AND POTENTIAL ENERGY

Potential energy is closely linked with forces. If the work done by a force on a body that moves from *A* to *B* does not depend on the path between these points. then the work of this force measured from *A* assigns a scalar value to every other point in space and defines a scalar potential field. In this case. the force can be defined as the negative of thevector gradient of the potential field.

For example. gravity is a conservative force. The associated potential is the gravitational potential. often denoted by ϕ or V . corresponding to the energy per unit mass as a function of position. The gravitational potential energy of two particles of mass *M* and *m* separated by a distance *r* is

$$U = -\frac{GMm}{r},$$

The gravitational potential (specific energy) of the two bodies is

$$\phi = -\left(\frac{GM}{r} + \frac{Gm}{r}\right) = -\frac{G(M+m)}{r} = -\frac{GMm}{\mu r} = \frac{U}{\mu}.$$

where μ is the reduced mass.

The work done against gravity by moving an infinitesimal mass from point A with $U = a$ to point B with $U = b$ is $(b - a)$ and the work done going back the other way is $(a - b)$ so that the total work done in moving from A to B and returning to A is

$$U_{A \to B \to A} = (b - a) + (a - b) = 0.$$

If the potential is redefined at A to be $a + c$ and the potential at B to be $b + c$. where is a constant (*i.e.* can be any number. positive or negative. but it must be the same at A as it is at B) then the work done going from A to B is

$$U_{A \to B} = (b + c) - (a + c) = b - a$$

as before.

In practical terms. this means that one can set the zero of U and ϕ anywhere one likes. One may set it to be zero at the surface of the Earth. or may find it more convenient to set zero at infinity. A conservative force can be expressed in the language of differential geometry as a closed form. As Euclidean space is contractible. its de Rham cohomology vanishes. so every closed form is also an exact form. and can be expressed as the gradient of a scalar field. This gives a mathematical justification of the fact that all conservative forces are gradients of a potential field.

POTENTIAL ENERGY: TAPPING AFRICA'S RENEWABLE RESOURCES

Historically oil. gas and coal have been the mainstay of the economies of Europe. the US. Japan and other members of Organisation of Economic Cooperation and Development (OECD). These energy resources. particularly oil. enabled them to reach and maintain their current levels of development and lifestyle. Many countries wishing to transform their economies and societies have tended to follow the line of fossil fuels. However. many energy economists agree that the current oil driven development is unsustainable due to several factors including dwindling global reserves. the impact of fossil fuel consumption on the planet. and the costs and security associated with the production and transportation of fossil energy.

USING OIL

The transportation and industrial sectors of many African countries – from Ghana to Tanzania to Zambia – rely on oil imports. and these countries spend a large proportion of their GDPs on oil. This has led to trade imbalances and debt.For example. the debt incurred by the Tema Oil Refinery (TOR) in Ghana made it difficult for the company to import crude oil. leading to several shutdowns which affected economic activities across the country. The government of Ghana was forced to settle the arrears before TOR could lift crude into the country again.These debts are linked to high global oil prices. The high prices mean that African oil-importers have to use their limited foreign exchange to compete with the likes of the US and China.China's demand for oil – which is expected to grow from 8 million barrels a day in 2010 to 17.5 million barrels a day by 2030 – coupled with demand from the likes of Argentina. Brazil. India. Turkey. and the OECD. means that competition for access to global oil reserves will increase. The increase in demand is likely to push up world energy prices over the medium term making it even harder for many African economies to remain competitive.

ENERGY POVERTY

Africa in general. and sub-Saharan Africa in particular. remains one of the most energy-poor regions in the world. The continent accounts for more than a quarter of the 2.5 billion people globally who are without access to convenient. reliable and modern cooking technologies that can help meet their basic needs and support their economic development. Africa also accounts for the biggest share of the 1.6 billion people globally who are without electricity.

In 2008. a report by energy expert Anton Eberhard noted that Africa's electricity infrastructure capacity remains the lowest in the world. Eberhard noted that the 48 sub-Saharan African countries with a combined population of over 800 million produced around the same amount of electricity as Spain's population of 45 million.

Another report. authored by Vivian Foster for Africa Infrastructure Country Diagnostic. which studied business activities and energy infrastructure in 26 countries in sub-Saharan Africa found that "for an important subset of countries. power emerges as by far the most limiting factor. being cited by more than half of firms in more than half of countries as a major business obstacle". The firms reported losing 5% of their sales as a result of frequent power outages. The figure rose to 20% for informal sector firms unable to afford backup generators. TaTEDO. a Tanzanian NGO. points out that more than 40% of agricultural products go to waste due to post-harvest losses and lack of appropriate energy to process or preserve them.

However. it is not only businesses that face energy challenges. households are also confronted with electricity problems. Only 16 African countries have a national electricity coverage of 20% or more and there is a huge gap in electricity accessibility between rural and urban areas.

In Tanzania. for instance. while about 12% of households in the country have electricity coverage. only 2% of those in rural areas – who make up 75% of the population – have access to electricity.

The IEA's 2010 Energy Development Index which tracks progress in a country or a region'stransition to the use of modern fuels shows that sub-Saharan countries are not moving fast enough to tackle energy poverty and increase the use of modern fuels. According to the World Bank the more than 580 million Africans who are without access to modern forms of energyspend more than $10 billion annually buying low quality energy services such as kerosene. candles and firewood. Available figures indicate that death associated with the use of these services in Sub Sahara Africa is 400.000 per annum - Cuvilas.

FIREWOOD AND CHARCOAL AS MAIN ENERGY SOURCES

The lack of electricity and other forms of modern energy mean that firewood and charcoal for cooking. and kerosene and candles for lighting. remain the primary source of energy in many households. and there is every indication that the dependence on low forms of energy is growing.

For instance. in 1986 about 66% of Zambia's energy use came from woodfuel; by 2010. this figure had risen to 76%. Elsewhere. 92% of energy used in the DRC. 65% of Ghana's energy. and over 92% of Ethiopia's energy derives from combustible biomass. mostly woodfuel.

The use of charcoal. firewood. candles and kerosene as the dominant source of energy effectively classifies Africa as one of the least energy intensive economic regions. heavily constrained by both low quality of fuel type and low per capita energy.

THE RENEWABLE ENERGY POTENTIAL

While global attention has focused on the development of renewable energy resources as a way to promote sustainable development and contain the threat posed by climate change. progress in developing the Africa's abundant renewable energy resources has been slow. Eberhard et al. for example. estimate that 93% of Africa's hydropower potential remains idle.

But given the global demand and competition for fossil fuels. coupled with the associated price increase and debt burden for oil importing African countries. it is obvious that Africa cannot take the development path driven by fossil energy. Renewable energy. on the other hand. has the potential to help African countries invigorate their economies. wean themselves from dependence on fossil fuels and reduce the debt burden associated with oil importation.

Renewable energy can also help increase household access to modern energy services. reduce energy poverty. improve quality of life. empower women. create jobs and bridge urban-rural inequality. It has the potential to protect the environment. reduce natural resource conflicts (*e.g.* around firewood collection); slow down rural-urban migration and the associated urbanisation; and reduce carbon emissions.

The influential global energy outlook report prepared by BP suggests that the contribution of renewables to global energy growth will increase from 5% up to 2010 to 18% by 2030. But Africa's share in terms of production and consumption of this growth is calculated to be very small.

There is therefore the need for African governments to begin working seriously with the private sector and other relevant bodies to aggressively develop the necessary policies. institutions and infrastructures to take advantage of Africa's huge renewable energy resources. Efforts must also focus on addressing the human. financial and management capacity challenges associated with the renewable energy sector so as to the make the sector a catalyst for achieving economic growth. development and prosperity in Africa.

CONSERVATION OF MECHANICAL ENERGY

We have just established that $\Delta U = -W$. and we know from the Work-Energy Theorem that $\Delta K = W$. Relating the two equations. we see that ΔU

$= -\Delta K$ and thus $\Delta U + \Delta K = 0$. Stated verbally. the sum of the change in kinetic and potential energy must always equal zero. By the associative property. we can also write that:

$$\Delta(U+K) = 0$$

Thus the sum of U and K must be a constant. This constant. denoted by E. is defined as the total mechanical energy of a conservative system. We can now generate a mathematical expression for the conservation of mechanical energy:

$$U+K=E$$

This statement is true for all conservative systems. and thus for all systems in which U is defined.With this equation we have completed our proof of the conservation of mechanical energy within conservative systems.

The relation between U. K and E is elegantly simple. and is derived from our concepts of work. kinetic energy. and conservative forces. Such a relation is also a valuable tool in solving physical problems. Given an initial state in which we know both K and U. and asked to calculate one of these quantities in some final state. we simply equate the sums at each state: $U_0 + K_0 = U_f + K_f$. Such a relation further bypasses our kinematics laws. and makes calculations in conservative systems quite simple.

USING CALCULUS TO FIND POTENTIAL ENERGY

Our calculation of the gravitational potential energy was quite easy. Such an easy calculation will not always be the case. and calculus can be a great help in generating an expression for the potential energy of a conservative system. Recall that work is defined in calculus as $W = \int_{xv}^{xf} F(x)dx$. Thus the change in potential is simply the negative of this integral.

To demonstrate how to calculate potential energy using vector calculus we shall do so for a mass-spring system.

Consider a mass on a spring. at equilibrium at $x = 0$. Recall that the force exerted by the spring. which is a conservative force. is: $F_s = -kx$. where k is the spring constant. Let us also assign an arbitrary value to the potential at the equilibrium point: $U(0) = 0$. We can now use our relation between potential and work to find the potential of the system a distance x from the origin:

$$U(x) - 0 = -\int_0^x (-kx)dx$$

Implying that

$$U(x) = \frac{1}{2} kx^2$$

This equation is true for all x. A calculation of the same form can be completed for any conservative system. and we thus have a universal method for calculating potential energy. Though Newtonian mechanics provide an axiomatic basis for the study of mechanics. our concept of energy is more universal: energy applies not only to mechanics. but to electricity. waves. astrophysics. and even quantum mechanics. Energy pops up again and again in physics. and the conservation of energy remains one of the fundamental ideas of physics.

ENERGY CONSERVATION: THE ONLY WAY TO AVOID ECONOMIC AND ECOLOGICAL RUIN

Energy conservation is our best strategy for pre-adapting to an inevitably energy-constrained future. And it may be our only real option for averting economic. social. and ecological ruin. The world will face limits to energy production in the decades ahead regardless of the energy pathway chosen by policy makers. Consider the two extreme options—carbon minimum and carbon maximum. If we rebuild our global energy infrastructure to minimize carbon emissions. with the aim of combating climate change. this will mean removing incentives and subsidies from oil. coal. and gas and transferring them to renewable energy sources like solar. wind. and geothermal. Where fossil fuels are still used. we will need to capture and bury the carbon dioxide emissions.

We might look to nuclear power for a bit of help along the way. but it likely wouldn't provide much. The Fukushima catastrophe in Japan in 2011 highlighted a host of unresolved safety issues. including spent fuel storage and vulnerability to extended grid power outages. Even ignoring those issues. atomic power is expensive. and supplies of high-grade uranium ore are problematic.

The low-carbon path is littered with other obstacles as well. Solar and wind power are plagued by intermittency. a problem that can be solved only with substantial investment in energy storage or long-distance transmission. Renewables currently account for only a tiny portion of global energy. so the low-carbon path requires a high rate of growth in that expensive sector. and therefore high rates of investment. Governments would have to jump-start the transition with regulations and subsidies—a tough order in a world where most governments are financially overstretched and investment capital is scarce.

For transport. the low-carbon option is even thornier. Biofuels suffer from problems of high cost and the diversion of agricultural land. the transition to electric cars will be expensive and take decades. and electric airliners are not feasible.

Carbon capture and storage will also be costly and will likewise take decades to implement on a meaningful scale. Moreover. the energy costs of building and operating an enormous new infrastructure of carbon dioxide pumps. pipelines. and compressors will be substantial. meaning we will be extracting more and more fossil fuels just to produce the same amount of energy useful to society—a big problem if fossil fuels are getting more expensive anyway.

So. in the final analysis. a low-carbon future is also very likely to be a lower-energy future.What if we forget about the climate? This might seem to be the path of least resistance. After all. fossil fuels have a history of being cheap and abundant. and we already have the infrastructure to burn them. If climate mitigation would be expensive and politically contentious. why not just double down on the high-carbon path we're already on. in the pursuit of maximized economic growth? Perhaps. with enough growth. we could afford to overcome whatever problems a changing climate throws in our path.

Not a good option. The quandary we face with a high-carbon energy path can be summed up in the metaphor of the low-hanging fruit. We have extracted the highest quality. cheapest-to-produce. most accessible hydrocarbon resources first. and we have left the lower quality. expensive-to-produce. less accessible resources for later. Well. now it's later. Enormous amounts of coal. oil. gas. and other fossil fuels still remain underground. but each new increment will cost significantly more to extract (in terms of both money and energy) than was the case only a decade ago.

After the Deepwater Horizon oil spill of 2010 and the Middle East–North Africa uprisings of 2011. almost no one still believes that oil will be as cheap and plentiful in the future as it was decades ago. For coal. the wake-up call is coming from China—which now burns almost half the world's coal and is starting to import enormous quantities. driving up coal prices worldwide. Meanwhile. recent studies suggest that global coal production will max out in the next few years and start to decline.

New extraction techniques for natural gas (horizontal drilling and "fracking") have temporarily increased supplies of this fuel in the United States. but the companies that specialize in this "unconventional" gas appear to be subsisting on investment capital: Prices are currently too low to enable them to turn much of a profit on production. Costs of production and per-well depletion rates are high. and energy returns on the energy invested in production are low. Recent low prices resulted from a glut of production produced by rampant drilling in 2005–2007. which only made economic sense when gas prices were much higher than they are now. All of this suggests that rosy expectations for what "fracking" can produce over the long term are overblown.

Exotic hydrocarbons like gas hydrates. bitumen ("tar sands"). and kerogen ("oil shale") will require extraordinary effort and investment for their development and will entail environmental risks even higher than those for conventional fossil fuels. That means more expensive energy. Even though the resource base is large. with current technology the nature of these materials means they can be produced only at relatively slow rates.

But if the hydrocarbon molecules are there and society needs the energy. won't we just bite the bullet and come up with whatever levels of investment are required to keep energy flows growing at whatever rate we need them?

Not necessarily. As we move toward lower-quality resources (conventional or unconventional). we have to use more energy to acquire energy. As net energy yields decline. both energy and investment capital have to be cannibalized from other sectors of society in order to keep extraction processes expanding. After a certain point. even if gross energy production is still climbing. the amount of energy yielded that is actually useful to society starts to decline anyway. From then on. it will be impossible to increase the amount of economically meaningful energy produced annually no matter what sacrifices we make. And the signs suggest we're not far from that point. In one sense it matters a great deal whether we choose the low-carbon or the high-carbon path: One way. we lay the groundwork for a sustainable (if modest) energy future; the other. we destabilize Earth's climate. shackle ourselves ever more tightly to energy sources that can only become dirtier and more expensive as time goes on. and condemn myriad other species to extinction.

However. in another sense. it doesn't matter which path we choose: With human population numbers growing and energy constraints looming. we will have less energy to burn per capita in the future. Plot any scenario between the low-carbon and high-carbon extremes and that conclusion still holds. which means less energy for transport. for agriculture. and for heating and cooling homes. Less energy for making and using electronic gadgets. Less energy for building and maintaining cities.

Efficiency can help us obtain greater services for each unit of energy expended. Research has been proceeding for decades on how to reduce energy inputs for all sorts of processes and activities. Just one example: The electricity needed for illumination has declined by up to 90 percent due to the introduction first of compact fluorescent light bulbs. and now LED lights. However. efficiency efforts are subject to the law of diminishing returns: We can't make and transport goods with no energy. and each step Towards greater efficiency typically costs more. Achieving 100 percent efficiency would. in theory. require infinite effort. So while we can increase efficiency and reduce total energy consumption. we can't do those things and produce continual economic growth at the same time.

Humanity is at a crossroads. Since the Industrial Revolution. cheap and abundant energy has fueled constant economic growth. The only real discussion among the managerial elite was how to grow the economy—whether in planned or unplanned ways. whether with sensitivity to the natural world or without.

Now the discussion must centre on how to contract. So far. that discussion is radioactive—no one wants to touch it. It's hard to imagine a more suicidal strategy for a politician than to base his or her election campaign on the promise of economic contraction. Denial runs deep. but sooner or later reality will expose the delusion that endless growth is possible on a finite planet.

Sooner or later we must make conservation the centerpiece of economic and energy policy. The term "conservation" implies efficiency—building cars and appliances that use less energy while delivering the same services. But it also means cutting out Non-essential uses of energy. Rather than continuing to increase economic demand by stimulating human wants. we must begin to think about how to meet basic human needs with minimum consumption of resources. while discouraging extravagance. If we move Towards renewable and intermittent energy sources. a larger portion of society's effort will have to be spent on processes of energy capture. Energy production will require more land and a greater proportion of society's total labour and investment. We will need more food producers. but fewer managers and salespeople. We will be less mobile. and each of us will own fewer manufactured products—though of higher quality—which we will reuse and repair as long as possible before replacing them.

The transition to a more durable and resilient but lower-energy economy will go much better if we plan it. Wherever it is possible for households and communities to pre-adapt. and wherever clever people are able to show innovative ways of meeting human needs with a minimum of consumption. there will be advantages to be enjoyed and shared.

Much of the current public discussion about our energy future tends to turn on the questions of which alternative energy sources to pursue and how to scale them up. But it is even more important to broadly reconsider how we use energy. We must strategize to meet basic human needs while using much less energy in all forms. Since this will require major societal effort sustained over decades. it is important to start implementation of conservation strategies well before actual energy shortages appear.

USING OIL REVENUES TO RESEARCH ALTERNATIVE FUELS

With regard to our food system. it is essential to understand that lower energy inputs will result in the need for increased labour. Thus the energy transition could represent economic opportunity for millions of young farmers. Agricultural production must be adapted to substantially reduced applications of nitrogen fertilizer and chemical pesticides and herbicides since these will grow increasingly expensive as their fossil fuel feedstocks rise in price. And higher transport energy costs mean that food systems must be substantially relocalized.

Transport systems must be adapted to a regime of generally lowered mobility and increased energy efficiency. This would most likely require widespread reliance on walking and bicycling. with remaining motorized transport facilitated by car-share and ride-share programmes. Electric vehicles and rail-based public transport systems should be favored. and new highway construction halted.

Reduced overall mobility will require substantial changes in urban design practice and land use policies. Neighborhoods within cities must become more self-contained. and cities must be reintegrated with adjacent productive rural areas. Buildings—including tens of millions of homes in the United States alone—must be retrofitted with insulation to minimize the need for heating and cooling energy. New buildings must require net zero energy input. Incentives for installing residential solar hot water systems. and using solar cookers and clotheslines. should be effective and widespread.Most new sources of energy will produce electricity—and in the cases of solar and wind. electricity will be produced only intermittently. Electricity storage systems (such as pumped water or compressed air) must be built to overcome at least some of the problems of intermittency.

Reconfiguration of electricity grids. distributed generation. and alignment of household and industrial energy usage patterns to fit intermittent power availability are other strategies for adaptation.

The historically close relationship between increasing energy use and economic growth suggests that the global economy probably cannot continue to expand as world energy production falters. Therefore. adaptive measures must include efforts to restructure the economy to meet basic human needs and support improvements in quality of life while reducing debt and reliance on interest and investment income. Family planning must be encouraged. as adding more people to a stagnant or shrinking economy simply means there will be less for everyone.

The costs to ecological integrity and to human health of the ever-increasing scale of society's production and transport systems have become the subject of broadening concern in recent decades. Air and water pollution. resource depletion. soil erosion. and biodiversity loss are just some of those costs. With reduced energy use must come the realization that the scale of our human presence on the planet must be appropriate to the Earth's limited budgets of water. energy. and biological productivity.

Altogether. this will constitute a historic shift away from continual societal growth and Towards conservation. It will not be undertaken except by necessity. but necessity is inevitably approaching. Barring some technological miracle. we will have less energy. like it or not. And with less energy. we will no longer be able to operate a consumer society.

The kind of society we will be able to operate will almost certainly be as different from the industrial society of recent decades as that was from the agrarian society of the nineteenth century.But suppose this analysis is wrong. or that a new miracle technology appears. and energy proves to be abundant rather than scarce. Even then. conservation makes sense: Increasing energy use leads to greater consumption of natural resources of all kinds. and the degradation of wild natural systems. Sooner or later we must rein in consumption—and since signs of ecological decline are already frighteningly prevalent. sooner is clearly better than later.The shift to a conserver society could hold benefits for people as well as for nature. As we begin to measure success not by the amount of our consumption. but by the quality of our culture. the beauty of the built environment. and the health of ecosystems. we could end up being significantly happier than we are today. even as we leave a far smaller footprint upon our finite planet. But those benefits will be delayed and diluted for as long as we deny the conservation imperative.

5

Energy Security: A 'Common but Differentiated' Concern

Although energy is a concern for all countries alike. the degree to which energy becomes a vital component or even a determinant of a country's national security strategy is a result of other influencing factors. Not least important amongst these 'other influencing factors' is domestic resource endowment.

Energy concerns become a security threat primarily when countries cannot or can no longer meet their increasing demand for energy (to fuel economic growth as well as ensure a basic standard of living to their people) domestically (that is. independently). or when they have to depend on other countries for energy resources or the technology to be able to make use of available resources. Therefore. energy becomes a security concern for countries when they do not have access to sufficient energy resources at affordable prices.

For energy importing countries therefore. the loss of independence (of being able to rely on their own resources) is perhaps the first sign of energy becoming a national security concern. Access to markets (for energy suppliers) and sources (for importers) is only one part of the energy security dilemma. Affordability too is a particularly important aspect of energy security; although again the degree to which it is a security concern for a country depends on the financial ability of the country to access resources at higher prices or opt for alternative sources of energy that imply higher investment/technology costs. Countries with the wherewithal can bankroll access to energy at comparatively higher costs than countries that are poorer and developing. Non-etheless. the pinch of the high price of energy resources is felt by almost all energy importing countries alike.

Affordability also determines the extent to which countries have the room to manoeuvre when it comes to choosing between sources of energy. Thus. rather than being only a simple financial consideration. 'affordability' also implies the relative 'ease' with which countries can make the choices they make. That is. countries naturally have to factor into their calculations of 'affordability' not only the comparatively higher prices of renewable energy technologies. or the rising price of oil. but also other costs that make certain choices more 'costly'. such as international pressure to cut-back on dirty fossil fuels. domestic and international pressure against going nuclear. civil society activism against big hydropower projects and so on. Differences in the degree of energy insecurity experienced by countries is to a great extent inherent in the very nature of resource distribution in the world.

Given that energy resources are disproportionately apportioned in the world. availability and consumption patterns are rarely co-terminus. As a result. centres of demand are distinct from centres of supply; hence creating what is baldly perceived as a hierarchy of power relations; with energy-rich and exporting countries at the top. transit countries in the middle and energy-deficient and importing countries at the bottom. Another reason for the differences in levels of energy security in the world can be grasped from the financial capability of countries to bankroll access to resources at higher prices. further away. or alternative sources of energy that are comparatively costlier than fossil fuels.

Therefore. although energy is a concern for all countries in the international system. the extent to which energy is a security concern depends on assured supplies (both domestic and overseas) to meet demand or the financial capability to look for alternative sources - if not seek energy independence. This would seem to suggest that energy. given its fungibility. is closely linked to power in the international system. To the extent that energy is critical to not only economic wealth. but also military prowess. energy security can be seen as an important element of state power. However. the linkage between energy and power requires closer study and analysis; an issue we turn to next.

ENERGY SECURITY

When the price of oil on world markets increased dramatically in 1973. several countries which were major energy importers reviewed their energy policies and took steps to reduce their vulnerability to political and economic uncertainties. France embarked upon a major programme of nuclear power construction to replace most of its fossil fuel imports used for electricity. and Japan set out to diversify its electricity generation. including a significant proportion of nuclear power. alongside coal and gas.

The following graph on primary energy illustrates the dependence of some countries on net primary energy imports. and raises the question of supply and price vulnerability in those. It also shows the significance for four countries of net exports. with major economic implications and in one case political influence. But the import side is the point here:

France imports half of its net primary energy. and this is a significant justification for its heavy reliance on nuclear power for electricity. since uranium is a small part of the power cost. This policy of having three quarters of its electricity from nuclear power was set in 1973. France is a world leader in nuclear fuel cycle and reactor building. and uranium is easily stockpiled. Germany imports more than half its net primary energy and in the past it has addressed this vulnerability with one third of electricity from nuclear. and also major incentives for renewables. Japan imports nearly 85% of its primary energy and has framed energy policies in the light of this vulnerability. Its policy since the 1970s has been to have a balance among coal. gas and nuclear. with this changing since 2000 to increase the nuclear proportion. However. since the Fukushima accident this is being reviewed.

The UK imports less than 20% of its net primary energy. but this is set to increase with depletion of North Sea gas. Continuing a high reliance on gas would make it vulnerable to supply interruptions from Siberia and the Middle East.

The USA imports almost 20% of its net primary energy today (less than in the 2007 diagram). mostly as oil and gas. and this is regarded as having a major influence on its defence budget. The advent of low-cost shale gas is helping its situation in the short term. Italy. which is the world's largest net importer of electricity – 44 TWh net in 2010. about 15% of its consumption – which has been typical for a decade. Most of the imported power comes from French nuclear plants. South Korea imports almost all of its energy and had a 12-fold increase in electricity demand from 1980 to 2009. It now gets 35% of its electricity from nuclear power while planning to increase this to 43% in 2020 and 59% by 2030.

IMPLICATIONS OF ENERGY IMPORTS

There are geopolitical. economic and availability implications of a country relying on energy imports. The early 1970s 'oil shocks' showed that fuel supplies from international sources could not be taken for granted. France's response to this for its electricity generation is evident in the following graph.

Today. much of the internationally-traded oil and gas comes from relatively few sources. and political instability there or in countries traversed by pipelines is a constant risk to supplies and hence a major economic vulnerability.Coal supplies are more diverse geographically and less uncertain. Uranium is sourced from a still wider variety of countries geographically and politically. which gives it a very high rating in respect to energy security. It also comprises a very small part of the cost of power generation. so is a more affordable fuel to stockpile than fossil fuels.

In April 2014. following Russia's annexation of Crimea. the Polish prime minister called for a Europe-wide energy union including a single body charged with purchasing gas supplies. as a means of confronting "Russia's monopolistic position with a single European body charged with buying its gas". The dependence of at least ten of the EU's 28 members on Russian state-controlled gas exporter Gazprom for more than half their consumption highlighted the need for greater EU infrastructure. notably gas interconnection and storage. Member states should work more closely together on energy infrastructure to guarantee the security of supplies and better utilise fossil fuel resources in eastern EU states. particularly coal and shale gas. he said. LNG imports from the USA and Australia should be used. The EU's Euratom facilitates joint purchasing of uranium for nuclear power. showing what could happen with gas. Bilateral energy contracts should be made transparent and contract templates. along with a role for the European Commission. should be introduced. In the past seven years Poland had invested more than EUR 2 billion on gas storage and other infrastructure to diminish reliance on Russia.* It is also planning to build two large nuclear power plants totaling 6 GWe.

* Financial Times 21/4/14.

Uranium's low cost per unit of contained energy and its wide geographical and political availability do not remove all concerns regarding energy security. Some countries see the prospect of trade restrictions or transport disruptions affecting their security of supply. so seek to maximize not only indigenous sources of uranium (and other fuels) but also the transformation of uranium into reactor fuel – notably enrichment. But because so little uranium is needed to produce a large amount of electricity. and a few years supply is easily stockpiled. it is sometimes considered to be effectively an indigenous energy source.

STOCKPILING FUELS FOR ELECTRICITY GENERATION

Any country or power utility may see the need to stockpile reserves of fuel sufficient to endure a major political upheaval in a source country.(If this is a large reserve supply there are obvious constraints in both paying for it and storing it securely.

Most kinds of coal can be stored. but with over 3 million tonnes required annually for a 1000 MWe power plant. that storage has space. dust and visual implications. Natural gas can be stored underground. but capacity in most countries is not great – a few months' supply at best. Uranium can very readily be stored long-term. and with only about 200 tonnes of natural uranium. or less than 30 tonnes of fabricated fuel. required per year for a 1000 MWe power plant. the advantage is obvious.

EMERGING NUCLEAR POWERS: A SAFE PATH TO ENERGY SECURITY?

It's impossible to rely solely on natural gas or sources of renewable energy to meet this demand. (File photo: Reuters) Demand for electricity in the emerging economies is growing very strongly – between 5% and 6% each year. on average. compared to 1% or less in developed economies – and will continue to rise in the decades ahead. Moreover. many of these same countries have goals to improve energy security and avoid emissions of greenhouse gases and other air pollutants.

It's impossible to rely solely on natural gas or sources of renewable energy to meet this demand. Nor is it possible to rely exclusively on coal. the most carbon-intensive fossil fuel. From our past work it is clear that almost all of the increase in nuclear power capacity over the coming decades is set to come from emerging countries. There are three that are particularly crucial: China. India and Russia. Within the OECD. South Korea is the only country expected to see any notable expansion. There are also many other countries that are considering the introduction of nuclear power for the first time. Although significant caution should be exercised in assessing which might actually succeed and over what timeframe as doing so will require a lot of time. expertise and determination.

Countries pursuing an expansion of nuclear power face big challenges. Nuclear power plants have high upfront investment costs and long construction times. which creates particular issues in competitive markets where utilities face significant market and regulatory risk. Nuclear power also faces intense public concern about a wide range of issues. Safety is the dominant concern – safety in plant operation. safe radioactive waste disposal and safeguards against the proliferation of nuclear weapons. And perhaps most importantly. there is the need to improve confidence in the competence and independence of regulatory oversight. If these challenges are not adequately addressed. the nuclear component of future generation may be lower than many expect.

Our world is facing twin challenges of climate change and energy security. Nuclear power can be part of the solution and I believe it will remain an important part of the electricity generation mix in the decades to come in many countries.

SAFEGUARDING NUCLEAR MATERIAL

You cannot stop the transmission of knowledge. There is no way that you can prevent people learning how to build a nuclear power plant. how to enrich uranium. or even how to make a bomb. If every nation is to have the right to use nuclear energy. there must be disciplined Behaviour in its use. both in terms of safeguarding the environment and resisting the temptation to use it as a weapon. Beyond that. the greater challenge is to apply this discipline in a world that is increasingly unstable. The key to ensuring this is to control and manage the materials that serve as nuclear fuel. such as uranium-235 and plutonium-239. We must reach a global consensus on how to manage these substances: it could be that a multinational company is empowered to control most of the nuclear fuel worldwide. which it then leases to each country. and when the fuel is spent. it is safely returned. This last stage is crucial. as some spent materials can be used for the production of nuclear arms. In theory. such an arrangement is workable. but it's up to the politicians to decide if we can reach that kind of agreement. To get to the negotiation table. we must first stabilize Eastern Europe. the Middle East and North Africa; only then can we begin the necessary process of diplomacy and understanding. Because it goes without saying that this cannot be achieved without cooperation and consensus between the world's superpowers.

NUCLEAR POWER AND THE EUROPEAN ENERGY SECURITY STRATEGY

The serious nuclear accident in Fukushima. Japan. in 2011 and the difficulties in financing the high cost of building power plants appeared to have dampened the prospects for nuclear power to play a significant role in a more integrated approach to energy. However. following the events in Ukraine in early 2014—which raised the possibility of disruptions to gas supplies. as occurred in 2006 and 2009—policy proposals have focused on improving the security of energy supply. emphasizing the need to develop energy resources within the EU in a sustainable way. Such an approach would seem to enhance the prospects for nuclear power as part of an energy mix—since electricity from nuclear power plants constitutes a reliable. emission-free base-load electricity supply.A number of EU member states now seem to be advancing plans to keep nuclear power in their energy mix. British plans to develop nuclear power are probably the most ambitious in Europe. with proposals for up to 11 new reactors by the mid-2020s. Other member states—including Bulgaria. Finland. France. Hungary. Lithuania. Poland. Romania and Slovakia—are either reviving projects that were put on ice. building nuclear reactors or moving forward with plans to do so.

The European Commission has spent more than a decade developing a policy framework for climate and energy. as well as the 'Energy Roadmap 2050'. However. its recent Communication laying out the European Energy Security Strategy is explicitly linked to the consequences of the recent political crisis in Ukraine and preventing coercion by threats of denial of access to resources. In the nuclear context. this approach to security—encompassing security of supply—contrasts sharply with the focus of the three Nuclear Security Summits. held in Washington. Seoul and most recently in The Hague. These summits have progressively narrowed the scope of nuclear security to reducing the risk of mass impact terrorism. largely through technical measures to protect sensitive nuclear materials and radioactive sources.

OBSTACLES TO INCORPORATING NUCLEAR POWER INTO THE EUROPEAN ENERGY SECURITY STRATEGY

While the need to ensure that nuclear material does not fall into the wrong hands is uncontested. the role of nuclear power in an EU energy mix is more controversial. Furthermore. while a broader and more inclusive debate is certainly desirable. a number of obstacles to such a debate have also become apparent. First. the level of technical knowledge considered necessary to participate in nuclear security discussions deters engagement. and linking the discussion to counterterrorism has tended to reduce information flows. The narrow framing of nuclear security issues around measures to reduce the risk of mass-impact terrorism has excluded large parts of the interested public—including proponents and opponents of nuclear energy—and abandoned the public policy sphere to special interests.

Second. there are some specific problems in promoting dialogue on nuclear science as an aspect of public policy. The reaction to the accident in Fukushima underlined the powerful psychological impact of a nuclear safety failure. The deaths. physical damage and economic impact caused by the earthquake and tsunami were far greater than those caused by the resulting nuclear safety failure at Fukushima.

However. the impact on the public discourse of the nuclear event was greater—not only in Japan but around the world. When discussing nuclear science. the expert community is unwilling to state that risks can be eliminated. while political decision makers are reluctant to admit publicly that some degree of risk is unavoidable. Methodologies and processes for risk assessment cannot repair this disconnect between science and public policy in the nuclear field.

Third. there is no agreement on the scope of nuclear security beyond physical protection of nuclear material. In general. industry has worked to differentiate between civilian and military nuclear domains. as demonstrated by the Nuclear Security Summits. where discussion has been confined to the civilian nuclear-fuel cycle.

However. there are significant countries where the civilian and military fuel cycles remain intertwined. For many interested constituencies in Europe. it is neither possible nor desirable to treat these issues entirely separately. and bridging that gap in understanding may also be necessary to find a common European approach to the proper role of nuclear in any future energy mix.

EXTERNAL DIMENSIONS OF AN ENERGY SECURITY STRATEGY

Some specific questions related to the external dimensions of an energy security strategy will also need to be thought through carefully. EU member states that build new nuclear power stations will have to be certain that they can buy the natural uranium that is the raw material for nuclear fuel. As noted in a 2013 SIPRI Policy Paper. African countries already account for a significant share of world natural uranium output. and many are prospecting to identify new uranium reserves. Given the emphasis in EU documents on diversifying external supplies and speaking with one voice in external energy policy. future EU uranium-extraction projects could be the basis for a more fair. transparent and commercially viable approach to Africa than was displayed in past national programmes.

Increasing security of supply through energy production inside the EU would probably involve the construction of nuclear reactors of non-European origin. EU documents emphasize the development of energy technologies. and EU industry already has advanced capabilities throughout the whole nuclear fuel cycle. Although purchasing nuclear fuel for long-term operation (or even the whole lifetime of the nuclear reactor) and storing it on-site is feasible. member states might want to avoid any risk of disruption by further developing the capability to manufacture fuel for reactors of non-EU origin.

The energy security strategy calls for making the possibility of fuel supply diversification a condition for any new investment in nuclear power. However. in the case of Russian-supplied reactors. the certification of non-Russian fuel for their operation would need to be prepared for in advance—something that would require close consultation with Russian partners.

NUCLEAR PLANT SECURITY MEASURES

The nuclear energy industry maintains very strict security to prevent unauthorized persons from gaining access to critical equipment or approaching close enough to harm the facility with land- or air-borne explosives. Security measures include:

- Physical barriers. electronic detection and assessment systems. and illuminated detection zones
- Electronic surveillance and physical patrols of the plant perimeter and interior structures
- Bullet-resisting protected positions throughout the plant
- Robust barriers to critical areas
- Background checks and access control for employees
- Highly trained. well armed security officers.

CONCENTRIC CIRCLES OF ESCALATING SECURITY

Security measures are based on concentric circles or perimeters. with the level of security increasing as distance to the reactor decreases.

Owner-controlled area. The outer perimeter. called the "owner-controlled area." is sufficiently distant from the reactor that only minimal security is deemed necessary. Explosives. firearms and alcohol are prohibited in this area.Protected area. The level of security increases dramatically at the boundary of the "protected area." which is fenced. protected by sophisticated security systems and guarded by armed security officers. Industrywide. the security force includes some 9.000 officers. many with military or law-enforcement backgrounds.

Individuals who are granted unescorted access to the protected area must first undergo a background check. psychological evaluation and fitness-for-duty testing (drug testing). Once inside the protected area. personnel are subject to behavioral observation and random drug testing. Each day. before entering the plant. they must pass through metal and explosives detectors and biometric screening. Visitors are screened and must be escorted at all times.

Vital area. The innermost circle is called the "vital area." which contains equipment needed to safely shut down the reactor and keep it in a safe condition. The control room. used fuel pool and main security alarm stations are in this area in addition to the reactor and associated safety equipment. Access is protected by card readers. security doors and sometimes staffed guard stations.

In response to a new NRC rule issued in 2009. the industry increased both the amount of live-fire weapons training and the frequency and scope of drills and exercises. This enhanced training ensures that each officer will participate in numerous security drills and exercises facing a mock adversary each year. While the scenarios are closely held. the drills themselves are announced in advance to ensure that drill participants are not exposed unnecessarily to lethal force.Each nuclear plant site has developed an integrated security and response plan with federal. state and local law enforcement agencies and emergency responders who can assist in the unlikely event of an attack.

FEDERAL OVERSIGHT OF NUCLEAR PLANT SECURITY

The U.S. Nuclear Regulatory Commission holds nuclear power plants to the highest security standards of any American industry. and the industry exceeds those standards. In response to public concern over nuclear plant security. Congress included in the Energy Policy Act of 2005 several provisions that increase security requirements or capabilities. This included allowing the NRC to authorize security officers to carry certain advanced weaponry and increasing federal penalties for sabotage and for bringing unauthorized weapons onto a nuclear power plant site. The act also directed the NRC to increase the scope of the "design basis threat"—that is. the threat against which nuclear power plants must be protected.

The NRC develops the design basis threat based on its regular interactions with federal intelligence and law enforcement authorities. It is currently characterized as a well-trained and dedicated paramilitary force. armed with automatic weapons and explosives and intent on forcing its way into the plant to commit radiological sabotage. Such a force may have the assistance of an "insider." who could pass along information and help the attackers. The threat also includes bomb-laden land and waterborne vehicles.

The NRC reviews the design basis threat each year and. since 2001. has revised it twice to reflect a higher number of possible attackers and greater weapons capabilities. In addition. the NRC conducts regular security briefings for senior executives and security managers in the nuclear industry to ensure they are up to date on the latest relevant intelligence.

The terrorist attacks of Sept. 11. 2001. prompted another look at the potential for an airplane crash to cause serious damage. NRC analysis shows that areas of a nuclear power plant housing the reactor and used reactor fuel would withstand the impact of a wide-body commercial aircraft. However. to enhance safety. NRC required nuclear plants to have response procedures to address an aircraft threat or loss of large areas of the facility due to explosions or fire. The agency's aircraft impact assessment rule requires design features for new plants to mitigate the effects of an airplane crash. and post-9/11 NRC orders require existing plants to implement similar measures.

The NRC provides regulatory oversight of nuclear power plant security through its routine inspection programme as well as evaluations in which a specially trained mock adversary attacks the plant. The agency conducts these force-on-force exercises at each nuclear power plant at least once every three years. The NRC also has at least two resident inspectors at each site.

ENERGISING POWER IN THE INTERNATIONAL SYSTEM

Maintaining economic growth rates and projecting power without requisite supplies of energy is a serious issue for all countries. particularly for resource deficient countries with rising or high demand. While it is clear that energy is a critical component of state power. there are few studies on the role of energy in the rise and fall of powers in the international system. Interestingly. in the context of the rising power of China and India. there are several studies/reports that highlight the potential for conflict or competition between the two countries as well as between India and China vis-a-vis the main energy-consuming countries of the developed world.

As countries make efforts to secure energy resources and transit/transportation routes (either countries or sea lines of communication [SLOCs]). they are more and more likely to brush up against each other. given that there are only a handful of countries that have exportable surpluses of energy resources. This is as true for oil and natural gas as much as it is for uranium and rare earth minerals that are important for renewable energy technologies. Energy therefore is a very useful arena to analyse whether the emergence of new powers in the international system can upset the prevailing balance of power and/or create potential for conflict. If those who portend that energy geopolitics is essentially zero-sum or conflictual are to be believed. then energy can be seen as a factor that affects power balances in the international system. If we agree that the military and economic power equations that exist between the major powers of the international system depend on the predictability and security of access to energy resources in the world. then the emergence of new powers would naturally imply more pressure on resources that are geophysically limited in nature. In the short to medium term. the ability of the great and rising powers of the international system to secure sources and routes to energy resources in the world would be competitive. if not conflictual. and would mean a reformulation (and not necessarily a longterm change or shift) of power equations in the world. However. this understanding of energy relations and power equations in the world fails to take cognizance of critical features that are specific to the energy sector.

CO-DEPENDENCE

For countries that are dependent on energy imports. particularly in the short to medium term (until they push for alternatives that give them more energy independence mostly possible in the medium to long term). ensuring security is not achievable independently of energy exporting or transit countries. What this means is that the notion of power and security in a realist sense is not possible. particularly in the context of energy. that is. through self-help means. Countries need to depend on energy-rich countries for their security. Undoubtedly. emerging and great powers alike seek to secure energy resources by bringing into their strategic fold important energy-rich countries. either through mutually beneficial trade relations or military partnerships. However. energy-rich countries that are trading partners of emerging or great powers in the international system would wield a certain degree of influence over the latter. given the competitive nature of demand and supply. For example. Russia can threaten the energy security of its Western European buyers if the geopolitical equations between Russia and its Eastern European neighours sour. as in the case of Ukraine in 2009; or America's fear of resource nationalism in Venezuela; even though Saudi Arabia is a key partner of the US. because Saudi Arabia is also a member of OPEC. it is constrained by OPEC decisions to cut production (in order to raise prices) rather than its strategic interests in maintaining close military relations with the US. Similarly. countries that are important for transit (between energy producing and importing countries) can also leverage their power. even though they are merely conduits. As India is learning. good relations in the neighbourhood are critical for the success of gas pipeline projects that have been in the pipeline for long. namely the Turkmenistan-Afghanistan-Pakistan-India (TAPI) and Iran-Pakistan-India (IPI) pipelines. Therefore. in order to achieve selfsufficiency in terms of energy needs. countries. particularly energy-importing countries. must build mutual stakes that are attractive and beneficial for longterm energy security.

Securing Demand for Energy

Although energy producing and transit countries appear to be more powerful in the international system. it is necessary to ask whether this is indeed so. From the examples. and the simple fact that demand is continuously falling short of supply as new emerging powers. such as China and India. join the market. it would seem that energy-rich countries can play a particularly powerful role in the international system. The reality however is far more complicated than this simplistic inference would have us believe. Notwithstanding the 'resource curse' that several analysts suggest afflicts resource-rich countries. there is another basic reason why energy-rich countries are not and indeed have not been also the most powerful states in the international system. That is. that although energy-deficient and importing countries are definitely in a comparatively dire situation. the fact of the matter is that even energy exporting countries need stable demand. This therefore highlights the need to broaden our understanding of energy security from one that focuses on supply for energy importing countries. to one that also includes the concern of energy-rich countries as well their stake. albeit less 'dire'. in ensuring that demand and supply complementarities remain intact.

It is only in this light that the following developments can be read. For example. although Russia can threaten to use its energy supplies as a political tool. it is also interested in ensuring that it can export its energy supplies to its importing partners. The fact that bad relations with transit countries could seriously hamper delivery to end markets can be seen as the motivating factor behind Russia's interest to look eastwards. In December 2009. Russia decided to launch the Eastern Siberia- Pacific Ocean (ESPO) pipeline to capture markets in Asia (hitherto. Russia's pipeline infrastructure was directed westwards—to Europe). The steep drop in oil prices in 2009 (as well as the world financial crisis) intensified Russia's economic troubles. which in turn led to country-wide demonstrations. During the months when oil prices were on a steady rise. it was not only energy-dependent and importing countries that were concerned. but also OPEC countries who were worried about a possible beginning of a shift from fossil fuel imports by key energy-importing countries of the world. Other countries such as the UAE are taking steps to be ready for a world keen on getting off its 'oil addiction'.

Dubai for instance has introduced a subsidy for solar panels. in an attempt to expand its oil exports in the future. while at the same time cutting down its own use of hydrocarbons. What the foregoing analyses and examples seek to highlight is the fact that the link between energy and state power is often not linear or direct. On the one hand. particularly in the short to medium term. energy-rich countries would continue to wield a certain degree of influence over both the great powers of the international system. as well as the emerging powers. Indeed. the greater and diversified the demand for energy. the more influence and power the energy-rich countries acquire. However. this does not mean that being rich in energy resources is a corollary of power in the international system. A trade logic that is built on demand and supply complementarities often trumps energy geopolitics where energy is seen as merely a power game and a zero-sum affair. Also. the importance of transit (between suppliers and consumers) gives transit countries greater importance in the pecking order. What this therefore means is that energy exerts a distinct kind of logic on countries that does not necessarily correspond to a realist understanding of international relations and power equations.

ENERGISING ECONOMIES WITH SOLAR POWER

For all the energy innovations in the 21st century. over 1.2 billion people worldwide still do not have electricity at home. And yet on any given day. only one hour's worth of energy from the sun is enough to sustain the energy consumption of the entire world for a year.

Recognizing the huge potential for solar energy to address existing energy poverty. Swiss power and automation giant ABB recently hosted a session on solar energy on the sidelines of the World Economic Forum in Manila. The discussion. held on May 22. called "Sharing the sun: The future of solar energy in East Asia". centred on advancements in solar. as well as the opportunities and challenges for this sector in the region in the context of achieving equitable progress – the theme of the WEF.

Experts on the panel highlighted Asia's energy poverty woes. particularly in archipelago nations like the Philippines and Indonesia where millions still do not have electricity. hindering development. Policies promoting deployment of solar and innovative business models that capitalise on existing solar technologies are key factors that can drive sustainable and inclusive economies. they said.Maxene Ghavi. head of ABB's solar industry segment initiative and a panellist at the Manila discussion. noted that ABB supports both traditional power applications and applications for off- or microgrids. especially in Asia where energy security and access to energy is "very. very critical".

ABB is the world's second-largest supplier of solar inverters. It also provides products that cater to the entire range of the solar photovoltaic (PV) value chain – from generation and transmission to distribution and maintenance. Some of its specific solutions include inverters for large-scale PV power plants and grid stabilization technology that integrates renewable energy into microgrids or off-grid locations for a reliable supply of power.

ABB believes solar energy decouples economic growth from energy consumption and improves lives. especially across various appliations. said Ghavi.

The firm recently announced a technology partnership with Solar Impulse SA. a Swiss solar aviation research and development (R&D) company that is attempting the first round-the-world flight powered by the sun in 2015. Ghavi said ABB's decision to support Solar Impulse was due to an alignment of vision. which is essentially to power a better world.

The solar aviation firm's Solar Impulse 2 – a single-seater solar plane with a 72-metre wingspan with 17.000 solar cells – recently completed its maiden flight on June 2 in Switzerland. Commending the project. founders Betrand Piccard and André Borschberg said Si2 incorporates a vast amount of new technology to render it more efficient. reliable and in particular. better adapted to long-haul flights.

Solar Impulse aims to prove that exploration and aviation. which currently accounts for two per cent of global manmade CO2 emissions. can be done without fuel or pollution. Their ambition. they added. is to "contribute to the cause of renewable energies [and] to demonstrate the importance of clean technologies for sustainable development..."

SOLAR'S POTENTIAL

Posing a provocative question. Satinder Bindra. former CNN South Asia bureau chief and ADB principal director for external relations who moderated the discussion. asked: "If a solar plane can potentially travel the world. how come we are lagging behind in getting solar energy out there?"

He highlighted Asia's continued dependence on fossil fuels. citing statistics from the Asian Development Bank (ADB) that the consumption of coal. oil and natural gas is set to increase by 2035 in the region. Demand for coal. which is the primary energy source in the energy mix. is projected to increase by 53 per cent by 2035 in Asia and the Pacific. according to a 2013 ADB publication.In addition. electricity demand in the region is forecasted to more than double between 2010 and 2035. while CO2 emissions from the energy sector will increase to over 22 billion tonnes. a growth rate of two per cent per year.

Panelist Eric Berkowitz. chief investment officer of impact investing at private equity firm Bamboo Finance. noted that solar is the way to provide clean and affordable electricity to the over one billion people in the world who live off the grid. and to the other two million people who have limited or unreliable access to energy.

These people should use safe. affordable solar lanterns that can be upgraded to a solar home system or microgrid for their energy needs. in place of kerosene or candles. which not only provides poor lighting but also produces hazardous fumes and is a fire hazard. said Berkowitz.

"Solar can transform communities. It creates vibrancy and stimulates economic activity. People can open and operate their businesses after dark. kids can study at night and – a frequent feedback from the communities – it even prevents snake bites." he added.Ghavi similarly stressed the existence of solar options in the market. highlighting the availability of solar technologies and its competitive pricing compared to conventional energy sources.

She said the reason that the world is lagging behind in the use of solar energy. particularly in rural communities. is not for a lack of technology but the lack of policies and government support. – it's about what policies are in place and what governments are able to support. "We need to have policymakers that enable the technology for deployment." she added.

SMALL SOLUTIONS. BIG IMPACT

In a recent op-ed in Eco-Business. ABB region president for South Asia. Haider Rashid. argued that smallsolar farms. for example. can bring electricity to far-flung rural communities. which usually rely on generators running on expensive diesel fuel. Routing electricity to remote towns and villages from power plants can be very costly and communities typically have to wait years for the power to start flowing. he pointed out.

Unlike this traditional method and its requisite infrastructure. solar can easily provide electricity just as mobile phones have given those in distant provinces a means of communication despite the lack of telephone lines. explained Jim Ayala. a panellist and founder and chief executive of Philippine social enterprise Hybrid Social Solutions.

"Without electricity. they can't develop. But with solar. we don't have to wait for the grid." said Ayala. one of 24 awardees in the 2013 Social Entrepreneurs of the Year by the Schwab Foundation. For example. once a household in the Philippines has a simple solar lamp where they can also charge their cellphones. their household income goes up by 25 per cent. Ayala noted. That's about US$40. of which $10 is savings usually spent on kerosene. batteries. and charging their cellphones in the village; while. the $30 is earnings from becoming more productive. since they have more time and they can use light in aid of their business. he explained.

Fishermen likewise benefit from affordable solar products. Rather than spend US$7 per night on kerosene. they can use light from a lamp with stored solar energy to attract fish. said Ayala. "So instead of spending $200 a month. you spend $200 on a system. and from then on it's pure savings for the next five to ten years or until the system lasts." he added.

Orb Energy in India is one example. he cited. The company helps underprivileged communities attain basic services like electricity and water through solar photovoltaic and solar water heating systems through their vast retail network of 150 stores that also works with local banks. This leads to rural electrification. he noted.

Solar is an ideal solution to provide light and other essential services in the developing world. especially to the millions of people in India who are still reliant on kerosene for basic lighting. said Orb Energy.

NATIONAL POLICIES

India's new Prime Minister Narendra Modi is likewise keen to tap on solar energy as a means to stir sustainable development. Prior to his win. he announced a solar revolution for the sub-continent as a way to eliminate power outages and achieve economic growth. In a post-election pledge. he said his government's goal is to bring solar power to every home by lighting at least one light bulb by 2019.

In the Philippines. although there is a Renewable Energy Bill that promotes the development of renewable energy resources. there is still a need to make solar energy attractive. said Professor Alvin Culaba. head of the Solar Energy Centre in De La Salle University who also spoke at the ABB solar session.

He explained that since energy is still dependent on technology. large-scale solar infrastructure or production of electricity from renewable energy will still involve higher upfront costs compared to traditional energy sources – unless the government removes market distortions to conventional fuels and also adds in environmental and social costs.

While the off-grid set-up is the clear advantage of solar. grid connection is also crucial for the economy. particularly to power industries. Ghavi pointed out. "So you need to have a grid and to invest in that infrastructure. That's as critical. and that's very dependent on what the government wants to enable and what policies they have in place." she said.Both clear policies from the government and economically viable solutions from the private sector are needed. she emphasised. Ambiguous policies are not effective since this only inhibits financing from investors. she added. Still. despite any hiccups amidst the growing solar uptake. Culaba said. "With the sun always there. the future is always bright."

THE MULTIDIMENSIONALITY OF ENERGY SECURITY

A fact already alluded to above is that energy security is simultaneously a concern for energy importing countries as well as energy exporting countries. The nature of energy resource endowment in the world necessitates a reciprocity that ties together countries that are major consumers and producers. However. energy security is more than just about managing the demand-supply dynamic or energy trade between nations. It is a muddier arena. primarily due to the various levels at which energy security can be and must be addressed. as well as the multiple constraints and pressures countries have to increasingly work within. Energy security is addressed not merely by managing import dependency and ensuring the security of demand and supply. In reality. countries attempt to address their energy needs in multiple ways at multiple levels. Because energy resources are not unlimited in supply—energy at comparatively cheaper rates is definitely not unlimited in supply—countries need to manage their demand in a much more efficient and rational manner. Therefore. addressing energy security is equally about putting in place effective domestic regulations and frameworks as it is about energy diplomacy. Furthermore. it is increasingly important for countries to make sure that the two aspects of their energy securing strategy connect with each other. That is. a decision to expand nuclear energy is not only about sourcing uranium and inking civil nuclear energy deals with leading nuclear energy countries. but equally about putting in place a financial plan that apportions priority to nuclear energy infrastructure and mining efforts; a regulatory framework to allow greater foreign and private sector participation and a grievance redressal mechanism that is capable of addressing the consequences of going nuclear in a bigger way. Bringing in energy efficiencies is also an important aspect of reducing losses and making the economy less energy intensive.

Similarly. countries have also been keen on building strategic petroleum reserves so that they are not exposed to sudden supply disruptions in international markets. Increasingly. countries are also working within an environment in which there are multiple constraints and pressures that add to the 'cost' of their energy choices. What this means in terms of strategy is that energy security has to be addressed simultaneously at multiple levels. and that there needs to be greater coordination between the various strategies. the priorities of the government. the demand projection and the resources the country has at its disposal.

A holistic understanding and approach to achieving energy security that stresses energy efficiency (in consumption patterns and production) and sustainable development practices has emerged as part of the strategy of several countries; particularly energy importing countries. While putting in place an energy strategy at the national level. almost all countries need to keep in mind this multidimensional and holistic understanding to energy security. We turn to what role energy plays in India's energy security strategy. and whether to what extent energy can be seen as exerting a structure and imperative of its own to India's national security strategy.

MULTIDIMENSIONAL APPROACH TO ENERGY SECURITY

Energy security is an issue of primary concern for decision-makers worldwide. This is especially true in many post-Soviet countries. where the current dependency on Russian energy imports is being reinforced by the high energy intensity of these economies – a legacy of the energy inefficient Soviet technologies coupled with a lack of technological modernization over the past two decades.

Belarus. a landlocked country with a population of 10 million people. is one of the countries struggling to solve an energy security puzzle in the midst of perturbations of the energy markets and important changes in regional geopolitics.

Belarus' economy has been growing steadily in the early 2000s with an impressive 7.7% average annual GDP growth – a figure surpassing the economic performance of its closest post-Soviet neighbors. Ukraine (7.6%) and Russia

(7.5%). The 2010 economic crisis resulting in substantial downturns in Ukraine (-15.0%) and Russia (-7.9%). had very mild impact on the Belarusian economy. which grew 0.2% in 2010.

Despite the apparent robustness of the Belarusian economy as compared to its neighbors. the crisis revealed a major weakness of the Belarusian economic model. the country's utmost dependence on economic and political relations with Russia. Belarus is trying to move away from the Russia-centered economic model. in an attempt to diversify the sources of its economic growth. Not surprisingly. Russia is using a number of economic and political levers. of which oil and natural gas are the most important ones. in an attempt to tame a rebellious ex-vassal.As a result. Belarus recently faced a variety of new energy challenges that must be successfully tackled for the country to preserve its political and economic independence.

THE BELARUSIAN ECONOMIC GROWTH DRIVERS

Belarusian economic growth in the late 1990s-early 2000s was primarily driven by the combination of three main factors: (*i*) privileged access to Russian markets for Belarusian industrial and agricultural exporters and energy importers; (*ii*) preferential support of the enterprises and sectors with a large state share. especially those producing for export. and (*iii*) governmental policies on wage and price control. which resulted in temporary cost advantages for traditional exports (WB 2005). These factors were reinforced by the low capacity utilization that experienced a sudden drop in the early 1990s as the Soviet Union collapsed.

Immediately prior to the 2010 economic downturn. productivity growth was the main driving force of the industrial growth in Belarus (WB 2010a). For most economies in transition. productivity growth is driven by (*i*) productivity increases within the firms and (*ii*) labour reallocation. In Belarus. most of the productivity increase occurred due to the former driving force. Recent data show that productivity growth is slowing down – a sign that productivity improvements has so far been gained through "low hanging fruit" type of investments. but these are now coming to an end. (WB 2010a).

Productivity growth in 2004-2008 was reinforced by increasing capacity utilization from approximately 45% in 1996 to 57% in 2004 to almost 70% in 2009. Yet. it is commonly perceived that most of the underused capacities are outdated and need rehabilitation or replacement.

Thus. the actual figures of the unused capacities may be well inflated. Therefore. the years of reclaiming unused capacities will soon become history. and Belarus is gradually approaching a point at which output growth would require either costly capacity expansion or increase of capacity-usage efficiency. Of these two alternatives. improvements in energy efficiency are the one that does not show signs of being exhausted in the near future.

Belarusian energy efficiency increased by nearly 50% between 1996 and 2008 as the government began designing and enforcing a comprehensive energy efficiency policy. The measures included among others (i) establishing a Committee for Energy Efficiency in 1993. which evolved into Energy Efficiency Department of the Committee for Standardization with a mandate to develop and implement the energy efficiency improvement strategy; (ii) substantial financing. amounting to USD 4.2 billion in 1996-2008 and USD 1.2 billion in 2008 alone; (iii) political commitment to energy efficiency. as illustrated by two National Energy Savings Programmes approved in 1996 and 2001 respectively and the 1998 Law on Energy Savings (WB 2010b).

Currently. Belarus' energy intensity is the lowest compared to the neighboring CIS countries. Specifically. in 2008 Belarus used 1.17 tons of oil equivalents (toe) to produce USD 1.000 of its GDP – a substantial advantage compared to Ukraine's 2.55. Russia's 1.60 and Moldova's 1.50 toe/USD 1.000. Yet. despite substantial recent progress and good standing in its regional sub-group.

Belarus is still far from its energy efficiency potential. as showed by comparison with the closest Western neighbors: Poland and Lithuania use respectively 0.41 and 0.46 toe/USD1.000 (IEA 2010). Economic modeling suggests that a baseline scenario of 50% decline in energy intensity within the next decade would be a source of an additional annual GDP growth by 3.5-7%.

OVERVIEW OF THE ENERGY SECURITY DIMENSIONS IN BELARUS

Energy security is a multidimensional issue. which requires considerations with respect to:

- Primary energy sources distribution
- International trade and the geopolitical context
- Impact of energy on the environment

Primary Energy Security Dimensions in Belarus

A reasonable diversification of energy sources results in a more sustainable energy model of the economy. Currently Belarus' primary energy source is natural gas. which accounts for 63% of its energy supply. Natural gas is primarily used for heat production (55% of the total natural gas supply) and electricity production (20%). Over 80% of Belarusian centralized heating stations use natural gas and nearly 95% of electric energy in the country is produced with natural gas as primary fuel.

The second biggest share (29%) is crude oil and petroleum products. mainly used in the transport sector as well as the residential. commercial and public services sectors. All other primary energy sources account for less than 10% of the total primary energy supply. Renewable sources of energy are virtually unused in Belarus.

In sum. the analysis of the Belarusian energy balance reveals a disproportionately large share of natural gas use. especially in electricity and heat generation. It is therefore clear that. in the context of emerging tensions over the imported Russian natural gas. substantial changes in the electricity and heat generation sector will be needed.

International Trade Considerations and Geopolitical Context

Belarus produces only 14% (4 Mtoe per year) of its total primary energy demand and nearly 15% of its oil and gas consumption. thus being totally dependent on fossil fuels imports from Russia. Prior to the escalation of the conflict with Russia. almost the entire demand for natural gas and oil was satisfied by Russian imports at discounted prices. which was often viewed as an implicit subsidy of the Belarusian economy. Currently Russia is reducing these implicit subsidies by narrowing the gap between prices charged to Belarus and to the EU. An important difference between natural gas imports and oil imports is that while natural gas imports are entirely consumed by the Belarusian domestic market. a large share of crude oil imports is processed and exported as petroleum products. Therefore. while reducing dependency on Russian gas imports may be achieved. to a large extent. by a transition to alternative energy sources and improvements in energy. the same approach is unlikely to work for oil imports. since no transition to other sources of energy is possible for oil refineries and efficiency increase is limited to losses minimization. Thus. the only alternative to reduce dependency on Russian oil imports is diversification of oil suppliers.

In early 2010. the Belarusian government has signed an agreement with Venezuela on continuous supply of crude oil to Belarus. The first delivery was made by a railroad transfer from the Ukrainian sea port of Odessa; the following deliveries were made through the Estonian Muuga seaport and the Lithuanian Klaipeda seaport by railroad. Belarusian government has announced that it expects nearly 4 million tons of Venezuelan oil to be delivered in 2010. and the quantity is expected to grow to 10 million tons (*i.e.*, 42.5% of the current oil imports) in 2011 and onwards. The average price for Venezuelan crude in 2010 was USD645 per ton (compared to USD 402 per ton of Russian oil). according to the national statistics committee.

Land transport of Venezuelan oil from seaports remains the most questionable issue. While railroad transfer proved to be a reasonable intermediate solution. a sustainable and cost-efficient transportation of Venezuelan oil is possible only through pipelines. Although the Lithuanian and Latvian legs of the former Soviet Druzhba pipeline system can be used. they require major investments to allow for reverse transfer from Baltic seaports to Belarus. The Ukrainian Odessa-Brody oil pipeline. in reverse direction. is the most likely route for a large share of Venezuelan oil. as Ukrainian government signed an agreement with Belarus for transfer of 9 million tons of Venezuelan crude in 2011. Yet. the deal is heavily threatened by Russia which was using the Odessa-Brody pipeline in the opposite direction until 2010 and is losing an important lever of influence over Belarus as the country diversifies its oil imports.Another crucial energy security consideration from the geopolitical perspective for Belarus is its own pipeline systems.

Until recently. Belarusian oil and gas transit capacity has been a powerful lever in its relationships with Moscow. In an attempt to diversify its hydrocarbon export routes. however. Russia has announced the construction of an alternative Nord Stream pipeline system in 2005. The two-legged 1.200 km pipeline system will transport natural gas from Russian Vyborg to German Greifswald under the Baltic Sea. thus making it the longest sub-sea pipeline in the world. Each leg has a projected capacity of 27.5 billion cubic meters per year (55 billion cubic meters for the entire system). The first leg is projected to be in full operation by late 2011. the second by late 2012.

Although the Nord Stream transfer capacity is below the annual transfer of natural gas through Belarus. it represents an important strategic instrument in Russian foreign policy to manipulate Belarus and Ukraine as they compete for a residual share of the Russian natural gas transfer. Recent trends in European energy security policy headed towards increase of energy efficiency. diversification of hydrocarbons importers and shale gas revolution will undoubtedly lead to a decrease in the European demand for Russian gas. which. in the worst case scenario. may completely eliminate Belarus from the Russian gas transfer system. as Belarusian and most of the Ukrainian gas pipeline capacity become redundant.

Impact of Energy on the Environment

Belarus lies around the average. both in Europe and in the Eastern European region. when it comes to pollution intensity of its energy use. While there is room for improvements in terms of the impact of energy on the environment. this concern is of second order as compared to the above discussion on energy intensity. Moreover. it is believed that improvement of energy efficiency of the economy through implementation of modern technologies will bring along reduction of pollution intensity as well.

About 20% of Belarusian territory was affected by the accident and nearly 17% of its agricultural land. Costs to the economy are estimated in the order of 32 to 35 times the Belarus state budget in 1985. Nearly 22% of the national budget was spent in 1991 on remediation measures. although the figure has contracted to 6% in 2002 and 3% in 2006%. The total spending of Belarus due to consequences of the Chernobyl disaster over the period 1991-2003 exceeded USD 13 billion. Besides the direct impacts on health. several social problems followed the worst civil nuclear accident. including the loss of rural livelihoods and outward migration of qualified workforce accompanied by inward migration of unqualified workforce and people who have economic difficulties elsewhere. A significant amount of agricultural land in the area of the radioactive fallout is still unavailable for cultivation. Development of the area remains a challenge. especially in small towns accommodating migrants from outside Eastern Europe. predominantly from Central Asia. Radioactive pollution is still a concern in the affected areas.

Not surprisingly. Belarusian population remains cautious about plans to construct the first nuclear power plant in Astravets. in the Hrodna Voblast. as nuclear power is still considered a source of substantial risks. despite extensive media campaigns and policy assurances on the exceptional nature of the Chernobyl accident.

6

India and its Energy Security Strategy

Undoubtedly. energy has become an important aspect of India's domestic and foreign policy over the past few years. At the domestic level. energy is a critical component of India's governmental planning and implementation. On the other hand. in the area of foreign policy. energy diplomacy has emerged as a distinct area of focus. These developments at the domestic and international levels together point out that energy plays a big role in India's national strategy. However. whether this means that India has a clearly enunciated and coherent 'national' 'security' strategy on energy is unclear. Rather. from an analysis of the various government documents. policy pronouncements and the country's energy diplomacy. we can piece together the chief features and priorities of India's energy security strategy. For analytical purposes. the discussion is divided into its domestic and foreign policy dimensions. While this is largely in keeping with the way the country has expressed its energy security concerns. in several instances. the two do come together. if not in intent. then definitely in purpose. Although here we identify the developments and characteristics of India's strategy in the context of energy at both the domestic and international level. the focus shall be mainly on the latter. while the former will be discussed briefly.

INDIA'S ENERGY SECURITY

GROWING ASIAN ENERGY DEMAND

The growth in demand for energy in Asia is forecast to surpass growth rates in all other regions over the next decade and beyond. By 2020. the world is projected to consume three times the amount of energy it used before the 1973 oil crisis.1 The US Energy Information Agency predicts that nearly half of the world's projected incremental demand will occur in developing Asia. in which they include principally India. China and the members of the Association of South-East Asian Nations (ASEAN). but not Japan. New Zealand and Australia. Asia's current economic crisis has slowed the energy demand growth trends in East Asia. but has not reversed them. Energy analysts around the world have anticipated the Asian economic crisis to be severe but not protracted.2 The dimensions of Asia's demand for energy will shape the international energy world in a number of important ways and have significant consequences. For example:Oil demand growth in Asia is expected to be the fastest of any region in the world. The region's oil demand in the year 2000 is expected to average 13.3 million barrels per day (mb/d)—close to Western Europe's 14.3 mb/d. Experts anticipate that by 2020. Asia will consume 28.6 mb/d. which is greater than projected consumption in the United States (24.4 mb/d).3 China's demand for oil will drive this significant increase. growing at approximately 5 per cent per annum. By 2020. China's oil consumption is expected to be approximately 9.5 mb/d.4

Natural gas is expected to be the fastest growing primary energy source over the next two decades both worldwide and in Asia. Gas consumption in developing Asia is predicted to grow by more than 7 per cent annually from 1995-2020. increasing consumption six fold. from 4.7 trillion cubic feet in 1995 to 27.7 trillion cubic feet by 2020. In industrialised Asia (Australia. Japan. and New Zealand) gas use will grow at a more conservative rate of 1.6 per cent annually. increasing consumption 50 per cent. from 3.1 trillion cubic feet in 1995 to 4.6 trillion cubic feet in 2020.5 Natural gas is abundant in the region. it has minimal environmental effects and relative price stability. which makes it the preferred fuel in many Asian countries and the candidate to reduce reliance on Middle East oil and to make up for potential shortfalls in the nuclear sector.

Asia consumes far more coal than any other region of the world. Asia's share of total world coal consumption will increase from 40 per cent in 1995 to 60 per cent in 2020 (on a tonnage basis). Coal consumption in the region is projected to increase by more than 3.1 billion tons. from 2.0 billion tons in 1995 to almost 5.2 billion tons in 2020.6 China will account for the majority of the increase in coal consumption. but increased coal consumption is likely to be widespread throughout the region. Only in Japan is coal use likely to decline in response to increasing environmental pressures.Across Asia. nuclear capacity is projected to increase from 85.8 to 129.4 gigawatts by 2020. A number of Asian countries currently operate nuclear power plants. including Japan. China. South Korea. Taiwan. India and Pakistan. At the end of 1996. these six countries had 60.0 gigawatts of nuclear capacity on line. with Japan accounting for 42 gigawatts. With the exception of Japan and South Korea. these programmes are small. but all anticipate some growth in the future. Ambitious government plans to expand nuclear power production in India and China contrast with the limited growth potential in Japan and South Korea. where development of the nuclear sector increasingly is constrained by adverse popular opinion.

IMPLICATIONS OF GROWING ASIAN ENERGY DEMAND

What do these trends in energy consumption mean for Asian actors?

As Asian energy demand grows. its regional resources. particularly oil resources. are being depleted. As a result. Asia's dependence on extra-regional imports will rise. Dependence on oil imports is expected to rise to approximately 77 per cent by 2010 of which 93 per cent is predicted to come from the Middle East.7 The strategic reality is clear: the Middle East will become more important as the primary supplier of energy to Asia. not less.

Growing energy demand across the region could heighten competition for imports in Asia's regional market. This regional energy market. traditionally dominated by Japan. is now characterised by a number of industrialising economies. all of which will be seeking to meet their growing energy demands. We will likely see Japan's share of oil imports decline relative to the growing demand of other regional consumers. most of whom will have energy-intensive economies; growing energy-consuming middle classes; and few effective energy-conservation measures. China and the ASEAN will make up the largest increase in imports between 2000 and 2010. The economic crisis may have slowed this trend. but it is almost certain that more economies in the region will be dependent on energy imports from outside their region.

More tanker traffic from the Persian Gulf to Asia will be a direct result of this trend. The increased number of oil and liquified natural gas (LNG) tankers coming from the Middle East will increase the pressures on already congested strategic chokepoints and raise new security questions. The Strait of Malacca. in particular. will be a critical chokepoint for a dangerously high amount of energy-related tanker traffic. Even with the slowdown of regional energy demand. it is likely that at least 14 mb/d of oil will flow through the Strait of Malacca from the Middle East to East and North-East Asia by 2010. Recently. this strait has experienced rising levels of piracy. much of it by unflagged Chinese vessels. Environmental problems related to tanker traffic are also a concern. To ease pressure on the Strait of Malacca. future tanker traffic could be partially routed through the Sunda and Lombok Straits. which are controlled by Indonesia. However. instability in Indonesia could make these and other alternative routes problematic. causing new and complex challenges for the energy security of many Asian states. One possible safety valve has not materialised: Malaysia has proposed building a 500.000 b/d trans-peninsular pipeline to alleviate the oil-filled tanker traffic. but the economic crisis has postponed these ambitious plans.

Allow us to make two important points related to the economic crisis and current low oil prices. First. as we know. more than two-thirds of the world's oil reserves are located in the Persian Gulf. In the next two decades. we will see the importance of the Middle East increase as smaller reserves in non-Gulf countries are depleted. Moreover. the persistence of low oil prices also will focus attention on the low-cost production in the Middle East at the expense of other high-cost. non-Organisation of Petroleum Exporting Countries (OPEC) regions. such as the Caspian and the Russian Far East. Consequently it bears repeating frequently that the strategic reality is that Asian states will become more dependent for energy on the Persian Gulf. not less. as conventional wisdom—which tends to exaggerate the size of energy supplies elsewhere and understate the difficulties in bringing them to market—might suggest.

Second. low oil prices and depressed demand during the last 18 months have encouraged a misguided sense of complacency in the policy processes of many states with regard to energy security. This complacency discourage serious thinking on energy security and diversification strategies at a time when both should be receiving more attention. A number of large-scale energy projects—particularly natural gas projects designed to reduce regional reliance on Middle East oil—have been postponed or delayed since the economic crisis. A recent Asia Pacific Economic Cooperation (APEC) energy outlook report warns that lower investment in energy infrastructure and production could induce bottlenecks that prevent the efficient delivery of energy to satisfy increased regional demand growth beyond 2000.8

This is the general picture of energy trends in Asia. Of course. there are many sources of data. and some offer different versions of this picture—but only on the margin. give or take a few hundred thousand barrels per day. However. nearly all data confirm the general trends in Asia. Asian energy consumption will increase across all energy sectors and Asian actors will be forced to search beyond East Asia for the energy to satisfy their growing energy demands.

INDIA: PART OF THE DEVELOPING ASIAN PICTURE

How does India fit into the Asian energy picture? As the world's sixth largest energy consumer. India is not only affected by these energy dynamics but is a major part of the trends that we have outlined. India is endowed with a variety of energy resources. Unfortunately. it lacks substantial indigenous supplies of oil and gas. Demand for these commercial fuels has been growing at an average of approximately 5 per cent p.a. and is projected to continue at this rate into the next century.9 Coal is India's most abundant indigenous energy resource. supplying over half of India's total energy demand. India imports coal to meet only 20 per cent of its total energy demand. but it must import approximately 60 per cent of its oil.10 India currently does not import natural gas. but natural gas consumption is expected to double by 2000 and will likely reach 2.3 trillion cubic feet by 2005.11 The Oil and Natural Gas Commission (ONGC) and Gas Authority of India Ltd (GAIL) both stress the importance of natural gas in India's middle and long-term future. and both have formulated ambitious plans to expand gas infrastructure to and in India. Again. it is worth emphasising that the rapid increase in consumption will only to be met through imports. Like other Asian states. India will continue to be dependent on the Middle East for oil and will expect a growing dependence on imported natural gas coming from a variety of directions. It is clear that the government is concerned about meeting India's growing energy demand. Based on our research of publicly available information. we see four major components of an energy strategy emerging:

Increase the Development of Indigenous Resources—Oil. Gas and Coal. Self-sufficiency appears to be the centrepiece of India's energy strategy. reflecting an ingrained tradition of self-reliance. Increased production will come from discovering new reserves and from employing new exploration and recovery techniques to maximise yields from existing fields. Particularly in the natural gas sector.

India seeks to improve efficiency in its production techniques and in its internal distribution infrastructure. The government is heavily dependent on foreign capital and technology to achieve its ambitious goals. and. therefore. appears to be committed to rapid reform and liberalisation of the energy sectors. Incremental reforms began in 1991. but the urgency of India's energy demands has consolidated political support for reforms. thus. accelerating the pace of implementation in the past two years.

Expand Foreign Exploration Activities. ONGC currently operates in Iraq. Iran. Egypt. Tanzania. Vietnam and Abu Dhabi. and is actively seeking to expand its foreign activities. Of particular interest is a link ONGC has forged with the China Natural Gas Exploration and Development Corporation for developing the Caspian energy resources.

Increase Natural Gas Consumption. Natural gas is projected to be India's fastest growing energy sector. increasing to 15-18 per cent of total demand in the next century.12 A large portion of that increase will be in the power generation sector. as gas-powered power generators replace coal-fired generators. The natural gas will come from indigenous supply. LNG contracts and pipelines. In the medium term. LNG shows great promise. The government plans to import over 10 million tons/year of LNG in the next 10 years and has introduced a plan to build the necessary LNG infrastructure.13 LNG supplies will come from the Middle East and South-East Asian states—Oman. Qatar. Iran. Indonesia. Malaysia and Australia.

Pipeline networks will help meet demand in the longer term. India has discussed a number of pipeline options to import oil and gas. but is wary and cautious about their security. which we will discuss in more detail presently.Strengthen Relationships with Middle Eastern Suppliers. As noted. the strategic importance of the Middle East for India. like much of Asia. will increase with respect to the supply of oil and gas. India appears to be cultivating and maintaining relationships with the states in the Persian Gulf astutely. This engagement is by no means one way. The Middle East oil producers have recognised the attractiveness of the Indian market and are actively engaged in India's refining sector in order to secure the Indian market for their crude.

THE EMERGING GEO-POLITICS OF ASIAN ENERGY

India will be forced to calculate its energy security requirements within a more general geo-political environment that is characterised by rapid change and unpredictability. The geo-politics of Eurasia's new energy security equation is complex and challenging. and we do not intend to overly simplify a complex subject. However. we are prepared to make three generalisations about the nature of geo-politics in the region from Central Europe to the Pacific and from the Arctic Ocean to the Indian Ocean—the geographic and political contexts in which India and many other countries seek to solve their energy requirements in the next two decades.

First. we have traditionally thought of the geo-politics of energy in Eurasia as having a strong north-south orientation. with Russia playing a central. and. in some cases. dominant role. But the emerging energy security environment is shaping up to be more east-west (or west-east. depending on where one is standing) in the nature of its political. economic and social developments. What is happening in Central Asia illustrates this shift. When the Soviet Union collapsed. many pundits argued that the former republics would never be able to escape Russia's economic and political web. Clearly. some of these new states retain ties to Russia. especially trade ties. but consider this: the leading direct foreign investor in Uzbekistan today is the United States. followed by South Korea; in Georgia. Ireland. the United States. the Netherlands and Israel are all strongly represented; in Azerbaijan and Kazakhstan. multinational energy investment is coming from American. European and Asian companies; Armenia's leading trading partner is probably Iran; Georgia's is probably Turkey. Other states with significant investment across this region include Turkey. China. Indonesia. Malaysia. Japan. Germany. Pakistan. the Gulf Arab states and. increasingly. India.

While Russia will remain important to the economies of the Central Asian and Caucasian states. all of them are embarked on a rapid diversification of economic and trade interests that ultimately will pull them east. west and south. that is away from Russia. Russia's influence. already diminished everywhere. will probably continue to fade. Nowhere do we see this more cogently than in the development of the Eurasia Transport Corridor (ETC). which is now several years in the making and gaining momentum quickly. The ETC is an inspiration of the European Union (EU). and until recently the EU was most interested in promoting it. currently with investments of more than $5 billion. In the last 18 months or so. the US government has also taken an interest in the ETC's development—including the introduction in Congress of a New Silk Road Act—and US companies are now scouring the region for opportunities. The ETC is intended to be a network of telecommunications. energy pipelines and transport infrastructures that link Central Europe to China. European politicians refer to the ETC as a "west-east" link. which is intended. pointedly and explicitly. to reduce Russia's ability to dominate these regions politically and economically. The Chinese are excited about the development of the ETC. and in their writings describe it as an east-west link whose logical endpoints from the Chinese perspective are Rotterdam and Antwerp.

Our point may be summarised this way: north-south dynamics are rapidly giving way to east-west dynamics. not simply in the flow of goods but in the thinking of the peoples affected by them. This shift in thinking will probably have profound consequences in and on Eurasia in the next few decades. and it will ultimately change geo-political relationships. the risk and opportunities calculus. and strategic thinking. For example. as Russia declines. one can imagine that India will assume greater responsibilities for the security. stability and defence of its region. India's logical partners in this endeavour are its strategic neighbours to the east and west. such as Iran. Israel and ASEAN.

Second. the new Eurasia may be characterised by the political and economic weakness at its core. None of the Central Asian or Caucasian states is politically stable. with the possible exception of Georgia. None has its economic house in order. though again Georgia stands out as continuing to sustain positive growth. All. except Georgia and possibly Armenia. lack adequate mechanisms for transferring political power. When the current leaders die. which will be soon. it will set off wild scrambles among elites representing the claims of diverse families. tribes. clans. hordes. cities. and mafias. If energy revenues fail to flow soon. as appears likely. both the supplier states and those that will transport energy will suffer grievous economic setbacks. For example. Kazakhstan. which has most of the Caspian's wealth. is facing a looming budget deficit of at least three per cent of Gross Domestic Product (GDP) due to low oil prices and slow energy development. And if oil and gas do flow. there is every likelihood that the "Dutch disease"—that is. unsustainable debt spending on infrastructure—will ultimately cause serious economic infections.

Third. this unsettled region may be characterised by its troubled periphery. whch is almost everywhere unstable. In the north. Russia is likely to remain weak and incoherent for a long time. perhaps two decades or more. It could fragment into pieces of different size and political complexity that command dramatically unequal resource bases. China is likely to remain economically strong. but. again. its development is at best uneven across regions and ethnic boundaries. Moreover. China's east is inherently unstable and may be subject to severe disruption. Afghanistan is unlikely to become a coherent state in the foreseeable future. and will continue to be unbalanced by competing ethnic. regional and religious forces. Pakistan constantly flirts with failing as a state. and its collapse would affect everything around it. Iran remains an outcast. at least to Washington. and faces severe economic challenges that have already led to some internal turmoil. The North Caucasus is on the verge of general disruption. which has serious implications for Georgia. Armenia and Azerbaijan.

The bottom line is sobering. Nowhere around the periphery of Central Asia and the Caucasus can one find political stability. and in most places the dominant feature is instability. Worse. it is hard to imagine where stabilising influences might come from. India is the exception to this pattern. which suggests to us. again. that India's role as a facilitator of political stability in the region could become an important mission.

These three conditions—north-south dynamics becoming east-west dynamics. a soft political and economic core. and potentially tumultuous and unstable peripheries—are key defining characteristics of the new Eurasia.

NEW GEO-POLITICAL DYNAMICS

What. then. are some of the new geo-political dynamics that should capture our attention?

First. new actors with historical claims or more recent interests in Eurasia are expanding into the political void left by the collapse of the USSR and the inability of Russia to dominate it. Turkey has established a strong grass-roots position in commerce and education—and to some extent religion—throughout the region. Iran. which sees itself foremost as an Asian power rather than a Gulf power. has also extended economic tentacles throughout Central Asia and the Caucasus. where it. too. has historical preoccupations. Pakistan's influence is felt mostly through trade and subversive religious influences. particularly Wahhabism. which. though currently exaggerated by outside analysts and host governments. could grow into a menacing force within a decade. India has returned to Central Asia after nearly a century's respite. Strategic thinkers in India now refer to Central Asia as "India's extended strategic neighbourhood." Both India and Pakistan share a vision of Central Asia as an important energy supplier. China. which shares borders and population with Central Asia and which is experiencing a rapidly growing appetite for energy. could be the most important and aggressive new player. We believe that China has a long-term plan to expand into Central Asia. and that its economic influence will be hard to resist. It is thinkable that within a short period of time. perhaps within two decades or less. Kazakhstan—which will be tied to China by energy umbilical pipelines—will be firmly within China's economic and political orbit. By this time. much of the Russian Far East and eastern Siberia might also have been absorbed by China. on the strength of Japanese capital investment in the substantial Siberian gas fields and against minimal Russian resistance.

India's interests could be challenged if the new politics of Eurasia result in major geo-political realignments that affect its interests. China's strong economic and political offensive in Eurasia to expand its influence for energy and political gain could become worrisome to India. Moreover. the commitment of some states in Eurasia to possess nuclear weapons could intensify in the wake of tests by India and Pakistan. We may expect that Iran will become nuclear in the near future. and that this will push Turkey to develop its own capability or to shelter closely under Israel's. Nearly everywhere. the impetus will be on going nuclear. not getting rid of these weapons. We may even anticipate that formerly nuclear states—Kazakhstan and Uzbekistan. for example—could seek to regain their former status or to connect themselves closely to another nuclear state. Because no one will possess second strike capabilities. impediments to the first-strike use of nuclear weapons could be dangerously low.

We must anticipate that all of these players. as well as nearby outsiders like Israel. will develop strategies for pursuing interests in the region and that some of these strategies will conflict. We need to develop a better understanding of what the new of geo-political games will look like. what the strategies of the contestants might be. and where India's interests could be intersected.

Second. energy exploration and transport could come to dominate some of the economies of the region and be major sources of revenue in others. Caspian energy has already attracted many new actors into the region. and it could attract still more. Competition for supply and strategies for protecting transport and possibly targetting the transport of opponents will gradually come to define the link between energy strategy and military strategy in most countries. In other words. we may anticipate that the quest to find and protect energy will drive states to develop particular kinds of military capabilities.

We would also point to the potentially destabilising effects of energy not meeting expectations in the Caspian. It is fully conceivable to us that the Caspian has been badly over-sold. that the amounts claimed by optimists are not there. and that the low price of oil and lower-cost exploration opportunities elsewhere will force many economic players—principally Western energy companies—out of the Caspian. leaving only the strategic players—China. perhaps a weakened Russia and India. perhaps in concert with other regional actors like Iran—to dominate the Central Asian energy sector and the heart of central Eurasia. We suspect that this will change the rules of the game in ways that will affect India's interests and strategies.

Third. Russia will not have sufficient power to re-conquer any of this territory. but it will have relatively more power and the ability to project it than any of the objects of its attention. A highly nationalist Russia that places reconstituting the empire at or near the centre of its ideology will have the motive and means to destabilise most of the countries along its periphery. It might do this with the explicit intent of causing turmoil that impedes particular states from consolidating their own sovereignty. with the idea that Russia will step in to reassert its own claims at a later date when it is more powerful. Russia's ability to meddle thus could be a key factor in the new strategic universe. On the other hand. Russia will remain militarily weak. politically incoherent. economically destitute and demographically sick. But we should not expect Russia to play a constructive role as a balancer of interests in Eurasia.

Fourth. few of Central Asia's borders make sense. All are political borders that were created for a different politics. We should anticipate that some. perhaps many. will become the objects of change. Contemplate Afghanistan for a moment. Its Turkic/Tajik north will be a chief concern for Uzbekistan. which will become the Central Asian hegemon; its Shiite east is already a concern to Iran. which recently threatened war over events there; and its Pushtun south relates closely to Pakistan. We find it fairly easy to imagine a complete dismemberment of Afghanistan along ethnic lines. Nearly every Central Asian and Caucasian state is at some risk in this regard. as are many Middle East states. for example Iraq.

Fifth. demographic change will drive profound internal. and perhaps cross-border change throughout the region. In two decades. both Turkey and Iran will have over 100 million people; Pakistan will have a larger population than Russia; India will be close to becoming the world's most populous country; and Russia will suffer severe population disorders. including absolute decline. The southern rim countries will be exceedingly young; Russia. and increasingly China. will be growing old. We can anticipate mass urbanisation across the region. with all of its attendant social pathologies. These pathologies will be fed by political and economic breakdowns. local conflicts and environmental disasters. We can anticipate human disasters that will require international assistance. such as public health crises. large scale migrations. refugee flows. epedimics and other major social dislocations. Sixth. non-state actors—terrorists. crime syndicates. ethnic separatists. and others—will proliferate across the region. especially as governments disintegrate and order is harder to maintain. Access to Weapons of Mass Destruction (WMD) and off-the-shelf information warfare technology will grow. Some non-state groups may become more powerful than the governments of the states they inhabit.

Seventh. some states will become increasingly non-viable. and they may simply collapse into chaos and conflict. Pakistan is a good candidate; Afghanistan is mostly there already. Iran. if pushed to the logical conclusion of current sanctions against it, might eventually follow suit. The nightmare scenario is everything coming apart at once. which given the overlapping and reinforcing dynamics. is not entirely far-fetched. Thus. we would be faced with most of Eurasia in turmoil.

We could probably extend this list. but already it is long enough to paint a picture of what might take place. We wish to re-emphasise that we are not trying to predict the future. Rather. we are trying to come to grips with how one might think about these problems. India's energy security strategies need to be informed by these possibilities.

How Should India be Thinking About its Energy Security?

The geo-political and energy trends in Eurasia that we have outlined.

intersect or will intersect at many levels to affect India's national security interests. How should India be thinking about this intersection of plausible geo-political trends and probable energy trends? In this dynamic Eurasian context. we see a range of challenges and opportunities for India.

The Myth of Self-Sufficiency. Energy self-sufficiency is a laudable. but elusive goal for India. In the first place. improving energy efficiencies in the system is costly and will not keep up with the growth in India's energy demand. In the second. environmental problems associated with burning coal will put downward pressure on coal consumption. In the third. long lead times. political sensitivities on the international stage and difficulties in attracting the necessary foreign investment will complicate India's ambitious plans to expand the nuclear power sector. Therefore. unless India is able to increase its use of renewable resources—solar. biomass. hydro—it will become increasingly dependent on foreign oil and gas. While India undoubtedly can reduce the rate of growth in demand for outside energy. like virtually all other Asian states. it should plan for the risks of having to import oil and gas through pipelines and by sea over possibly considerable distances and across potentially hostile territory.

Multiple Energy Fronts Require Multiple Strategies. Currently. India conducts international energy relations mostly in one direction: it imports most of its oil from the Middle East. In a decade. India's energy—oil and gas—could come from three or four different directions—the Middle East. Central Asia. Bangladesh and South-East Asia. Protecting energy supplies coming from many directions by pipeline and tanker will require a variety of new strategies for developing and maintaining alliances. for political and economic engagement in new directions. and for possible military engagement. What strikes us as particularly important about this new world is that each of the emerging energy fronts poses a different combination of challenges. In the north. India will be faced with its historical problems with Pakistan and the spectre of cascading instability there and in neighbouring states. The challenge will be choosing more secure routes and providing security for energy transport. In the Gulf. India will have to compete with many other Asian states for energy and access. which suggests that the challenge will be one of alliance building. diplomacy and an ability to project some military power. probably naval power. In the Bay of Bengal. India will face direct competition from China in off-shore regions. Gas from Bangladesh must cross potentially hostile territory. Moreover. Bangladesh is increasingly influenced by India's main rivals in the region. Pakistan and China. and in this regard. energy could become a convenient strategic lever on India. The challenge will comprise security. access. diplomacy and intelligence. And in the east. India will face the prospects of a fragmenting Indonesia. an increasingly assertive Japan and a China that aggressively pursues its energy opportunities in its own maritime borderlands. The challenge for India in this theatre will be a bit of security. alliance building. military alertness.

and access. In our view. India will need a number of energy security strategies. not a one-size-fits-all solution. The Need to Compete. India will be no different from any other major developing economy that is increasingly dependent on foreign energy. As all the Asian economies begin growing again. India will find itself in competition with others for energy coming from all four directions. In the Middle East. access to energy could bring India and China into direct competition or conflict. as we may anticipate that China will take steps to secure its own energy from the Persian Gulf. which it will see as threatened by. among others. India. We have no difficulty imagining a Chinese naval build-up in the Gulf and around India's maritime periphery.

In Central Asia. the number of cconomic actors may decline if the projects are not economically viable. but the strategic actors—especially China—will probably remain. Energy security thus creates a new. and somewhat unfamiliar context for India. namely having to compete with other major actors outside its immediate defence periphery.

Safeguarding Energy will Become a Strategic Priority. Although oil and gas are plentiful now—few are worried about energy security in a world awash with oil—in 15 years the market could change and become increasingly tight. India will likely have to form energy alliances to secure access to supplies and to protect energy transport by pipeline and by sea through strategic chokepoints. The Straits of Malacca and Hormuz will be critical chokepoints for India's energy imports. India should be thinking about a naval strategy capable of protecting these chokepoints effectively. This may require increasing naval resources and capabilities and/or forming strategic alliances with others. such as the United States. Japan. Australia and Indonesia. Similarly. pipelines that connect India to Central Asia will be vulnerable to a variety of threats. India will wish to consider these threats and challenges with a view Towards developing strategies to pre-empt or reverse adverse situations.

Pakistan: Energy Conflict or Energy Cooperation. Energy strategies might be a way to engage Pakistan in an area of mutual concern and interest. Without cooperation with Pakistan. India's cnergy vulnerabilities will be much more serious. Both countries look to Central Asia as a key energy supplier in the future. This raises the possibility of an important symmetry that can be exploited to mutual advantage. On the one hand. no pipeline is viable unless Pakistan provides India with a certain security comfort level. On the other. pipelines from Central Asia are feasible economically only if they address the Indian market. Without both security and economic viability. no pipelines are likely to be built. but neither country can provide both security and economic viability. Mutual interest is so well served by cooperation on vital energy security issues that a strategic context divorced from other more contentious issues. such as the Kashmir problem. might be possible. Perhaps cooperation on energy security could be one of the first efforts for India and Pakistan to cooperate on a broader range of issues. On the other hand. it is difficult to imagine what kind of security guarantees Pakistan can give India that Indian leaders will believe. Therefore. India may wish to pursue energy cooperation with Pakistan. but it must still plan for the possibility of conflict over energy.

Plan for the Worst Case Scenario. We are trained to think about worst case scenario. so we ask to be forgiven if we stress these over the happy endings. But we are struck by the number of "things that can go wrong" in Eurasia that are increasingly plausible. For example. India's energy security strategy could be affected by the collapse of fragile regimes in the Middle East. which could precipitate a political crisis in the region and interrupt the flow of energy; by an Indonesia that implodes and/or fragments. jeopardising both production levels and destabilising transportation through the Strait of Malacca and throughout Asia; by a Japan that expands its military influence into South-East Asia and the Indian Ocean. or that forms an energy alliance with China; by an Iran that dissolves into civil war; or by a China that aggressively asserts economic and/or political hegemony in Central Asia. And. of course. by a Pakistan that is either dangerously aggressive or dangerously unstable. If several of these scenarios occur simultaneously. India's energy security could be severely challenged.The United States May Depart. India's energy security interests will be complicated by the fact that US energy interests increasingly will be focussed elsewhere. Over the next 10-15 years. it is likely that the US will be less dependent on the Middle East. Unless oil prices remain extremely low. increasingly imports from Latin America. West Africa. the North Sea and domestic US production will satisfy US energy demand. (Europe has already reduced its dependence on the Middle East dramatically.) If US strategic interests in the Middle East wane as a result. and consequently domestic political pressures to withdraw from the region mount. US military presence in the Gulf is likely to be reduced. US presence could be replaced by other Asian actors whose interests and dependence on the Middle East are rising. for example by China. whose future dependence will be paramount. Consequently. the Middle East could become a new arena of competition for Asian actors without the US there as a broker. The new actors could be faced with China as a mediator. not the US.

The United States May Increase its Presence. If you view a map of Eurasia from the standpoint of potential US interests. one feature emerges starkly: an almost total absence of allies. From Japan and Korea in North-East Asia to the Persian Gulf. the United States in fact has not a single substantial ally (Singapore bases barely qualify). Moreover. we could be looking at a world in which Japan's interests—and hence the character of the US-Japan relationship—change dramatically. If the United States wishes to pursue strategic interests seriously throughout this region—for example. protection of energy flows—it will need new allies. Yet the US government has put little effort into strengthening its relationship with the world's largest democracy. India. which also happens to be located at a critical geo-political crossroads. and it has openly sought to build a hostile relationship with Eurasia's other key player. Iran. If the United States is serious about forward presence in this region. its leaders need to engage in some focussed alliance building.

INDIA FOCUSES ON ENERGY SECURITY STRATEGY

India's top foreign government official is seeking new strategies to enhance international relationsto meet the demand for a continuous energy supply.Speaking at the 2012 Energy Security Conference in New Delhi. Indian Foreign Minister Salman Khurshid said. "Demand for energy is growing at a terrifying pace in India and yet not fast enough if we take into account the per capita consumption in India."

India imports 80 percent of its crude oil requirements which accounts for $120 billion of the country's wealth. If oil prices increase. the import bill increases and will impact India's economic growth. By 2030. India's oil import is expected to increase to 90 percent.India imported 186.7 million tons of crude oil and fuel products in fiscal year 2012. according to the Indian Oil Ministry data. In 2011. the amount was 148 million tons.

During a speech to India Oil shareholders. Chairman R.S. Butola spoke about the implications of world-wide energy issues on India's financial affairs.

"The global economic environment continues to be weak and challenging." Butola said. "The year 2011-12 saw unfolding of many new challenges."Emphasizing the importance of the strategy and economics of energy security. Khurshid said. demand for energy is escalating in India but sources of energy are depleting at the same pace. "Going forward. if [demand continues] to grow at 8 percent to 9 percent. import dependence is likely to increase and India would be importing 35 percent to 57 percent of coal. 90 percent to 94 percent of oil. and 20 percent to 57 percent of gas by 2031-32.

"We have made progress in linking India's electricity grid. the second-largest in the world. with Nepal. Sri Lanka and Bangladesh." Khurshid said.

In addition. India plans to have an additional gas pipeline network of 15.000 kilometers and increase its liquefied natural gas [LNG] capacity to 49 million tons annually from its current 14 tons. India plans to have the Turkmenistan TAPI Gas Pipeline commissioned by 2017. according to Khurshid.

OVERSEAS ACQUISITION A KEY FOR ENERGY SECURITY

CII Director General Chandrajit Banerjee said energy security has clearly emerged as a key concern for India. To succeed in winning international energy assets. India urgently needs a value-added strategic road map Towards acquiring overseas energy assets. CII President Adi Godrej. who also serves as chairman of Godrej Group. emphasized the need for strengthening the domestic energy sources as well as acquiring energy assets overseas."Measures to scale up renewable energy and expedite the exploration and production of oil. gas and coal to enhance domestic production need to be put in place. The strategic alliances and joint ventures as well as the establishment of a sovereign energy fund will enable successful acquisition of energy assets overseas." he said.

Godrej also said increasing energy requirements coupled with a slower-than-expected increase in domestic crude oil and natural gas production have led to a strong reliance on imports and have drawn attention to the importance of energy security.

"Ministry of External Affairs has been working with the line ministries. public and private sector to enable energy asset acquisition and there is a need to explore how synergies and tradeoffs can be developed; cooperation enhanced and opportunities leveraged to ensure the nation's energy security." India Economic Relations Secretary Sudhir Vyas said in his address.India targets reductions in hydrocarbon importsIndian Petroleum and Natural Gas ministry plans to reduce the dependence of hydrocarbons by 50 percent by 2017.

Under the plan. the ministry will establish a policy framework to increase investor confidence and facilitate investments in this segment as well as increase domestic production and accelerate the acquisition of hydrocarbon assets overseas.

INCREASE IN NATURAL GAS USAGE AND PIPELINE NETWORK

The ministry also is looking to diversify into new and unconventional energy sources such as coal bed methane and shale gas."The single most important global development was the discovery of shale gas. which is acknowledged as a game changer. In India. we have adopted a two-pronged approach with respect to shale gas — overseas acquisition and domestic exploration. Recognizing the importance of policy direction. we have also prepared a draft policy for shale gas." Indian Minister for Petroleum and Natural Gas Veerappa Moily said in his talk to the CII's National Council.

"The whole natural gas value chain including domestic production. LNG imports and pipeline transportation and gas pricing are key focus areas as we take measures to increase the share natural gas in the energy basket from the current 9 percent towards the global ratio 23 percent. This will require collective action by the government. industry and consumers." Moily said.

ENERGY SECURITY: KEY TO INDIA'S FUTURE

For an India aspiring for double digit economic growth. the central question is 'How would India meet its energy needs in the coming years? '. The India Energy Security Summit 2011 will focus on the need for an enduring strategy which India could adopt towards Nuclear Power and Gas. the two energy sources which may meet the requirements of striking a balance between clean energy and energy availability. Additionally. the two day summit would also look at changes in the renewable energy sector post Cancun. the rising cyber security threats to the energy sector. and the paradox of harnessing energy in the light of renewed concerns about the environment and the impact of climate change on the way we live and work.With China moving rapidly towards acquiring energy sources across the world. but also in India's neighbourhood. the challenge for India's policy makers is to provide alternatives on an urgent basis and the formulation of a strategy for the same.

Moreover. India's dependence on import of most fuels has repercussions on its economy. making it vulnerable to global price fluctuation. As China's hunger for energy continues. thc issuc of Encrgy Security needs to be examined. in terms of both competition and cooperation. The depletion of fossil fuels. coupled with the environmental concerns of their emissions. has led experts to push for the aggressive adoption of renewable sources of energy. along with demand side management (DSM). Though DSM. energy efficiency measures and mass deployment of renewable sources of energy are a must. the fact that about 500 million Indians do not have formal access to electricity needs to be kept in mind.

Fortunately. we have reached a point where alternative energy sources that offer low carbon emission. economic growth and can meet our energy requirements. are within our grasp. such as the Nuclear. Gas and Renewable energy. Rapid and enduring development of these energy sources may be the key to ensuring energy security for India. But these too have there own political. economic. social and implementation challenges.

NUCLEAR POWER: THE CHALLENGES AHEAD

While Nuclear power has been the most in the news for a number of reasons. the passing of the Nuclear Liability Bill has paved the way for India to have a capacity of 20 GW by 2020 and 63 GW by 2032. But critics of the drive for Nuclear energy argue that while nuclear energy only makes up for a mere 4% of India's currcnt cncrgy baskct. by adding several more reactors – the safety hazards apart – nuclear energy would not substantially add to India's energy basket. But with India developing at an average rate of 8% for the last five years. the peak electricity deficit will only increase the current deficit. Thus. to fill this gap nuclear power would play a critical role with its long gestation period in comparison to Coal and Gas based power plants.

The questions now are: who will invest and finance nuclear projects. as the estimated cost of building 20 GW of nuclear plants. India needs 1lakh crore? Who will invest this money? Moreover with regulatory policies. plus the fixation of tariff and capital are yet to be defined. and the Central and State Commissions are yet to define their operational parameters. to fix tariff for nuclear plants. the investors still lack clarity on the policies of the government on nuclear power.

GAS: THE EMERGING ALTERNATIVE

With the opening up of the market in the 1990s. the appointment of independent regulators and the increase in private investment in the sector. led to a level playing field for Private and Public Sector Undertakings. But the recent Supreme Court Judgement confirming the right of the government to fix the price of gas and it's buyer. has deterred those private investors keen to participate in India's NELP round. Despite that. the huge potential for international and domestic investments in the Gas sector remains. along with the prospects of huge employment opportunities and cheaper fuel. will make Gas as a preferred alternate fuel option for power generators and industrial users favouring environmental considerations and facing coal supply constraints.

INDIA'S MIDDLE EAST ENERGY STRATEGY

India is the seventh largest country in the world in terms of geographic landmass. and the second largest in terms of population – with 1.2 billion people. When gross domestic product is considered. the country falls into the ten largest economies. Further. the country has been experiencing economic growth of around 7% per annum since 2000. despite the 2008 economic crisis. The country enjoys an abundance of traditional and non-traditional energy sources. but these sources are insufficient to meet India's growing needs. It therefore resorts to importing most of its energy from abroad. especially from Middle East crude oil and natural gas exporters.

India's energy quandary is illustrated by the statistic that. in 2011. it was the fourth largest energy consumer after the United States. China and Russia. Furthermore. despite average per capita consumption in India remaining low relative to that of western countries. the growth in energy use has meant that the country's consumption levels have doubled since 1990. Making this situation even direr is the estimate that over 44% of Indian homes do not receive electricity and more than 90% of them rely on biomass such as wood. waste and gas.

Meeting the growing demand for energy is a major challenge that is constantly confronting Indian leaders. The country has crude oil imports from around 40% in 1990 to 70% in 2011. In 2012. over 64% of these imports came from the Middle East. a trend that is expected to continue. By 2032. over 91% of the country's energy needs will need to be imported. Thus. in an effort to secure both best prices and energy security. the country has concluded a number of short- and long-term contracts at government level and. to a lesser extent. through private companies.

However. despite the country's dependence on the Middle East for the provision of this vital and strategic resource. no clear political. economic. or even energy policies directed at the region have been formulated. The establishment of diplomatic relations with Israel in 1992 marks one of the clearest and most important turning points in India's interaction with the region. These relations have flowered and now encompass both the strategic and security realms. When it began. the relationship was opposed by the country's Muslims and leftists. and was met with moderate protests from Arab states. At the core of these relations was the perception within part of the Indian ruling elite that the country's strong pro-Arab stance was not being reciprocated with support for Indian claims over Kashmir.

Although India has not yet clearly determined its goals in the Middle East. it is slowly treading a path that will eventually lead to a clearly defined role in the region. The most significant step in this regard was the country's May 2005 appointment of an ambassador extraordinary and plenipotentiary to the region. This was followed by the 2006 naval entrance into the area to supplement diplomatic efforts. So far. India's navy has conducted exercises with countries including Saudi Arabia. Kuwait. Bahrain. Qatar. and the United Arab Emirates. An important characteristic of Indian diplomacy has been its ability to maintain amicable relations with countries that oppose each other. such as Iran. Saudi Arabia. and Israel. It is significant that India still maintains strong relations with Iran. despite ongoing US pressure to revaluate this relationship.

ENERGY SOURCES

India enjoys a number of energy sources: non-renewable energy such as coal. lignite. oil and natural gas; and renewable energy such as wind. solar energy. hydropower. biomass. and sugarcane bagasse. Knowing the size and amount of these sources is necessary to assess the extent of the country's need for consumable and imported energy. and develop strategies to secure the required energy from external sources. India is trying hard to develop alternative local sources to meet the energy challenge and reduce its dependence on external sources.

LOCAL RESERVES

On 31 March 2011. India's coal reserves were estimated at 286 billion tons. and its lignite at 41 billion tons. In March 2011. its estimated oil and natural gas reserves amounted to 757 million tons and 1.241 billion cubic metres respectively. Some 43% of India's oil reserves are in fields off the western coasts. and 22% in the Assam fields of northwest India. Of its natural gas reserves. 35% is in fields off the eastern coast. and 33% in fields off the western coasts. The size of the renewable energy was estimated at 89.760 megawatts on 31 March 2012. and was divided as follows:

- Wind energy: 49.132 MW (55%);
- Small hydro-energy sources: 15.358 MW (17%);
- Biomass: 17.538 MW (20%); and
- Sugar cane bagasse: 5.000 MW (6%).

POTENTIAL FOR GENERATING ELECTRIC POWER

As of 31 March 2013. the potential for energy generation amounted to 206.526 megawatts. compared to 16.271 MW on 21 March 1971. representing an increase of 6.4% per annum. About 64% of this is expected to be provided by thermal electric generating stations and 18.2% is to be acquired from hydro-electric stations. The electricity production of nuclear powered plants did not exceed 2.31% in 2011.

Coal is currently the traditional source of power generation in India. but due to the low quality of local coal. it is imported from Australia and Canada. Coal imports have increased from 20.93 million metric tons in the 2000-01 period to 73.26 million metric tons in 2009-10. During the same period. domestic coal exports increased from 1.29 million to 2.45 million metric tons. However. the importation of coal witnessed a 59.2% decline in 2010. while coal exports increased by 80%.

India relies heavily on imported crude oil and its derivative petroleum products to meet its growing needs. Imports have been increasing year after year. Imports jumped from 11.68 million metric tons in 1970-71 to 163.59 million metric tons in 2010-11. The 2010-11 period witnessed an increase of 2.72% over the previous year. India currently imports about 70% of its crude oil and petroleum products from countries across the world.

There are 20 oil refineries in India. 17 of which are owned by the public sector with the remaining three owned by private entities. By 31 March 2011. the total annual capacity of these refineries was 187 million metric tons. The refineries had been operating at 105.7% of their capacity in 2009-10 and at 110% during the 2010-2011 year. The country has. in recent years. succeeded in setting up facilities for refining and processing crude oil and its derivatives. to the extent that it now is an exporter of oil products. Its oil derivatives increased from 0.33 million tons in 1970-71 to 59.13 million tons in 2010-11. These statistics are even more astounding when we note that the 2010-11 figure represents an increase of 16% over the 2009-10 figure.

Further. the country has the fifth largest wind electricity generation network in the world. Its generation capacity currently stands at over 11.800 megawatts. and solar energy generation targets have been set at 20.000 megawatts for 2022.

CRUDE OIL PRODUCTION AND CONSUMPTION

India is currently responsible for around 1% of total crude oil production. which in 2010-11 was calculated at 38.9 million tons. However. in the same period. the country consumed 155.5 million tons of crude. representing 3.9% of global production for that year. And. in the 2010-11 period. India produced 1.6 per cent of global natural gas production (45.8 million tons). Over 70% of India's energy usage is currently comprised of fossil fuels. Coal represents around 40% of this whilst 2.4% is made up of crude oil. with natural gas constituting 6%. These figures illustrate the dilemma of power in India. which can be summarised as an increasing shortage of energy products and the relentless attempt to source the shortfall from alternative and renewable sources – specifically solar. nuclear and wind energy.

India hopes to attain. by 2032. 25% energy self-sufficiency through the use of renewable sources. and has already enacted various laws to enable this. For this purpose. the state established a ministry of renewable energy in 1992. Furthermore. it has encouraged and provided incentives for energy produced from waste. solar projects and wind energy. Companies have been incentivised to produce renewable energy through 'green energy' financial bonds. customs duty reductions on imported equipment for renewable energy generation. and the provision of soft loans and financial concessions. These incentives aim to increase especially water. wind and solar capacities. Undoubtedly. the country seeks to reduce the cost gap between traditional energy generation and renewable energy. The construction of green buildings to reduce the country's overall energy consumption is also encouraged.

Although India is a major importer of crude oil. it is also a huge exporter of refined oil. It has established a number of refineries for this purpose. especially in Gujarat. Two companies. Essar Oil and Reliance. export naphtha. benzene and refined petroleum products to Singapore. the United Arab Emirates. Indonesia. Sri Lanka. Iran and other countries. Petroleum products are also exported to the US market by Reliance Group.

NEEDS

By 2025. India will be the second largest pressure. after China. on global energy resources. The country is trying to respond to this through two ways: by expanding the base of domestic renewable energy and increasing its nuclear power capacity which is scheduled to rise to 9% of total energy capacity in the next 25 years from its current 4.2% level. India has five nuclear reactors. and is working to build 18 more by 2025. If this is achieved. the country will have the highest amount of energy nuclear reactors in the world. The seriousness of India's energy requirements can be gleaned from the fact that over 56% of rural households receive no electricity.

FOREIGN INVESTMENT

Besides expanding the power network internally. India has sought partnerships with both foreign governments and companies. and exploration rights abroad. The government encourages its departments and private companies to acquire exploration and production rights abroad as a way to protect the domestic market from international price fluctuations. It has achieved these gains despite opposition from the United States. India has. thus far. acquired rights in over 24 countries. The government-owned Oil and Natural Gas Corporation Limited (ONGC) alone has invested 11 billion dollars in such contracts. and currently has a presence in 15 countries where it is involved in over 40 projects. Countries where the ONGC is active include Vietnam. Russia. Sudan. Myanmar. Colombia. Cuba. Syria. Iran. Iraq. Libya. Brazil. Venezuela and the joint development zones between Nigeria and São Tomé. and Principe. Nigeria and Egypt. Reliance has been involved in the purchase of US shale natural gas project rights. Likewise. private companies such as Hindustan Petroleum. Essar and Bharat Petroleum have undertaken similar activities. The Indian government is vigorously seeking more opportunities and Indian embassies are tasked with this responsibility.

India has also decided to invest in the Israeli energy sector. It has invested an unknown amount in the Leviathan natural gas field. located in the eastern Mediterranean Sea. Kuwaiti protests. interpreted as being orchestrated by Saudi Arabia. have failed to force India to alter this policy.

In the context of energy provision and diversification of energy sources. India has signed the Trans-Afghanistan Pipeline (or the Turkmenistan–Afghanistan–Pakistan–India Pipeline. TAPI) Treaty. which will run from Turkmenistan through Afghanistan and Pakistan. It has not yet signed the treaty for the Iranian gas pipeline that passes through Pakistan. Indian authorities argue that this is mainly a result of security concerns and the fear that Pakistan may exploit the situation during crises. However. it has more to do with US opposition and the threat of sanctions. which have dissuaded India from signing onto a project which would go a long way in solving the current and expected future energy crises and provide it with natural gas at lower prices and better terms then current international prices. India's November 2009 vote against Iran at the International Atomic Energy Agency (IAEA) almost destroyed its relations with the Islamic republic. halting pipeline negotiations. Amends were made by India. reviewing its stance and adopting a neutral position.

American threats have also led to the reduction of India's imports of Iranian crude oil from 18.1 million tons in the past year to 13 million tons in the current year. This quantity is transported via oil tankers to India's western shores. It has refused to fully comply with US pressure which demands that it does not import any oil or gas from Iran. In addition. India has used creative means. including non-dollar payments and barter exchanges. to circumvent US bank sanctions on Iran. and has even created a 3.7 billion dollar insurance fund through its General Insurance Corporation to insure Iranian oil and gas tankers which western insurers have been prohibited from ensuring.

REDUCING DEPENDENCE ON THE MIDDLE EAST

India is currently trying hard to reduce its dependence on Middle East sources. mainly as a result of political instability. It has been attempting to compensate through energy procurement from other internal and external sources. *e.g.* by investing in fields outside the Middle East and improving relations with neighbouring Myanmar. India has also allowed for ONGC and Reliance's extensive oil exploration. specifically on its coasts. In addition. foreign companies. including Canadian company Kern. have been allowed to explore for oil. especially in the desert state of Rajasthan. which is similar to Arab countries that produce oil. and the Krishna Godavari Basin in South India as well as areas in north-east India. around the state of Assam. where oil was discovered in 1889.

With the exception of Israel. India is uninterested in pursuing a strategic alliance or even close cooperation with any Middle Eastern country. including Iran. Since adopting a policy of economic liberalisation in 1992. under the control of then economic adviser to the central Indian government and now prime minister. Manmohan Singh. India has attempted to become close to western countries. especially the United States and Israel. It has thus sought harmony and coordination with these countries' policies in terms of politics and security. Its previously strong and longstanding relations with Arab countries such as Egypt have been downgraded. This was best demonstrated by India's coldness during Egyptian President Mohamed Morsi's official visit to New Delhi in March. It was clear during the visit that India was not interested in rekindling its relations with the countries with which it once led the Non-Aligned Movement. India had also previously enjoyed close relations with former Iraqi President Saddam Hussein. Saddam sold oil to India at lower prices and with preferential conditions. However. in 2003. when the United States invaded Iraq. India was ready to deploy a large military contingent to join the US-led coalition. It did not join the coalition only because of the huge pressure from the public. opposition parties. and Indian Muslims. In 2006. the government also replaced its oil minister. Mani Shankar Aiyar. who was enthusiastic about the Iranian gas pipeline and wanted close relations with Arab countries. with pro-American Murli Deora.

India's strong and strategic relations with Israel is due to the belief of many members of the Indian ruling elite that the Jewish lobby in Washington is an important entrance point for influencing American decisions. India believes that good relations with the United States are the key to good relations with Arab Gulf states. In addition. the country has attempted to initiate free trade treaties with some Arab countries but these attempts have. for the most part. been unsuccessful – except for the August 2004 economic cooperation treaty signed with Gulf Cooperation Council countries. However. this treaty. rather than being a practical treaty on economic cooperation. is more of a goodwill document. Hundreds of Indian companies have. however. opened representative offices and warehouses for their goods in the GCC. and some Indian companies have established projects in the Egyptian free zones. Last March. India signed a joint venture treaty paving the way for the establishment of a solar energy generation project in the Egyptian oasis of Siwa. A key outcome of the treaty was the attempt to illuminate an Egyptian village in the Matrouh governorate through solar energy as an initial pilot project. India has also established a fertilizer plant in Oman to exploit gas resources.

POTENTIAL FOR COOPERATION

Due to the geographic proximity between India and many Middle East countries. located just three to four hours away by air. there is great potential for cooperation. However. the indifference of both sides has led to the loss of many opportunities. Arab countries have not realised India's full potential and only in the last few years have they acknowledged the country – mainly as a result of western media reports around the many leaps in the country's information technology sector and its status as an emerging power. In an attempt to secure closer economic and industrial relations between the two countries. the January 2006 visit of Saudi Arabia's King Abdullah to India. raised hopes but has not borne any fruit. Saudi Arabia has invested much in India. but only a few sectors.India remains a non-preferred destination for Arab investments. which commenced about a decade ago when Arab investors reoriented towards the east. specifically Towards India.

However. the country's many administrative complexities. lack of clear legislation. and rampant corruption at all levels have greatly inhibited a substantial flow of Arab investments. Arab investment remains light. including Saudi Arabia's five oil refinery investments through the state-owned Aramco.

Similar problems exist with Indian investments in Arab countries. especially in the oil. gas and industrial sectors.

Indian companies. both government and private. do not feel welcome in Arab countries. believing that these countries are more likely to align themselves with Pakistan. The clearest evidence of this is India's exclusion from membership in the Organisation of Islamic Cooperation (OIC) as a result of Pakistani objections. despite the existence of 180 million Muslims in India. who represent the second largest Islamic bloc in the world after Indonesia.

Recently. India has sought security relations with countries in the region within the framework of the fight against terrorism and organised crime. and concluded an extradition treaty with the United Arab Emirates and Saudi Arabia. It also participated in a 2004 Saudi conference on terrorism. and has supported the Saudi proposal for the establishment of a regional centre for combating terrorism.

AXES OF INDIAN POLITICS IN THE MIDDLE EAST

The most pertinent factors influencing Indian interests in the Middle East revolve around four axes:

1. Continued access to crude oil and natural gas at lower prices and better payment terms whenever possible. India believes conditions in the Middle East are likely to improve in its favour and that the 'liberation' of the United States from dependence on Middle Eastern oil as a result of expansion in US production of natural gas will create a new geopolitical situation in the region. Shivshankar Menon. India's National Security Adviser. expressed this sentiment in a speech to the Indian Council for Energy. the Environment and Water in August 2012. "The Middle East now counts for less sources of energy." he said. This has made it easier. he added. for the world to bear the current crisis in the Middle East. Also. the energy crisis. which had been predicted as a result of the Arab Spring and the impasse of the Iranian nuclear programme. did not materialise. However. he added. if all energy sources were activated. the world could witness an energy glut similar to that of the 1980s.
2. India is always looking for opportunities to participate in energy exploration as is the case in Iraq. Libya and Sudan. Many of these efforts have. however. met US opposition.
3. Indian policy aims to secure Arab markets for Indian goods. This is mainly because Arab countries. especially in the Gulf. are large importers of Indian-manufactured goods. The UAE is currently the largest importer of Indian goods in the Gulf. with these subsequently being distributed to Arab. Iranian and African markets. The volume of Indian trade with the UAE stood at 8 billion dollars in 2006. India is also the fourth largest trading partner for Saudi Arabia; however. this trade mainly consists of oil imports as the kingdom is India's largest oil supplier.
4. India regards caring for and protecting the interests of Indian workers in the Middle East as one of its priorities. It is keen that the region. and especially the Gulf states. continues to provide employment for millions of Indians, skilled and unskilled. There are at least 3.5 million Indian workers in the Gulf who remit large sums of money to India (6 billion dollars in 2006). This provides the largest source of hard currency to the country. and is both politically and economically cheap as no special demands are made by these workers to the state.

News this April that thousands of Indians will be deported from Saudi Arabia as a result of the kingdom's 'saudiisation' regulations and the tightening of labour regulations shook both the Indian government and its people. The Indian government intervened at the highest level in Saudi Arabia. and secured a two-month grace period for violators to take corrective measures.

Despite the fog surrounding India's policy towards the Middle East. it can be concluded that the country has adopted two principles: first. maintaining

India's energy security. that is. guaranteeing India's access to its oil and natural gas needs without interruption and at the best prices and terms possible; and second. a continuation of Nehru's policy. which specifies non-interference in the internal affairs of other countries. This policy is likely to be altered in the future. however. when India's geopolitical position changes as a result of its economic growth. It is expected that India and China will both gain a great deal of influence in the region at the expense of the United States. whose lack of future oil dependence on the region will mean that it will retreat. It will be in the interests of the countries of the region to establish close relations with both emerging powers so that neither one of them does not control the important resources of this region.

DECIPHERING INDIA'S ENERGY SECURITY STRATEGY AT THE DOMESTIC LEVEL

The last decade has witnessed several vision and strategy documents that *pertain* to the energy sector. The listing of these documents reveals two important features: one. the rising importance of energy in the country—an importance that has emerged in sharp relief only in the last decade; and two. the range of ministries/departments that are simultaneously involved in the energy sector— demonstrating the often disjointed and often overlapping nature of the Indian government's efforts to set the agenda and devise a strategy on energy.

Apart from these documents. there are other ministries that are also involved in work that pertains to the energy sector; and their annual reports or plan documents spell out in detail their plans and agenda for addressing India's energy security. These include the ministry of external affairs. ministry of power. the ministry of water resources. the department of atomic energy and the ministry of coal. Important acts and policies. such as the Electricity Act of 2003 and the New Exploration Licencing Policy (NELP) (currently in its 9th round) have sought to make the energy sector more transparent. market friendly and efficient. Based on these documents and policy pronouncements. the institutional structure of India's energy sector can be put together.

An analysis of these documents and the projected plans that the different ministries have identified for themselves help delineate the basic contours of India's strategy on energy as well as highlight the country's evolving and expanding priorities in the energy sector.

These are - briefly:

- A recognition of India's growing demand for energy has brought about a multi-faceted attention to energy that straddles reform in the regulatory sector. inclusion of greater efficiencies in the whole value chain. from mining and exploration. to transmission. distribution and pricing. policy changes to make way for greater private sector participation. deregulation of the energy sector (particularly power and natural gas). reduction of losses and so on.

- The main driver behind all policy pronouncements and governmental action on energy security is providing energy access to the people of the country. About 400 million people remain without access to electricity while a number of households in both rural and urban areas use inefficient and harmful sources of energy. A project carried out by The Energy and Resources Institute (TERI) studied household energy transitions. which revealed that there was very little change in the percentage of rural households dependent on firewood and chips (75-78 per cent) given their cheap availability in rural areas. The *Integrated Energy Policy* stated the internal 'energy poverty' dimension clearly:
- The broad vision behind the energy policy is to reliably meet the demand for energy services of all sectors at competitive prices. Further. lifeline energy needs of all households must be met even if that entails directed subsidies to vulnerable households. The demand must be met through safe. clean and convenient forms of energy at the least cost in a technically efficient. economically viable and environmentally sustainable manner.
- A major component of India's energy security strategy can be discerned as being about seeking self-reliance and energy independence. It is in this light that several of the vision/mission documents and recent governmental actions can be read. For example. the *Hydrocarbon Vision 2025* document focused on primarily assuring energy security by 'achieving self-reliance through increased indigenous production (and investment in equity oil abroad). This resulted in the NELP. under which exploration in India (through the inclusion of the private sector) has expanded from 11 per cent before 2000 (before NELP was started). to more than 40 per cent. Diversification of India's energy basket has been another major plank of the country's energy strategy. The nation's Biofuel Policy. the Solar Mission and the III-Stage Nuclear Programme seek to implement what the IEP mentions as essentially:
- Meet[ing] this vision [providing energy security to all] requires that India pursues all available fuel options and forms of energy. both conventional and non-conventional. Further. India must seek to expand its energy resource base and seek new and emerging energy sources Planning Commission 2006: xiii).
- The Solar Mission and the III-Stage Nuclear Programme are fundamentally about pushing for technologies that India can use on the basis of its resource endowment (ample sunlight and thorium

supplies). India plans to target the deployment of 20.000 MWe of nuclear energy by 2020 while the Solar Mission is equally ambitious—hoping to put in place 20.000 MW of solar power capacity by 2020. To achieve this objective. as ambitious as it does sound. would mean the government providing a subsidy of Rs 900 billion over 20 years from the day the mission kicks off. Natural gas is also being promoted for India's energy security. particularly as a bridge fuel towards shifting to more sustainable energy choices. As India becomes a bigger energy consumer. it needs to ensure that energy services are provided in an efficient. transparent and accountable manner. The Electricity Act as well as several of the more recent stay orders on mining projects by the ministry of environment and forests (MOEF). particularly on the sustainability of several energy projects. is an important development. Even the debate on the Civil Nuclear Liability Bill must be read in this light—about protecting the people of the country from externalities attached to providing energy from certain sources. such as nuclear energy. Several proposed hydropower projects in the Northeast face similar opposition from local communities due to the negative fallout ranging from the environmental to the socio-economic. to health and geopolitical security concerns. In the context of both nuclear energy as well as hydropower. it has been pointed out that the Environmental Assessment Reports and the public hearing system put in place have not been carried out properly. Apart from the sustainability aspect. India has also shown a concern about adequate compensation due to the linkage between lack of compensation for developing local resources and intra-state conflict. particularly in the Naxal/Maoist-affected parts of the country. According to Jason Miklian and Scott Carney. although 'revenues from mineral extraction in Chhattisgarh and Jharkhand topped $ 20 billion in 2008. and more than $1 trillion in proven reserves still sit in the ground'. because this 'geological inheritance has been managed so disastrously that many locals—uprooted. unemployed. and living in a toxic and dangerous environment. due to the mining operations—have thrown in their lot with the Maoists'. Carrying the local community along is emerging as an important aspect of expanding India's domestic energy resource base. The opposition that the Indian government (particularly the Uranium Corporation of India Limited [UCIL]) has faces for uranium mining in Meghalaya's Khasi hills is a case in point that demonstrates that the government needs to think increasingly about putting in place benefit sharing mechanisms with the local community and make them stakeholders in the development of local energy resources.

INDIA'S ENERGY DIPLOMACY

Just over the last decade. it is interesting to note that energy has become a critical component of almost all bilateral and regional/plurilateral high level meetings that India has been part of. The IEP portends an increased energy import dependency for India across all fuel types. While India has been importing coking coal for years. it has also recently begun to import thermal coal. Even in the area of nuclear energy. India is going to be dependent on uranium imports. The amount India has been spending on importing its energy needs (oil. coal and natural gas). Hence. India's energy diplomacy around the world is a direct result of the growing import dependency that the country is experiencing.

The creation of an Energy Security Cell in the MEA. which was upgraded to a full-fledged division in 2009. is a recognition of the importance energy has as a foreign policy concern. Interestingly however. the MEA does not yet have a vision document on the role energy plays in the country's strategic sphere and what the priorities of the division are for the future. Nonetheless. just as it was possible to glean the main elements of India's energy security strategy at the domestic level. it is possible to piece together the main aspects of India's external energy strategy.

Some of the pertinent ones are discussed below:

- Most of India's energy imports still come from West Asia. The Pre-eminence of West Asia notwithstanding (and Australia. Indonesia and South Africa for coal). India has been making concerted efforts to cast its net wide—looking for energy imports not only from Africa. but also faraway Latin America and a comparatively inaccessible Central Asia. According to the IEP. the Americas and Central Asia respectively accounted for 3.55 per cent and 4.74 per cent of India's oil imports in 2006. However. the figures are not indicative of the pace at which energy diplomacy has become central to foreign policy and the consistency with which energy figures in regional and bilateral meetings and discussions. The most tangible presence for India in Central Asia has been Kazakhstan. when the two countries signed a civil nuclear deal in January 2009 for the supply of uranium and a comprehensive cooperation in civil nuclear energy programme. Table illustrates the India's current and potential energy partners across the major fuel types.
- The diversification of import sources is at the heart of India's energy diplomacy. The diversification of fuels has also lead to new energy partnerships for the country. In the context of uranium and nuclear energy for example. in the last two years alone. India has inked civil nuclear agreements with six countries. namely. the US. France. Russia. Namibia. Mongolia and Kazakhstan. While Australia has refused to enter into nuclear commerce with India. countries such as

Canada. Brazil. South Africa and Gabon have offered to supply uranium to India in the future. Energy has been the stimulus for India to build new partnerships with countries while in other cases. it has provided the impetus to reinvigorate old connections. particularly with Russia and some African countries.

- Along with the diversification of sources and imports of energy. technology collaboration and partnerships are equally important if India is to move towards greater energy self sufficiency. India joined the International Renewable Energy Agency (IRENA). which was set up in 2009 to expand the use of renewable energy worldwide. The IRENA membership is seen as a means for enabling India to forge partnerships with other member countries at a multilateral level for accelerating development and deployment of renewable energy technologies. The Asia-Pacific Partnership on Clean Development and Climate (APP). which also India is a member of. is a private-public partnership of seven countries to develop and accelerate deployment of cleaner. more efficient energy technologies to meet national pollution reduction. energy security and climate change concerns in ways that reduce poverty and promote economic development.
- Apart from the diversification of sources. India's external energy strategy has also included within its purview the identification of alternative routes. focusing on the possibility of not only pipelines (overland as well as undersea). but also swap arrangements that would circumvent routes considered otherwise unsafe. 'India's energy security depends as much on diversifying its energy partners as it does on ensuring secure and reliable routes for ensuring the supply of its energy imports...transportation routes are open to risks and threats from more than one country. given the transnational nature of shipping lanes and pipelines. as well as physical disruptions caused by natural disasters. accidents at sea and traffic constrictions at maritime chokepoints'. The Iran- Pakistan-India (IPI) and Turkmenistan-Afghanistan-Pakistan-India (TAPI) pipelines are not only about being able to access the energy resources of Central Asia. but also about accessing that energy in a relatively troublefree manner. if the region were not riddled by intra-state conflict and troubled political relations. Other pipelines that have been proposed seek to circumvent the Strait of Hormuz that could bring oil from as far north as Iraq—through Kuwait. Saudi Arabia and the UAE to the Omani capital of Muscat on the Arabian Sea. Other than pipelines. the Indian government has also mooted the idea of swap arrangements. 'Like laying pipelines and monitoring/patrolling SLOCs. swap arrangements too require a high degree of collaboration between

countries. However. unlike the other more proactive measures. swap arrangements can be seen as reactive responses to the insecurity of sea lanes'.

- Closely connected to the diversification of routes and identifying secure ways of bringing energy to India is the recognition that India has to play a bigger role in the maritime security of the Indian Ocean. not least because of its energy security concerns. The Indian navy has been involved in a 'sea-lane sanitising role'. Countries such as Indonesia. Singapore and Malaysia have looked to India as a 'reliable and non-controversial ally' in keeping SLOCs and chokepoints. such as the Malacca Straits. clear of piracy and other anti-state elements. India already has a series of joint patrolling exercises with Indonesia as 'part of a 200 nautical mile-long energy feeder path'. The Quadrilateral Naval exercises in the Bay of Bengal in September 2007 were a collaborative exercise geared to enhance maritime security in the Indian Ocean between countries such as India. the US. Australia. Japan and Singapore. In October 2009. India joined Indonesia and the Maldives to patrol the Indian Ocean waters to protect them against sea-based piracy. According to C. Raja Mohan. it would bode India well to work within a free but regulated Indian Ocean region and not strive for a narrow and exclusivist interpretation of maritime security.
- Much has been written about the growing competition between India and China in Africa. West Asia and Central Asia. This perception is grounded in projections that suggest India and China will account for 43 per cent of the global increase in oil demand between 2005 and 2030. according to the IEA. One region where this perception of a growing competition between India and China is well-entrenched is Africa's resource sector. For instance. in 2006. ONGC India was a contender for a deepwater block in Nigeria for a $ 2.6 billion deal that CNOOC eventually acquired a 45 per cent stake in OML 130. Due to proximity (for example the Central Asia Republics) and historically closer relations (with Myanmar. China has been able to clinch deals in the energy sector. leaving India far behind. India's response to this has seemed to be partly reactive and partly ill thought out. Falling for the rhetoric that pits China against India as if they were at par. has meant that India has ended up trying to outbid country that has superior financial capabilities and has a different political agenda. Equity investments in overseas oil and gas fields have been another crucial aspect of India's energy security strategy. While these are essentially commercial in nature. the government has acknowledged the role they can play in the context of providing

a fillip to India's energy security. particularly at a time when there is an international energy-related crisis or a sudden spike in prices.

- Last but not least. corresponding to India's growing role in the energy arena is its growing participation in the various energy-related institutional frameworks—from the regional to the multilateral. Along with like-minded countries. such as the IBSA/BRICs/SCO (Shanghai Cooperation Organisation). India has been stressing the importance of energy as an arena where greater complementarities can be identified and developed. India has already been involved in the International Energy Forum (IEF). and is seeking to expand its current interaction with the IEA and the Energy Charter Treaty.

A NATIONAL ENERGY SECURITY STRATEGY FOR INDIA: PLUGGING THE GAPS AND CONNECTING THE DOTS

Absence of a cohesive energy security strategy for India raises several concerns. The problems arise particularly because energy. being a multidimensional policy arena with cross-cutting issues and challenges. requires a holistic and long-term strategy. It is important to highlight some of the gaps and linkages that need to be addressed (both at the domestic and the external level) in order to move towards a future where India can seek to achieve its energy security in the most efficient and rational manner.

REGIONAL FOCUS AND PRIORITISATION

As long as India's energy basket is fossil-fuel centric. West Asia's predominance will not wane. According to the New Policies Scenario spelled out in the World Energy Outlook (WEO) of 2010. India will become the third largest spender on oil imports by 2020. thereby implying that although diversification of its import sources will continue to be an objective. the primacy of West Asia will remain a reality. What is required is a concerted focus on managing India's dependence on West Asia in the short to medium term. while continuing to press for greater diversification. Also. there is a need for a region-specific prioritistion of India's energy securing strategy. which takes into consideration several important parameters. not least among them. the role of other energy importing countries. developments in the energy sectors of those countries. the need to continually evolve India's own engagement with the country beyond the energy sector and so on. After West Asia. it would appear that South East Asia and Africa would be of immediate importance to India's energy security. while Central Asia and the Caspian Sea can be thought of as more medium to long term interests.

RISK ASSESSMENT AND ENERGY SECURITY

At the moment. it appears as though India is trying to source its energy from everywhere. However. there is a need to think of equity investments as well as energy trade in a more enduring manner. taking into consideration the groundlevel security threats as well as the larger geopolitical ramifications of that energy partnership.

On-ground security threats require an assessment that provides the investing/trading country a real picture of the risks involved. This would help in making assessments and prioritisations. which might not substantially impact India's import options (that is. India. as well as other countries will continue to trade with energy-rich countries that are otherwise politically risky); Nonetheless. these inputs are crucial to look at possible alternatives in place before costly disruptions occur.

DEVELOPING MUTUALLY BENEFICIAL STAKES BEYOND THE ENERGY SECTOR

While it is important not to over-extend the nature of engagement that India seeks to put in place with the energy-rich countries (as China does by offering soft loans. arms sales and so on). it is equally important that India look beyond the energy sector to ensure that its energy partnerships are robust. For example. in 2009-10. energy resources accounted for 96.8 per cent of total imports from the country.

India does not figure amongst Nigeria's top five partners. while China. the US. Belize. Germany and Belgium do. Even in terms of energy exports from Nigeria. India accounts for 10 per cent of Nigeria's total energy exports. while the US accounts for almost 30 per cent. This shows that India ranks quite low in terms of Nigeria's import needs. India must think proactively about building partnerships that go beyond the energy sector.

RENEWABLE ENERGY: DOMESTIC REGULATORY FRAMEWORK AND SECURITY CONCERNS

Renewable energy. particularly solar energy. is part of India's long-term push for meeting India's energy security concerns. However. there is a need to match the projections on the domestic front with the security and foreign policy implications it will pose for the country. something that the Solar Mission does not do. Therefore. there needs to be better synchronicity between India's solar ambitions and the countries with the technology and the raw material (rare earth minerals) that is necessary to achieve the former.

Also. more sustainable energy pathways are not without their geopolitical implications. as Japan is learning from China and over the rare earth exports imbroglio. There needs to be a greater understanding of the geopolitical implications of the energy transitions India seeks to chart. If China. Bolivia and Afghanistan are important for minerals that are important for renewable energy technologies. then strategic partnerships need to be put in place accordingly.

INTEGRATED ACTION NEEDS TO PRECEDE INTEGRATED PLANNING

The IEP was laudable in its effort to deal with a whole gamut of issues pertaining to energy within one policy document. However. what has been severely lacking is the linkages between the different ministries. This is perhaps the greatest obstacle to devising a national security strategy on energy in India. While the group of ministers for energy set up in June 2010 is a welcome step. it is not enough. The GOM under Finance Minister Pranab Mukherjee has been set up to coordinate energy security issues that have an international angle and guide and coordinate the external interface on energy security matters. More needs to be done in order to integrate the two arms of India's energy security strategy. This means not necessarily creating another institution but bringing the prevailing institutions together in a decision-making mechanism that includes the strategies and priorities of each ministry. as well as the private sector.

ASSESSMENTS OF INDIA'S OWN STRENGTHS

India needs to be careful about not getting trapped in an unnecessary competition with China. It seems that too much energy is spent in being unduly concerned about China's financial capability to outbid and 'corner' overseas equity investments in the energy sector. India needs to go beyond Western literature on the matter and get inputs from the private sector. academia and civil society organisations working in the energy-rich countries as well as within India. Also. there is a need to accord more 'agency' and 'voice' to the energy-exporting countries. particularly the African countries. Their security lies in being able to leverage the fact that more than one country is interested in them. which allows them to pick and choose their partnerships according to what they seek to get out of them. While learning from other countries' experiences. there is an equal necessity for India to recognise and study closely the perceptions and the ground realities of the countries India imports energy from and work that into the strategy. India needs to be aware of the fact that vis-à-vis energy. China's strategy is not all that state-driven and focused. while India's is not all that confused or ad hoc.

THE WEAKEST LINK: THE NEIGHBOURHOOD

A real stumbling block to India's energy security. particularly at the foreign policy level. is the immediate neighbourhood. India's energy security is dependent on a stable region that is conducive to establishing energy links beyond the South Asian region itself. particularly with land-locked Central Asia. Building synergies in the energy sector by putting in place cross-border power grids might go far in tapping the hydropower and natural gas potential of some of India's immediate neighbours. However. even if building demand-supply synergies between India and its neighbours is not possible in the short to medium term (for example. Bangladesh does not want to export its natural gas. anticipating its own rise in demand in the near future). a neighbourhood that is conducive to building energy linkages beyond the region are crucial. Sri Lanka. Myanmar. Pakistan. Nepal. and Bangladesh all highlight lost opportunities for India. The SAARC Energy Secretariat has been a relative non-starter. At the regional level within SAARC. there have been several attempts to push for energy cooperation in South Asian. but they seem to lack vigour.

ENERGY GOVERNANCE: STEERING THE DISCUSSIONS

'Encrgy governance is an area that is growing in importance—if not in tangible results. then definitely in terms of rhetoric. As an emerging power. India can illafford to not be part of this field and make its mark'. The latest World Energy Outlook of the IEA flags the importance of governments in the area of energy.

Energy governance has emerged as a critical area of research and policy making because energy use and deployment in a sustainable and holistic manner depends on good governance practices.

- India needs to take the initiative and play a larger role in determining any future governance structure or mechanism in the energy sector. The world needs to constantly strive for an understanding of energy security that moves away from a zero-sum approach and that seeks to promote principles and norms that engender long-term energy cooperation. transparency. non-discrimination. accountability and best practices'.

Given that several of the challenges that the world will face in the future will spring from the energy sector. it is important for India to not only be a part of these governance frameworks on energy. but also ensure that they reflect its own interests and concerns adequately.

INDIA'S ENERGY DIPLOMACY: UNDER CHINA'S SHADOW

With an economy that is projected to grow at a rate of 7 to 8 percent over the next two decades. meeting its rapidly increasing demand for energy is one of the biggest challenges facing India. Burgeoning population. coupled with rapid economic growth and industrialization. has propelled India into becoming the sixth-largest energy consumer in the world. with the prospect of emerging as the fourth-largest consumer in the next four to five years.

Rising incomes in India. along with generating prosperity. are pushing demand for energy resources even further. India is not only rated as one of the highest energy-intensive economies in the world. energy intensity being a measure of energy required by an economy to produce one unit of GDP growth. but Indians also pay one of the highest prices for energy in purchasing power parity terms. India faces a growing imbalance between the demand for energy and its supply from indigenous sources resulting in increased import dependence.

Though it has the third-largest reserves of coal after China and the United States. dependence on imported oil is India's greatest vulnerability. because it imports about 70 percent of its oil. and this dependence is likely to increase to around 92 percent by the year 2020. Hydrocarbons have been viewed as better alternatives to the less efficient and more polluting coal energy. While natural gas is India's most important potential alternative to coal. the effective exploration and distribution infrastructure is yet to develop. And despite some recent attempts to think seriously about nuclear power. oil retains its primacy in India's energy matrix.

The recent fluctuations in global oil prices have been a worrying trend for India. It has been estimated that a sustained 5 percent rise in the oil prices over a year could dampen India's GDP growth rate by 0.25 percent and raise the inflation rate by 0.6 percent. India can only sustain its high rates of economic growth in the long term if it is successfully able to bridge the increasing demand-supply gap. According to the Integrated Energy Policy Report of the Indian Planning Commission. India will have to quadruple its energy supply to sustain an 8 percent rate of growth for the next twenty-five years. which calls for an energy regime that ensures supply. manages demand. and balances pricing to enable growth. The report goes on to recommend that India pursue all available fuel options and forms of energy.

The Indian government has only recently woken up to the challenge of managing the nation's energy security with the realization that it has already fallen behind other major players. such as China. Despite this. India continues to lack an overarching energy strategy because of a lack of consensus on crucial choices that the nation needs to make in the domestic political as well as global context. In so far as India's engagement with the outside world is concerned. four schools of thought have been identified: the "self-sufficiency" school; the "cooperation with Asian states" school; the "greater integration into the global energy markets" school; and the "free-for-all" school that calls for India to pursue its interests by all necessary means. The last school. not surprisingly. seems to have an upper hand at the moment. which is more a result of confusion in Indian policymaking circles than any attempt on the part of the government to evolve a coherent policy framework. India is now trying to work at multiple levels by opening up the domestic energy market to multiple players. thereby making it more competitive; by adopting relatively rational principles for energy pricing; by establishing credible energy pricing regulatory framework; by diversifying beyond oil to access alternative energy sources such as nuclear power and natural gas; and by focusing greater on exploration activities with its borders. India is trying to increase fuel efficiency by slashing state subsidies on all petroleum products. But this is a politically contentious policy issue. and subsidizing of household necessities is viewed as essential for supporting the poor in the country. India is also trying to put its emphasis on the import of natural gas. Various proposals are in the offing to import natural gas from Central Asia. the Middle East. and even from its neighbors such as Bangladesh. India is also trying to promote investment in the exploration and production of domestic oil and gas. and it has had some successes in that regard in the last few years.

But these attempts are aimed at the long-term management of the nation's energy security. India's greatest challenge as of now is to ensure successful diversification of sources for oil procurement to minimize possibilities of disruption in supplies. It is Towards this end that India has devoted its diplomatic energies in recent times as it encourages its public sector companies to acquire energy stakes in oil and gas fields abroad.

India. like China. is reshaping its diplomacy to serve energy needs. because its booming economy also needs new supplies of oil to ensure its continued growth. Not surprisingly. perhaps. the focal point of India's energy diplomacy has been the Middle East. because around 65 percent of its energy requirements are met by this region. India's large and growing energy demand and Iran's pool of energy resources make the two nations natural economic partners. India's search for energy security in a rather volatile energy market makes Iran. with its fourthlargest reservoir of oil and second-largest reserves of natural gas. highly attractive. Iran has described India as one of its best customers and had offered to supply more crude oil to India in case of a disruption caused by an American military attack against Iraq in 2003.

This energy relationship between India and Iran is at the heart of a strong bilateral partnership between the two countries. despite the fact that Indo-Iranian relations have significantly diversified across various sectors in recent years. The proposal to build a gas pipeline between India and Iran has consumed a lot of diplomatic energy.

Various options. such as offshore and overland routes. have been under consideration for quite some time now. Both these options have their problems. especially the problem of relying on Pakistan for the security of these pipelines. The United States has also been discouraging the pipeline proposal. Yet. India officially continues to insist that the 1.625-mile-long. $4.16 billion pipeline project intended to carry gas from Iran through Pakistan to energy-starved India remains firmly on track. India has enjoyed traditional ties with Iran and Iraq for long. partly to meet its energy requirements. However. with Tehran adopting an aggressive anti- Western posture and pursuing an independent nuclear programme in defiance of its obligations under the Nuclear Non-Proliferation Treaty. and the ongoing instability in Iraq. India has been looking to expand its influence beyond the Persian Gulf to the Saudi peninsula.

As with Saudi Arabia's relations with China. energy has become the driving force in its relations with India. with India emerging as Saudi Arabia's fourth-largest destination for oil exports and Riyadh being the largest supplier of oil to India. India's crude oil imports from the Saudi kingdom are projected to double in the next twenty years. During his visit to India last year. the Saudi king emphasized his country's commitment to uninterrupted supplies to a friendly country such as India regardless of global price trends. During the state visit. King Abdullah bin Abdul-Aziz Al Saud and Indian prime minister Manmohan Singh signed an Indo-Saudi "Delhi Declaration." calling for a wide-ranging strategic partnership. putting energy and economic cooperation on overdrive. and committing to cooperate against terrorism.

Reliance. a private Indian energy firm. has decided to invest in a refinery and petrochemicals project in Saudi Arabia. and India's state-owned energy firm. Oil and Energy Gas Corporation (ONGC). is also planning to engage Saudi Arabia as its equity partner for a refinery project in the Indian state of Andhra Pradesh. The recent upheavals in India's relationship with Iran and Iran's decision to renege on some of its oil supply commitments in the aftermath of India's vote against Iran at the IAEA have also alerted India to the importance of having a diversified set of suppliers in the Middle East.

However. the Middle East remains a highly volatile region. forcing India to look beyond its regional confines in search of energy security. Following the disintegration of the Soviet empire. Central Asia has emerged as an important region. where many countries. including the United States and China. have evinced a keen interest. especially since it has emerged as a major oil-producing region. India has also actively nurtured its relations with the Central Asian states. Most notably. it has stationed troops in Tajikistan. provided it with $40 million in aid. and is refurbishing an air base near Dushanbe. The North-South International Transportation Corridor agreement signed in 2000 by India. Iran. and Russia and the Agreement on International Transit of Goods between India. Iran. and Turkmenistan. signed in 1997. are also significant. because they go a long way in cutting time and costs in the transit of goods. thereby giving a boost to India's trade with Iran and other Central Asian nations. Though India has expressed an interest in joining the proposed 1.700-kilometer Turkmenistan-Afghanistan-Pakistan gas-pipeline project as the final destination. it continues to remain Non-committal to receiving the 3 billion-cubic-feet-per-day pipeline amid doubts expressed by Afghanistan and Pakistan that Turkmenistan has enough gas to make the venture viable. apart from security issues posed by the passage through Afghanistan.

It is significant that India and Iran have agreed to intensify collaboration on transport projects that could link India with the Persian Gulf. Afghanistan. Central Asia. and Europe. India will cooperate with Iran in the development of a new port complex at Chah Bahar on the coast of Iran that could become India's gateway to Afghanistan and Central Asia. There is also another project that involves linking Chah Bahar port to the Iranian rail network. which is also well connected to Central Asia and Europe. India hopes to make Pakistan marginal to its relationship with the Central Asian region so that India's relations with Central Asia can no longer be hostage to Islamabad's policies.

India's growing interest in the acquisition of energy assets in African states as diverse as Sudan. Congo. Gabon. Cameroon. Nigeria. Chad. Ghana. and Angola has also been very prominent in recent years. India has decided to offer lines of credit up to $1 billion on a government-to-government basis to a number of oil-rich but poor African countries for infrastructure projects in exchange for oil exploration rights. A $6 billion infrastructure investment deal struck in Nigeria by ONGC Mittal Energy. a joint venture between India's state-run Oil and Natural Gas Corporation and the world's largest steel maker. Mittal Steel. is seen as a major breakthrough in this strategy. Nigeria is India's biggest supplier of oil from Africa and India hopes to source an even greater share of oil from Nigeria in the next few years. India will now look to a group of eight West African countries in a special cooperation model called the Team-9 initiative. under which India offers credit for projects set up by Indian companies through the Export Import Bank of India. Team-9 countries include Burkina Faso. Chad. Ivory Coast. Equatorial Guinea. Ghana. Guinea-Bissau. Mali. and Senegal. India is exploring the possibility of high-level cooperation and investment in oil and gas sectors across various African states with India offering assistance in developing a pipeline network and infrastructure for transportation of the LNG.

India's energy diplomacy is also now forcing India to undertake a more substantive engagement with Latin America. ONGC Videsh Ltd. (OVL). the overseas arm of India's state-owned ONGC. has finalized the acquisition of 15 percent stake in a Brazilian oil company. making its foray into the South American territory. Venezuelan president Hugo Chavez signed various energy related trade deals during his visit to India in 2005. One of these agreements is expected to result in the OVL picking up a 49 percent stake in a major Venezuelan oil field. Chavez told the representatives of Indian big business that Venezuela had the capacity to meet India's annual requirement of 100 million barrels of crude. He emphasized that Venezuela wanted to become a permanent partner of India in the hydrocarbon sector and invited Indian oil companies to follow the example of their Russian and Chinese counterparts and become more active in Venezuela's oil sector.

India's relations with Russia are also becoming energy focused. with Russia being the world's second-largest oil producer and its leading gas producer. Both sides have expressed their keenness to expand cooperation further in this sector. which is already playing an important role in bilateral relations. India's OVL. in partnership with Exxon-Mobil. a U.S. company. runs a profitable offshore project in Sakhalin. The public sector company. in one of the biggest oil deals signed in Russia. purchased a 20 percent share in the Sakhalin-I project with an investment of 1.7 billion. According to the terms of the contract. 40 percent of the production will belong to the ONGC for the first five to six years. The Sakhalin venture will tap gas that will then be piped into northern Japan. The Sakhalin group of islands lies just north of Japan. There are an estimated 340 million metric tons of oil and 420 billion cubic meters of gas in the Sakhalin oilfield. India and Russia have also decided to cooperate in the Caspian Sea basin and have identified a few other areas for exploration. Already. OVL has signed a confidentiality agreement to evaluate the data of Sakhalin-III (Kirinsky block). This investment alone is expected to be in the range of $1.5 billion. ONGC and Russia's natural gas monopoly. Gazprom. have signed a memorandum of understanding pledging to explore possibilities for joint ventures in India. Russia. and third countries to produce oil and gas and to build trunk pipelines. The Russian company Gazprom and the Gas Authority of India Limited are also jointly developing a block in the Bay of Bengal. While India is scouring far and wide to quench its thirst for energy. it is in its immediate neighborhood that it has been most disappointed. It is embroiled in territorial disputes that prevent the launch of a free-for-all energy foreign policy. While its troubled relationship with Pakistan continues to create problems for its plans to import oil from Iran. its other neighbor. Bangladesh has also reneged on its earlier commitment to the tripartite agreement for transportation of gas from Myanmar to India via a pipeline running through Bangladesh. India wants to pursue this project seriously. because of all the pipeline options to bring natural gas from the Shwe fields in offshore Myanmar. the overland option via Bangladesh is possibly the most economical.

The India-Bangladesh-Myanmar pipeline idea was initially seen as a landmark in Indo-Bangladesh relations. with Bangladesh agreeing to its territory being used for transport of any commodity to the Indian market for the first time in three decades. While India seems willing to pay $125 million as transit fee to Bangladesh. Dhaka also wants transit facility through India for hydroelectric power from Nepal and Bhutan to Bangladesh. a corridor of trade between Nepal and Bhutan. and measures to reduce bilateral trade imbalance before it can conclude this agreement.

The one reality that Indian diplomacy has to confront in its search for nation's energy security is the presence of China almost everywhere and its relative success in achieving desirable outcomes. more often than not. to India's detriment.

INDIA'S STRATEGIC OBJECTIVES

The previous Delhi government. the Bharatyia Junta Party (BJP) and its coalition partners. brought a paradigm shift from a Nehruvian perspective to realism in India's foreign and security policies. Nehruvians and realists share the same objective of achieving a Great India. The former. however. hold that India should obtain the status of major power through moral superiority. whereas the realists want to achieve that status through power politics. This paradigm shift resulted in increased arms procurement and development by the Indian armed forces. The return of the Congress Party to power. after a lapse of nine years. did not bring a shift in the arms development and procurement policy of the BJP government. According to the Congress leadership. its government would ensure that all delays in the modernization of armed forces would be eliminated. and funds budgeted for modernization would be spent to the fullest. More precisely. Congress is committed to maintaining a credible missile and nuclear weapons programme as well as conventional military muscle.

The Congress government has been maintaining the BJP policy in the sphere of Indo-US relations because in the post–Cold War international order. New Delhi seems comfortable with the emergence of the United States as a sole superpower and a dominant Indian Ocean player. P.S. Das. the former commander-in-chief of the Indian Navy's Eastern Naval Command. stated: 'However. there is no basic conflict between core American interests and Indian concerns. and in fact there are several areas of convergence. It is. therefore. possible to evolve strategies which further our interests in the new global environment.' As for China. the Indians consider it a potential adversary. China's relations with Myanmar and Pakistan. its facilities in the Coco Islands (off the Andaman). and its ability to influence political postures in South Asia and in many Indian Ocean littoral states figure prominently in India's security calculus. Mohan Malik argued that 'the US and India have similar geo-strategic concerns about China's growing power and influence.

For India. which has long regarded China as a strategic adversary. the Bush administration's characterization of China as a "strategic competitor" rather than a strategic partner was a welcome development.' The preceding discussion offers evidence that Washington wants to establish strategic relations with New Delhi because India can be used as a core element in balancing Beijing in the post–Cold War international arena. At the same time.

India has been trying to secure US support – or at least US understanding – for strengthening its pre-eminent position in South Asia and the Indian Ocean region via transfers of advanced military technologies. training in modern modes of warfare. and so on. The relationship between India's quest for greater US support and the simultaneous objective of eventually securing US military withdrawal from the South Asian–Indian Ocean region also has merit in Delhi's strategic calculations. It is argued that India's position within the region would grow with US support and understanding. If in the future Washington decides to pull out of the region. it would leave India as the exclusive. paramount power.

BRIEF OVERVIEW: INDO-US STRATEGIC COOPERATION IN THE 21ST CENTURY

President Bush brought a dramatic shift in the Indo-US strategic relationship. He counted India as a key power requiring substantially greater American attention. C. Raja Mohan argued. 'Convinced that India's influence will stretch far beyond its immediate neighbourhood. Bush has reconceived the framework of US engagement with New Delhi. He has removed many of the sanctions. opened the door for high-tech cooperation. lent political support to India's own war on terrorism. ended the historical US tilt towards Pakistan on Kashmir. and repositioned the US in the Sino-Indian equation by drawing closer to New Delhi.' In September 2002. President Bush spoke of developing a strategic relationship with India as a component of the US national security strategy. Both states have been engaged in charting a new course for the relationship. Consequently. since April 2003 the US intelligence community has discontinued its semi-annual unclassified reporting to Congress on India's nuclear and missile programmes. The suspension of information might have undermined the US Congress's efficacy in intervening in the Indo-US nuclear and missile cooperation. Certainly. it would have helped facilitatc thc dcal approval process.

New Delhi. for the sake of cultivating good relations with Washington. endorsed Bush's Ballistic Missile Defence project – even before his closest strategic allies backed it – and remained silent over the abrogation of the Anti-Ballistic Missile Treaty. It is pertinent to note that India opposed President Ronald Reagan's Strategic Defence Initiative. In contrast. when President George W. Bush unveiled a 'new framework for security and stability' in May 2001 and revived strategic defences by discarding the Antiballistic Missile Treaty. the then Indian minister of external affairs. Jaswant Singh. immediately endorsed the plan. On 11 May 2001 he stated. 'We are endeavouring to work out together a totally new security regime which is for the entire globe.' It was probably the first time in decades that India had extended such support to the United States on any global armament issue.

This shift in the Indian stance was due to the promise of technological cooperation. which was critical to India. India offered military bases to the United States for Operation Enduring Freedom in Afghanistan after 9/11 (something it never offered to the former USSR. despite the Treaty of Peace and Friendship). There are a number of areas in which India gave up its traditional stances and endorsed the US position. These include climate change – incorporating its latest avatar. the Asia-Pacific Partnership – and helping the United States get rid of a Third World director-general of the Organisation for the Prohibition of Chemical Weapons. New Delhi also agreed to work with the United States on multinational military operations outside of the United Nations framework. Twice. in 2005 and 2006. India voted with Washington against Iran

– an erstwhile Indian ally – at the International Atomic Energy Agency. India came close to sending a division of troops to Iraq in the summer of 2003. before pulling back at the last moment. During the Defence Policy Group (DPG) meeting held 6–7 August 2003 in Washington. the two sides agreed to establish a high-level dialogue on defence- technology security issues. They reaffirmed their shared view that missile defence enhances cooperative security and stability. They decided to hold a missile defence workshop in India within six months. as a follow-on to an international conference. The workshop. attended by US and Indian delegations. was held at the Multinational Ballistic Missile Defence Conference in Kyoto. Japan. in June 2003. The Indian delegation also accepted invitations to the July 2004 Multinational Ballistic Missile Defence Conference in Berlin and the 2005 Roving Sands missile defence exercise.

Also at the August 2003 DPG meeting. Indian and American delegates approved a range of activities for the coming year. including:

- Specialized training programmes and joint exercises to be carried out by the armed services of the two countries. including an air combat training exercise.
- A multinational planning exercise to develop standard operating procedures. hosted by India in coordination with the United States.
- Continued development of a defence supply relationship. including the Government-to-Government Foreign Military Sales programme. The US team was to travel to India in September to discuss details of a possible sale of P-3 maritime patrol aircraft.
- US sale to India of training materials and specialized equipment to support India's peacekeeping training capabilities.
- A Defence Planning Exchange to enable US and Indian experts to conduct discussions on defence strategy and planning.

In June 2004. a high-level American delegation visited New Delhi to negotiate the transfer to India of technology related to the missile defence system. The United States also licensed Boeing's satellite systems to the Indian Space Research Organization for construction of a communications satellite. Moreover. the United States did not oppose the transfer of Arrow and Cruise missile technologies to India by Israel and the Russian Federation respectively. Arrow missile technology is very much part of the Indian missile defence system programme. Before Prime Minister Singh's visit to Washington on 28 June 2005. Pranab Mukherjee and Donald Rumsfeld – who were. at the time. Indian defence minister and American secretary of Defence. respectively – signed a new framework that would guide the defence relations of the two states for the next decade. They planned to expand defence trade. improve cooperation between their armed forces. and co-produce military hardware.

The July 2005 summit between US President George Bush and Indian Prime Minister Manmohan Singh in Washington provided a roadmap for the transformation of bilateral strategic ties. Both sides agreed to broaden their strategic engagement. They agreed on several joint ventures that highlight the breadth of the new Indo-US relationship. Among these were revitalized economic and energy dialogues. a CEO forum. a global democracy initiative. a disaster response initiative. the completion of the Next Steps in the Strategic Partnership (NSSP) process. and a partnership to fight HIV/AIDS. They initiated new efforts in education. agriculture. science. and space exploration. and agreed to send an Indian astronaut on the Space Shuttle for the first time. On 17 October 2005. US Secretary of State Condoleezza Rice and Indian Minister of State for Science and Technology Kapil Sibal signed an umbrella science and technology agreement designed to boost cooperation in areas ranging from health to space technology. The purpose of the agreement was threefold: to strengthen the science and technology capabilities of the United States and India; to expand relations between the extensive scientific and technological communities of both countries; and to promote technological and scientific cooperation in areas of mutual benefit. On 22 February. President Bush stated. 'We have an ambitious agenda with India. Our agenda is practical. It builds on a relationship that has never been better. India is a global leader. as well as a good friend.... My trip will remind everybody about the strengthening of an important strategic partnership. We'll work together in practical ways to promote a hopeful future for citizens in both our nations.' On 2 March 2006. the United States and India reiterated their intention to build the foundation of a durable defence relationship that would continue to support their common strategic and security interests.

They agreed to pursue the following objectives:

- Maritime security cooperation: The United States and India are committed to a comprehensive cooperative effort to ensure a secure maritime domain.
- Counterterrorism: The United States and India are jointly expanding the scope of our counterterrorism cooperation. including work on bioterrorism and cybersecurity.
- Military logistics support: The United States and India will soon sign an agreement to facilitate mutual logistical support during combined training. exercises. and disaster relief operations.
- Defence trade: The United States reaffirmed its goal to help meet India's defence needs and to provide the important technologies and capabilities that India seeks.
- Non-proliferation: Both countries support efforts to limit the spread of enrichment and reprocessing technologies. and also to support the conclusion of a Fissile Material Cutoff Treaty.

NUCLEAR COOPERATION

It was briefly mentioned earlier that on 18 July 2005. the Bush administration announced civil nuclear cooperation with India. President Bush offered to modify US non-proliferation laws and revise the global nuclear order to facilitate full cooperation with India on civilian nuclear energy. In simple terms. the administration agreed to lift a ban on civilian nuclear technology sales to nuclear-armed India. despite its refusal to sign the nuclear non-proliferation treaty or give up its nuclear arms. This cooperation would effectively grant India highly sought-after access to sensitive nuclear technology only accorded to states in full compliance with global Non-proliferation standards. It would also treat India in much the same way as the five original nuclear weapon states by exempting it from meaningful international nuclear inspections. It is a virtual endorsement of India's nuclear weapon status. In contrast. previous US administrations adopted the stance that India's nuclear arsenal. which was first tested in 1974. was illegitimate and should be eliminated or at least seriously constrained.

The nuclear deal is very much to India's advantage because it would enable India to obtain enriched uranium to fuel its nuclear reactors. acquire nuclear reactors from the international market. and participate in international nuclear research and development. The implementation of the civil nuclear energy cooperation deal requires the US Congress to alter US laws and policies. According to the reports. the Senate Foreign Relations Committee indicated that it would judge the efficacy of the Indian separation plan in terms of three criteria: compliance with International Atomic Energy Agency (IAEA) safeguards; non-assistance to India's nuclear weapons programme; and transparency. Under the Bush-Manmohan pact. India agreed to separate its civilian and military facilities in return for full civilian nuclear energy cooperation from the United States.

In this context. instead of 'perpetual' safeguards arrangements between India and the IAEA. which would signal finality to civilian separation. New Delhi agreed to a 'voluntary' safeguards arrangement with the IAEA. This arrangement allows Delhi to pull nuclear facilities out of the civilian list in the future and put them back to military use. It seems that the Bush administration has given in to the demands of the Indian nuclear lobby – especially when it is considered that the United States exempted large portions of Indian nuclear infrastructure from international inspections.

To settle the nuclear deal. India classified 14 of its 22 reactors as civilian. These 14 facilities would be under safeguards and opened to international inspections. Eight reactors are deemed military. making them exempt from inspection. Additionally. there was no mention of facilities such as research reactors. enrichment plants. or reprocessing facilities being declared civilian. Reportedly. implementation would be conducted in phases from 2006 to 2014. India's fastbreeder reactor programme – the Fast Breeder Test Reactor and the Prototype Fast Breeder Reactor is not included in the civilian list.

Whether the perpetual safeguards arrangement would have been able to prevent the Indians from using material from the declared civilian nuclear facilities for military purposes is debatable. The Senate Foreign Relations Committee criteria contain loopholes and do not offer an alternative to comprehensive safeguards. Moreover. India's past record indicates that it would violate the agreement. For example. the 40-megawatt Canadian-supplied CIRUS reactor. located north of Mumbai. was subject to an apparent diversion. It would be difficult to resolve problems when a reactor intended for peaceful use was diverted for military purposes. Since March 2006. the process of finalizing a nuclear deal between New Delhi and Washington has not been confronted with any impediment. In the last week of July. there was a major development in Indo-US relations. specifically in the realm of civil nuclear cooperation. The US House of Representatives approved an agreement to share civilian nuclear technology with India. The bill was passed by a vote of 359 to 68. a month after the Senate Foreign Relations Committee endorsed the bill by a 16-to-2 margin. Prior to the endorsement of the Senate (the upper house). some analysts thought that it might seek a few amendments to the nuclear agreement. New Delhi. however. had conveyed to Washington that the final legislation must not deviate from earlier agreements between the two countries.

The Indian negotiators had categorically rejected any change to the original agreement signed on 2 March 2006. Consequently. the Senate approved the bill on 17 November 2006 with 85 votes in favour and 12 against. President Bush signed the legislation. called the Henry J. Hyde United States–India Peaceful Atomic Energy Cooperation Act of 2006. on 18 December. The votes indicate that the Indo-US nuclear deal received significant and bipartisan Congressional support. The proposed agreement reverses Washington's policy of restricting nuclear cooperation with New Delhi because it has not signed the nuclear Non-Proliferation Treaty (NPT) and has tested nuclear weapons. in 1974 and 1998. The nuclear deal would have serious ramifications for the nuclear non-proliferation regime and for South Asian security. US Representative Edward Markey. Democrat of Massachusetts. argued. 'The administration's move to launch nuclear cooperation with India has grave security implications for South Asia and the entire world.' The deal would assist India in increasing its nuclear weapons: by virtue of acquiring nuclear fuel from the United States for civilian use. India would free up its own stocks for weapons.

ENERGY SECURITY ATTAINMENT FOR INDIA ENVIRONMENTAL SCIENCES

Energy has become need for everyone in current dynamic environment. Every country is trying to exploit different source of energy to meet their daily requirements and India is one of these country. India has shifted its focus from the source of Non- renewable energy. which is depleting at higher rate. to renewable source of energy. It is trying to strike a balance between both sources of energy. This paper will address strategy adopted by Indian government for energy security.

India is one of the fastest developing countries of the world and its GDP is more than $1 trillion. It needs to sustain 8-10% economic growth rate to remove poverty and meet its economic as well human development goals. It creates a huge demand of energy right from the households need to industrial need but the supply is less. In order to balance the supply and demand. government has taken some of major steps. These steps will not only be able to meet demand but also produce safe. clean and convenient energy at least cost. The availability of Non- rcncwablc cncrgy sources is limited and may not be adequate in the long term to maintain the growth rate. The focus should also to increase the efficiency of current power plant running across country as well as to look out for stakes in overseas energy assets. Another vital aspect is to provide clean and convenient energy for social and environment welfare at the cheapest cost so that even poor can get access to it. Assured supply of such energy and technologies at all times by taking into account. the shocks and disturbance is vital to provide energy security to all.

The major contribution of primary energy source comes from coal which is followed by oil and natural gas (about 96.5%). These fossil fuel are not only exhaustible energy source but also harmful to environment. Nuclear energy production produces lot of harmful radiations which affect the living being and ozone layer. Hydro power plants are renewable source of energy but dependency on this source is limited to 2.5% (approx.).

There is some alternate source of energy like wind and solar has drawn attention of the government to meet its energy needs. These alternative sources hold huge potential especially in India where it is still in infancy stage of exploitation.

The energy need of India is growing fast and competition to meet the needs with rest of the world is on rise. The vision of attending energy security in future dcpcnds on thc stratcgy adopted by government of India. It requires hunting for all available fuel options and forms of energy. both renewable and Non- renewable. as well as new and budding technologies and energy sources.

STRATEGY FOR OIL AND NATURAL GAS

The percentage share of commercial primary energy resources of oil and natural gas account about 36% and 9% respectively. As per estimate by Bureau of Energy Efficiency (BEE). the share of oil and natural gas will be 22.71% and 23.86% in 2031-32. To meet the requirements India needs to diversify its acquisition resources. India's energy strategies for oil and natural gas incorporate: acquiring upstream assets. pursuing transactional pipeline routes. securing oil navigation sea routes. expanding supply agreements. accessing new technologies and sheltering foreign investments. In order to implement these strategies successfully India would require close collaboration with energy rich countries along with many energy importing economies.

According to estimates. India may need to double its oil requirements in the next 20 years so it is important to increase its current capacity. Besides other pipeline routes. Turkmenistan- Afghanistan- Pakistan [TAP] pipeline project and Iran- Pakistan- India pipeline projects plays a vital role for Indian Energy Security.

As a part of exploration programme of oil and natural gas India has identified different zone known as NELP. In these zone companies are allowed to bid and the winner can exploit for oil and gas available there. Even the recent discovery of fossil fuel by Reliance and Crains Energy is not sufficient to meet its need so bilateral agreement with other countries will play pivotal role to meet the demand.

STRATEGY FOR COAL

Coal is the most important source of fuelling the power plant in India. It accounts for around 50% of the total commercial primary energy produce in India. The high depletion rate of coal is basically due to large dependency on coal for household consumption and other industrial sectors.

India strategies to have coal as energy security incorporate: expanding bilateral supply contracts. improving the raw material quality and processing as well as exploring new sites. India has signed different agreement with the African and Asian countries that holds large deposit of unexploited coal. The main purpose of signing these agreements is to procure more amount of coal from other countries and thereby save our own coal reserves.

The quality of coal used by power plant is poor. hence their efficiency is poor. India is trying to improve the quality of coal by processing the poor quality of coal. Processing enriches the different elements present in coal and thus it improves the per unit energy production.

STRATEGY FOR WATER ENERGY

Hydro is renewable source of energy. The energy produce from it is clean and does not have adverse effect on the environment. Till date the contribution of hydro as commercial primary source is about 2.14%. It is estimated that by 2030 the contribution will increase to 2.36%. In order to increase the contribution of this clean and eco friendly source of energy India has designed a proper strategy.India is a country of different rivers but still some river face shortage of water during needy season.

To short out this problem. India government has launched programme of linking all the rivers of the country by constructing dam across them. The government has planned to set up hydro power plant near the newly constructed major dams. Apart from new construction government is investing more amount of money to increase the capacity of existing plant by borrowing new technology from other countries.

STRATEGY FOR NUCLEAR ENERGY

Nuclear energy is another form of energy which is able to contribute about 1.5% of the total energy production in India. India has abundant amount of uranium which is raw material for the production of energy. But it lacks the technology to enrich uranium fuel rod.

In order to meet future needs for enriched uranium. India signed popular "123 Agreement" with America in 2008. Along with this agreement the banned for importing enriched uranium from other countries was lifted. India is now cash cowing from this agreement.

It has started building civil nuclear plant to harness maximum benefit. India is also procuring uranium enriching technology from other capable countries as well as has set up research and development laboratory in collaboration with other country. India has started stockpile of nuclear fuel in order to counter the risk of interruption of international fuel supply.

STRATEGY FOR WIND AND SOLAR ENERGY

Wind and sun are clean and environmental friendly source of renewable energy. India has huge potential to harness these energy sources but their full potential has not been exploited. In order to attract private companies to make significant investment in these sources of energy generation. Indian government is providing subsidies and tax benefits. Government is also going for bilateral agreement.To exploit the wind as source of energy NHPC is working with state government to set wind power plant. For solar power government launched Jawaharlal Nehru National Solar Mission that aims at installing extra 20000 MW of power by 2020. It also aims at making country global hub for solar energy power with solar science. engineering. R&D etc. to make huge business out of it.

STRATEGY FOR NEW AND BUDDING TECHNOLOGIES

The new emerging trends like biogas. bio-diesel. ethanol. wood gasifier and clean coal are now being promoted by Indian government. These can meet at least household needs and to a little extend industry needs. To promote usage of biogas in manufacturing firm especially food and textile sector government has made stringent effluent discharge code. Based on these codes. firm has to treat the effluent before discharge. During treatment some amount of biogas. ethanol are produced which are used to meet some of their firm energy needs. For other emerging technologies government is dependent on foreign help.

INDIAN ENERGY POLICY AND STRATEGY

With the largest population and the 12th largest economy in the world. India is currently the world's sixth largest energy consumer. Interest in the energy policies of the central and individual state governments and the related strategies is increasing due to their huge impact on global energy prices. geopolitical relations and climate change. For a comprehensive understanding of Indian energy policy and strategy options we need to examine the sources of primary energy. the purposes for which this energy is being consumed and the trends of relevant indicators over the recent past.

India's energy policies in the context of climate change and the recent international negotiations. Rather than give details of the policy and strategy options. we outline some of the innovative changes in policies as well as the challenges and constraints that India is to overcome if it is to make the transition to sustainable development. After a brief discussion of India's energy needs we highlight the nation's energy policies with respect to development needs. energy demand and supply-side dynamics. We then outline the challenges and constraints of Indian energy policies in general and those specific to a transition to a low-carbon economy.

The Indian government needs to overcome barriers that have constrained its previous attempts at improving quality of life for its citizens by providing them with a framework that ensures energy security as well as optimal material and energy utilisation. A holistic vision that questions consumer patterns associated with development and strives to improve human development with decoupled growth (growth based on reduced consumption of resources) is the need of the hour.

SHIFTS IN INDIAN ENERGY TRENDS: IMPLICATIONS FOR POLICY

India's primary energy consumption in 2007 was 19.885.302 terajoules (TJ).1 of which 30 per cent was imported (EIA. 2009. 2010a). Most of this energy was from fossil fuels. while only 1.8 per cent was from hydroelectric. 0.7 per cent from nuclear and 0.2 per cent from other renewable sources that included wind and solar energy. Almost 70 per cent of India's population lives in rural areas that have limited access to electricity and automobile ownership.

The nation consumes a large quantity of biomass (firewood. agricultural residues and animal waste) for household and cottage-scale industry energy needs in rural areas. Of the total energy consumed in 2007 by India. 27.2 per cent could be considered combustible renewables such as firewood. agricultural residues and animal waste. Supply-side estimates of this biomass consumption are highly uncertain because it is not subject to market transaction; there may be between 201 and 352 million tonnes of biomass use per year. Variation in moisture and calorific content of wood adds further uncertainty to the energy content of this biomass.

India's primary energy consumption in 2006 (18.636.242 TJ) was five times less than that of the United States (US). four times less than that of China. 14 times more than that of Switzerland and 17 times more than that of Nigeria.

India's political development objectives have centred on the establishment of a social democracy that aims to ensure equal opportunity (but not necessarily equal outcomes) in political and economic institutions. Over the past 63 years of independence India has maintained parliamentary democracy and civil liberties to an extent that is exceptional for an extraordinarily diverse country colonised for more than 200 years. However. equal rights. social justice and reduced poverty still remain distant ideals. The government needs to deal with an extremely large population. severe poverty and limited resources. Moreover. the current state of affairs is a consequence of an evident failure in governance.

Improving human development could lead to considerably increased consumption of electricity if India follows the development path chosen by most other countries that have made the transition from low to moderate levels of development. The Ministry of Power and the Ministry of Environment and Forests estimate that over 600 million Indians. that is 53 per cent of India's population. had no access to electricity in 2007 (Government of India. 2007).

Demographic trends may also directly affect energy consumption. The Indian population began to spiral in the 1920s. Birth control policies were undertaken from the 1950s on. Thanks to family planning initiatives. the growth rate has edged down to the current level of 1.5 per cent. India now represents 17.3 per cent of the world population.

Between 1980 and 2007 India's Human Development Index (HDI) rose by 1.33 per cent annually from 0.427 to 0.612. In 2007 India's HDI rank was 134 among 182 countries. with China's rank being 92.

A wide disparity in energy accessibility exists across India's urban and rural divide. Indeed. 54.9 per cent of rural households. in comparison to 92 per cent of urban households. had access to electricity in 2005; 9 per cent of rural households. in comparison to 57 per cent of urban households. had access to liquefied petroleum gas for cooking. Approximately two-thirds of rural households still depend on biomass such as firewood. crop residues. and dung cakes. The lack of cleaner fuels and energy-efficient cooking devices results in indoor pollution. This reduces life expectancy and increases associated medication expenses which further reduce incomes. Additionally. these devices emit larger quantities of greenhouse gas (GHG) per unit of energy and result in a need for more time to gather fuel. which also hinders education. India's energy policies targeting the 28.6 per cent of the population living below the poverty line aim to raise the HDI. Measures such as the National Biogas Programme (1981–82) and subsidies for liquefied petroleum gas and kerosene. through smart cards for families living below the poverty line. are aimed at enhancing access to cleaner fuels. However. both the National Biogas

Programme and the subsidies on liquefied petroleum gas and kerosene have failed to enhance access. The main reasons for failure of the National Biogas Programme are: lack of sense of ownership by the community. inappropriate match between the design of the biogas plant and its environment due to inadequate understanding of biomass flow. difficulty in establishing price for input and output. lack of coordination between organisations involved in the programme and lack of follow-up. Subsidies for liquefied petroleum gas and kerosene have ended up favouring the rise of a black market for these fuels. which forces poorer families to pay higher costs. The Rajiv Gandhi Grameen Vidyutikaran Yojana Programme (begun in 2005) and the Remote Village Electrification Programme (begun in 2001) aim to provide basic electricity to rural and remote areas by extending free connections to households living below the poverty line and subsidising capital costs by 90 per cent through Indian government grants.

Although there is no precise Millennium Development Goal regarding energy. the United Nations (UN) Millennium Project highlights the role of energy services as a prerequisite for development and for achieving the Millennium Development Goals. India accounts for about a third of the world's population without access to electricity. that is 40 per cent of India's population in 2005 (Bhattacharyya. 2010). India spends around 30 per cent of its export earnings on importing energy (UNDP. 2010). This dependence depletes scarce foreign exchange and increases exposure to the balance of payments impact of oil price shocks. India's Integrated Energy Policy. in combination with more specific programmes like the National Biogas Programme. the Integrated Rural Energy Programme and the Remote Village Electrification Programme. and targeted subsidies for liquefied petroleum gas and renewable technology. are all steps towards promoting rural access to energy services through increased use of improved technology. However. these programmes have had limited success in achieving their goals. mainly because of an extensive decentralisation of policy implementation at the level of individual states and difficulties in spreading proper understanding of new energy technologies in rural areas.

ENERGY USE: DEMAND. INTENSITY AND EFFICIENCY

Although the first industrial revolution began in England in the late eighteenth century. the British actively discouraged Indians from taking up modern technology with access to fossil fuel and electricity. At the time of independence India's population was around 350 million and most depended primarily on biomass for energy. Since independence in 1947 the demand for energy. particularly electricity and fossil fuels. has grown exponentially. primarily due to the rapid increase in urbanisation. industrialisation and population. The average growth rate in energy consumption from 1980 to 2006 was 5.4 per cent. In 2006 India accounted for about 3.7 per cent of the world's commercial energy demand. However. this is still 7–11 per cent short of the demand for energy in India. Despite this increase in overall energy consumption. the average per capita energy consumption in India is only 16.8 GJ. in comparison to the world average of 76 GJ in 2006. In 2007 India was ranked 61st out of 207 countries classified from lowest to highest energy consumption. This low per capita consumption could be partially due to the large amount of biomass that is consumed without being recorded.

In 1991 India imported just 17.8 per cent of its commercial energy; in 2008 it imported more than 30 per cent. This growth in import is due to a growth in demand. scarcity of fossil fuels and the inefficiency of state-run enterprises in energy exploration. production and distribution. as illustrated by the huge transmission and distribution losses in electricity. In 2004 India. with losses amounting to 26.29 per cent. was ranked 13th out of 131 countries listed from highest to lowest transmission and distribution losses. Despite these inefficiencies and the inability of energy corporations to keep up with demand. India has achieved moderate levels of increased energy efficiency (Government of India. 2007). From 2002 to 2007 some INR 140 billion (USD 3.1 billion) of taxpayers' money went towards reducing transmission and distribution losses. which decreased by 9.62 per cent over those five years. Yet. the investment did not include programmes to improve collection and reporting of data by the individual state electricity boards so as to continually monitor improvements in reducing such losses.

Energy intensity (the amount of energy consumed per unit of gross domestic product (GDP)) has decreased in India ever since the early 1970s. However. compared to other countries. energy intensity in India is still extremely high. that is 1.5 times the world average. 1.47 times the average of all Asian countries and 1.55 times that of the US. To some extent. subsidised prices of certain forms of energy (fossil fuels) and the continuing inability of the government to pass on the true cost of oil to consumers have led to end-use inefficiencies. For example. the price paid by consumers for electricity. liquefied petroleum gas and kerosene was respectively 48 per cent. 61 per cent and 69 per cent of the true production and supply costs in 1992. Although this pricing has gradually changed and today these prices are approaching the true production and supply costs. end-use inefficiencies due to subsidisation of electricity for specific sectors of the economy (agriculture. for example) are acting as key barriers to improving the energy intensity of the Indian economy.

Despite these inefficiencies. the rate of energy growth from 1997 to 2007 (4–5 per cent per annum) has been much lower than India's economic growth (9 per cent per annum). While India's energy intensity has always been lower than that of China. the decrease in energy intensity has not been as remarkable.

When only commercial sources of energy are accounted for in India the industrial sector consumes the largest percentage. Major energy-consuming sectors such as cement. steel. aluminium and fertilisers have reduced their energy intensity over the years; thermal-specific energy consumption in the Indian cement and iron/steel sectors has decreased by 7.5 per cent and 3.5 per cent per annum respectively (Government of India. 2007).

This decline in India's energy intensity is due to various policies:

1. Energy Conservation Act (2001) that has identified nine major energy-consuming sectors for observance of mandatory energy efficiency standards;
2. linking of tariffs to energy efficiency by the Electricity Regulatory Commissions. thereby providing an incentive for efficiency improvement;
3. high ratio of recycling and consequently decreased demand for virgin raw material for the steel. aluminium and copper sectors;
4. Energy Labelling Programme (launched in 2006) for electrical appliances. distribution transformers. fluorescent tube lights. air conditioners and so on;
5. Energy Conservation Building Code (launched in 2007) that has been incorporated into the compulsory Environmental Impact Assessment requirements for new large commercial buildings;
6. Mandatory execution of energy audits in large-scale units in nine high-energy-consuming sectors that are also required to report energy conservation and consumption data annually;
7. Implementation of 538 clean development mechanism (CDM) projects (registered by India's CDM Executive Board) accounting for a reduction of 43.5 million tonnes of carbon dioxide (CO_2) annually and associated efficiency improvements; 1.023 more projects have been approved by the CDM National Designated Authority and are currently being implemented.

As with most policies in India the level of enforcement and implementation is variable. Each act is implemented by appropriate government agencies that are controlled by the individual states. Each of India's 28 states has a different level of enforcement depending on the efficiency of the ruling party of each state government. Therefore. the government has to make extra efforts for efficient implementation and enforcement of policies in general.

When non-commercial sources of energy (biomass not subject to market transaction) are included the residential sector in India is the largest consumer of energy. Within the residential sector almost 85 per cent of total energy consumed between 1999 and 2000 was non-commercial; therefore. this sector is very important but is often neglected in policies aimed at energy conservation. Some 35–40 per cent of the energy consumed by the residential sector is for cooking. High energy intensity in this sector is due to use of cheap and inefficient cooking stoves. The Ministry of Non-Conventional Energy Sources (now the

Ministry of New and Renewable Energy) funded a large-scale National Programme on Improved Chulha (*chulha* means stove in Hindi) from 1984 to 2002. The main objective of the programme was to reduce demand for firewood by providing subsidised (up to 90 per cent of cost) energy-efficient stoves to rural households. In 2001 the programme had distributed such stoves to 32.77 million households (27 per cent of existing rural households); however. this number may not represent the number of operational stoves.

Despite such programmes. there has been an increase in the per capita consumption of firewood in rural areas from 16.2 kg in 1988 to 17.3 kg in 1994. This increase is partially due to the failure of the National Programme of Improved Chulha because of poor coordination between the Ministry for Non-Conventional Energy Sources and the individual state-level implanting agencies. subsidies granted to the builders of the stoves that cause their motivation to be directed more towards the government than the consumers and lead to hasty production of faulty stoves. lack of after-sales servicing and maintenance and greater focus on merely achieving targets without building capacity to maintain and service these stoves for years to come. This problem of continued usage remains a challenge to the myriad companies and organisations that are still distributing these stoves in rural and semi-urban India. In urban areas the shift from biomass to commercial fuels is significant. Government policies that subsidise the prices of liquefied petroleum gas and kerosene and control their distribution have played a key role in this transition.

DYNAMICS OF ENERGY SUPPLY IN INDIA IN THE KYOTO-COPENHAGEN CONTEXT

The total primary energy demand in 1960–61 in India was only approximately 2.400 TJ. In a single decade this increased to 2.940 TJ. with over 20 per cent of supply in coal/peat and over 60 per cent in biomass (IEA. 2010b). Over three decades the demand due to Indian population and economic growth resulted in a three-fold increase in the country's total primary energy supply (IEA. 2010b). In 1999 coal provided 32 per cent of total primary energy supply. while the share of biomass had dropped to 42 per cent. This was at the time when the Kyoto Protocol had just come into existence.This was also the same period when India had just finished enacting a series of policies to liberalise the economy. Srivastava (1997) predicted that India would need 19.147.000 TJ from coal and 6.560.000 TJ from oil by 2011–12 to sustain a 6 per cent GDP growth per annum. While these projections did not include biomass. Sudha and Ravindranath (1999) projected that about 457 million tonnes of biomass would be needed for use as firewood and industrial energy in 2010. Since then India has grown at a rate higher than 7 per cent per annum and has exceeded the original growth target set in the 9th Five-Year Plan (Planning Commission. 1997). Total primary energy use. including biomass. shot up from 19.6 million

TJ in 1999 to 25.4 million TJ in 2008. a 29 per cent increase in less than a decade. Coal provided around 40 per cent of primary energy. Oil became the second largest source with 25 per cent. whereas biomass slipped to 24 per cent.

India has taken large and innovative steps to reduce GHG emissions and thereby address climate change through its National Action Plan on Climate Change (2008). announcing a reduction in emissions intensity of the economy (CO_2 per unit of GDP) by 20–25 per cent by 2020. However. in all climate change negotiations India has been persistent about two points. namely taking per capita GHG emissions into consideration when constructing a global strategy to reduce emissions. on the one hand. and supporting strategies that are only based on equitable burden-sharing. on the other; the latter strategies take the impact of accumulated GHG into consideration as well as the economic capability of a country to reduce its emissions (Government of India. 2009a).

Despite this commitment to reduce emissions. India's development path is characterised by a large allocation of funds to create and maintain expensive fossil-fuel-dependent infrastructure. Such allocation has reduced the budgets available to improve critical sectors such as health. education. energy-efficient infrastructure that includes non-motorised transportation. renewable energy and further energy efficiency initiatives. India has a rare opportunity to adopt a different development paradigm; the Indian government should focus more on integrating energy efficiency and renewable energy technologies and strategies in all development policies.

At the UN Climate Change Conference in Copenhagen in December 2009 Indian Prime Minister Manmohan Singh indicated that. irrespective of the outcome of Copenhagen. India would go ahead and meet its intensity reduction targets. In the most recent Five-Year Plan (Planning Commission. 2007) the Indian government has targeted an additional 30 gigawatts (GW) of capacity from renewables. Through the National Solar Mission the target is an additional 22 GW by 2022. Moreover. the recently approved National Mission on Enhanced Energy Efficiency aims to save 943.000 TJ by 2015. However. India's Integrated Energy Policy (Planning Commission. 2006a) still depends on coal and oil as the main sources of primary energy in the near future and this is unlikely to change without radical action.

REALITY OR MYTH OF THE TRANSITION TO A LOWER-CARBON ECONOMY

Technical constraints and opportunities

In 2007 India's 1.9 billion tonnes of CO_2 emissions were less than a third of those in the US. But they are growing fast with an increase in use of fossil fuels. India's power sector is one of the most CO_2-intensive in the world and contributes 60 per cent of its total CO_2 emissions. The power grid emission factor of 0.82t CO_2/MWh in 2008–09 (Central Electricity Authority. 2009) was more than 50 per cent higher than the world average (OECD and IEA. 2007). Yet. this is predicted to decrease because of increases in the shares of renewables. nuclear power and the newly developed ultra-supercritical technology for coal-based power plants; a prototype plant is planned to be commissioned by 2017 (Bhaskar and Koshy. 2010). Nearly 70 per cent of India's electricity supply comes from coal due to large indigenous reserves. With modernisation of these coal-fired plants India could be looking at emissions cuts of between 10 and 13 million tonnes of CO_2 equivalent each year (World Bank. 2009). Additionally. switching to a cleaner fuel such as natural gas for power generation would reduce CO_2 emissions by about 50 per cent. However. shortage of domestic resources along with constraints in regulation. pricing. supply and infrastructure have led to gas demands going unmet in recent years.

Although gas use in India amounted to 59 billion cubic metres in 2009–10. up from 43 billion cubic metres in 2008–09. total demand for 2008–09 was estimated at 30 billion cubic metres higher than actual consumption (OECD and IEA. 2010). Wind power capacities of 12.009.28 megawatts (MW) as well as with other renewables provide over 10.6 per cent of India's grid capacity (Ministry of New and Renewable Energy. 2010). The New and Renewable Energy Policy promotes utilisation and development of renewables through indigenous design. but its potential is hindered by fiscal and technological constraints. India has approved a National Solar Mission 'Solar India' (Government of India. 2009b). at an estimated cost of INR 43.37 billion (USD 963.7 million). with the aim of installing 20.000 MW of solar energy capacity by 2022 and achieving an estimated cut of 42 million tonnes of CO_2 emissions. India is endowed with vast solar energy potential. with most areas receiving 4–7 kWh per square metre incident energy per day. India is looking to use a mix of thermal as well as photovoltaic solar energy to achieve its mission. The mission has been termed realistic by experts. but great stress is put on critical environmental and certain economic aspects of this very expensive technology. Currently solar generation costs in India are INR 15–20 (USD 0.33–0.44) per kWh (Ministry of New and Renewable Energy. 2010) and. while plans for subsidies have been made for the initial years. grid parity is anticipated by 2022. contingent on factors such as the scale of global deployment. the pace of advancements and research and development (R&D).

There is great scope for improvement in energy efficiency across all sectors in India. The target set by India for reductions in emissions intensity of economy (CO_2 per unit of GDP) is 20–25 per cent by 2020 (Dasgupta and Sethi. 2009). McNeil et al. (2008) showed that total electricity consumption could be reduced by about 4.7 per cent by 2020 by improving the efficiency of household appliances. In addition. new vehicles abiding by mandatory pollution limits could cut 10–15 per cent of GHG emissions by 2015. Promoting non-motorised mobility by improving cycling and pedestrian paths would also aid in reducing emissions.

India has a technical advantage in that it is in the process of building its energy. transport and industrial infrastructure. Therefore. it should invest in energy-efficient technologies helping it to 'leapfrog' carbon-intensive phases of development and move towards an advanced low-carbon economy.

Economic constraints and opportunities

India's economy has accelerated with GDP growth averaging close to 7 per cent per year since 2000; up until 2030 it is projected to average between 5.8 and 6.5 per cent. reflecting improving economic efficiency through liberalisation. foreign direct investment (FDI) and industrialisation. In order to meet its energy demands. India should invest about USD 1.25 trillion in energy infrastructure from 2006 to 2030 (OECD and IEA. 2007). bringing a need for an explicit financing mechanism and thus substantial investment opportunities. Shifting to a low-carbon economy would require a major reorientation of India's energy strategy. It would call for a shift from coal. its most abundant resource. to renewable energy-based and biofuel-based energy systems. A shift to oil and gas would increase India's dependence on imports due to low domestic reserves. According to Prasanna (2009). current subsidies for fossil fuels are acting as a primary barrier to enabling economic viability of these renewable energies.

Energy prices in India are indeed heavily subsidised. Policies should ensure that energy costs reflect the real economic as well as environmental costs of providing them to the consumer. Targeted subsidies should only be provided to help improve the living conditions of the poor.

Renewable energy options often require high initial investments. The Indian government offers investment support through various schemes and tax benefits. Estimates indicate that more than USD 600 million could be yielded per year through the National Clean Energy Fund. The fund. financed by levying a tax of INR 50 (USD 1.1) per tonne of coal. has been created to support the development of renewable energy. India is also host to CDM projects which promote technology transfer from industrialised nations and offset emissions through carbon credits. While Indian companies see CDM projects as very relevant. the extent of CDM implementation may remain low unless the host country is given the right to replicate and innovate in technology gained through transfer. thereby removing the monopoly of investing countries on its price. CDM projects as well as the Electricity Act (2003). which encourages independent private electricity production. have facilitated the setting up of several renewable energy-based electricity plants (CDM India. 2010). Currently renewable resources represent a generating capacity of 14.538 MW (Chandramouli. 2010b).

Institutional constraints and opportunities

The presence of a robust institutional mechanism is critical in India's transition to a low-carbon economy. Although India has undertaken initiatives to anticipate climate change impacts. it typically has difficulty executing its plans promptly and effectively due to pervasive corruption. inefficiency and the lack of accountability in its bureaucracy.

The energy sector in India is split between five different ministries and several government agencies. This often leads to administrative bottlenecks in the implementation of planned and proposed policies. In 2008 the Indian cabinet agreed to bring together the various ministries and agencies involved. The National Development Council is the umbrella organisation in charge of reviewing and approving the Integrated Energy Policy set forth in the Five-Year Plan by the Planning Commission.

India's energy sector has been dominated largely by state-owned companies. This results in controlled and subsidised energy prices. Recent reforms are slowly removing barriers to private participation and are ensuring competitive energy prices that reflect true resource costs in the energy sector. In 1997 the government announced a New Exploration Licensing Policy to provide a more attractive framework for private domestic investment and FDI in oil exploration. This became a success story with the discovery of 424 billion cubic metres of natural gas by Reliance Industries in the Krishna Godavari Basin in 2002. the largest gas discovery in the world that year. The find has relieved shortage of gas in some individual states. Although the government officially abolished the administered pricing mechanism in 2002 for all petroleum products. customers have been paying the true cost of petrol. diesel and kerosene only since 2010 (BBC. 2010). Most states in India provide electricity to farmers for free or near-free rates. On a countrywide basis 28 per cent of electricity is consumed by this segment which has no incentive to improve efficiency or reduce wastage. India has given host-country approval to numerous CDM projects. many of which are being developed by Indian companies. Their expected emissions reductions by 2012 amount to about 260 megatonnes of CO_2 equivalent (CDM India. 2010). Increased cooperation between the government. financial institutions and industry would be very valuable in defining optimal mechanisms for reducing energy consumption and emission levels and in continually evaluating them.

SOCIAL CONSTRAINTS AND OPPORTUNITIES

Home to around 1.1 billion people and with about 27 per cent of the population living below the poverty line and 400 million people without access to electricity. India needs to sustain high economic growth and ensure proper allocation of funds if it is to eradicate poverty and meet its human development goals (Planning Commission. 2006a). With close economic ties to natural resources and climate-sensitive sectors such as agriculture. water and forestry. India seems to be in a tight situation because it needs to continue to develop at a rapid rate in order to serve rural energy needs while striving to make the transition to a lower-carbon economy.

In reality the poor contribute very little towards global carbon emissions as they live lives below subsistence level and essentially use biomass for cooking. thereby saving energy at the cost of human welfare. An increase in energy use to improve the living conditions of the poor is seen as their due right. therefore. even if it increases India's GHG emissions. Introduction of biomass technology for improved burning of rural fuels is already helping lower their carbon footprint further.

It is estimated that land-use change in developing countries could contribute towards global emissions to the extent of 1.6 billion tonnes of carbon. A rapidly growing population and the consequent increase in requirement of land and biomass resources are a cause for concern regarding forests and their ability to ensure carbon sequestration. The Indian Prime Minister has announced a Green India Mission campaign for the afforestation of 6 million hectares. thus covering a total land area of 33 per cent (compared with 23 per cent currently). An initial amount of INR 60 billion (USD 1.3 billion) has been earmarked by the Compensatory Afforestation Management and Planning Authority to commence work. Compared to many other developing countries. India has been commendable in maintaining a relatively high percentage of forests on its territory; for example. over 2.5 million hectares of forests are lost in Brazil every year. However. India lags behind China's achievement of gaining 4 million hectares of forests annually. From 1999 to 2009 the forest cover in India grew by 3.31 million hectares. with an average 0.46 per cent annual increase.

ENERGY HOPES AND FEARS

LOOPHOLES AND BARRIERS

India has pledged to reduce the carbon intensity of its economy. but without absolute limits. arguing that they would unfairly curb its development. It insists that the developed world should take the lead in cutting global carbon emissions. Although overall development and improving the living conditions of the poor are most important. there is a concern that these priorities might become an excuse for a relaxed attitude towards carbon mitigation.

The lack of a comprehensive framework to cover policy formulation. compliance and verification provides numerous loopholes for industry to conduct 'business as usual' in India. For example. in 1988 the Forest Conservation Act of 1980 was amended to stop wood-based industries sourcing raw material from forestlands. leaving them for the needs of the forest-dependent communities.

However. the amendment did not prohibit forestry departments from undertaking plantations. Using this loophole. politicians tried to allow industrial firms access to government forestlands.

Market barriers. ranging from inadequate access to capital. energy subsidies and information asymmetry. inhibit energy efficiency in India. The government needs to remove these by facilitating access to capital through low-interest loans for energy efficiency such as the 5 per cent interest loan available for renewable energy projects from the Indian Renewable Energy Development Agency. It also needs to improve access to information via workshops. courses and help lines aiming to enhance industrial energy efficiency. Assessing a project's contribution towards sustainable development is difficult due to varying emission sources. unreliable data and estimates that can be interpreted in a range of ways. leaving room for manipulation. Thus. determining the baseline for calculating 'additionality' of CDM projects is very difficult. Much literature has suggested that CDM effects on non-Annex I countries are not positive in sustainable development. Two case studies of Indian CDM project proposals show that 'packaging' of information plays a decisive role in 'additionality' assessment by the CDM Executive Board. Despite both above-mentioned projects being clearly non-additional. only one was rejected as the project developer himself praised the project's attractiveness in the absence of the CDM.

POVERTY ALLEVIATION IN A LOWER-CARBON ECONOMY

The impact of carbon emission policies on economic growth and poverty alleviation is crucial for a low-income country like India because the most pressing need is to reduce poverty rather than control carbon emissions. While emissions growth to provide minimum energy requirements to India's poor is inevitable. it is still modest relative to developed countries' emission levels. The additional electrical energy required to provide electricity to India's 450 million poor is less than 8 per cent of the US electricity supply. However. the redistribution of energy from over-consumers to the poor must also play a role. As Haavelmo (1990) puts it: 'Only raising the bottom without lowering the top will not permit sustainability.'

India's poor population is stuck in a vicious circle. Energy and firewood deficits lead to deforestation. and crop residues and dung being diverted from agriculture. which further intensifies land degradation. hunger and poverty. In order to emerge from this vicious circle. innovative strategies such as bio-agricultural production that can be used for carbon sequestration and poverty alleviation are needed. Such synergies between land-use change and poverty alleviation must be found so that participation in carbon sequestration may benefit the poor. Various options such as cleaner fuels. more efficient technology and localised renewable energy projects have begun making a small but positive contribution towards poverty alleviation along with a low-carbon economy. While CDM projects claim the potential of poverty alleviation thanks to supplementation of agricultural income through non-farm employment and improved availability of energy and other infrastructural facilities via investment and technology. nearly all such projects have a business orientation and do not contribute towards rural poverty alleviation to any notable extent.

INDIAN POLICY RESPONSES

Lowering energy intensity through higher efficiency is equivalent to creating a virtual source of untapped domestic energy in India (Planning Commission. 2006a). The National Mission on Enhanced Energy Efficiency is developing polices that include establishing benchmarks of energy consumption for all energy-intensive industries. allowing trade of energy-savings certificates. energy incentives and reduced taxes on energy-efficient appliances. It also calls for energy policies to put greater emphasis on urban waste management and recycling. including power production from waste. to strengthen enforcement of automotive fuel economy standards. to use pricing measures to encourage the purchase of efficient vehicles and to offer incentives for the use of public transportation (National Action Plan on Climate Change. 2008). These policies will be implemented by the Bureau of Energy Efficiency.

The Indian government has also begun moving towards a rational energy pricing policy by removing a variety of energy subsidies. thus permitting energy prices to reflect their economic as well as environmental costs. and only allowing subsidies targeting poverty alleviation. Such a policy. if properly respected. would influence the choice of technology. fuel and energy and result in fair allocation of costs among consumers according to the burden they impose on the system.

While the Integrated Energy Policy covers all sources of energy. the Indian government is considering further means to re-enforce it so as to achieve more rapid and more inclusive growth. Several policy considerations have been highlighted in the National Action Plan on Climate Change. Exploiting non-conventional energy. especially solar power. and developing the thorium cycle for nuclear power offer possibilities for India's energy independence beyond 2050 (Planning Commission. 2006b). In order to enhance the National Solar Mission. policies supporting the establishment of a solar research centre. increased international collaboration on technology development. the strengthening of domestic manufacturing capacity as well as increased government funding and international support are being considered.

SOLAR POWER RULES TO BOOST INDIA'S ENERGY SECURITY

Regional governments are increasingly looking to solar power to solve the problem. An estimated 300 million Indians have no access to electricity. The governments of four Indian states – Tamil Nadu. Gujarat. Rajasthan and Madhya Pradesh – have already put in place policies to support solar power.In January. the government of southern Karnataka too launched a rooftop solar policy. to install 2GW of capacity by 2020. This will allow households and enterprises that generate their own power to sell their excess electricity to the state grid.

Starting this month. citizens and enterprises across New Delhi will also be able to generate their own solar power. This will cut the load on an overburdened national grid while shaving off precious rupees from their own power bills.Delhi Electricity Regulatory Commission (DERC). the power regulatory watchdog. last week announced regulations for the net metering of renewable energy. That will allow stakeholders to supply power to the grid. receive energy credits and adjust the amount against their electricity bills.Malls. hospitals. schools. hotels. government buildings and residents have been generating solar power for private consumption for some time.

The new regulation gives them the right to be connected to the grid. so the best use can be made of their power. If customers generate more than they use. they get energy credits to use in the next billing cycle.Deepak Khokar. a retired official from the department of environment. said: "Solar energy is a cheap and sustainable option for bridging the supply-demand gap in the city. It can empower citizens to become more independent and whenever parity is reached for a consumer segment it can reduce their power tariffs."

AIR POLLUTION

The step will also reduce the city's dependence on coal for power generation. he added. Forests are being cut down to clear the way for coal mining. while burning the fuel causes air pollution. According to World Health Organization data. New Delhi is the world's most polluted city. It has an average of 153 micrograms of small particulates. known as PM 2.5. per cubic metre. As many as 10.000 people a year may die prematurely in Delhi as a result of air pollution.

Delhi also has a history of power shortages. Despite borrowing power from neighboring states. each summer the capital city of Asia's third largest economy grapples with a power crisis.The landscape of power supply is also changing fundamentally: grid power prices continue to rise as the power supply deficit continues to widen.

"Generating stations within Delhi have a capacity of 1.345 MW (55% coal and 45% gas) which leaves Delhi with a shortfall of 4.297 MW from its peak demand of about 5.642 MW." an official at the ministry of power explained.Despite the dire power situation. the Delhi government ditched a rooftop power plan in 2011 as "unfeasible" due to the cost of solar panels. Since then. a sharp drop in the cost of solar power (by as much as 50% in the last two years). has prompted the government to reconsider. A Greenpeace report says Delhi could generate 2GW of solar power by 2020. This could rise to 123GW. more than 20 times peak power demand. if the whole territory were covered in solar panels.

Leadership?

Prime minister Narendra Modi has been an advocate of clean energy projects. He even penned a book on Gujarat's response to climate change.

However Modi's recent actions and words belie his image as an environmental crusader. To the consternation of the environment lobby. he dismissed the science of climate change in a speech to school students on 5 September."Climate has not changed. We have changed...our tolerance and habits have changed. If we change then God has built the system in such a way that it can balance on its own." he said.

Modi is not expected to attend this month's United Nations summit on climate change. signalling tepid support for a global pact to slash greenhouse gas emissions. India's contribution is significant. as the world's third highest emitting country.But whatever Modi's views on climate change. renewables are seen as an important way to boost energy security. Regulatory officials say clean energy sources could generate up to 70% of India's electricity by 2030.

INTEGRATING ENERGY CONCERNS INTO INDIA'S NATIONAL SECURITY STRATEGY

India's prodigious economic growth refuses to let up. While the 2008-09 world financial crisis caused a brief interruption (GDP growth dipped from pre-crisis averages of 9% to less than 7%). it quickly rebounded and now approaches double-digit levels again.

This economic expansion. coupled with India's billion-plus population. has triggered soaring energy demand. By 2030. India is expected to become the world's third-largest energy consumer. Predictably. projections forecast the need for dramatic increases in energy generation in the coming decades. New Delhi's Planning Commission estimates that to maintain 8% GDP growth through 2031-32. India's primary energy supply must be tripled and electricity generation quintupled.

India's indigenous sources of energy are woefully insufficient to meet this demand. As a result. the country is heavily dependent on overseas resources. Presently about two-thirds of oil consumption comes from overseas. with (according to International Energy Agency estimates) the quantum projected to increase to 90% by 2030. (Presently. oil makes up about a third of India's primary energy mix. with the figure expected to drop a few percentage points by 2030.) Also by that year. India is expected to import half of its natural gas. and even a third of its coal – presently the country's chief domestic energy resource. (In 2030. coal and natural gas are expected to comprise a combined 55% of India's energy mix.) Together. this suggests that by 2030. more than 80% of India's energy mix will be dependent. to a significant extent. on foreign importation

Accordingly. India places a premium on its ability to obtain energy assets abroad. To this end. in September 2007 the External Affairs Ministry established an energy security division to coordinate global energy diplomacy efforts (with the goal of concluding energy-related MOUs and bilateral agreements). Today India's energy diplomacy. while modest in comparison to China's. extends across Central Asia. the Middle East. Africa. and Latin America. Diplomatic campaigns smooth the way for the international activities of India's national oil and gas companies (NOGCs). which expend billions of dollars on dozens of assets in about 20 nations.

IMPLICATIONS FOR NATIONAL SECURITY

India's externally oriented energy security strategy holds troubling implications for national security. First. with many of its prized energy assets (and the sea-lanes needed to convey them back home) situated in volatile regions. Indian nationals – from overseas-based NOGC staff to seamen transporting energy supplies – operate under dangerous conditions. The Middle East – convulsed by uprisings and violence in 2011 – houses Indian hydrocarbon blocks from Egypt and Iran to Syria and Yemen. Indian energy trade must navigate the piracy-choked coast of Somalia. And war in Afghanistan and perennial unrest in Pakistan will pose security risks for Indians involved with the envisioned Trans-Afghanistan (TAPI) pipeline. which. if ever constructed. will pass through both of those nations.

Second. India's race for overseas energy resources brings it into close competition with China. The latter. which is already embroiled in a border conflict with India. often angers New Delhi with its aggressive efforts to acquire oil and gas reserves in and around the Indian Ocean Region (IOR). which India regards as its backyard. Some Indians believe that such activities constitute part of a Chinese "string of pearls" strategy. meant to encircle India from East Africa to Burma and the Bay of Bengal. India makes little secret of the fact that its current military modernization is driven by a desire to accelerate efforts to keep up with China's own modernizing trend.

Critically. even the more modest internally oriented elements of India's energy security policies endanger national security. For instance. India is blessed with ample hydropower resources in Kashmir. With economic growth and energy demand soaring. the nation has increased its development of hydro dams along the western rivers of the Indus Basin. This policy enhances energy security but adds to tensions with neighboring Pakistan. where the anti-India militant group Lashkar-e-Taiba (LeT) routinely accuses India of "water theft" and threatens to retaliate with violence. Additionally. one of the rallying cries of the summer 2010 uprising in Jammu and Kashmir revolved around the perception that India's state-owned hydro companies were not allocating sufficient electricity to energy-starved locals.

Meanwhile. sizable quantities of India's coal reserves are located in the central and eastern portions of the country that serve as the bastions of a virulent Maoist insurgency. This has implications for both access and security. On the one hand. it is difficult to extract these reserves. On the other hand. when coal is excavated from these areas. locals are often displaced and living conditions become toxic. In so doing. New Delhi and the nation's powerful mining corporations fan the flames of the insurgency. which India's top leadership repeatedly describes as the country's gravest internal security threat.

The great significance of political instability in India's coal-rich areas cannot be emphasized enough. Coal constitutes the majority resource in India's energy mix (53%). and about 70% of the country's electricity generation occurs in coal-fired power plants. In India. no indigenous energy resource occurs in greater supply than coal (in fact. only two countries produce more coal than India does). If access to coal is jeopardized in India. the country's energy security is immediately imperiled.

INTEGRATING ENERGY INTO NATIONAL SECURITY STRATEGY

With India's energy needs increasing exponentially. and with the volatile regions housing its energy assets – from Maoist-infested Chhattisgarh to strife-torn Libya – demonstrating few signs of stabilizing. implications for India's national security will grow more serious. It is increasingly apparent that India's policymakers and strategists must take account of energy security issues as they craft national security policies. How. then. can this be done?

To be sure. India's government and military have demonstrated an understanding of how energy needs are tied to national security. Back in 2009. Shekhar Dutt. the country's deputy national security adviser. described energy shortages as a future threat. Addressing this challenge constitutes "part of a broad national security plan." he stated. of which Defence is only one part.

Meanwhile. India's navy depicts its modernization efforts as energy security-driven. According to the *Financial Times*. senior naval planners have identified India's "future energy and mineral resources" as a motivation for basing more powerful warships in the Indian Ocean.Such power projection is meant to protect assets deep in the southern Indian Ocean. including faraway Diego Garcia Island – a thousand miles from home. Meanwhile. India expert Juli A. MacDonald has argued (based on discussions with Indian military officers) that the proliferation of Indian naval activities and leadership across the IOR–such as the navy's hosting of the first Indian Ocean Naval Symposium in 2008 – is meant to help "keep the sea-lanes open and safe for energy transport."

The navy. more so than any other branch of India's armed forces. recognizes the links between energy and national security. The official Maritime Doctrine states that disruption of India's Persian Gulf-based oil supplies "could critically affect the country's interests." and that offshore oil and gas facilities are "extremely vulnerable to disruptive attacks." The document lays out strategies for enhancing what the navy describes as "security of energy." or the military means to address energy supply vulnerabilities. These include investments in maritime capacities to protect littoral-area energy infrastructure. and better protection of energy-assets. Accordingly. India places a premium on its ability to obtain energy assets abroad. To this end. in September 2007 the External Affairs Ministry established an energy security division to coordinate global energy diplomacy efforts (with the goal of concluding energy-related MOUs and bilateral agreements). Today India's energy diplomacy. while modest in comparison to China's. extends across Central Asia. the Middle East. Africa. and Latin America. Diplomatic campaigns smooth the way for the international activities of India's national oil and gas companies (NOGCs). which expend billions of dollars on dozens of assets in about 20 nations.

CHALLENGES

Such developments are welcome. yet insufficient. Consider that even as India's navy seeks to boost its power projection capacities (it plans to add 100 new warships over the next decade). it still lags far behind China's forces. which have three times the number of combat vessels and five times the personnel. India also lags behind China in the overseas energy acquisitions race (this is due in part to non-military factors such as China's longer time spent in the acquisitions business and to the onerous Indian government regulation of energy diplomacy and deal-making). Delhi's unease about Beijing's IOR-based energy activities is deepened whenever it is outbid as was recently the case with a natural gas deal with Burma. Complicating matters further is India's notoriously inefficient Defence procurement and modernization process. which is at best bureaucratic and at worst corrupt.

Another. more fundamental. challenge to India's efforts to enshrine energy security imperatives in national security planning is what some describe as a lack of strategic thought. Arun Prakash. a former Naval Chief of Staff. has written that Indian politicians and statesmen simply do not demonstrate a commitment to long-term planning and strategic foresight. "Every military operation since independence." he notes. "has been guided more by political rhetoric than strategic direction." One indication of this lack of strategic thinking is the fact that India's navy – despite its self-defined prime role in protecting energy assets – has traditionally been the least well-resourced of the three military branches. a consequence of what US Naval War College professor Andrew Winner labels India's "sea blindness." While naval budgets have increased each year for much of the last decade. the same is true for the army and air force. The difficulties in furthering the integration of energy concerns into security planning are thrown into sharp relief by a study published by Booz Allen Hamilton (BAH) in 2007 ["Energy Futures in Asia: Perspectives on India's Energy Security Strategy and Policies." Prepared by Bethany A. Danyluk. Juli A. MacDonald. and Ryan Tuggle. Prepared for Director. Net Assessment. Office of the Secretary of Defence]. The report depicts Indian military officers as very wary about involving themselves in energy matters. The armed forces surveyed for the report assert that energy matters are essentially a commercial issue. They refuse to commit to interventions if Indian energy assets abroad are imperiled. contending that the nations hosting these assets are expected to provide security. Military officers demonstrate little concern about energy insecurity sparking conflict (with the exception of some scenarios involving India-China competition). and argue that in past conflicts with Pakistan. energy supplies were never disrupted – intimating. falsely. that such disruptions remain unlikely in the present day.

Recommendations

The BAH report acknowledges that such views are beginning to evolve. with some in the military (particularly in the navy and air force) speaking of the need to create more strategic reach and power projection. Such doctrinal evolutions. it concludes. will facilitate India's "ability and willingness" to carry out energy security-related operations.

In the few years since the report was released. India's energy-linked security vulnerabilities have been sharply exposed. The LeT's sea-based assault on Mumbai in 2008 demonstrates the ability of militants to penetrate India's shores – and hence its offshore energy infrastructure. Rumors in the spring of 2011 about militants' infiltration of the Pakistani navy will only deepen the perception that India's shores are vulnerable to attack. Meanwhile. the worsening Maoist insurgency – the nearly 1200 casualties last year represent the most killed in any year since the rebellion began in the 1960s – reveals the constraints India faces in exploiting its most heavily consumed indigenous energy resource. According to media reports. Maoist violence now afflicts 40% of India's top-50 mineral-rich districts.

The time is ripe to shift from mouthing platitudes about energy-national security links to implementing actual policies that solidify this nexus. What are some possible steps Towards consummating this shift?

ENHANCE COORDINATION AT HOME AND ABROAD

The government and military will struggle to incorporate energy issues into national security planning so long as energy policies remain as poorly coordinated as they are today. India does not have an overarching energy ministry. and as a result a number of different ministries (Petroleum and Natural Gas. Coal. Power. Renewable Energy. and External Affairs) perform redundant energy-related duties. One improvement would be to reduce duplication between the MEA's energy security division and the Petroleum and Natural Gas Ministry's international cooperation division (according to Indian energy specialist Shebonti Ray Dadwal. the latter cell even has a senior MEA officer posted to it).

With India's military not presently in a position to secure the nation's far-flung energy assets. New Delhi must also better coordinate security-related arrangements with the nations housing these assets. Specifically. Indian energy firms and the government should elicit guarantees from host nations that plans are in place to protect both the holdings and the Indian personnel managing them. While the armed forces have generally expressed satisfaction with the security provided by the. the unrest unfolding in the Middle East over the last few months – home to about two-thirds of India's oil imports – starkly illustrates the need to revisit and reexamine the security plans of any existing arrangements.

STRENGTHEN CAPACITY FROM NAVAL RESOURCES TO STRATEGIC OIL RESERVES

India needs to enlarge the navy's resources. As the nation enhances its power projection capacities to better enable it to protect its energy holdings (both offshore and overseas). the navy will remain on the front lines. The navy has been pushing the army and air force to expand their conception of security from one of sub continental conflict to one of global conflict (a broader framework that encompasses energy security). and these two branches readily acknowledge that they view the navy as an agent of change.

Furthermore. with the exception of indigenous coal reserves in Maoist bastions. India's energy security threats are largely sea-based. India's sea-based energy assets have increased significantly in recent years. and while much of this expansion has occurred abroad (thanks to India's decision to geographically diversify its source of supplies). it is also happening closer to home. The country has constructed over 3.000 kilometers of pipeline to facilitate the flow of oil and gas from offshore platforms to onshore terminals. Additionally. to facilitate increasing crude imports. India seeks to become a refining hub. and refining capacity has already tripled since 1998. While it is unrealistic that the naval budget will leap ahead that of the air force. much less of the army. it is undeniable that the navy needs more resources to ensure the security of the country's growing array of sea-based energy assets.

India should also boost the capacities of its strategic reserves for civilian use in the event of war or other supply interruptions (India's military has a separate reserve to meet war-fighting needs). According to Dadwal. India's strategic reserves are expected to have. at most. a capacity of 15 metric tons – insufficient for energy security. The*Financial Times* calculates that this reserve. expected to be operational by the end of 2012. will be able to hold little more than two weeks' worth of imports. India's Integrated Energy Policy. a government assessment released in 2006 (and not updated since then). argues that because "today's local wars are not likely to last beyond a few weeks." buffer stocks need not be large. Such an observation. however. ignores the fact that most of today's conflicts are driven by non-state actors and exemplified by long. grinding insurgencies or episodic periods of violence. Reserves must be equipped to weather the long. drawn-out conflicts that imperil international security (and particularly the Subcontinent) today. While one cannot expect India to strive for the whopping 100 days' worth of imports envisioned by China's strategic reserve. it should aim for a reserve capacity approaching three months (a level maintained by many nations).

ENABLING THE ENERGY SECURITY-PEACE NEXUS

Above all. India's national security planning must make more robust efforts Towards regional peace. The connection between peace and security may be clear; less so is the link between peace and energy. In essence. stability and strong ties with its neighbors can dramatically enhance India's energy security. An obvious example. albeit one that extends beyond regional matters. is relations with the United States. For much of the Cold War. US-India relations were poor. However. in the post-Cold War era. the bilateral relationship strengthened to the point that the two governments were able to conclude a landmark civil nuclear agreement. The US Energy Information Agency projects that with the new inflow of nuclear energy and technology into India. the nation's nuclear power generation will increase at an average annual rate of nearly 10% until 2035. To be sure. however. even with such a ramp-up in generation. nuclear energy will remain a relatively modest component of India's energy mix; it is projected to account for small percentages of India's energy supply even in 2030 (anywhere from 2% to 6%. depending on the estimate). Closer to home. warmer regional ties would enable forward movement on pipelines. a critical means of delivering natural gas resources to India without fear of sea-based threats. Granted. some areas envisioned as part of pipeline projects (such as the eastern portions of Afghanistan figuring in the TAPI pipeline) are convulsed by endemically driven instability that would not magically disappear if peace were to break out across South Asia. Yet India-Pakistan rapprochement. for example. would remove one of the major impediments to constructing the TAPI.

Perhaps most beneficial to India's energy security would be improved ties with Beijing (a goal that. despite vocal opposition from hardliners and hawks in the Indian security establishment. is fervently pursued by New Delhi's civilian leadership). With more cordial Sino-Indian ties. China's forays into the Indian

Ocean Region would likely be more freely accepted in India as a natural outgrowth of China's immense economic and energy needs. India could then proceed with its own energy-oriented activities in the IOR (and. by extension. in Southeast Asia) without fear of provoking Beijing's anger. In other words. instead of responding to a Chinese "string of pearls" strategy with a retaliatory "string of diamonds" effort (rhetoric used in today's highly charged debates about Sino-Indian energy competition). India would simply carry out its own energy diplomacy alongside that of China.

Most critically. such energy cooperation would boost opportunities to bid jointly for contracts abroad. India has actually teamed up with China on certain occasions previously. though such arrangements have been rare more recently. Joint bids would be a particular boon for India. given that the nation so often loses out to its Chinese competitor.

STRENGTHENING ENERGY SECURITY AND NATIONAL SECURITY THROUGH DEMAND-SIDE MANAGEMENT

Better inter-agency and international coordination. enhanced naval and reserves capacity. and greater efforts Towards regional peace can all bring positive outcomes for both energy and national security. Admittedly. however. they do little to lessen India's dependence on overseas hydrocarbons – an addiction that fuels the very insecurity these three recommendations are meant to reduce. Therefore. New Delhi's official policy of energy resource diversification –particularly in terms of focusing on a broader array of indigenous supplies – is a welcome one. In the last few years. 15 trillion cubic feet of natural gas deposits have been discovered in the Bay of Bengal off Andhra Pradesh state. and ample oil reserves unearthed in the state of Rajasthan.

Such finds have prompted the Indian energy giant Reliance to promise that it will increase indigenous oil and gas output by 40%. Indeed. while gas currently constitutes only 9% of India's primary energy mix. Reliance has taken major steps to ensure that the fruits of the Bay of Bengal discovery are exploited to the fullest. Soon after the gas deposits were found. the firm built a pipeline of nearly 50 diameters. with production capacity of nearly 3 billion cubic feet per day. This should prove advantageous for India's energy security. given that natural gas consumption in India has risen faster than any other fuel in recent years (demand has grown at a 6.5% rate over the last decade). Additionally. the power generation. fertilizer. and petrochemical production industries are all moving Towards natural gas.

The gas discovery may prove to be more of a boon for energy security than the oil one. Even with the oil found in Rajasthan. India houses less than 0.5% of the world's proven reserves of crude oil. Not surprisingly. a significant majority of India's oil consumption (two-thirds) originates from abroad. Furthermore. oil constitutes a relatively small portion of electricity generation in India. Meanwhile. efforts to exploit local renewable electricity sources are coming along well. Increases in solar and wind power investment have averaged 10% per year. while India's wind power programme is already the world's fifth largest. Wind now constitutes about 14.000 MW of electricity capacity. with solar now expected to approach 20.000 MW by 2020. Together. they represent a modest share of India's total electricity capacity (presently about 173.000 MW). yet represent a considerable increase from years past.

However. despite such achievements. the sheer volume of India's energy demand ensures that the nation will remain dependent on overseas energy into the foreseeable future. To blunt the impact of supply shocks on energy security and national security. India should promote better energy demand-side management. In other words. India should respond to energy demand by managing existing resources more judiciously – and not simply by generating new supply.There are some hopeful signs on this front. The government has already announced its intent to root out electricity theft and poor energy billing practices – problems that the government's Planning Commission estimates cost distribution companies more than $6 billion per year. The government also needs to take more decisive action against energy wastage; this can be done with more robust regimes of energy infrastructure maintenance that minimize the possibility of leakage and other inefficiencies.

However. from a national security standpoint (and particularly from the vantage of internal security). energy equity measures are important as well – and sorely lacking today. Some of India's top security threats emerge from grievances about unjust exploitation of local energy resources. The Maoists. for example. seize on the sentiments of locals unhappy about how local coal reserves are mined by outsiders and promptly trucked away. And in J&K. locals resent how hydro firms tied to New Delhi take away their electricity. The government and private energy firms alike must ensure that local (and often impoverished) communities are guaranteed a proper supply of energy.

To this end. last year Indian legislators attempted in vain to pass a bill that would have allocated 26% of mining company profits to local populations. This unsuccessful attempt to promote greater energy resource equity must not dissuade policymakers from undertaking similar efforts in the future. More equitable energy use can help calm volatile populations and weaken insurgencies. thereby strengthening national security. This goes to show that bringing energy issues into the national security fold is not only a matter of enhancing the navy's capacities to protect offshore energy holdings. or of promoting peace with neighbors to yield more energy cooperation. It is also a basic matter of governance: ensuring that those in need of energy resources are provided with them. in order to head off any unrest and violence that could ensue if such resources remain elusive.

7

Energy and Power System

Indian economy has reached to historical important point (turning point) of 9% GDP in 2007-08. Robust agricultural sector has pushed the GDP to 9% even when the manufacturing sector fails to live up the expectations of higher growth. The economy has boomed at 9 per cent in 2007-08. more than 8.7% what was estimated. The time period from 2003-04 to 2007-08 has seen a 5 progressive years in the India's economy history with a 8.8% annual average GDP growth rate. The 2007-08 9% GDP has put India into the group of one of the fastest growing major economy after China. It is the 3rd year in a row. in which nation's GDP has touched the mark of 9% or above India. an emerging economy. has witnessed unprecedented levels of economic expansion. along with countries like China. Russia.

Mexico and Brazil. India. being a cost effective and labour intensive economy. has benefited immensely from outsourcing of work from developed countries. and a strong manufacturing and export oriented industrial framework. With the economic pace picking up. global commodity prices have staged a comeback from their lows and global trade has also seen healthy growth over the last two years. The pace of growth has been recorded fast as compare to what was expected by market. The government had earlier estimated annual growth of 8.7 percent for the whole of 2007-08.

The government exuded confidencc that thc cconomy will achieve the same or more GDP growth in 2008 year also. The industrial market is considered it as a good sign from trading point of view. as year 2007 witnessed high turbulence in stock exchange and financial markets. Energy intensity in India had a decreasing trend in 1990-2007. It means that energy efficiency in economy of India has increased. Then it is a necessary which India has a programme to ensure energy for all of sectors. Energy security has an important role in future energy consumption in India. According to the Indian government. 30 percent of India's total energy needs are met through imports. The combination of rising oil consumption and relatively flat production has left India increasingly dependent on imports to meet its petroleum demand. In 2006. India was the seventh largest net importer of oil in the world. With 2007 net imports of 1.8

million bbl/d. India is currently dependent on imports for 68 percent of its oil consumption. The EIA expects India to become the fourth largest net importer of oil in the world by 2025. behind the United States. China. and Japan. The government of India's largest crude oil import partner is Saudi Arabia. followed by Iran. Nearly three-fourths of India's crude oil imports come from the Middle East. The Indian government expects this geographical dependence to rise in light of limited prospects for domestic production.

ROLES AND FUNCTIONS OF THE POWER AND ENERGY DIVISION

- Servicing the Energy coordination Committee under the Chairmanship of Prime Minister;
- Evolving an integrated energy policy covering commercial and non-commercial sources of energy;
- Proposing policies and institutions for the management of supply and demand in different sub-sectors of the energy sector. assessing the availability of different forms of energy and suggesting appropriate arrangements to meet the country's energy needs keeping in view the need to tap all available technology options. improve energy efficiency and conserve energy to lower energy intensity and thereby deliver a suitable growth trajectory;
- Analysing issues pertaining to the energy security of the country;
- Suggesting policies to meet lifeline requirements of poorer households and vulnerable households;
- Examining Plan proposals and finalisation of scheme- wise outlays in respect of Central Ministries and PSU's covering the Energy sector. These include the ministries of Power. Coal. Petroleum and Natural Gas and New and Renewable Energy Sources. the department of Atomic Energy and PSUs under their respective administrative control;
- Examining all proposals related to Policy. Regulation. CoS/ GoM/ Cabinet Notes and Acts mooted by various ministries covering the energy sector;
- Examining/ suggesting policy and regulatory frameworks that facilitate competition and private sector participation in the Energy Sector. Restructuring of PSUs in the sector. need for reducing the dominance of the Government through disinvestment;
- Examining technical. financial and economic viability of investment projects in the energy sector and their appraisal.
- Crafting. evaluating and monitoring key initiatives such as Rajiv Gandhi Grameen Vidyutikaran Yojana (RGGY). Bharat Nirman. Accelerated Power Development and Restructuring Programme (APDRP). Remote Village Electrification and Village Energy Security;

- Preparing Annual and Five year plans for the Energy Sector. Monitoring and appraisal of Plan programmes and schemes of respective ministries;
- Reviewing annual financial performance of State power utilities;
- Evaluating strategies and policies for promotion of emerging issues in all energy sub-sectors such as for Clean Coal Technologies. In-situ Coal Gasification. extraction of Coal Bed Methane. Coal Liquefaction. Carbon Capture and Sequestration. Low Carbon Growth. LNG import. transmission pipelines. New Exploration Licensing Policy (NELP) etc.
- Examining and suggesting policies related to pricing of fuels.
- Promoting growth of industries in the energy in the areas from exploration for natural resources. exploitation. refining and product processing. transportation including pipelines.
- Promoting energy efficiency through various programmes including education. demand side management. infusing commercially or near commercial technologies. developing new technologies etc.
- Reviewing progress of R and D in the Energy Sector. Managing the National Energy Fund for R and D.

ENERGY POLICY

The importance of Planning Commission's role in energy policy arises from the need for an integrated energy policy because the responsibility for different energy sources is distributed over a number of different Ministries. *e.g.* Petroleum. Coal. Power. Water Resources (in the case of hydroelectricity). Atomic Energy and New and Renewable Energy. Several other Ministries are also involved in determining policies which affect energy demand (Transport. Urban Development. Industry. Steel. etc.) and the Finance Ministry determines tax rates for different fuels. Policies applicable to different energy sources need to be consistent with each other and the overall framework for energy must be consistent with achieving the objective of inclusive growth. In many areas policies relevant for energy are in the hands of State government *e.g.* urban transport. city planning. building codes. etc. and these policies also need to be made consistent with the overall energy policy. Guiding principles of an Integrated Energy Policy are as follows:

Energy markets should be competitive wherever possible for economic efficiency and for promoting optimal investment in energy. However. competitive markets alone will not ensure efficiency in this area because of negative environmental externalities associated with some fuels. potential supply risks and also the scope for exploitation of temporary shortages. These problems can only be addressed through appropriate fiscal policies to take care of externalities and independent regulation to take care of anti-competitive market Behaviour. Given the need to expand supplies of energy public sector investment in energy must be supplemented by private investors. The removal of distortions and impediments that discourage investment in expanding domestic energy capacity is vital. as is the maintenance of an investor friendly environment for energy development.

In general. both the tax structure and regulatory philosophy applied in each energy sector should be consistent with the overall energy policy should provide a level playing field to all players whether public or private. Taxes should be neutral across energy sources except where differentials in taxation across energy sources are specifically intended to counter differential externalities. such as differences in pollution.

Subsidies are relevant but they must be transparent and targeted. Consideration should be given to alternative means of achieving the social objectives sought to be achieved by energy subsidies through different methods. including direct transfers to eligible households. The most efficient method of schemes and the objective should be chosen.

Energy-efficiency is extremely important and can be promoted by setting appropriate prices and this is particularly important where energy prices are rising. However. appropriate prices by themselves may not suffice and non-price incentives/disincentives are therefore also required. This includes standards of energy efficiency that are forward looking. *i.e.* anticipate future price changes or pollution penalties. These standards should be determined on the basis of rational considerations and must be set in an expanding range of applications. with continuous dynamic adjustment of these standards. The standards should also be effectively enforced. There is scope to use both. mandatory and voluntary standards. the latter being reinforced by public opinion combined with appropriate tax incentives.

Public Sector Undertakings operating in the energy sector must operate with autonomy and also full accountability to ensure incentives for adequate investment through their own resources and improvements in efficiency in energy production and distribution.

ELASTICITY OF ENERGY DEMAND

Contrary to other developed and developing countries. total primary commercial energy requirement in India has been falling with respect to the growth in GDP largely because higher energy prices have led to its efficient use. The elasticity for per capita primary commercial energy supply with respect to per capita GDP (*i.e.* percent increase in per capita energy consumption for one percent increase in per capita GDP) estimated from the time series data of India over 1990-91 to 2003-04 comes to 0.82 which is significantly lower than 1.08 estimated for the period since 1980-81. Similarly the elasticity for per capita electricity generation is only 1.06 for the period from 1990-91 to 2003-04 compared to 1.30 for the period since 1980-81. However. the energy elasticity of GDP growth in India may not fall as much in the future as rising income levels will foster life style changes that are more energy intense.

Comparing India's energy elasticity with other countries. using cross-country regression based on data of 2003. the elasticity for total primary energy supply (TPES) comes to 0.83 for all countries and to 0.79 for countries with a purchasing power parity (PPP) GDP between $2000 and $8000 (India's GDP in PPP terms based on 2000 dollars was $2732 in 2003 and by 2031-32 might reach the upper end of the range). India's energy elasticity for commercial energy is comparable to the elasticity estimates for TPES using cross country data. The elasticity for electricity consumption comes to 1.24 for all countries and to 1.25 for PPP adjusted GDP per capita range of $2000 to $8000. India's elasticity for electricity generation is comparable to that of countries with per capita GDP exceeding $8000 in PPP terms. Importantly. the trend of falling elasticity with rising income levels is demonstrated even by cross country data.

India 's primary energy use is projected to expand massively to deliver a sustained GDP growth rate of 9% through 2031-32 even after allowing for substantial reduction in energy intensity. In order to fuel this on sustained basis. the growth of around 5.8% per year in primary energy supply including gathered non-commercial such as wood and dung of would be required. Commercial energy supply would need to grow at about 6.8% per annum as it will replace non-commercial energy. but this too involves a reduction of around 20% in energy use per unit of GDP over a period of ten years. Requirement of India's dominant fuel Coal including Lignite will expand from around 500 million tonne in 2006-07 to over 2.5 billion tones per annum based on the quality of available domestic coal over a period of 25 years. The primary energy use by 2031-32 will increase by 4 to 5 times and Power generation capacity would increase six-folds from the 2006-07 level of around 1.60.000 MW inclusive of all captive plants.

Putting India's likely energy demand in 2031-32 in a global perspective. one sees that China's current energy consumption is 1100 1200 Mtoe and USA's current consumption is 2400-2500 Mtoe. In comparison. India consumed about 421 Mtoe of commercial energy in 2007-08. With a projected population of just under 1.47 billion in 2031-32. India's per capita energy consumption will be marginally above China's current per capita consumption or be about one seventh of the current US per capita consumption. What this means is that India on per capita basis. currently consumes under 6% of what the US consumes and under 41% of what China consumes and will. by 2031-32. consume just under 15% of current US consumption levels and equal China's current per capita consumption. More importantly. India's per capita energy consumption that is less than 27% of 2003-04 level of global average energy consumption shall in 2031-32 also remain just about 74% of the current global average.

SUPPLY SCENARIO AND ENERGY MIX

India 's energy basket has a mix of all the resources available including renewables. The choice before the country in reference to pursuing for different sources of energy is not choosing among the available ones but to develop them all and to seek what else? The dominance of coal in the energy mix is likely to continue in foreseeable future.

Primary Energy Consumption Mix in 2007-08

Energy Type	Units	in Original Units	in Mtoe	per cent share in Primary Commercial Energy	per cent share in Total Primary Energy Consumption
Coal	Mt	501.52	215.48	53.54	39.50
Lignite	Mt	34.65	9.71		
Oil	Mt	139.73	139.73	33.22	24.51
Natural Gas	BCM	32.27	29.07	9.34	6.89
LNG	Mt	8.24	10.21		
Nuclear Power	MkWh	16777	4.38	1.04	0.77
Hydro Power	MkWh	128702	11.07	2.63	1.94
Wind Power	MkWh	11410	0.98	0.23	0.17
Primary Commercial Energy	Mtoe	–	420.62	100.00	73.78
Non-Commercial Energy	Mtoe	–	149.50	–	26.22
Total Primary Energy consumption	Mtoe	–	570.12	–	100.00

Energy Equivalence

The energy labeled as 'final energy' such as electricity. petrol. gas. coal. firewood. etc. is obtained from the sources available in nature. labeled as 'primary energy'. and includes hydrocarbons (coals. oil. and natural gas). fissile or fertile elements primarily uranium. the kinetic energy of natural elements (wind. water. etc.). and the electromagnetic rays of the sun and the natural heat of the Earth (geothermal energy). As per convention. final energy consumption is generally expressed as weights of fuels burnt. or from kWh consumed if it is electricity. Each fuel. while burning. produces certain amount of energy in the form of heat that can be measured in standard units such as kilocalories or Joules. Fuels are compared using their calorie content with that of oil in tonnes or million tonnes of oil equivalent (Mtoe). One tonne of oil is worth 42 billion Joules or 10 billion calories whereas one tonne of Indian thermal coal has 4.1 billion calories. Thus 1 Mt of Indian thermal coal is 0.41 Mtoe.

Electrical energy measured in kWh is also converted in to the thermal energy kcal or kJ using the definition and finally expressed as Mtoe (1 billion kWh = 0.86 billion calorie or 0.086 Mtoe). Taking the thermal efficiency of the power plant and other losses in the system. the equivalence between electricity and fossil fuels would be 1billion kWh = 0.28 Mtoe (in case of coal-fired boilers) and 0.261 Mtoe (in case of nuclear electricity). 1 billion kWh generated from hydroelectricity or wind power. however. are considered as equivalent to 0.086 Mtoe since there is no intermediate stage of heat production while using these primary energies. It is possible to argue that the efficiency of thermal power plant should be used to convert hydroelectricity and wind power also. In this case. 1 billion kWh of hydroelectricity would be equivalent to 0.28 Mtoe. This has an important bearing when one considers how much of energy is renewable. Thus in 2007- 08. renewable energy was 2.86% or 8.76% of India's total primary commercial energy depending on the conversion factor used.

POWER SECTOR PERFORMANCE

Rapid growth of the economy places a heavy demand on electric power. Reforms in the power sector. for making it efficient and more competitive. have been under way for several years and while there has been some progress. shortage of power and lack of access continues to be a major constraint on economic growth. Average peak shortages excluding scheduled load shedding was estimated at 12% and average energy shortages at 11 per cent in 2008-09. The persistent shortages of electricity both for peak power and energy indicate the need for improving performance of the power sector in the country. Power shortages are an indication of insufficient generating capacity and inadequate transmission and distribution networks. To a great extent this is the outcome of poor financial health of the State Electricity Utilities having high levels of Aggregate Technical and Commercial (AT and C) losses. AT and C losses of most of the State Power Utilities (SPUs) are currently high at above 35 per cent. This has made them financially sick and unable to invest adequately in additional generating capacity. For the same reason. these utilities have had only limited success in attracting private investors to set up power plants.

Accelerated Power Development and Restructuring Programme (APDRP) was promoted in the year 2003 with the mission of bringing down Accumulated Technical and Commercial (AT and C) losses up to 15% in over five years period but the actual performance in last seven years has not come anywhere close to the targeted level. The scope for further tariff increase is limited since tariffs for paying customers are already among the highest in the world and it may make sense for them to opt out for captive generation. It may be noted that the reported AT and C loss is an underestimate as SEBs' accounts conceal more than they reveal. There are several incidences of unaccounted ghost billing. manipulated consumer mix and recording of sales accrual and expenditure on cash basis etc.

Viability of State Utilities Not Improving

	2001–02 (Actual)	2002–03 (Actual	2003–04 (Actual)	2004–05 (Actual)	2005–06 (Actual)	2006–07 (Actual)	2007-08 (Actual)	2008-09 (Prov.)
Energy sold/ available. (in per cent)		66.02	67.46	67.47	68.75	69.58	71.35	72.42

74.55								
Revenue from sale of electricity	68135	76640	85942	91738	101366	117267	123423	154398
Cost of elec tricity sold	98541	102247	110553	118975	129110	153036	173886	204800
Loss on sale of electricity	30407	25607	24611	27237	27743	35768	41462	50402
Average cost of supply (paise/kWh)	374.57	351.72 (-6.10%)	353.80 (-5.54%)	357.35 (-4.60%)	367.62 (-2.03%)	392.17 (4.07%)	404.66 (8.03%)	436.09 (16.42%)
Average tariff (paise/kWh)	258.99	263.63 (1.79%)	275.04 (6.20%)	275.55 (6.39%)	288.63 (11.44%)	300.51 (16.03%)	308.17 (18.99%)	328.77 (26.94%)
Gap between the cost of supply and tariff (paise)	115.58	88.09	78.76	81.80	79.00	91.66	96.49	107.32

Notes:

Financial Performance of 20 major states excluding Delhi and Orissa—as reported.

Figure in brackets are growth rates over 2001–02.

Approved tariffs hikes exceed average tariff increases estimated above.

Generating Capacity addition during the Tenth Plan (2002-2007) and Anticipated generating capacity by the end of the Eleventh Plan (2007-2012) (in MW)

	Hydro	Thermal	Nuclear	Wind and Renewables	Total
Installed capacity as on 31 March 2002	26269	74429	2720	1628	105046
Addition during Tenth Plan	7886	12114	1080	6132	27212
Installed capacity as on 31 March 2007	34654	86015	3900	7760	132329
Proposed Addition during Eleventh Plan	15627	59693	3380	14000	92700
Total capacity anticipated as on 31 March 2012	50281	145708	7280	21760	225029

INDIA'S EMISSION EFFICIENCY

Fossil fuels are made up of hydrogen and carbon. When fossil fuels are burned. the carbon combines with oxygen to yield carbon dioxide. The amount of carbon dioxide produced depends on the carbon content of the fuel; for example. for each unit of energy used. natural gas emits about half and petroleum fuels about three-quarters of the carbon dioxide by coal. The carbon emission factor of a fuel simply tells us how much carbon will be released per unit energy used.

India is a large. fast growing economy with a very low consumption of energy but with a significant share of coal in its primary energy mix. CO_2 emissions from consumption of fossil fuels constitute more than half (~54% in 2000) of total GHG emissions in India. India's CO_2 emissions from fossil fuel combustion in the year 2004 were estimated at about 1.1 billion tonne. The CO_2 emissions will continue to grow for some time. because there is a need to increase the currently low per capita levels of energy use to support growth.

reach the Millennium Development Goals and eventually provide modern living standards to all her citizens.Most of the available projections undertaken by reputed independent international organizations indicate that India's CO_2 intensity per unit of GDP is likely to continue to decline through 2030-2050. India is a relatively low carbon economy by global comparison by two measures. CO_2 emissions per capita and CO_2 emissions per unit of GDP in PPP terms.

Energy Units. Calorific Values of various Fuels and Terminologies:

Unit	Energy Units Equivalence in Joules	Other equivalence
Joule		
Electron Volt	1.0622 x10 -19	
Erg (erg)	10 -7	
Calorie (cal)	4.187	
British Thermal Unit (BTU)	1.055 x 10 3	
Kilo calorie (K cal)	4.1868 x 10 3	
Mega Joule (MJ)	10 6	238.85 k cal
Kilo Watt Hour (kWh)	3.6 x 10 6	3.6 MJ or 1 Unit or 860 k cal
Therm	1.055 x 10 8	10 5 BTU
Giga Joule (GJ)	10 9	278 kWh
Million BTU (MMBTU)	1.055 x 10 9	
Terajoule (TJ)	10 15	
Exajoule (EJ)	10 18	
Quad (Quadrillion BTU)	1.055 x 10 18	~172 million barrels of Oil equivalent
Terawatt-year (TWyr)	3.1536 x 10 19	8760 Billion Units

Calorific Value of Various Fuels

Fuel	Unit	Calorific Value in Million tonnes of Oil equivalent (Mtoe)
LNG	Mt	1.23
LP	Mt	1.13
Motor Spirit (MS)	Mt	1.10
Kerosene	Mt	1.064
Oil (crude)	Mt	1.00
Diesel (HSD)	Mt	0.95
Furnace Oil	Mt	0.904
Natural gas	Bm 3	0.90
Charcoal	Mt	0.693
Soft coke	Mt	0.6292
Biogas	Bm 3	0.4713
Firewood	Mt	0.45
Indian Thermal Coal	Mt	0.41
Coal gas	Bm 3	0.4004
Indian Lignite	Mt	0.2865
Nuclear Electricity	BkWh	0.261
Cow-dung Cakes	Mt	0.21
Electricity	BkWh	0.086
Hydro Electricity	BkWh	0.086
Wind Electricity	BkWh	0.086

THE ECONOMICS OF NUCLEAR POWER

Assessing the relative costs of new generating plants utilising different technologies is a complex matter and the results depend crucially on location. Coal is. and will probably remain. economically attractive in countries such as China. the USA and Australia with abundant and accessible domestic coal resources as long as carbon emissions are cost-free. Gas is also competitive for base-load power in many places. particularly using combined-cycle plants. though rising gas prices have removed much of the advantage.

Nuclear power plants are expensive to build but relatively cheap to run. In many places. nuclear energy is competitive with fossil fuels as a means of electricity generation. Waste disposal and decommissioning costs are included in the operating costs. If the social. health and environmental costs of fossil fuels are also taken into account. the economics of nuclear power are outstanding.

ASSESSING THE COSTS OF NUCLEAR POWER

The economics of nuclear power involves consideration of several aspects:

Capital costs. which include the cost of site preparation. construction. manufacture. commissioning and financing a nuclear power plant. Building a large-scale nuclear reactor takes thousands of workers. huge amounts of steel and concrete. thousands of components. and several systems to provide electricity. cooling. ventilation. information. control and communication. To compare different power generation technologies the capital costs must be expressed in terms of the generating capacity of the plant (for example as dollars per kilowatt). Capital costs may be calculated with the financing costs included or excluded. If financing costs are included then the capital costs change in proportion to the length of time it takes to build and commission the plant and with the interest rate or mode of financing employed. It is normally termed the 'investment cost'. If the financing costs are excluded from the calculation the capital costs is called the 'overnight cost'. because it imagines that the plant appeared fully built overnight.

Plant operating costs. which include the costs of fuel. operation and maintenance (O&M). and a provision for funding the costs of decommissioning the plant and treating and disposing of used fuel and wastes. Operating costs may be divided into 'fixed costs' that are incurred whether or not the plant is generating electricity and 'variable costs'. which vary in relation to the output. Normally these costs are expressed relative to a unit of electricity (for example. cents per kilowatt-hour) to allow a consistent comparison with other energy technologies. To calculate the operating cost of a plant over its whole life (including the costs of decommissioning and used fuel and waste management). we must estimate the 'levelised' cost at present value. It represents the price that the electricity must fetch if the project is to break even (after taking account of the opportunity cost of capital through the application of a discount rate). External costs to society from the operation. which in the case of a nuclear power is usually assumed to be zero. but could include the costs of dealing with a serious accident that are beyond the insurance limit and in practice need to be picked up by the government. The regulations that control nuclear power typically require the plant operator to make a provision for disposing of any waste. thus these costs are 'internalised' (and are not external). Electricity generation from fossil fuels is not regulated in the same way. and therefore the operators of such thermal power plants do not yet internalise the costs of greenhouse gas emission or of other gases and particulates released into the atmosphere. Including these external costs in the calculation gives nuclear power a significant advantage over fossil fuelled electricity generation.

Considering these costs in turn. with information from numerous studies:

CAPITAL COST

Construction costs comprise several things: the bare plant cost (usually identified as engineering-procurement-construction – EPC – cost). the owner's costs (land. cooling infrastructure. administration and associated buildings. site works. switchyards. project management. licences. etc.). cost escalation and inflation. Owner's costs may include some transmission infrastructure. Recent studies have shown an increase in the capital cost of building both conventional and nuclear power plants.

The term "overnight capital cost" is often used. meaning EPC plus owners' costs and excluding financing. escalation due to increased material and labour costs. and inflation. Construction cost – sometimes called 'all-in cost' – adds to overnight cost any escalation and interest during construction and up to the start of construction. It is expressed in the same units as overnight cost and is useful for identifying the total cost of construction and for determining the effects of construction delays. In general the construction costs of nuclear power plants are significantly higher than for coal- or gas-fired plants because of the need to use special materials. and to incorporate sophisticated safety features and back-up control equipment. These contribute much of the nuclear generation cost. but once the plant is built the cost variables are minor. The OECD Nuclear Energy Agency's (NEA) calculation of the overnight cost for a nuclear power plant built in the OECD rose from about US$ 1.900/kWe at the end of the 1990s to US$ 3.850/kWe in 2009.

The NEA figures for the 1990s must be treated with caution as they are not in line with some other data sources. The US Energy Information Administration (EIA) calculated that. in constant 2002 values. the realized real overnight cost of a nuclear power plant built in the USA grew from US$ 1.500/kWe in the early 1960s to US$ 4.000/kWe in the mid-1970s. The EIA cited increased regulatory requirements (including design changes that required plants to be back-fitted with modified equipment). licensing problems. project management problems and mis-estimation of costs and demand as the factors contributing to the increase during the 1970s. Its 2010 report.*Updated Capital Cost Estimates for Electricity Generation Plants*. gave an estimate for a new nuclear plant of US$ 5.339/kW.

There is also significant variation of capital costs by country. particularly between the emerging industrial economies of East Asia and the mature markets of Europe and North America. which has a variety of explanations. including differential labour costs. more experience in the recent building of reactors. economies of scale from building multiple units and streamlined licensing and project management within large civil engineering projects. With few new orders. the data set for new build costs is lacking. The shift to Generation III reactors has added further uncertainty. Other non-nuclear generation technologies also show variation and as do major infrastructure projects such as roads and bridges. depending upon where they are built. However. the variation is particularly crucial for nuclear as its economics depend so much on minimising its capital investment cost.

The French national audit body. the Cour des comptes. said in 2012 that the overnight capital costs of building NPPs increased over time from □ 1.070/kWe (at 2010 prices) when the first of the 50 PWRs was built at Fessenheim (commissioned in 1978) to □ 2.060/kWe when Chooz 1 and 2 were built in 2000. and to a projected □ 3.700/kWe for the Flamanville EPR. It can be argued that much of this escalation relates to the smaller magnitude of the programme by 2000 (compared with when the French were commissioning 4-6 new PWRs per year in the 1980s) and to the subsequent loss of economies of scale.

In several countries. notably the UK. there is a trend to greater vendor involvement in financing projects. but with an intention to relinquish equity once the plant is running.A presentation by Dr. N. Barkatullah. UAE Regulation and Supervision Bureau. at the World Nuclear Association 2014 Symposium showed the risk in construction costs (per kilowatt of capacity). much of it due to financing cost incurred by delays:

By way of contrast. China has stated that it expects its costs for plants under construction to come in at less than $2000/kW and that subsequent units should be in the range of $1600/kW. This estimate is for the AP1000 design. the same as used by EIA for the USA. This would mean that an AP1000 in the USA would cost about three times as much as the same plant built in China. Different labour rates in the two countries are only part of the explanation. Standardised design. numerous units being built. and increased localisation are all significant factors in China.Financing costs will depend on the rate of interest on debt. the debt-equity ratio. and if it is regulated. how the capital costs are recovered. There must also be an allowance for a rate of return on equity. which is risk capital.

Long construction periods will push up financing costs. and in the past they have done so spectacularly. In Asia construction times have tended to be shorter. for instance the new-generation 1300 MWe Japanese reactors which began operating in 1996 and 1997 were built in a little over four years. and 48 to 54 months is typical projection for plants today.

OPERATING COSTS

Fuel costs have from the outset given nuclear energy an advantage compared with coal. oil and gas-fired plants. Uranium. however. has to be processed. enriched and fabricated into fuel elements. and about half of the cost is due to enrichment and fabrication. In the assessment of the economics of nuclear power allowances must also be made for the management of radioactive used fuel and the ultimate disposal of this used fuel or the wastes separated from it. But even with these included. the total fuel costs of a nuclear power plant in the OECD are typically about a third of those for a coal-fired plant and between a quarter and a fifth of those for a gas combined-cycle plant. The US Nuclear Energy Institute suggests that for a coal-fired plant 78% of the cost is the fuel. for a gas-fired plant the figure is 89%. and for nuclear the uranium is about 14%. or double that to include all front end costs.

In June 2013. the approx. US $ cost to get 1 kg of uranium as UO2 reactor fuel (at current spot uranium price):

Uranium:	8.9 kg U_3O_8 x $130	US$ 1160
Conversion:	7.5 kg U x $11	US$ 83
Enrichment:	7.3 SWU x $120	US$ 880
Fuel fabrication:	per kg	US$ 240
Total. approx:		US$ 2360

At 45.000 MWd/t burn-up this gives 360.000 kWh electrical per kg. hence fuel cost: 0.66 c/kWh.Fuel costs are one area of steadily increasing efficiency and cost reduction. For instance. in Spain the nuclear electricity cost was reduced by 29% over 1995-2001. This involved boosting enrichment levels and burn-up to achieve 40% fuel cost reduction. Prospectively. a further 8% increase in burn-up will give another 5% reduction in fuel cost.

Uranium has the advantage of being a highly concentrated source of energy which is easily and cheaply transportable. The quantities needed are very much less than for coal or oil. One kilogram of natural uranium will yield about 20.000 times as much energy as the same amount of coal. It is therefore intrinsically a very portable and tradable commodity.

The contribution of fuel to the overall cost of the electricity produced is relatively small. so even a large fuel price escalation will have relatively little effect. Uranium is abundant and widely available.There are other possible savings. For example. if used fuel is reprocessed and the recovered plutonium and uranium is used in mixed oxide (MOX) fuel. more energy can be extracted. The costs of achieving this are large. but are offset by MOX fuel not needing enrichment and particularly by the smaller amount of high-level wastesproduced at the end. Seven UO2 fuel assemblies give rise to one MOX assembly plus some vitrified high-level waste. resulting in only about 35% of the volume. mass and cost of disposal.Operating costs include operating and maintenance (O&M) plus fuel. Fuel cost figures include used fuel management and final waste disposal. These costs. while usually external for other technologies. are internal for nuclear power (*i.e.* they have to be paid or set aside securely by the utility generating the power. and the cost passed on to the customer in the actual tariff).

This 'back end' of the fuel cycle. including used fuel storage or disposal in a waste repository. contributes up to 10% of the overall costs per kWh – rather less if there is direct disposal of used fuel rather than reprocessing. The $26 billion US used fuel programme is funded by a 0.1 cent/kWh levy.

Decommissioning costs are about 9-15% of the initial capital cost of a nuclear power plant. But when discounted. they contribute only a few percent to the investment cost and even less to the generation cost. In the USA they account for 0.1-0.2 cent/kWh. which is no more than 5% of the cost of the electricity produced.

SYSTEM COSTS

System costs are the total costs above plant-level costs (capital and operating) to supply electricity at a given load and given level of security of supply. They include grid connection. extension and reinforcement. short-term balancing costs and long-term costs of maintaining adequate back-up.

They are external to the building and operation of any power plant. but must be paid by the electricity consumer. usually as part of the transmission and distribution cost. From a government policy point of view they are just as significant as the actual generation cost. but are seldom factored in to comparisons among different supply options. especially comparing base-load with dispersed renewables. In fact that the total system cost should be analysed when introducing new power generating capacity on the grid. Any new power plant likely requires changes to the grid. and hence incurs a significant cost for power supply that must be accounted for. But this cost for large base-load plants is small compared with integrating renewables to the grid.

The integration of intermittent renewable supply on a preferential basis despite higher unit cost creates significant diseconomies for dispatchable supply. as is now becoming evident in Germany. Austria and Spain. compromising security of supply and escalating costs.

An OECD study found that the integration of large shares of intermittent renewable electricity is a major challenge for the electricity systems of OECD countries and for dispatchable generators such as nuclear. Grid-level system costs for variable renewables are large ($15-80/MWh) but depend on country. context and technology (onshore wind < offshore wind < Solar PV). Nuclear system cost is $1-3/MWh.

EXTERNAL COSTS

External costs are not included in the building and operation of any power plant. and are not paid by the electricity consumer. but by the community generally. The external costs are defined as those actually incurred in relation to health and the environment. and which are quantifiable but not built into the cost of the electricity.

The report of a major European study of the external costs of various fuel cycles. focusing on coal and nuclear. was released in mid 2001 – ExternE. It shows that in clear cash terms nuclear energy incurs about one tenth of the costs of coal. If these costs were in fact included. the EU price of electricity from coal would double and that from gas would increase 30%. These are without attempting to include the external costs of global warming.

The European Commission launched the project in 1991 in collaboration with the US Department of Energy. and it was the first research project of its kind "to put plausible financial figures against damage resulting from different forms of electricity production for the entire EU". The methodology considers emissions. dispersion and ultimate impact. With nuclear energy the risk of accidents is factored in along with high estimates of radiological impacts from mine tailings (waste management and decommissioning being already within the cost to the consumer). Nuclear energy averages 0.4 euro cents/kWh. much the same as hydro. coal is over 4.0 cents (4.1-7.3). gas ranges 1.3-2.3 cents and only wind shows up better than nuclear. at 0.1-0.2 cents/kWh average. NB these are the external costs only.

COMPARING THE ECONOMICS OF DIFFERENT FORMS OF ELECTRICITY GENERATION

In 2013 the US Energy Information Administration published figures for the average levelized costs per unit of output for generating technologies to be brought on line in 2018. as modeled for its *Annual Energy Outlook*. These show advanced nuclear. natural gas (advanced combustion turbine). and conventional coal in the bracket 10-11c/kWh. Combined cycle natural gas is 6.6 cents. advanced coal with CCS 13.6 cents. and among the non-dispatchable technologies: wind onshore 8.7 cents. solar PV 14.4 cents. offshore wind 22.2 cents and solar thermal 26.2 c/kWh. The actual capital cost of nuclear is about the same as coal. and very much more than any gas option.

A 2010 OECD study Projected Costs of generating Electricity set out some actual costs of electricity generation. from which the following figures are taken:

Actual Costs of Electricity (US cents/kWh)

Technology	region or country	At 10% discount rate	At 5% discount rate
Nuclear	OECD Europe	8.3-13.7	5.0-8.2
	China	4.4-5.5	3.0-3.6
Black coal with CCS	OECD Europe	11.0	8.5
Brown coal with CCS	OECD Europe	9.5-14.3	6.8-9.3

CCGT with CCS	OECD Europe	11.8	9.8
Large hydro-electric	OECD Europe	14.0-45.9	7.4-23.1
	China: 3 Gorges	5.2	2.9
	China: other	2.3-3.3	1.2-1.7
Onshore wind	OECD Europe	12.2-23.0	9.0-14.6
	China	7.2-12.6	5.1-8.9
Offshore wind	OECD Europe	18.7-26.1	13.8-18.8
Solar photovoltaic	OECD Europe	38.8-61.6	28.7-41.0
	China	18.7-28.3	12.3-18.6

Source: OECD/IEA-NEA. 2010. Projected Costs of Generating Electricity This shows the levelised cost. which is the average cost of producing electricity including capital. finance. owner's costs on site. fuel and operation over a plant's lifetime.

It is important to distinguish between the economics of nuclear plants already in operation and those at the planning stage. Once capital investment costs are effectively "sunk". existing plants operate at very low costs and are effectively "cash machines". Their operations and maintenance (O&M) and fuel costs (including used fuel management) are. along with hydropower plants. at the low end of the spectrum and make them very suitable as base-load power suppliers. This is irrespective of whether the investment costs are amortized or depreciated in corporate financial accounts – assuming the forward or marginal costs of operation are below the power price. the plant will operate.US figures for 2012 published by NEI show the general picture. with nuclear generating power at 2.40 c/kWh. compared with coal at 3.27 cents and gas at 3.40 cents.

Doubling the uranium price (say from $25 to $50 per lb U3O8) takes the fuel cost up from 0.50 to 0.62 US cents per kWh. an increase of one quarter. and the expected cost of generation of the best US plants from 1.3 US cents per kWh to 1.42 cents per kWh (an increase of almost 10%). So while there is some impact. it is comparatively minor. especially by comparison with the impact of gas prices on the economics of gas generating plants. In these. 90% of the marginal costs can be fuel. Only if uranium prices rise to above $100 per lb U3O8 ($260/kgU) and stay there for a prolonged period (which seems very unlikely) will the impact on nuclear generating costs be considerable.

Nevertheless. for nuclear power plants operating in competitive power markets where it is impossible to pass on any fuel price increases (ie the utility is a price-taker). higher uranium prices will cut corporate profitability. Yet fuel costs have been relatively stable over time – the rise in the world uranium price between 2003 and 2007 added to generation costs. but conversion. enrichment and fuel fabrication costs did not followed the same trend.

In February 2014 the US Nuclear Energy Institute presented figures from the Electric Utility Cost Group on US generating costs comprising fuel. capital and operating costs for 61 nuclear sites in 2012. The average came to $44/ MWh. being $50.54 for single-unit plants and $39.44 for multi-unit plants (all two-unit except Browns Ferry. Oconee and Palo Verde). The $44 represented a 58% increase in ten years. largely due to a threefold increase in capital expenditure on plants which were mostly old enough to be fully depreciated. Over half of the capital expenditure (51%) in 2012 related to power uprates and licence renewals. while 26% was for equipment replacement.

For prospective new nuclear plants. the fuel component is even less significant. The typical front end nuclear fuel cost is typically only 15-20% of the total. as opposed to 30-40% for operating nuclear plants.

Competitiveness in the context of increasing use of power from renewable sources. which are legally preferred. is a major issue today. The most important renewable sources are intermittent by nature. which means that their supply to the electricity system does not necessarily match demand from customers. In power grids where renewable sources of generation make a significant contribution. intermittency forces other generating sources to ramp up their supply or power down at short notice. This volatility can have a large impact on non-intermittent generators' profitability.A variety of responses to the challenge of intermittent generation are possible. Two options currently being implemented are increased conventional plant flexibility and increased grid capacity and coverage. Flexibility is seen as most applicable to gas and coal fired generators. but nuclear reactors. normally regarded as base-load producers. also have the ability to load-follow. eg. by the use of 'grey rods' to modulate the reaction speed.

As the scale of intermittent generating capacity increases however. more significant measures will be required. The establishment and extension of capacity mechanisms. which offer payments to generators prepared to guarantee supply for defined periods. are now under serious consideration within the EU. Capacity mechanisms can in theory provide security of supply to desired levels but at a price which might be high. for example. Morgan Stanley has estimated that investors in a 800 MWe gas plant providing for intermittent generation would require payments of □80 million per year whilst Ecofys calculate that a 4 GWe reserve in Germany would cost □140-240/year. Almost by definition. investors in conventional plant designed to operate intermittently will face low and uncertain load factors and will therefore demand significant capacity payments in return for the investment decision. In practice. until the capacity mechanism has been reliably implemented. investors are likely to withhold investment. Challenges for EU power market integration are expected to result from differences between member state capacity mechanisms.

FUTURE COST COMPETITIVENESS

Understanding the cost of new generating capacity and its output requires careful analysis of what is in any set of figures. There are three broad components: capital. finance and operating costs. Capital and financing costs make up the project cost. Calculations of relative generating costs are made using levelised costs. meaning average costs of producing electricity including capital. finance. owner's costs on site. fuel and operation over a plant's lifetime. with provision for decommissioning and waste disposal.

It is important to note that capital cost figures quoted by reactor vendors. or which are general and not site-specific. will usually just be for EPC costs. This is because owner's costs will vary hugely. most of all according to whether a plant is Greenfield or at an established site. perhaps replacing an old plant.

There are several possible sources of variation which preclude confident comparison of overnight or EPC (Engineering. Procurement and Construction) capital costs – eg whether initial core load of fuel is included. Much more obvious is whether the price is for the nuclear island alone (Nuclear Steam Supply System) or the whole plant including turbines and generators – all the above figures include these. Further differences relate to site works such as cooling towers as well as land and permitting. Financing costs are additional. adding typically around 30%. and finally there is the question of whether cost figures are in current (or specified year) dollar values or in those of the year in which spending occurs.

MAJOR STUDIES ON FUTURE COST COMPETITIVENESS

There have been many studies carried out examining the economics of future generation options. and the following are merely the most important and also focus on the nuclear element.

The 2010 OECD study *Projected Costs of generating Electricity* compared 2009 data for generating base-load electricity by 2015 as well as costs of power from renewables. and showed that nuclear power was very competitive at $30 per tonne CO2 cost and low discount rate. The study comprised data for 190 power plants from 17 OECD countries as well as some data from Brazil. China. Russia and South Africa. It used levelised lifetime costs with carbon price internalised (OECD only) and discounted cash flow at 5% and 10%. as previously. The precise competitiveness of different base-load technologies depended very much on local circumstances and the costs of financing and fuels.

Nuclear overnight capital costs in OECD ranged from US$ 1556/kW for APR-1400 in South Korea through $3009 for ABWR in Japan. $3382/kW for Gen III+ in USA. $3860 for EPR at Flamanville in France to $5863/kW for EPR in Switzerland. with world median $4100/kW. Belgium. Netherlands. Czech Rep and Hungary were all over $5000/kW. In China overnight costs were $1748/kW for CPR-1000 and $2302/kW for AP1000. and in Russia $2933/kW for VVER-1150. EPRI (USA) gave $2970/kW for APWR or ABWR. Eurelectric gave $4724/kW for EPR. OECD black coal plants were costed at $807-2719/kW. those with carbon capture and compression (tabulated as CCS. but the cost not including storage) at $3223-5811/kW. brown coal $1802-3485. gas plants $635-1747/kW and onshore wind capacity $1821-3716/kW. (Overnight costs were defined here as EPC. owner's costs and contingency. but excluding interest during construction.)

OECD electricity generating cost projections for year 2010 on - 5% discount rate. c/kWh

country	nuclear	coal	coal with CCS	Gas CCGT	Onshore wind
Belgium	6.1	8.2	–	9.0	9.6
Czech R	7.0	8.5-9.4	8.8-9.3	9.2	14.6
France	5.6	–	–	–	9.0
Germany	5.0	7.0-7.9	6.8-8.5	8.5	10.6
Hungary	8.2	–	–	–	–
Japan	5.0	8.8	–	10.5	–
Korea	2.9-3.3	6.6-6.8	–	9.1	–
Netherlands	6.3	8.2	–	7.8	8.6
Slovakia	6.3	12.0	–	–	–
Switzerland	5.5-7.8	–	–	9.4	16.3
USA	4.9	7.2-7.5	6.8	7.7	4.8
China*	3.0-3.6	5.5	–	4.9	5.1-8.9
Russia*	4.3	7.5	8.7	7.1	6.3
EPRI (USA)	4.8	7.2	–	7.9	6.2
Eurelectric	6.0	6.3-7.4	7.5	8.6	11.3

* For China and Russia: 2.5c is added to coal and 1.3c to gas as carbon emission cost to enable sensible comparison with other data in those fuel/technology categories. though within those countries coal and gas will in fact be cheaper than the Table above suggests.

At 5% discount rate comparative costs. Nuclear is comfortably cheaper than coal and gas in all countries. At 10% discount rate nuclear is still cheaper than coal in all but the Eurelectric estimate and three EU countries. but in these three gas becomes cheaper still. Coal with carbon capture is mostly more expensive than either nuclear or paying the $30 per tonne for CO2 emissions. though the report points out "great uncertainties" in the cost of projected CCS. Also. investment cost becomes a much greater proportion of power cost than with 5% discount rate.

OECD electricity generating cost projections for year 2010 on - 10% discount rate. c/kWh

Country	Nuclear	Coal	Coal with	CCSGas CCGT	Onshore wind
Belgium	10.9	10.0	–	9.3-9.9	13.6
Czech R	11.5	11.4-13.3	13.6-14.1	10.4	21.9
France	9.2	–	–	–	12.2
Germany	8.3	8.7-9.4	9.5-11.0	9.3	14.3
Hungary	12.2	–	–	–	–
Japan	7.6	10.7	–	12.0	–
Korea	4.2-4.8	7.1-7.4	–	9.5	–
Netherlands	10.5	10.0	–	8.2	12.2
Slovakia	9.8	14.2	–	–	–
Switzerland	9.0-13.6	–	–	10.	23.4
USA	7.7	8.8-9.3	9.4	8.3	7.0
China*	4.4-5.5	5.8	–	5.2	7.2-12.6
Russia*	6.8	9.0	11.8	7.8	9.0

EPRI (USA)	7.3	8.8	–	8.3	9.1
Eurelectric	10.6	8.0-9.0	10.2	9.4	15.5

* For China and Russia: 2.5c is added to coal and 1.3c to gas as carbon emission cost to enable sensible comparison with other data in those fuel/technology categories. though within those countries coal and gas will in fact be cheaper than the Table above suggests. A 2004 report on *The Economic Future of Nuclear Power* from from the University of Chicago. funded by the US Department of Energy. compared the levelised power costs of future nuclear. coal. and gas-fired power generation in the USA. Various nuclear options were covered. and for an initial ABWR or AP1000 they range from 4.3 to 5.0 c/kWh on the basis of overnight capital costs of $1200 to $1500/kW. 60 year plant life. 5 year construction and 90% capacity. Coal gives 3.5 - 4.1 c/kWh and gas (CCGT) 3.5 - 4.5 c/kWh. depending greatly on fuel price.

The levelised nuclear power cost figures include up to 29% of the overnight capital cost as interest. and the report notes that up to another 24% of the overnight capital cost needs to be added for the initial unit of a first-of-a-kind advanced design such as the AP1000. defining the high end of the range above. For more advanced plants such as the EPR or SWR1000. overnight capital cost of $1800/kW is assumed and power costs are projected beyond the range above. However. considering a series of eight units of the same kind and assuming increased efficiency due to experience which lowers overnight capital cost. the levelised power costs drop 20% from those quoted above and where first-of-a-kind engineering costs are amortised (eg the $1500/kW case above). they drop 32%. making them competitive at about 3.4 c/kWh.

Nuclear plant: projected electrcity costs (c/kWh)

Overnight	capital cost $/kW	1200	1500	1800
First unit	7 yr build. 40 yr life	5.3	6.2	7.1
	5 yr build. 60 yr life	4.3	5.0	5.8
4th unit	7 yr build. 40 yr life	4.5	4.5	5.3
	5 yr build. 60 yr life *	3.7	3.7	4.3
8th unit	7 yr build. 40 yr life	4.2	4.2	4.9
5 yr build. 60 yr life *		3.4	3.4	4.0

* calculated from above data

The study also shows that with a minimal carbon control cost impact of 1.5 c/kWh for coal and 1.0 c/kWh for gas superimposed on the above figures. nuclear is even more competitive. But more importantly it goes on to explore other policy options which would offset investment risks and compensate for first-of-a-kind engineering costs to encourage new nuclear investment. including investment tax breaks. and production tax credits phasing out after 8 years. (US wind energy gets a production tax credit which has risen to 2.1 c/kWh.)

In May 2009 an update of a heavily-referenced 2003 MIT study on *The Future of Nuclear Power* was published. This said that "since 2003 construction costs for all types of large-scale engineered projects have escalated dramatically. The estimated cost of constructing a nuclear power plant has increased at a rate of 15% per year heading into the current economic downturn. This is based both on the cost of actual builds in Japan and Korea and on the projected cost of new plants planned for in the United States. Capital costs for both coal and natural gas have increased as well. although not by as much. The cost of natural gas and coal that peaked sharply is now receding. Taken together. these escalating costs leave the situation [of relative costs] close to where it was in 2003." The overnight capital cost was given as $4000/kW. in 2007 dollars. Applying the same cost of capital to nuclear as to coal and gas. nuclear came out at 6.6 c/kWh. coal at 8.3 cents and gas at 7.4 cents. assuming a charge of $25/tonne CO2 on the latter.

The French Energy and Climate Directorate published in November 2008 an update of its earlier regular studies on relative electricity generating costs. This shied away from cash figures to a large extent due to rapid changes in both fuel and capital. but showed that at anything over 6000 hours production per year (68% capacity factor). nuclear was cheaper than coal or gas combined cycle (CCG). At 100% capacity CCG was 25% more expensive than nuclear. At less than 4700 hours per year CCG was cheapest. all without taking CO2 cost into account.

With the nuclear plant fixed costs were almost 75% of the total. with CCG they were less than 25% including allowance for CO2 at $20/t. Other assumptions were 8% discount rate. gas at 6.85 $/GJ. coal at EUR 60/t. The reference nuclear unit is the EPR of 1630 MWe net. sited on the coast. assuming all development costs being borne by Flamanville 3. coming on line in 2020 and operating only 40 of its planned 60 years. Capital cost apparently EUR 2000/kW. Capacity factor 91%. fuel enrichment is 5%. burnup 60 GWd/t and used fuel is reprocessed with MOX recycle. In looking at overall fuel cost. uranium at $52/lb made up about 45% of it. and even though 3% discount rate was used for back-end the study confirmed the very low cost of waste in the total - about 13% of fuel cost. mostly for reprocessing.

At the end of 2008 EdF updated the overnight cost estimate for Flamanville 3 EPR (the first French EPR. but with some supply contracts locked in before escalation) to EUR 4 billion in 2008 Euros (EUR 2434/kW). and electricity cost 5.4 cents/kWh (compared with 6.8 c/kWh for CCGT and 7.0 c/kWh for coal. "with lowest assumptions" for CO2 cost). These costs were confirmed in mid 2009. when EdF had spent nearly EUR 2 billion. In July 2010 EdF revised the overnight cost to about EUR 5 billion.

A detailed study of energy economics in Finland published in mid 2000 was important in making the strong case for additional nuclear construction there. showing that nuclear energy would be the least-cost option for new generating capacity. The study compared nuclear. coal. gas turbine combined cycle and peat. Nuclear has very much higher capital costs than the others – EUR 1749/kW including initial fuel load. which is about three times the cost of the gas plant. But its fuel costs are much lower. and so at capacity factors above 64% it is the cheapest option.August 2003 figures put nuclear costs at EUR 2.37 c/kWh. coal 2.81 c/kWh and natural gas at 3.23 c/kWh (on the basis of 91% capacity factor. 5% interest rate. 40 year plant life). With emission trading @ EUR 20/t CO2. the electricity prices for coal and gas increase to 4.43 and 3.92 c/kWh respectively:

In the middle three bars of this graph the relative effects of capital and fuel costs can be clearly seen. The relatively high capital cost of nuclear power means that financing cost and time taken in construction are critical. relative to gas and even coal. But the fuel cost is very much lower. and so once a plant is built its cost of production is very much more predictable than for gas or even coal. The impact of adding a cost or carbon emissions can also be seen.

In 2013 the Nuclear Energy Institute announced the results of its financial modelling of comparative costs in the USA. based on figures from the US Energy Information Administration's 2013 Annual Energy Outlook. NEI assumed 5% cost of debt. 15% return on equity and a 70/30 debt equity capital structure. The report went on to show that with nuclear plant licence renewal beyond 60 years. power costs would be $53-60/MWh.

NEI 2013 Financial Modelling

	EPC cost	Capacity	Electricity cost
Gas combined cycle. gas @ $3.70/GJ	$1000/kW	90%	$44.00/MWh
Gas combined cycle. gas @ $5.28/GJ	$1000/kW	90%	$54.70/MWh
Gas combined cycle. gas @ $6.70/GJ	$1000/kW	90%	$61.70/MWh
Gas combined cycle. gas @ $6.70/GJ. 50-50 debt-equity	$1000/kW	90%	c $70/MWh
Supercritical pulverised coal. 1300 MWe	$3000/kW	85%	$75.70/MWh
Integrated gasification combined cycle coal. 1200 MWe	$3800/kW	85%	$94.30/MWh
Nuclear. 1400 MWe (EIA's EPC figure)	$5500/kW	90%	$121.90/MWh
Nuclear. 1400 MWe (NEI suggested EPC figure)	$4500-5000/kW	90%	$85-90/MWh
Wind farm. 100 MWe	$1000/kW	30%	112.90/MWh

5% cost of debt. 15% return on equity and a 70-30 debt equity capital structure.

The China Nuclear Energy Association estimated in May 2013 that the construction cost for two AP1000 units at Sanmen are CNY 40.1 billion ($6.54 billion). or 16.000 Yuan/kW installed ($2615/kW) – about 20% higher than that of improved Generation II Chinese reactors. but likely to drop to about CNY 13.000/kW ($2120/kW) with series construction and localisation as envisaged. Grid purchase price is expected to exceed CNY 0.45/kWh at present costs. and drop to 0.42 with reduced capital cost.

A striking indication of the impact of financing costs is given by Georgia Power. which said in mid 2008 that twin 1100 MWe AP1000 reactors would cost $9.6 billion if they could be financed progressively by ratepayers. or $14 billion if not. This gives $4363 or $6360 per kilowatt including all other owners costs. Finally. in the USA the question of whether a project is subject to regulated cost recovery or is a merchant plant is relevant. since it introduces political. financial and tactical factors. If the new build cost escalates (or is inflated). some cost recovery may be possible through higher rates can be charged by the utility if those costs are deemed prudent by the relevant regulator. By way of contrast. a merchant plant has to sell all its power competitively. so must convince its shareholders that it has a good economic case for moving forward with a new nuclear unit.

PROVIDING INVESTMENT INCENTIVES

As more electricity markets become deregulated and competitive. balancing supply and demand over the short-term can result in significant price volatility. Price signals in the spot market for electricity supply do not provide a guide on the return that might be achieved over the long term. and fail to create incentive for long-term investment in generation or transmission infrastructure. nor do they value diversity of supply.

Deregulated electricity markets with preferential grid access for renewables have left some utilities with stranded assets. which can no longer be used sufficiently fully to be profitable. As a result. many are being decommissioned. eg about 9 GWe by E.On and RWE in Germany to 2013. and a further 7.3 GWe expected there (apart from nuclear capacity).

The economic rationale for electricity from any plants with high capital cost and long life does not translate into incentive for investment unless some long-term electricity price is assured. This has been tackled differently in various countries.

In the USA. investment in new capital-intensive plant is going ahead only in states where cost-recovery can be assured. not in deregulated areas. Proposed merchant plants in Texas and some eastern states have been postponed indefinitely.

In Ontario. Canada. the refurbishment of Bruce A 1&2 was underwritten by a power purchase agreement (PPA) at about $63/MWh. slightly higher than the regulated price. The refurbishment of Bruce A 3&4 (1500 MWe) from 2016 and the C$ 8 billion needed for the Bruce B units (3480 MWe) from 2020 is likely to be underwritten similarly with PPAs.

In the UK. legislation from 2013 has three main elements:

- Feed-in tariffs (FIT). now relatively common in several countries. give particular low-carbon producers a predictable return per kWh over a set period regardless of prevailing market prices. The FIT can take several forms. In the UK it will be effected through contracts for difference (CfD) which remove long-term exposure to electricity price volatility. The FIT with CfD means that if the market price is lower that the agreed 'strike price'. the government or the transmission system operator (TSO) pays that difference per kWh. if the market is above the strike price the generator pays the TSO or government. They are long-term contracts which can be capped regarding quantity of power. helping developers secure the large upfront capital costs for low-carbon infrastructure while protecting consumers from rising energy bills. The first strike prices were published in the 2013-18 Delivery Plan: £155/MWh for offshore wind. £100/MWh for onshore wind and £125/MWh for large solar PV.

- A floor price for 'carbon' to support de-carbonisation. The idea is that a carbon floor price will drive the market towards any FIT or strike price level applied to clean sources.
- Capacity market measures will be introduced. These involve payments for dispatchable capacity maintained to ensure that demand can be met regardless of short-term conditions affecting other generators. They will work through penalties and availability payments to provide incentive for generators to be available when needed. in effect paying for reliability. The first capacity auction is scheduled for late 2014. for delivery during winter 2018-19.

In October 2013 the UK government announced that initial agreement had been reached with EDF Group on the key terms of a proposed £16 billion investment contract for the Hinkley Point C nuclear power station. The key terms include 35-year 'Contract for Difference'. the Strike Price of £89.50/MWh being fully indexed to the Consumer Price Index and conditional upon the Sizewell C project proceeding. If it does not for any reason. and the developer cannot share first-of-a-kind costs across both. the strike price is to be £92.50/MWh. EDF said that the agreement in principle is not legally binding. and is dependent on a positive decision from the European Commission in relation to State

Aid. following which it will make a final decision on the project. As well as price per MWh. the question of guaranteed load factor arises so that output is sufficient to amortise the investment. in the face of renewables' preferential grid access.In the Czech Republic. CEZ says that investment in two new 1200 MWe reactors at Temelin will not proceed unless it has some assurance of long-term electricity prices from them. The government and Ministry of Finance are resisting this.

The Industry Ministry was proposing £60/MWh. others suggest that £90 will be needed. indexed. CEZ requires £70/MWh for the new units to be profitable. compared with mid-2013 forward prices of under £40. In Turkey. in order to secure investment in the 4x1200 MWe Akkuyu nuclear power plant. a formula for long-term power prices was worked out. This involves the Turkish Electricity Trade and Contract Corporation (TETAS) buying a fixed proportion of the power at a fixed price of US$ 123.50/MWh for 15 years. or to 2030. The proportion will be 70% of the output of the first two units and 30% of that from units 3&4 over 15 years from commercial operation of each. Rosatom will initially have full ownership of the project.

ENERGY SUBSIDIES AND EXTERNAL COSTS

There are three main areas where. broadly speaking. subsidies or other support for energy may apply: government R&D for particular technologies. subsidies for power generation per unit of production (or conceivably per unit of capacity). including costs imposed on disincentivised alternatives. and the allowance of external costs which are either paid by the community at large or picked up later by governments.

ENERGY R&D

There has been a lot of government-financed energy research and development (R&D) in most developed countries. This has been driven by concern about energy security. as well as by the need to address environmental problems and social concerns. Reliable and affordable energy supplies are vital to any economy. while energy shortages or the threat of such have political and economic consequences. Therefore as concerns have evolved from oil shocks to climate change. each country's energy provision and infrastructure needs restructuring accordingly.

Government R&D expenditure on energy tends to be focused on long-term development of new technologies. with the aim of bringing them to commercialisation. while private R&D is mostly on the further development of existing and operational technologies. While there are notable exceptions both ways. there is a strong disincentive for industry working in a highly competitive market and needing to justify a return on capital to shareholders to undertake long-term. high risk R&D. This is because after all their investment they will still be selling kilowatt hours of electricity or another essentially undifferentiated product in a competitive and very price-sensitive marketplace.

In recent years. some controversy has surrounded the question of the relative levels of R&D expenditure on nuclear energy and on new renewables (essentially technologies to harness wind and solar energy). Unfortunately. IEA data available for the first edition of this paper is no longer available. hence some of the following is dated.

Serbia published new FITs early in 2013. which will be valid for 12 years from project commissioning and will be corrected annually every February in line with the level of inflation in the Eurozone. They include EUR 9.2 c/kWh for wind and 16.25 c/kWh for solar. but with low caps on the capacity covered.

Table. Expenditure by IEA countries on energy R&D.

Year	1975	1980	1985	1990	1995	2000	2005
Conservation	333	955	725	510	1240	1497	1075

Fossil Fuels	587	2564	1510	1793	1050	612	1007
Renewables	208	1914	843	563	809	773	1113
Nuclear Fission	4808	6794	6575	4199	3616	3406	3168
Nuclear Fusion	597	1221	1470	1055	1120	893	715
Other	893	1160	787	916			
Total Energy R&D	7563	15034	12186	9394	9483	9070	9586
Total: Japan	1508	3438	3738	3452	3672	3721	3905
Total: excluding Japan	6055	11596	8448	5842	5811	5349	5681

The above table and graph are from the OECD International Energy Agency's database (IEA. 2001 and 2006) regarding government expenditure in the 26 IEA member countries. The database does not include information about private companies' expenditure. nor funds spent by non-IEA countries. such as China. Russia or India.

The total amount of energy R&D expenditure by governments of IEA countries rose in response to the oil price shocks of the early 1970s and then fell away as associated concerns abated. with the conspicuous exception of Japan. Private R&D investment has apparently followed the same pattern outside Japan.

NUCLEAR ENERGY R&D VS RENEWABLES AND OTHER SOURCES

Throughout the period. the expenditure on nuclear fission dominated the overall figures. though falling from 64 per cent of the total in 1975 to 33 per cent in 2005. However. government R&D expenditure on nuclear fission fell significantly through the 1990s. to trivial levels - in fact below that spent on renewables. which has averaged about US$ 700 million per year for the last two decades but is now rising.

Table. Expenditure by IEA Countries on Fission R&D. (2005 US$ millions)

	UK	France	Japan	USA	Other IEA countries	All IEA countries
1975	929	0	763	2164	952	4808
1980	741	0	2098	2410	1160	6794
1985	638	895	2259	1241	1542	6575
1990	253	555	2298	737	356	4199
1995	17	599	2455	103	442	3616
2000	0	666	2393	39	308	3406
2005	4	?	2398	171	?	3168

IEA data shows R&D on nuclear fission peaking around 1980 and after 1985 declining steadily to less than half that level. Since 1990 Japan alone has been responsible for some two thirds of IEA R&D expenditure on nuclear fission. with France accounting for most of the remainder. If the French and Japanese figures are excluded. fission R&D expenditure in the rest of the IEA countries totalled US$ 308 million in 2000.

The extent of expenditure on renewables significantly outweighing that on nuclear fission everywhere except France and Japan would be unremarkable if the potential contribution from each were similar. In fact the potential scope for renewables contributing to electricity supply is very much less because the sources. particularly solar and wind. are diffuse. intermittent and unreliable. Their diffuse nature is simply a technical problem. But for intermittent and essentially opportunistic supply of wind- or solar-generated electricity to a grid system. the maximum potential appears to be about 20% of the total. and normally less. whereas that from nuclear energy is around 90%.

Partly as a result of the R&D expenditure. nuclear power now provides 14% of world electricity (more in those countries foremost in the R&D) - 2600 billion kWh per year. compared with a fraction of that for non-hydro renewables. Furthermore the scope for increasing the renewable contribution is not considered by the power producers to be very great.

The Japan Atomic Energy Agency (JAEA) is Japan's major integrated nuclear R&D organization. with 4400 employees at ten facilities and annual budget of 161 billion yen (US$ 1.7 billion).

A 2008 study by Management Information Services Inc looked at US energy more widely than just electricity. and took in all federal incentives. not simply R&D. from 1950 to 2006. Some $726 billion was identified (2006 dollars). Its conclusions included:

- The largest incentive category was tax concessions. especially for oil but also wind. No tax concession was for nuclear in this period.
- Total support for nuclear power over the 56 years was $65 billion. 9% of the total incentives. This compared with $50 billion (7%) for non-hydro renewables (wind and solar) plus geothermal.
- The main support was for oil and gas - $436 billion. 60% of total. with coal at $93 billion (13%).
- Most of the support for nuclear power was in R&D.
- Today nuclear power in the USA pays more than it receives due to contributions to the federal nuclear waste fund. which so far exceed disbursements from it by $14 billion. (There is no corresponding payment from other energy sources.)

Focusing on R&D:

- R&D comprised 19% of the total incentives. and half of this ($67 billion of $135 billion) was for nuclear. 16.5% for renewables plus geothermal. and 23% for coal. (Nuclear fusion was not included)
- Of the nuclear R&D. about $39 billion was spent before 1975 to explore a range of reactor concepts.
- Nuclear R&D peaked at $2.8 billion in 1978 and declined sharply to about $550 million in 1987. then steadily to a low of $75 million in 2001.
- Research on breeder reactors took 35% ($23.7 billion) of the nuclear R&D. though funding for this ceased in 1988. From 1976 to 1988. the breeder programme accounted for a high proportion of expenditure.
- Light water reactor technology accounted for only 8% ($5.3 billion)

of the nuclear R&D though it now provides almost 20% of US electricity.

- Other reactor types received $38 billion in R&D.
- Since 1988. spending on nuclear R&D has been less that for coal. and since 1994 it has been less than that for renewables as well.

US Department of Energy figures show the renewables total in the US R&D budget as $505 million in FY2007 and energy efficiency $676 million. compared with nuclear power at $300 million (double the 2003 level) and fossil fuels at $397 million. Nuclear fusion is additional at $319 million.

Other US DOE R&D data is as follows ($ million)

Years	currency	Renewables	Coal	Nuclear	End use
1988-2007	2007 $	6271	7593	13.500	5737
FY 2007	2010 $	717	582	1017	509
FY 2010	2010 $	1409	663	1169	832

EIA 2008 and 2011

In FY 2007. relating the support to actual energy produced. the figures are: wind 2.34 c/kWh. "clean coal" 2.98 c/kWh. gas. coal 0.044 c/kWh. nuclear 0.16 c/kWh.

Outside the IEA. Russia. India and China have substantial nuclear fission programmes and as the European Union also funds an amount of fission R&D. the worldwide totals for fission will be rather higher than the figure above. Non-etheless. given that the bulk of government-sponsored R&D into nuclear fission focuses on waste management and other fuel cycle back-end processes. it is clear that little is being spent at present by governments on new reactor designs.

SUBSIDIES FOR PARTICULAR ENERGY SOURCES AND DISINCENTIVES ON ALTERNATIVES

A simple definition of subsidy is difficult to find. The IEA points out that there is enormous confusion about what is meant by the term. The narrowest and perhaps most commonly used definition is a direct cash payment by a government to an energy producer or consumer. But this is just one way in which governments can stimulate the production or use of a particular fuel or form of energy.

Broader definitions attempt to capture other types of government interventions that affect prices or costs. either directly or indirectly. For example. an OECD study defined a subsidy as *any measure that keeps prices for consumers below market levels. or for producers above market levels. or that reduces costs for consumers and producers*. In a similar way. the IEA defines energy subsidies as *any government action that concerns primarily the energy sector that lowers the cost of energy production. raises the price received by energy producers or lowers the price paid by energy consumers.* What matters in practice is the overall impact of all subsidies and taxes on the absolute level of prices and costs and the competitiveness of each fuel or technology. In addition to front-end R&D expenditure there are ongoing operational subsidies for various forms and sources of energy. With government-controlled utilities. or regulated markets such as in the USA until the mid 1990s. utility costs could simply be passed on to the consumers. who effectively supplied a subsidy relative to cheaper alternatives. With deregulated and competitive markets this had to change.

In an open market. government policies to support particular generation options such as renewables normally give rise to explicit direct subsidies along with other instruments such as feed-in tariffs. quota obligations and energy tax exemptions. To provide disincentive on alternatives there can be targeted taxes including carbon taxes. or emission trading schemes for carbon.

SUBSIDIES FOR RENEWABLE ENERGY SUPPLYING ELECTRICITY

The IEA's *World Energy Outlook 2011* estimates that the total cost of subsidies for renewable energy will rise from $66 billion in 2010 to $250 billion in 2035. However. several countries are cutting back support for renewables due both to the high cost impacting electricity prices and also the costs and difficulties of integrating them into the transmission networks. Germany and Spain are cutting about $2.5 billion and $3.5 billion per year respectively from subsidies for renewables.

A feed-in tariff (FIT) obliges energy retailers to buy any electricity produced from specified. eg renewable. sources at a fixed price. usually over a fixed period of some years (eg 20 years in Germany). the price being significantly greater than that paid for power from mainstream sources. The rates usually vary for different sources. eg being greater for solar or offshore wind. In this case they may be called Advanced Renewable Tariffs (ART). differentiating by technology and perhaps project size. There is usually no amount or proportion specified. though a cap or quota on how much needs to be bought overall or from particular sources may be applied. With renewables. any supply offered must be taken by the grid operator. regardless of merit order considerations (normally applying. so that lowest marginal cost supplies are preferred). In Germany for instance. the grid operators buy the renewable kWh at the specified FIT rate and then sell them on the open market. The difference between the sales proceeds and the FIT they have paid to various suppliers is compensated by the end consumer through an 'EEG-surcharge' being applied to bills. Electricity-intense industry has this surcharge limited.

Feed-in tariffs (FIT) are now common in Europe. Canada. China and Israel and imminent in several Australian states. total at least 41 countries or provinces. They generally mean that the consumer pays the subsidy for power from the legislated sources. the cost being spread across all power purchases unless there is a special deal to buy renewable power at a premium. In Germany the additional cost of the FIT above normal wholesale market is recovered by a 'renewable energy surcharge' being added to retail electricity bills (with exemptions for industry). However. in some countries FITs have become unaffordable. and are being replaced with other mechanisms.

A variation on FIT is the contract for difference (CFD). which means that if the market price is lower that the agreed strike price. the government pays that difference per kWh. if the market is above the strike price. the generator pays the government. The key factor then is setting the strike price far enough ahead to enable investment. Another variation – short of a full FIT – is a bonus payment on market price.

A problem showing up in several countries. especially regarding FITs. is that they become increasingly costly to consumers as the take-up increases. In Germany. the cost of subsidies for solar power is expected to reach EUR 46 billion by 2030. In Spain the take-up was so high that the government had to renege on its subsidy commitments after investments had been made. France cut back subsidies in 2010. The UK in 2011 wound back the FIT levels for new plants. Slovakia in 2011-12 slashed FITs for solar from EUR 38 c/kWh to 11.9 c/kWh for small solar (up to 100 kW) in order to keep electricity prices down.

When governments change the FIT levels to adjust the incentive. the changes generally apply only to new sources.

EUROPE

In the EU. feed-in tariffs are widespread (in 18 of 25 EU countries as of 2007). European Environment Agency figures in 2004 gave indicative estimates of total energy subsidies in the EU-15 for 2001: solid fuel (coal) EUR 13.0. oil and gas EUR 8.7. nuclear EUR 2.2. renewables EUR 5.3 billion.

In the UK. a February 2010 report from Ofgem showed that subsidies for renewables. notably the Renewables Obligation. had risen from £7 in 2007 to £13.50 per year on the average household electricity bill. and in 2008-09 totalled £1.04 billion.

The UK Renewables Obligation (RO) requires retailers each to buy a certain proportion of the electricity they supply from renewable sources with certificates at whatever price they can. or to pay a penalty. In the UK proportion was 9.1% and the default buy-out price (or "fine") was 3.576 p/kWh in 2008-09. It had reached 11% at the end of 2010 and will be 15% by 2016 (ie suppliers needed to present to Ofgem 0.11 certificates per MWh sold in 2010-11). The buy-out price for 2010-11 was 3.7 p/kWh (£37 per MWh certificate) and in 2013 auction prices ranged £41.50 to £44/MWh. The price of the electricity from renewable sources is left to the market. The amount required to be bought can be adjusted annually. as in UK towards 15.4% by 2015 (2006-07 level was 6.7%. 2007-08 was 7.9%). In 2006-07 in England and Wales 12.87 billion kWh of renewable electricity was supplied and £218 million in fines was paid.

representing a shortfall of 6.55 billion kWh. (The actual UK system is more complex than outlined. because Ofgem issues to generators certificates which can be traded. and the price of these reflects the fact that fines are distributed to retailers or others in proportion to certificates they submitted. In 2010-11 this was £14.32 per certificate. so the value of a certificate to the generator was about £51. This compares with the wholesale electricity price of about £52/MWh.)

Due to the Renewables Obligation the UK subsidy on onshore wind generation is the highest in the EU. Under the *Energy Act 2008* the UK system was modified from 2009 to provide greater incentive to use offshore wind. biomass and emerging technologies. This is done by issuing one certificate (or 0.9 certificate) per MWh for onshore wind. 2 (or 1.9) per MWh for offshore wind. etc. and adjusting from time to time. Technologies such as wave and tidal power which are hopelessly uneconomic and likely to remain so. even if they are more useful. will get up to 5 certificates per MWh.

The Renewables Obligation provided about £1.4 billion support for renewables in 2010. at a cost of 3% on consumer bills. or about £20 per household. half of which is due to wind. DECC said it added £30 to an average household bill for 2013. By 2017 it is expected to be £50. A November 2011 estimate from DECC said every household in the UK had paid £320 on average so far to subsidise renewables. a total of £7 billion. bringing average household energy bills to £1300 pa. Ofgem estimates that in the course of achieving 30% of supply from renewables the amended Renewables Obligation for large-scale projects is predicted to cost consumers £6 billion per year by 2020. and the new feed-in tariff (FIT) for schemes up to 5 MWe will cost them £7.9 billion per year by 2030. on the basis of 5.2 pence/kWh for RO and 9.3 p/kWh for FIT*. Meanwhile it is seen by the Renewable Energy Foundation to be "both counterproductive and very poor value for money". The new government elected in 2010 is moving to replace the Renewables Obligation with a 'contract for difference' for new projects. effectively a long-term power price. which took shape in the draft energy bill released in May 2012. Three units of the Drax coal-fired power plant are being converted to run on biomass. mostly imported wood pellets. for a guaranteed power price of £105/MWh. However. in April 2014 the second unit converted to biomass was denied similar Investment Contract support. leaving it to recoup costs from Renewables Obligation Certificates (at 0.9 ROC/MWh. the average ROC price in May 2014 was about £41.70) plus the wholesale power price – about £50/MWh. A court appeal failed. However. the government has offered an Investment Contract with price guarantee for the third Drax unit. The Renewables Obligation is to be replaced in 2014 for new projects with a FIT effected through contracts for difference (CfD) which can be capped regarding quantity. Draft strike prices (FIT) for renewables include £155/MWh for offshore wind (declining to £135 in 2018).

£100/MWh for onshore wind (declining to £95 in 2018). and £125/MWh for large solar PV (declining to £110 in 2018).

The UK also has a Climate Change Levy of 0.43 p/kWh on non-renewable sources (at present including nuclear energy. despite its lack of greenhouse gas emissions). which corresponds to a further subsidy of renewables.

The UK government legislated to establish a carbon price floor from April 2013. to underpin the move to a low-carbon energy future. Per tonne of CO_2. this rises from £4.94 to £9.55 for 2014-15. £18.08 for 2015-16. and £18 to 2018. In Germany the Renewable Energy Sources Act (EEG) of 2000. revised in 2004 and 2007. governs subsidies. Germany applies a mixture of incentives for renewables. but principally relies on wholesale feed-in tariffs which are guaranteed for up to 20 years.

The average feed-in tariff (FIT) apart from solar PV was EUR 8.5 c/kWh. or 16.4 cents including solar PV in 2006 (solar PV being up to 49 cents). Wind provides nearly half of the renewable input and feed-in tariffs for new plants are 8.9 c/kWh on land and 15 c offshore. but dropping to 4.9c after five or twelve years respectively. Solar PV gets 12-18 c/kWh depending on size. for 20 years. The combined subsidy from consumers and government totals about EUR 20 billion per year – for some 25% of its electricity from wind and solar. Early in 2010 Germany announced a 15% cut in the solar feed-in tariff for new installations. after adding nearly 3000 MWe solar in 2009. and reportedly paying over $15 billion for solar power. Energy consumers will pay □100 billion over the next 20 years to subsidize domestic PV installed before the end of 2011. The first several months of 2012 added at least □5 billion to that amount. A public backlash is reported due to much of the economic benefit going to foreign solar module manufacturers.

In mid 2012 parliament agreed to cap solar FITs at 52 GW (about double the present level) and apply a new solar FIT of 18.5 cents/kWh for rooftop plants of 10-40 kW and 16.5 c/kWh for 40-1000 kW systems. For larger plants. none over 10 MW would be eligible for FITs. The four major German utilities and the Federal Network Agency and grid authority raised the surcharge that customers pay on their utility bills to fund renewable energy by a steep 47% in 2013. from 3.592 c/kWh in 2012 (yielding EUR 20.4 billion) to 5.277 c/kWh. Then in October 2013 they announced a further 18% rise to 6.24 c/kWh in 2014. taking the annual surcharge on consumers to about EUR 23.6 billion. This is to cover the increasing proportion from renewables and the fact that the utilities are obliged to pay for each renewable kWh much more than they can sell it for (eg 18 c/kWh for solar. sold for 4.5 c/kWh on wholesale market). Utilities charge most customers the EEG surcharge or *Umlage* to cover the difference. Some energy-intensive industries are exempt from this. Overall. the 2013 forecast EEG feed-in tariffs amount to about €18.5 billion. compared with projected revenues on the electricity market of about €2.6 billion. The difference between projected feed-in tariffs and marketing revenues forms the essential part of the EEG surcharge. However. the government is putting a cap on the surcharge until the end of 2014 and then allowing only 2.5% per annum increases. It also plans to tighten industry exemptions and possibly cut FITs for wind and biomass plants. calling into question investment security. The federal Economy Ministry calculates that electricity prices will increase by 3 to 5 c/kWh by mid-2013 from the early 2012 level of 3.59 cents in order to finance renewable energy subsidies and grid expansion. though other estimates put the figure at over 5 cents.

France cut subsidies for solar PV input to the grid by 25% early in 2010. from $0.80 set in 2006 to $0.61 c/kWh. Denmark has a wide range of incentives for renewables and particularly wind energy. In 2000 it produced 4 TWh (out of 36 TWh gross total. about 11%) thus. and is aiming at 15%. Its utility buy-back rates for privately-generated wind electricity in 1999 averaged DKr 0.60/kWh. including a DKr 0.27/kWh subsidy funded by carbon tax (now US$ 6.8 cents and 3.2 cents respectively). However. there is a further economic cost borne by power utilities and customers. When there is a drop in wind. back-up power is bought from the Nordic power pool at the going rate. Similarly. any surplus (subsidised) wind power is sold to the pool. The net effect of this is growing losses as wind capacity expands. Official estimates put the expected losses at DKr 1.5 billion per year. others reckon more than double this.

Early in 2009. Nord Pool announced that from October the spot floor price for surplus power would drop from zero to minus 20 Euro cents/kWh. In other words. wind generators producing power in periods of low demand will have to pay the network to take it. Nord Pool stated: "A negative price floor has been in demand for some time – especially from participants trading Elspot in the Danish bidding areas. In situations with high wind feed in Denmark there have been incidents where sales bids have been curtailed at price □0. Curtailment of sales may give an imbalance cost for the affected seller and thus creates a willingness to pay in order to deliver power in the market." This has increased the negative effect on the economics of wind power in Denmark. since a significant amount of its wind power production is affected.

Sweden subsidises renewables (principally large-scale hydro) by a tax on nuclear capacity. which (late in 2001) works out at EUR 0.32 cents/kWh. It also has a quota and certificate scheme which gives a price of 6.85 c/kWh on renewables apart from solar PV.

Italy had a quota (Renewable Portfolio Standard) and tradable and certificate scheme with average price 12.53 c/kWh for renewables apart from solar PV. 17.27 cents including solar PV. in 2006. This was replaced by FiTs. but due to the proliferation of solar PV capacity. its □6.7 billion cap on subsidies for 2013 was reached in mid-year. FiTs then were 10.6 to 18.2 c/kWh depending on size and location. Innovative plants got 21.7 to 24.2 c/kWh. Concentrating solar PV got 17.4 to 21.5 c/kWh. The FiTs are for 20 years. The government decided on a FiT reduction of 17-25% in 2014. In Norway the government subsidises wind energy with a 25% investment grant and then production support per kWh. the total coming to NOK 0.12/kWh. against a spot price of around NOK 0.18/kWh (US$ 1.3 cents and 2 cents respectively).

Spain has a feed-in tariff of EUR 7.32 c/kWh for wind energy. 27 c/kWh for solar thermal. and 31-34 c/kWh for solar PV. In 2010 cuts of 25% for roof-mounted solar systems and 45% for larger ones were announced. In February 2013 subsidies were cut further and indexed to an inflation estimate that strips out the effects of energy. food commodities. and tax changes. In 2000. the government had promised more than 20 years of large subsidies. and investment had proceeded on this basis.

At the end of 2012 Spain brought in higher taxes on power generation to address an EUR 24 billion energy tariff deficit after more than a decade of selling electricity at regulated rates which did not cover costs. with some EUR 7 billion per year subsidies on renewables. The cost of subsidies was not passed on to consumers. since this would have made power unaffordable. However. foreign investors put a lot of money into wind and solar projects due to the high FITs - some EUR 13 billion. But this power generation tax plus subsidy reductions in 2010 and further major cuts in February 2013 meant that the government had reneged on the terms of that investment. and legal action under the international Energy Charter Treaty was planned.

In July 2013 the Ministry of Industry. Energy and Tourism introduced further 'definitive reforms' to reduce the deficit by □4.5 billion per year. These measures remove the FIT system and substitute a new Regulated Asset Value-based system and will cut the payments for renewables by □1.3 to 1.4 billion per year. Overall they will cost utilities □2.7 billion per year. Solar companies are expected to be worst affected. due to debt load estimated at □30 billion. and widespread financial distress is predicted by solar and wind industry groups. In May 2013 renewables received an average subsidy of EUR 100/MWh.

Greece has a feed-in tariff of 6.1-7.5 c/kWh. whereas the Netherlands relies on exemption from energy taxes to encourage renewables.

Turkey. under its Dec 2010 Renewable Energy law. has a basic feed-in tariff of 7.3 c/kWh. slightly below market prices late in 2010. This can then be increased by up to 3.7c for wind. up to 9.2c for concentrating solar thermal. and up to 6.7c for solar PV. depending on the equipment used and its local content. Prior to this. the FIT was EUR 5.5 cents/kWh.

The Czech Republic had a mandated feed-in tariff for solar power of CZK 12($0.63) per kWh. about ten times the cost of power generated by CEZ. This was threatening grid stability and was reduced to CZK 5.5 for new PV projects over 100 kW and CZK 7.5 for smaller ones after the end of 2010. However. the impact of some 1600 MWe constructed by then was expected to lead to an increase in electricity prices of 13% for residential and 18% for industry consumers in 2011. and a 25-28% retroactive tax on solar electricity from installations over 30 kW was introduced. but was challenged. The International Photovoltaic Investors Club (IPVIC) had an arbitration complaint being lodged in the first quarter of 2013 with findings expected in 2014. The investors group is reportedly seeking up to CZK 2.5 billion in damages.

From January 2014 the Czech government will end all support for new renewables capacity coming on line from then. and set a CZK 495/MWh (□19/ MWh) cap on payments by consumers for renewable power - a 15% drop from 2013. The level of direct government payments to cover the costs of feed-in tariffs and green bonus scheme payments for electricity from renewables will rise to an estimated CZK 15.7 billion (□600 million) in 2014. Total Czech support for renewables is estimated at CZK 44.4 billion (□1.7 billion) in 2013. The 26% tax on new solar installations will drop to 10% in 2014.

Slovakia has drastically cut back on subsidies for solar power. after a boom in response to generous feed-in tariffs pushed the household price of electricity up by 5%. Only roof-mounted PV panels under 100 kW will now be eligible. The subsidy cost jumped from EUR 10 million in 2010 to EUR 117 million in 2011 (to 30 June). The planned 8 MWe of new solar capacity to the end of 2010 ended up with 145 MWe total. and 115 MWe more was expected by the end of June 2011 cut-off. Latvia has feed-in tariffs of EUR 9.6 to 18.2 c/kWh for wind. depending on size of generator. and 42.7 c/kWh for solar PV. Lithuania's feed-in tariff for wind is 8.7 c/kWh. Elsewhere in EU. small-scale photovoltaic (PV) input is encouraged by high feed-in tariffs. eg 50 c/kWh in Portugal.

NORTH AMERICA

The US government spent $24 billion on energy subsidies in 2011. $16 billion of this for renewables including $6 billion for ethanol tax credits. according to the Congressional Budget Office. The production tax credit for wind cost $1.6 billion. Fossil fuels got $2.5 billion in tax breaks.

In the USA a direct subsidy or Production Tax Credit (PTC. finally about 2.3 c/kWh net for wind) has been available to generators of renewable power over the first ten years of a project's operation so they can sell it that much below actual cost. The subsidy is granted as credit on taxes. though following the American Recovery and Reinvestment Act (ARRA) in mid-2009. an investment tax credit of 30% could be claimed instead for wind plant placed in service before 2013 if construction began before the end of 2013. A total of $16.8 billion had been provided in direct grants for energy efficiency and renewable energy projects under ARRA. This credit can be converted to a grant from the government. In the USA a Renewable Portfolio Standard is proposed. mandating a specified amount of renewable power from suppliers. and applying already in California and other states. The PTC is indexed to inflation. and was extended each year to the end of 2013. With a wholesale electricity price of around 2.8 c/kWh. the PTC meant that intermittent wind generators could dump power on the market to the extent of depressing the wholesale price so that other generators were operating at a loss. This market distortion has created major problems for the viability of dispatchable generation sources upon which the market depends. Several US states and municipalities are looking at FITs. Vermont enacted one in 2009 and Gainesville. Florida has one in 26-32 c/kWh range. In Ontario. Canada. under a 2009 Green Energy Act. feed-in tariffs were introduced. ranging from 11 c/kWh for landfill gas and 13 c/kWh for wind to 80.2 c/kWh for solar PV.

EAST ASIA

In Japan. since 2009 a feed-in tariff required utilities to buy surplus solar power produced domestically at up to JPY 48/kWh. This was extended to hydro. wind and geothermal power at JPY 17-20/kWh. compared with JPY 5-7 for base-load power. In mid 2012 the general FIT was increased to JPY 42/kWh for solar-generated electricity. double the tariff offered in Germany and more than three times that paid in China. The level is to be reduced in April 2014 to JPY 37/kWh residential and JPY 32/kWh for systems over 10 kW. Wind power FIT will be JPY 23.1/kWh for units above 20 kW and JPY 57.75 for smaller units. In China. the Global Wind Energy Council acknowledges "the fact that wind is heavily subsidised". This is under a variety of complex measures focused on capacity rather than output. and correlates with a low average capacity factor of 16% over 2006-07. partly due to grid constraints. China's 2006 Renewable Energy Law sets out a subsidized electricity tariff structure (though no feed-in tariff). a compulsory grid connection mandate for renewable energy projects. and a rule that requires utilities to purchase all the renewable electricity produced in their service area. In addition. carbon credits awarded under the UN Clean Development Mechanism (CDM) enable foreign investors in Chinese wind projects to sell carbon credits outside the country. this being essential to project viability.

Solar power has enjoyed substantial incentives in China since 2009. and in 2011 the national feed-in tariff was RMB 1.15 per kWh (18 cents). but in 2012 this was reduced to RMB 0.55 (8.7 cents). Late in 2012 subsidies for solar power were boosted by CNY 7 billion ($1.1 billion) to a total of CNY 13 billion. The subsidies are to allow support of 5.2 GWe of domestic solar energy production.

AUSTRALIA

Australia's Mandatory Renewable Energy Target (RET or MRET) has since 2001 required retailers each to buy a certain proportion of the electricity they supply from non-hydro renewable sources at whatever price they can. or incur a penalty by paying a shortfall charge. currently 4.2 c/kWh ($A). The original 10% target or 9500 GWh by 2010 was increased in 2009 to 20%. or about 45.000

GWh in 2020. representing a major increase from non-hydro sources. The shortfall charge goes up fro 4 cents to 6.5 c/kWh. The obligation is tradeable. Subsidies for renewables total an estimated $12 billion in the decade to 2011. which works out to about 0.6 c/kWh. Origin Energy estimates that the small-scale renewable scheme part of MRET will cost customers $3.2 billion over the current two years to 2012. Government-commissioned modelling suggests that the net overall power cost to consumers will be 0.5 c/kWh to 2015 and then 0.77 c/kWh to 2020. A 2011 study by Carbon Market Economics found that each tonne of CO2 emissions eliminated through the use of renewable energy plants commissioned by the end of 2010 cost $76 in subsidies. more than three times the proposed carbon price of $23 a tonne.

Feed-in tariffs are on a state basis. Victorian and NSW householders with solar PV sell power to the grid at 60 c/kWh. compared with about 8 c/kWh for coal-fired power delivered to the city.

SUBSIDIES FOR COAL (AND OTHER FOSSIL FUELS)

The OECD IEA estimates that globally. fossil fuel subsidies amounted to $409 billion in 2010. compared with about $300 billion in 2009. Its detailed inventory covers over 250 mechanisms that support fossil fuel production and use. Some 54% of the fossil fuel support went to the petroleum sector.

In the EU. coal is heavily subsidised by governments. particularly in Germany's Ruhrgebiet region. northwest Spain. and Romania's Jiu Valley. There have been proposals to phase out coal subsidies by 2022. reducing them by one quarter every three years. but some 100.00 jobs are involved. In 2010. some EUR 3.2 billion in coal subsidies were handed out in six EU countries: Germany. Hungary. Poland. Romania. Slovakia and Spain.

In July 2010 the European Commission unanimously approved a proposal to close uncompetitive hard coal mines in the EU that rely on subsidies by October 2014. and to phase out coal subsidies by 2018. The mines that rely on operating subsidies are located mostly in the Ruhr region in Germany. in northwest Spain and in the Jiu Valley in Romania. More than 40% of electricity in Germany is produced from coal. about half of which is hard coal and half lignite. In Romania. coal-produced electricity is also around 40%. most of which hard coal. In Spain the share is around 25%. also mostly hard coal. Under the approved rules. interim operating aid would only be allowed for coal mines with a closure plan in place. otherwise state aid will stop.

According to the EC in mid 2010. total aid to the hard coal sector has been halved from €6.4 billion in 2003 to € 2.9 billion in 2008. The amount of aid going towards actual production has fallen by 62% to € 1.3 billion in the same period. Germany has provided producer subsidies to its coal industry amounting to EUR 68 per tonne for 34 Mt coal in 2000 - total EUR 2.3 billion. Since the late 1980s the domestic hard coal production price has been at least EUR 100/t above the imported cost. and subsidies reached a high of EUR 7.9 billion in 1989. By 2002 production had declined to about 25 Mt/yr and the subsidy was down to EUR 3.5 billion and a later figure quoted EUR 2.5 billion. with EUR 130 billion over previous four decades.

ENERGY TAXES. AND SUBSIDIES FOR NUCLEAR POWER

Corresponding to subsidies in the other direction are taxes on particular energy sources. justified by climate change or related policies. and with low production costs providing opportunity. For instance Sweden taxes nuclear power at about EUR 0.67 cents/kWh. which makes up about one third of the operating costs for nuclear plants. Belgium is introducing a tax of 0.5 cents/kWh on nuclear. The UK has a Climate Change Levy which is a tax on energy used by business. The rate was 0.43 p/kWh but from 2006 has been indexed. Electricity from designated renewable sources is exempt from the levy. nuclear power is subject to it. Germany in 2010 legislated for a tax of €145 per gram of uranium or plutonium fuel for six years. yielding €2.3 billion per year (about 1.6 c/kWh). a levy on nuclear generators of €300 million per year in 2011 and 2012. and €200 million 2013-16. to subsidise renewables. and a tax of €0.9 c/kWh for the same purpose after 2016. Finland has been planning to introduce a tax on nuclear fuel to raise about €170 million per year from 2013. and countering the windfall profits from nuclear generators selling CO2 emission allowances. The Ministry of Employment and Economy in 2011 said that these so-called 'windfall' profits would be taxed at 43% to 45% of the market price of CO2 emission rights. depending on the model adopted. and at least € 0.2 cents/kWh. In the "minimum tax model". at €15 per tonne CO2 the tax would generate at least € 67 million per year. and at € 30 per tonne. the tax would be € 0.67 cents per kWh. generating some € 223 million.

In the "flexible tax model". the uranium tax would be € 0.17 cents per kWh. plus 30% of the windfall profit. An emission allowance price of €15 per tonne of CO2 would generate some € 57 million. and a price of € 30 per tonne would generate € 207 million. Under this model. if the emissions trading price fell to less than €9.3 per tonne of CO2. there would be a 'negative' tax which could be credited against subsequent years of 'positive' uranium taxes. The proposal has drawn criticism. as it counteracts a key goal of the EU's carbon market - to reward low-carbon production compared with high-CO2 sources. There is also occasionally a tax on excess wind production at times of low demand in Denmark and northern Germany. Nordpool requires generators to pay up to EUR 20 c/kWh for users to take excess electricity when demand is low. and in Germany the price has hit 50 c/kWh (at 5am on an October day in 2008). A similar situation arises locally in western Texas.

The USA is the only country which has offered any subsidy to nuclear power: a production tax credit of 1.9 c/kWh from the first 6000 MWe of new-generation nuclear plants in their first 8 years of operation (same as for wind power on unlimited basis). (In 2007 the USA subsidised renewables by $724 million and recorded $199 billion subsidy for nuclear power. The latter was entirely due to a change in tax rules related to decommissioning. under the 2005 Energy Policy Act.)

ESCALATING SUBSIDIES FOR RENEWABLES

A Eurelectric report in January 2004 looked at direct support levels for renewable electricity supply in 2001 and projections for 2010. assuming that present support mechanisms remained unchanged and that developments were in line with EU targets. The EUR 3.3 billion subsidy in 2001 was projected to grow to about EUR 11.5 billion in 2010. including EUR 7.4 billion for feed-in tariffs. The unit subsidy would then range from 0.4 c/kWh in Finland to 6.6 c/kWh in Germany. with a weighted average of 3.7 c/kWh in EU-15 countries (4.2 c/kWh in those with feed-in tariffs).

Table: Direct support for Renewable Electricity Supply

Country	Subsidy EUR million per yr		Subsidy EUR cents/kWh	
	2001	2010	2001	2010
Austria*	122	702	2.49	4.11
Belgium	27	55	2.7	2.70
Denmark*	273	499	4.19	3.87
France*	112	814	3.13	3.13
Germany*	1047	3326	6.21	6.58
Italy	1067	2493	6.31	5.88
Netherlands	59	679	1.98	5.69
Spain*	323	1537	2.78	2.65
Sweden	100	220	1.89	1.28
UK	96	547	1.73	1.45

* using feed-in tariff

CARBON TAXES AND EMISSION TRADING SCHEMES FOR CARBON

Despite much rhetoric and considerable experience with the European Emission Trading Scheme (ETS) for carbon applying to certain sectors. no country imposes an economy-wide tax on greenhouse gases or has in place an economy-wide ETS. The EU's cap-and-trade ETS. in its first six years of operation. raised a little more than $2.5 billion. Much of the justification for subsidising renewables is the avoidance of carbon dioxide emissions. due to the need for European countries to meet Kyoto targets. The 2004 Eurelectric report thus identifies cost of carbon emissions avoided. These in 2001 ranged from EUR 7/t of avoided CO_2 in Finland to EUR 64/t in Denmark. EUR 74/t in Germany and EUR 100/t in Italy. Projections for 2010 had much higher costs: EUR 55/t for Denmark. EUR 109/t for Germany and Italy. EUR 148/t for France. and EUR 155/t for Netherlands. The weighted average is EUR 88/t and that for countries with feed-in tariffs EUR 103/t.

In 2011 an Australian Productivity Commission report surveyed much of the world scene. The report calculates the subsidy equivalent. abatement achieved and implicit abatement subsidy for policies and aggregated by sector in each country. Those for electricity generation are addressed here. and the following is largely from that source. Estimates of abatement relative to counterfactual emissions in the electricity generation sector showed Germany significantly ahead. followed by the UK. then Australia. the USA and China. The estimated cost per unit of abatement achieved varied widely. both across programmes within each country and in aggregate across countries. Emissions trading schemes (ETS) were found to be relatively cost-effective when not crowded out by other policies. while policies encouraging small-scale renewable generation and biofuels produced little abatement for substantially higher cost. What all schemes have in common is that they involve a cost. which someone must pay. These costs can be expressed in subsidy equivalent or resource cost terms. and can be considered as the 'price' of abatement achieved by particular policies.

International comparisons for electricity generation. 2010

	Abatement per cent of emissions	Total electricity sector emissions. t CO2	Implicit abatement subsidy \$/t CO2	Electricity price uplift per cent
China	1-2	3370	35-37	1
USA	3	2270	43-50	-
Australia	3-5	196	44-99	1-2
UK	8-15	151	75-198	17
Germany	18-20	299	137-175	12-14
Japan	1	396	156-287	1
S.Korea	<1	191	225-401	-

The most widely applied emissions-reduction policies in the electricity sector are mandatory renewable energy targets (most with tradeable permits). feed-in tariffs. and capital subsidies (often in conjunction with feed-in tariffs). Mandatory renewable energy targets apply at the national level in Australia. Germany and the UK (under an EU mandate).

Japan. and South Korea (committed for 2012). Although the USA does not have a national level mandatory renewable energy target. over 41 states have renewable targets of one form or another. most mandatory. Feed-in tariffs apply at a national level in Japan. the UK. South Korea and Germany. and at a state level in Australia. China and India operate national and state/province-based schemes. Feed-in tariffs also exist in some US states. where they operate mainly as commercial arrangements between utilities and small-scale generators that the utilities use to meet their renewable energy targets. Capital subsidies are common. and provided for widely varying purposes.

EXTERNAL COSTS

However. the implicit subsidies where the waste products of energy use are allowed to be dumped into the biosphere are greater than these direct subsidies. The largest of them are given to fossil fuel producers. Nuclear energy has always had to cost in its own waste management and disposal (equivalent to about 5% of generation cost. with a further similar sum for decommisioning)*. Renewables only give rise to wastes in manufacturing. and while these are sometimes unpleasant they are dealt with in the same way as other manufacturing wastes.

Consideration. and if possible quantification. of external costs aids life cycle analysis and technology comparison as well as cost-benefit analysis generally.

The report of ExternE. a major European study of the external costs of various fuel cycles. focusing on coal and nuclear. was released in 2001 and further figures have emerged since. The European Commission launched the project in 1991 in collaboration with the US Dept of Energy (which subsequently dropped out). and it was the first research project of its kind "to put plausible financial figures against damage resulting from different forms of electricity production for the entire EU".The external costs are defined as those actually incurred in relation to health and the environment and quantifiable but not built into the cost of the electricity to the consumer and therefore which are borne by society at large. They include particularly the effects of air pollution on human health. crop yields and buildings. as well as occupational disease and accidents. The 2001 data excluded effects on ecosystems and the impact of global warming. but these are now included despite the high range of uncertainty in adequately quantifying and evaluating them economically.

The methodology measures emissions. their dispersion pathways and ultimate impact. Exposure-response models lead to evaluating the physical impacts in monetary terms. With nuclear energy the (low) risk of accidents is factored in along with high estimates of radiological impacts from mine tailings (since shown to be exaggerated) and carbon-14 emissions from reprocessing (waste management and decommissioning being already within the cost to the consumer).

The report shows that in clear cash terms nuclear energy incurs about one tenth of the costs of coal. Nuclear energy averages under 0.4 euro cents/ kWh (0.2-0.7). less than hydro. coal is over 4.0 cents (2-10 cent averages in different countries). gas ranges 1-4 cents and only wind shows up better than nuclear. at 0.05-0.25 cents/kWh average.

The EU cost of electricity generation without these external costs averages about 4 cents/kWh. If these external costs were in fact included. the EU price of electricity from coal would double and that from gas would increase around 30%. The report proposes two ways of incorporating external costs: taxing the costs or subsidising alternatives. Due to the difficulty of taxing in an EU context. subsidy is favoured. EC guidelines published in February 2001 encourage members states to subsidise "new plants producing renewable energy... on the basis of external costs avoided". up to 5 c/kWh. However. this provision does not extend to nuclear power. despite the comparable external costs avoided. EU member countries have pledged to have renewables (including hydro) provide 12% of total energy and 22% of electricity by 2010. a target which appears unlikely to be met. The case for extending the subsidy to nuclear energy is obvious. particularly if climate change is to be taken seriously.

In that connection it is interesting to note the significant state subsidies to the coal industry in the EU. reported to total EUR 6874 million or EUR 190 per tonne in 2000. This includes operating aid. 'aid for reduction of activity'. and other. In Germany alone. politically committed to phasing out nuclear energy and meanwhile finding new ways to tax it. EUR 4598 million was spent in subsidies to coal in 2000! Considerable effort was being given to finding ways to extend these subsidies beyond mid 2002.Another European treatment of production and external costs. specifically of power generation in Switzerland (the GaBE Project). has been done by the Paul Scherrer Institut and shows that the damage costs from fossil fuels are 10 to 350% of the production costs. while those for nuclear are very small. A summary is accessible on the web. and the figure below is from it:An earlier European study (Krewitt et al. 1999) quantified environmental damage costs from fossil fuel electricity generation in the EU for 1990 as US$ 70 billion. about 1% of GDP. This included impacts on human health. building materials and crop production. but not global warming.

The EC is undertaking a follow-on study to ExternE called NewExt to examine particular environmental costs and risks. mostly associated with fossil fuels. In October 2009 a US National Research Council report commissioned by Congress quantified and analysed a total of $120 billion in "hidden" external costs of energy production in the USA in 2005. The figures reflect mainly health damage and exclude the effects of climate change. Electricity generation accounted for more than half. practically all being from coal.

The external cost of damages. primarily caused from sulfur dioxide. nitrogen oxide and particulate matter emissions from burning coal. were $62 billion. or 3.2 cents per kWh of electricity produced from it. The report expects damages from coal to fall to 1.7 c/kWh by 2030. Electricity produced from natural gas produced $0.74 billion in damages (0.16 c/kWh) in 2005. primarily from air pollution. For nuclear the figure was about 0.02 c/kWh. Motor vehicles produced $56 billion in health and other non-climate damages. considering the full life cycle of vehicles - only one third was from their operation. Electric and plug-in hybrid vehicles resulted in higher non-climate damages than other technologies. due to reliance on fossil fuels for the electricity. Energy used to create the batteries and electric motors adds 20% of the manufacturing portion of life-cycle damages.

PUBLIC HEALTH

Consideration of external costs leads to the conclusion that the public health benefits associated with reducing greenhouse gas emissions from fossil fuel burning could be the strongest reason for pursuing them. Considering four cities - New York. Mexico. Santiago and Sao Paulo - with total 45 million people. a paper in *Science* presents calculations showing that some 64.000 deaths would be avoided in the two decades to 2020 by reducing fossil fuel combustion in line with greenhouse abatement targets. This is consistent with a 1995 WHO estimate of 460.000 avoidable deaths annually from suspended particulates. largely due to outdoor urban exposure.

The World Health Organisation in 1997 presented two estimates. of 2.7 or 3 million deaths occurring each year as a result of air pollution. In the latter estimate: 2.8 million deaths were due to indoor exposures and 200.000 to outdoor exposure. The lower estimate comprised 1.85 million deaths from rural indoor pollution. 363.000 from urban indoor pollution and 511.000 from urban ambient pollution. The WHO report points out that these totals are about 6% of all deaths. and the uncertainty of the estimates means that the range should be taken as 1.4 to 6 million deaths annually attributable to air pollution.

LIFE CYCLE CO_2 EMISSIONS

Turning to carbon dioxide. if all energy inputs are assumed to be from coal-fired plants. at about one kilogram of carbon dioxide per kWh. it is possible to derive a greenhouse contribution from the energy input percentage of output. However. For Sweden's Forsmark as many energy inputs are not fossil fuel. its life cycle analysis (2002 data) give it the very low CO_2 emission figure of 3.1 g/kWh.

In France. despite energy-inefficient enrichment plants which are run by nuclear power. the greenhouse contribution from any nuclear reactor using French-enriched uranium is similar to a reactor elsewhere using centrifuge-enriched uranium — less than 20 g/kWh overall.

Japan show 13 g/kWh. with prospects of this halving in future. Japan's Central Research Institute of the Electric Power Industry give life cycle carbon dioxide emission figures for various generation technologies. Swedish utility Vattenfall (1999) published a popular account of life cycle studies based on the previous few years experience and its certified Environmental Product Declarations (EPDs) for Forsmark and Ringhals nuclear power stations. and a similar exercise was undertaken in Finland by Kivisto et al. The sets of data compare as follows:

g/kWh CO_2	Japan	Sweden	Finland
coal	975	980	894
gas thermal	608	1170 (peak. reserve)	-
gas combined cycle	519	450	472
solar photovoltaic	53	50	95
wind	29	5.5	14
nuclear	22	6	10-26
hydro	11	3	-

The Japanese gas figures include shipping LNG from overseas. and the nuclear figure is for boiling water reactors. with enrichment 70% in USA. 30% France and Japan. and one third of the fuel to be MOX. The Finnish nuclear figures are for centrifuge and diffusion enrichment respectively.

ENERGY-RELATED ACCIDENTS

A November 1998 study from the Paul Scherrer Institut in Switzerland. more recently available in English. examines other aspects of external costs. The 400-page report was commissioned by the Swiss Federal Office of Energy. and draws on data from 4290 energy-related accidents. 1943 of them classified as severe. and compares different energy sources. It considers over 15.000 fatalities related to oil. over 8000 related to coal and 5000 from hydro - in total. about seven World Trade Centres. It points out that Full Cost Accounting. including both internal and external costs. is increasingly used for electric utility planning. though not on any standard basis. and not without considerable practical difficulty in assigning costs. Also it is notable that for any specific energy chain. different parts are often in different countries.

Considering only deaths and comparing them per Terawatt-year. coal has 342. hydro 883. gas 85 and nuclear power only 8 (/TWe.yr). (Nuclear power delivers some 2500 TWh per year. hence these 8 deaths would be spread over 3.5 years in the course of providing 14% of the world's electricity. whereas coal's 342 deaths can be expected every 19 months for slightly more than twice the amount of electricity.) In terms of number of immediate deaths per event from 1969 to 1996. hydro stands out with about 550 compared with coal at about 40.The new report updates and confirms an earlier study covering 1970-92.

ENERGY CONSUMPTION IN INDIA: AN INDICATOR ANALYSIS

India is the second largest commercial energy consumer in Non-OECD East Asia. comprising 19 percent of the region's total primary energy consumption.

Economic growth in India has largely been associated with increased energy consumption. While 60% of total energy needs in India are met by commercial energy sources. remaining 40% are comprised of non-conventional fuels. Over past few years. climate change has become one of the main concerns driving energy policy. More than 150 countries. including India. have committed themselves under the United Nations Framework Convention on Climate Change to formulate and implement mitigation and adaptation measures to climate change. India accounts for over 3.5% of world carbon emissions. Since energy use is a major source of emissions. it is necessary to focus on the management of energy demand and supply as a means to abatement. While energy demand grows significantly with economic growth. this coupling varies over time. depending on various other things. Technological progress. energy efficiency programmes and structural changes contribute towards the variation in energy demand. Understanding the various components of energy demand is therefore important and necessary in order to deal with future emissions. Energy use profile of the Indian economy

Sectoral demand for energy arises mainly from lighting and cooking in the household sector; irrigation and other operations in the agricultural sector; transport of passengers and freight and fuel input requirements in the industrial sector.

Sector-wise activity level and energy consumption pattern in India. India's commercial energy consumption has increased from 130.7 million tonnes of oil equivalent (mtoe) in 1991/92 to 176.08 mtoe in 1997/98. Per capita commercial energy consumption increased from 152.7 kilo grams of oil equivalent (kgoe) to 184.7 kgoe over the same period. Average annual growth rate for the agricultural GDP is 2.6 percent. the same figures for the industrial. transport and the service sectors are 6.8 percent. 7.6 percent and 6.4 percent respectively. Industrial sector has consistently remained the largest consumer of commercial energy. followed by the transport sector despite declining share of industrial sector from 50.4 percent in 1991-92 to 47.8 percent in 1997-98.

INDICATOR ANALYSIS

Energy use can be viewed as a function of total GDP. structure of the economy and technology. Aggregate energy intensity is taken as an energy performance indicator in energy demand analysis. Literature on indicator analysis adopts either of the two approaches: energy consumption approach or energy intensity approach. We follow the intensity approach and decompose total energy-GDP ratio into structural effect (S.E) and intensity effect (I.E). Structural effect shows that part of change in energy use which is attributable to change in activity composition of an economy. Intensity effect tells us that keeping GDP effect and structural effect unchanged. what has been the change in energy use solely due to conservation measures. Accompanying table show the respective values for the structural effect (Dstr). intensity effect (Dint) and the total effect (Dtot) comprising of these two effects. In last decade. India experienced a structural change that has worsened the overall energy intensity index as it is greater than one except in two intermediate years of 1992-'94. Beyond 1993-94 the structural effect shows a rising trend in energy intensity. Intensity effect showing the conservation effort had a fluctuating trend. though this effect alone could outweigh the structural effect and overall energy intensity index shows falling trend after 1995-96.

SECTORAL ENERGY INTENSITIES

Structural effect is dominated by sharp increase in the industrial and transport sector GDP. Energy intensity is higher in the industrial sector. followed by the transport sector. But. the industrial sector records a downward trend in energy intensity. The average annual decline in energy intensity during 1989-90 to 1997-98 is 2.14 per cent as compared to 0.33 per cent in the transport sector and 1.08 per cent in the service sector.

On the other hand. agriculture sector records an increase in the energy intensity over the same period (6.5 per cent). But. there seems to be significant energy efficiency improvements to curb the rising structural effect. and as a result of which the aggregate energy intensity index of the economy has improved after 1995-96.

This can be traced to demographic changes. including relatively faster growth in urban areas. high per capita GDP. penetration of more end use devices. technological improvements in conversion equipment and inter-fuel substitution with more efficient alternatives in the energy intensive industries.

Since sectoral output growth is the main contributing factor to rising energy intensity. one might think that policies should be designed to curb this growth. However. this would mean imposition of real cost on the economy. Hence. policy alternatives should see how to offset this increasing output effect by negative intensity and structural effects. Declining structural effect can be achieved by a greater shift towards non-energy intensive industries. expansion of service sector etc. Negative trend in intensity effects can be intensified by inter-fuel substitution. introducing efficient technology to improve energy productivity.

Other country studies reveal one thing in common that in most of the OECD countries energy intensity declined and improved energy efficiency played a substantial role in it. Intensity effect is smaller for India than for other countries. Energy demand can be restricted directly through economic instruments like prices. taxes or rationing etc. But they have their adverse welfare impact also unless supplemented by indirect policies in the form of introduction of more efficient technologies.

Conservation in industry sector has been successful in putting a break to rising overall intensity trend. Energy efficiency improvement through R&D. labels and standards. technology transfer may be a better policy tool to strengthen conservation effect to offset rising energy intensity due to structural change and activity growth.

Economic growth and structural change are the big drivers in positive growth in energy intensity in India. The structural component is driven mainly by incomes and by forces not directly related to energy or energy policies. Since it is difficult to restrict energy demand rising from increased output or activity directly. stress needs to be on conservation measures at the early stage of development. Sectoral policies on housing. commercial buildings. industry and transport must integrate energy efficiency at local. regional and national levels.

A STRUCTURAL DECOMPOSITION ANALYSIS OF ENERGY CONSUMPTION IN INDIA

During the fifty years that followed independence. the demand for energy. particularly for commercial energy. registered a high rate of growth contributed largely by the changes in the demographic structure brought about through rapid urbanisation. need for socio-economic development and the need for attaining and sustaining self reliance in different sectors of the economy.

The economic development of a country is often closely linked to its consumption of energy. Although India ranks fifth in the world so far as total commercial energy consumption is concerned. it still needs much more energy to keep pace with its development objectives. India's projected economic growth rate is slated at 7.4% in the period 1997-2012(DOE/EIA). This would necessitate commensurate growth in the requirement of commercial energy. most of which is expected to be from fossil fuels and hydroelectricity. India's proven coal reserves may last for about 200 years. but the limited known oil and natural gas reserves may last only a few more decades. which is a cause of concern. The continued trend of increasing share of petroleum fuels in the consumption of commercial energy will lead to more dependence on imports and energy insecurity.

India's energy intensity per unit of GDP is higher compared to Japan. U.S.A. and Asia as a whole by 3.7. 1.6 and 1.5 times respectively. This is mostly due to India being in a transition from an agricultural economy to an industrialized society. increased urbanization and consumerism. In addition. the large performance bandwidth of Indian Industries with respect to specific energy consumption is lowering the Indian average energy efficiency and contributing to higher energy intensity. The increasing global trade liberalization and growing global competition have enhanced productivity including energy cost reduction.

To uplift the economy and to accelerate its growth the government of India introduced a series of reform packages in the mid 1991 including the new strategies for the energy sector.

The energy strategies are: i) to initiate a shift from non-renewable sources of energy to renewable sources and to provide wider access for the rural and urban poor to adequate energy supplies at affordable costs. ii) to ensure efficiency in the use of energy in all production processes. iii) to review the use of all energy intensive materials and provide for their substitution by less energy intensive materials through Rand D. iv) to ensure efficiency in the use of equipment in the energy sector. especially in thermal and nuclear power generation through improved plant availability. v) to initiate measures aimed at reducing energy intensity in different sectors. through changes in technology and/or processes. vi) to optimise inter-fuel substitution. vii) to propagate renewable resources based on decentralised and environmentally benign non-conventional technologies and viii) to maximise the availability of indigenous energy resources such as oil. natural gas. coal and hydroelectric power. as well as non-conventional energy by way of bio-gas. solar energy and wind energy.

CONSERVATION INITIATIVES

Waste heat recovery systems. cogeneration. and the utilization of alternative sources of energy are also important for the conservation of energy. Technology. upgradation. modernization. and the introduction of control instrumentation are necessary to realize the full potential of energy conservation in industry.

The coal industry is both a source of energy and a consumer of energy. Energy can be conserved in both these areas. Coal reserves can be conserved through proper methods of exploration. improved recovery. and introduction of new mining technologies.Hydrocarbons continue to be the major source of energy. The conservation of this form of energy is essential as it will reduce environmental pollution. Here we can mention some relevant policies focusing on energy saving.

To initiate action to reduce the energy intensity of the different consuming sectors of the economy and promotes conservation and demand management through appropriate organizational and fiscal measures.In India energy demand can be restricted directly through economic instruments like prices. taxes or rationing etc. But they have their adverse welfare impact also unless supplemented by indirect policies in the form of introduction of more efficient technologies.Alternative technology has not yet been used up to required level. The first and foremost strategies should be to introduce alternative fuel like CNG. Natural gas and bio gas fuel instead of oil to cover up the extra strain arising due to price hike.

The trend in intensity effects can be intensified by inter-fuel substitution. introducing efficient technology to improve energy productivity. Other country studies reveal one thing in common that in most of the OECD countries energy intensity declined and improved energy efficiency played a substantial role in it. So a proper weightage should be given to review the use of all energy intensive materials and provide for substitution of less energy intensive materials. We have to encourage those industries which are using more energy efficient technologies and introduce new technology at a more rapid rate than in the past.

We have to ensure efficiency in the use of energy in all production processes extensively.Conservation in industry sector has been successful in putting a break to rising overall intensity trend. Energy efficiency improvement and speedy assimilation of technology through proper enhancement of expenditure on R&D. labels and standards. cost effective technology development and technology transfer may be a better policy tool to strengthen conservation effect to offset rising energy intensity due to the indirect role of the energy sectors.

Measures also needed for reducing technical losses in production. transportation and end-use of all forms of energy.From the above study it is noted that a paradigm shift in the approach to energy policy issues is needed – a shift from a supply dominated approach to an integrated approach incorporating a judicial mix of investment in energy supply side capacity. operational efficiency improvement of designated industrial consumers in particular existing power generating. transmission and distribution as well as end-use efficiency in households and commerce. The policy goals and concepts will have to be shifted from "energy conservation" to "energy efficiency". and from "energy inputs" to the effectiveness of energy use" and "energy services." Recognizing the importance and benefits of energy efficiency. the Government of India has enacted the Energy Conservation Act. 2001 which has already into force from 1st March. 2002. This act primarily stressed on energy conservation and energy efficiency. Hope the impact of this Energy Conservation Act will derive a better tomorrow for India.

ENERGY INTENSITY AND EFFICIENCY IN INDIA

Energy intensity is an indicator to show how efficiently energy is used in the economy. As was said energy intensity in India had a decreasing trend in 1990-2007and then it is a necessary which India has a programme to ensure energy for all of sectors. Energy security has an important role in future energy consumption in India. Going by the estimates released by the Central Statistical Organization. real GDP at factor cost was registered 9% in 2007-08 (9.6% in 2006-07). The main reason of robust 9 percent GDP growth rate can be credited to the higher investment rates. The gross fixed capital formation ratio to GDP which was 23.80 per cent in 2002-03. had shoot up to 24.94% in 2003-04. 28.41% in 2004-05. 30.98 per cent in 2005-06. 32.48 per cent in 2006-07 and 33.91 per cent in 2007-08.

Energy has been universally recognized as one of the most important inputs for economic growth and human development. There is a strong two-way relationship between economic development and energy consumption. On one hand. growth of an economy. with its global competitiveness. hinges on the availability of cost-effective and environmentally benign energy sources. and on the other hand. the level of economic development has been observed to be reliant on the energy demand. Energy intensity is an indicator to show how efficiently energy is used in the economy. The energy intensity of India is over twice that of the matured economies. which are represented by the OECD (Organization of Economic Co-operation and Development) member countries. India's energy intensity is also much higher than the emerging economies—the Asian countries. which include the ASEAN member countries as well as China. However. since 1999. India's energy intensity has been decreasing and is expected to continue to decrease.The indicator of energy–GDP (gross domestic product) elasticity. that is. the ratio of growth rate of energy to the growth rate GDP. captures both the structure of the economy as well as the efficiency. The energy–GDP elasticity during 1953–2001 has been above unity. However. the elasticity for primary commercial energy consumption for 1991–2000 was less than unity. This could be attributed to several factors. some of them being demographic shifts from rural to urban areas. structural economic changes towards lesser energy industry. impressive growth of services. improvement in efficiency of energy use. and inter-fuel substitution. The energy sector in India has been receiving high priority in the planning process. The total outlay on energy in the Tenth Five-year Plan has been projected to be 4.03 trillion rupees at 2001/02 prices. which is 26.7% of the total outlay. An increase of 84.2% is projected over the Ninth Five-year Plan in terms of the total plan outlay on energy sector.

The Government of India in the mid-term review of the Tenth Plan recognized the fact that under-performance of the energy sector can be a major constraint in delivering a growth rate of 8% GDP during the plan period. It has. therefore. called for acceleration of the reforms process and adoption of an integrated energy policy. In the recent years. the government has rightly recognized the energy security concerns of the nation and more importance is being placed on energy independence. On the eve of the 59th Independence Day. the President of India emphasized that energy independence has to be the nation's first and highest priority. and India must be determined to achieve this within the next 25 years The energy intensity of India is over twice that of the matured economies. which are represented by the OECD (Organization of Economic Co-operation and Development) member countries. India's energy intensity is also much higher than the emerging economies. However. since 1999. India's energy intensity has been decreasing and is expected to continue to decrease further. The indicator of energy–GDP (gross domestic product) elasticity captures both the structure of the economy as well as the efficiency in terms of energy consumption. The energy–GDP elasticity during 1953–2001 has been above unity in Indian case. However. the elasticity for primary commercial energy consumption for 1991–2000 was less than unity.

The variation in the energy intensity could be attributed to several factors. some of them being demographic shifts from rural to urban areas. structural economic changes towards lesser energy industry. impressive growth of services. improvement in efficiency of energy use. and inter-fuel substitution. Therefore. there is a major question arise what determine the energy intensity of the Indian economy in general and for the manufacturing industries in particular.

ENERGY CONSUMPTION IN AGRICULTURE SECTOR

The higher GDP growth rate has been ascribed to the good performance of the agricultural sector. It was increased to 4.5% as compared to projected 2.6%. This is seen as a result of bumper production of wheat. rice. maize. soya bean. cotton. pulses. which has reached to its maxim. The government says the buoyancy in agricultural sector is account to the revision made in the estimated agriculture crops production by the Department of Agriculture and Cooperation. The country inherited a stagnant agriculture at the time of Independence. The traditional tools and implements relied mostly on human and animal power and used a negligible amount of commercial energy. However. successive governments realized the importance of agriculture and initiatives were taken for the growth of this sector. Increased investment in irrigation infrastructure. expansion of credit. marketing. and processing facilities (therefore. led to a significant increase in the use of modern inputs. Till the 1950s. use of tractors for agriculture was very limited. Tractor manufacturing in India started in 1961 with aggregate capacity to manufacture 11 000 tractors. Joint efforts made by the government and private sector have led to steady increase in the level of mechanization over the years. Given that rains are not always timely and evenly distributed. farmers prefer pump sets as a more reliable and assured source of irrigation; as a result. energization of pump sets have been increasing rapidly.

As on 31 March 2004. 14.1 million pump sets had been energized. Maharashtra has the maximum number of energized pump sets (2.4 million). followed by Andhra Pradesh (2.3 million). Earlier. the average capacity of the pump sets was 3.68 kW and a pump set on an average consumed 6004 kWh of electricity in that year. However. owing to insufficient electricity supplies. some farmers have also procured diesel pump sets as a standby. In the recent past. concerted efforts of the government has led to an introduction of biomass and solar photovoltaic based pumping systems As a result of increased mechanization in agriculture. crop production and rural agro processing emerged as one of the major consumers of commercial energy. The share of mechanical and electrical power in agriculture increased from 40% in 1971/72 to 84% in 2003/04. The availability of farm power per unit area (kW/ha) has been considered as one of the parameters of expressing the level of mechanization. Power availability for carrying out various agricultural operations has increased from 0.3 kW/ha in 1971/72 to the tune of 1.4 kW/ha in 2003/04. Connected load in the agriculture sector in 2004 was estimated to be 51.84 GW. the number of consumers being 12.8 million. The electricity consumption in agriculture during 2003/04 was 87 089 GWh (second highest) 24.13% of the total electricity consumption. There was an increase of 3.08% in the electricity sales to the agriculture sector in 2003/04 over 2002/03. Electricity consumption in agriculture sector has been increasing mainly because of greater irrigation demand for new crop varieties and subsidized electricity to this sector. Moreover. due importance is not given to proper selection. installation.

operation. and maintenance of pumping sets. as a result of which they do not operate at the desired level of efficiency. leading to huge waste of energy. Agriculture (plantation/food) consumed 7 123 thousand tonnes of HSD (high-speed diesel) in 2003/04. accounting for 19.2% of the total HSD consumption during the year. Consumption of LDO (light diesel oil) and furnace oil for plantation in 2003/04 was 44 000 and 243 000 tonnes. respectively. accounting for 2.7% of the total LDO and 2.9% of the total furnace oil consumed in the country. Consumption of furnace oil for transport (agriculture retail trade) in the agriculture sector was 94 thousand tonnes. However. it is difficult to assess the total diesel consumption for agriculture from the available data.

ENERGY CONSUMPTION IN SERVICE SECTOR

Service sector emerged as one of the main driving force in country's high GDP. It grew by 10.8 per cent in comparison of 11.1 percent of 2006-07. It was increased by 12 per cent in trade. hotels. transport and communication sectors. while it was 11.8 per cent in the finance. insurance. business services and real estate. Government has recorded 7.3 per cent rise of GDP in social and personal services. community in 2007-08. Transport system in India is one of the largest in the world and serves a land area of 3.3 million square km and a population of over one billion. It consists mainly of roads. railways. and air services. Given its long coastline of approximately 7 517 km. India has a hub of over 150 seaports with inland water transport playing a small supplementary role in a few states. Transport plays a significant role in the overall development of a nations economy. In the past decade. the Indian economy has undergone many structural changes leading to decline of the share of the primary sectors (agriculture. forestry. and fishing) and increase in the share of the non-primary sectors (transport. communications. financing. manufacturing. etc.).

Transportation being a derived demand. arising out of a need to fulfill other means. is significantly influenced by such structural changes in the economy. The contribution to GDP (gross domestic product). of the transport sector (including transportation. communications. trade and hotels) in 1993/94. was 411 billion rupees (at 1993/94 prices) and escalated to 794 billion rupees in 2003/04. Also the largest contributor to GDP in the transport sector in 2003/04 was road transport with a share of almost 62%. In India transport demand. usually measured in passenger-km and freight-km. is increasing somewhat faster than the GDP. According to a World Bank study. India?s economy grew by 6% to 7% a year during the 1990s. and total transport demand grew by about 10% a year. The transport modes vary in their infrastructural requirements. carrying capacities. capital and operating costs. energy consumption. and environmental impacts. In the last three decades. owing to easy accessibility. flexibility. and reliability. the share of both freight and passenger traffic has experienced a rapid shift from rail to road. However. the capacity of the road has not been able to keep pace with the increasing demand. In terms of rail-road modal mixes. the freight traffic carried by road transport is estimated to have increased from roughly 35% in 1970/71 to 70% in 2003/04 whereas the passenger traffic has increased from 67% to 85% during the same period. The NTPC (National Transport Policy Committee) set up by the Planning Commission in 1978 had advocated a 72% share to rail and 28% to road for freight transport on the basis of resource costs. break-even points. and fuel costs by the year 2000. Similarly. in the case of passenger transport the recommendation was to adopt specific measures to encourage diversion of traffic from personalized modes of motor transport to public transport system. Yet. the share of rail transport in freight movement continues to decline. which has enormous implications for fuel consumption.

ENERGY CONSUMPTION IN INDUSTRY SECTOR

The industry has shown some signs of worries as its growth has been slowdown by more than 2% then what it was in 2006-07. In 2006-07 it was 11% but in 2007-08 it came down to 8.5%. All the expectations about the manufacturing sector and its rising share in economy pie now requires to be taken with some pinch of salt. As fallout has been seen in the manufacturing sector. where it dropped to 8.8% from 12% of 2006-07. Construction sector growth was 9.8 per cent vis-a-vis to 12% of 2006-07. The growth rate in electricity. gas and water supply shown a tad of 6.3 per cent from that of 6% in 2006-07. In the *IEO2009* reference case. India is projected to sustain the world's second-highest rate of GDP growth. averaging 5.6 percent per year from 2006 to 2030. This translates into a 2.3-percent average annual increase in delivered energy to the industrial sector. Although India is likely to achieve an economic growth rate similar to China's between 2006 and 2030. its levels of GDP and energy consumption continue to be dwarfed by those in China throughout the projection period. India's economic growth over the next 25 years is expected to derive more from light manufacturing and services than from heavy industry. so that the industrial share of total energy consumption falls from 72 percent in 2006 to 64 percent in 2030. and its commercial energy use grows nearly twice as fast as its industrial energy use. The changes are accompanied by shifts in India's industrial fuel mix. with electricity use growing more rapidly than coal use in the industrial sector. India has been successful in reducing the energy intensity of its industrial production over the past 20 years. A majority of its steel production is from electric arc furnaces. and most of its cement production uses dry kiln technology. A major reason is the Indian government's public policy. which provides subsidized fuel to citizens and farmers but requires industry to pay higher prices for fuel. Because the market interventions have spurred industry to reduce energy costs. India is now one of the world's lowest cost producers of both aluminum and steel. The quality of India's indigenous coal supplies also has contributed to the steel industry's efforts to reduce its energy use. India's metallurgical coal (which is needed for steel production in blast furnaces) is low in quality. forcing steel producers to import more expensive metallurgical coal from abroad. As a result. producers have invested heavily in improving the efficiency of their capital stock to lower the amount of relatively expensive imported coal used in the production process.The Indian government has facilitated further reductions in industrial energy use over the past decade by mandating industrial energy audits in the Energy Conservation Act of 2001 and mandating specific consumption decreases for heavy industry as part of the 2008 National Action Plan on Climate Change. The new plan also calls for fiscal and tax incentives for efficiency. an energy-efficiency financing platform. and a trading market for energy savings certificates. wherein firms that exceed their required savings level will be able to sell the certificates to firms that have not. Those measures contribute to a reduction in the energy intensity of India's GDP. which declines by an average of 2.9 percent per year from 2006 to 2030 in the *IEO2009* reference case.

ENERGY INDUSTRY

The energy industry is the totality of all of the industries involved in the production and sale of energy. including fuel extraction. manufacturing. refining and distribution. Modern society consumes large amounts of fuel. and the energy industry is a crucial part of the infrastructure and maintenance of society in almost all countries.

In particular. the energy industry comprises:

- The petroleum industry. including oil companies. petroleum refiners. fuel transport and end-user sales at gas stations
- The gas industry. including natural gas extraction. and coal gas manufacture. as well as distribution and sales
- The electrical power industry. including electricity generation. electric power distribution and sales
- The coal industry
- The nuclear power industry
- The renewable energy industry. comprising alternative energy and sustainable energy companies. including those involved in hydroelectric power. wind power. and solar power generation. and the manufacture. distribution and sale of alternative fuels
- Traditional energy industry based on the collection and distribution of firewood. the use of which. for cooking and heating. is particularly common in poorer countries

HISTORY

The use of energy has been a key in the development of the human society by helping it to control and adapt to the environment. Managing the use of energy is inevitable in any functional society. In the industrialized world the development of energy resources has become essential for agriculture. transportation. waste collection. information technology.communications that have become prerequisites of a developed society. The increasing use of energy since the Industrial Revolution has also brought with it a number of serious problems. some of which. such as global warming. present potentially grave risks to the world.

In society and in the context of humanities. the word *energy* is used as a synonym of energy resources. and most often refers to substances like fuels. petroleum products andelectricity in general. These are sources of *usable energy*. in that they can be easily transformed to other kinds of energy sources that can serve a particular useful purpose. This difference vis a vis energy in natural sciences can lead to some confusion. because energy resources are not conserved in nature in the same way as energy is conserved in the context of physics. The actual energy content is always conserved. but when it is converted into heat for example. it usually becomes less useful to society. and thus appears to have been "used up".

Ever since humanity discovered various energy resources available in nature. it has been inventing devices. known as machines. that make life more comfortable by using energy resources. Thus. although the primitive man knew the utility of fire to cook food. the invention of devices like gas burners and microwave ovens has increased the usage of energy for this purpose alone manifold. The trend is the same in any other field of social activity. be it construction of social infrastructure. manufacturing of fabrics for covering; porting; printing; decorating. for example textiles. air conditioning; communication of information or for moving people and goods (automobiles).

ECONOMICS

Production and consumption of energy resources is very important to the global economy. All economic activity requires energy resources. whether to manufacture goods. provide transportation. run computers and other machines. Widespread demand for energy may encourage competing energy utilities and the formation of retail energy markets. Note the presence of the "Energy Marketing and Customer Service" (EMACS) sub-sector.

MANAGEMENT

Since the cost of energy has become a significant factor in the performance of economy of societies. management of energy resources has become very crucial. Energy management involves utilizing the available energy resources more effectively that is with minimum incremental costs. Many times it is possible to save expenditure on energy without incorporating fresh technology by simple management techniques. Most often energy management is the practice of using energy more efficiently by eliminating energy wastage or to balance justifiable energy demand with appropriate energy supply. The process couples energy awareness with energy conservation.

CLASSIFICATIONS

Government

The United Nations developed the International Standard Industrial Classification. which is a list of economic and social classifications. There is no distinct classification for an energy industry. because the classification system is based on *activities. products.* and *expenditures according to purpose.*

Countries in North America use the North American Industry Classification System (NAICS). The NAICS sectors #21 and #22 (mining and utilities) might roughly define the energy industry in North America. This classification is used by the U.S. Securities and Exchange Commission.

Financial market

The Global Industry Classification Standard used by Morgan Stanley define the energy industry as comprising companies primarily working with oil. gas. coal and consumable fuels. excluding companies working with certain industrial gases.

ENVIRONMENTAL IMPACT

Government encouragement in the form of subsidies and tax incentives for energy-conservation efforts has increasingly fostered the view of conservation as a major function of the energy industry: saving an amount of energy provides economic benefits almost identical to generating that same amount of energy. This is compounded by the fact that the economics of delivering energy tend to be priced for capacity as opposed to average usage. One of the purposes of a smart grid infrastructure is to smooth out demand so that capacity and demand curves align more closely.

Some parts of the energy industry generate considerable pollution. including toxic and greenhouse gases from fuel combustion. nuclear waste from the generation of nuclear power. and oil spillages as a result of petroleum extraction. Government regulations to internalize these externalities form an increasing part of doing business. and the trading of carbon credits and pollution credits on the free market may also result in energy-saving and pollution-control measures becoming even more important to energy providers.

Consumption of energy resources. (*e.g.* turning on a light) requires resources and has an effect on the environment. Many electric power plants burn coal. oil or natural gas in order to generate electricity for energy needs.

While burning these fossil fuels produces a readily available and instantaneous supply of electricity. it also generates air pollutants including carbon dioxide (CO_2). sulfur dioxide and trioxide (SOx) and nitrogen oxides (NOx). Carbon dioxide is an important greenhouse gas which is thought to be responsible for some fraction of the rapid increase in global warming seen especially in the temperature records in the 20th century. as compared with tens of thousands of years worth of temperature records which can be read from ice cores taken in Arctic regions. Burning fossil fuels for electricity generation also releases trace metals such as beryllium. cadmium. chromium. copper. manganese. mercury. nickel. and silver into the environment. which also act as pollutants.

The large-scale use of renewable energy technologies would "greatly mitigate or eliminate a wide range of environmental and human health impacts of energy use".Renewable energy technologies include biofuels. solar heating and cooling. hydroelectric power. solar power. and wind power. Energy conservation and the efficient use of energy would also help.

In addition. it is argued that there is also the potential to develop a more efficient energy sector. This can be done by:

- Fuel switching in the power sector from coal to natural gas;
- Power plant optimisation and other measures to improve the efficiency of existing CCGT power plants;
- Combined heat and power (CHP). from micro-scale residential to large-scale industrial;
- Waste heat recovery

Best available technology (BAT) offers supply-side efficiency levels far higher than global averages. The relative benefits of gas compared to coal are influenced by the development of increasingly efficient energy production methods. According to an impact assessment carried out for the European Commission. the levels of energy efficiency of coal-fired plants built have now increased to 46-49% efficiency rates. as compared to coals plants built before the 1990s (32-40%). However. at the same time gas is can reach 58-59% efficiency levels with the best available technology. Meanwhile. combined heat and power can offer efficiency rates of 80-90%.

POLITICS

Since now energy plays an essential role in industrial societies. the ownership and control of energy resources plays an increasing role in politics. At the national level. governments seek to influence the sharing (distribution) of energy resources among various sections of the society through pricing mechanisms; or even who owns resources within their borders. They may also seek to influence the use of energy by individuals and business in an attempt to tackle environmental issues. The most recent international political controversy regarding energy resources is in the context of the Iraq wars. Some political analysts maintain that the hidden reason for both 1991 and 2003 wars can be traced to strategic control of international energy resources. Others counter this analysis with the numbers related to its economics. According to the latter group of analysts. U.S. has spent about $336 billion in Iraq as compared with a background current value of $25 billion per year budget for the entire U.S. oil import dependence

Policy

Energy policy is the manner in which a given entity (often governmental) has decided to address issues of energy development including energy production. distribution andconsumption. The attributes of energy policy may include legislation. international treaties. incentives to investment. guidelines for energy conservation. taxation and other public policy techniques.

Security

Energy security is the intersection of national security and the availability of natural resources for energy consumption. Access to cheap energy has become essential to the functioning of modern economies. However. the uneven distribution of energy supplies among countries has led to significant vulnerabilities.

Threats to energy security include the political instability of several energy producing countries. the manipulation of energy supplies. the competition over energy sources. attacks on supply infrastructure. as well as accidents.natural disasters. the funding to foreign dictators. rising terrorism. and dominant countries reliance to the foreign oil supply.

The limited supplies. uneven distribution. and rising costs of fossil fuels. such as oil and gas. create a need to change to more sustainable energy sources in the foreseeable future. With as much dependence that the U.S. currently has for oil and with the peaking limits of oil production; economies and societies will begin to feel the decline in the resource that we have become dependent upon.

Energy security has become one of the leading issues in the world today as oil and other resources have become as vital to the world's people. However with oil production rates decreasing and oil production peak nearing the world has come to protect what resources we have left in the world. With new advancements in renewable resources less pressure has been put on companies that produce the worlds oil. these resources are. geothermal. solar power. wind power and hydro-electric.

Although these are not all the current and possible future options for the world to turn to as the oil depletes the most important issue is protecting these vital resources from future threats. These new resources will become more useful as the price of exporting and importing oil will increase due to increase of demand.

DEVELOPMENT

Producing energy to sustain human needs is an essential social activity. and a great deal of effort goes into the activity. While most of such effort is limited towards increasing the production of electricity and oil. newer ways of producing usable energy resources from the available energy resources are being explored. One such effort is to explore means of producing hydrogen fuel from water. Though hydrogen use is environmentally friendly. its production requires energy and existing technologies to make it. are not very efficient. Research is underway to explore enzymatic decomposition of biomass.

Other forms of conventional energy resources are also being used in new ways. Coal gasification and liquefaction are recent technologies that are becoming attractive after the realization that oil reserves. at present consumption rates. may be rather short lived.

TRANSPORTATION

All societies require materials and food to be transported over *distances*. generally against some *force* of friction. Since application of force over distance requires the presence of a source of usable energy. such sources are of great worth in society.

While energy resources are an essential ingredient for all modes of transportation in society. the transportation of energy resources is becoming equally important. Energy resources are frequently located far from the place where they are consumed. Therefore their transportation is always in question. Some energy resources like liquid or gaseous fuels are transported using tankers or pipelines. while electricity transportation invariably requires a network of grid cables. The transportation of energy. whether by tanker. pipeline. or transmission line. poses challenges for scientists and engineers. policy makers. and economists to make it more risk-free and efficient.

INDUSTRIAL APPLICATIONS

Industrial applications for natural gas arc many. Industrial applications include those same uses found in residential and commercial settings – heating. cooling. and cooking. Click here for a review of residential uses. and here for a review of commercial uses. Natural gas is also used for waste treatment and incineration. metals preheating (particularly for iron and steel). drying and dehumidification. glass melting. food processing. and fueling industrial boilers. Natural gas may also be used as a feedstock for the manufacturing of a number of chemicals and products. Gases such as butane. ethane. and propane may be extracted from natural gas to be used as a feedstock for such products as fertilizers and pharmaceutical products.

Natural gas as a feedstock is commonly found as a building block for methanol. which in turn has many industrial applications. Natural gas is converted to what is known as synthesis gas. which is a mixture of hydrogen and carbon oxides formed through a process known as steam reforming. In this process. natural gas is exposed to a catalyst that causes oxidization of the natural gas when brought into contact with steam. This synthesis gas. once formed. may be used to produce methanol (or Methyl Alcohol). which in turn is used to produce such substances as formaldehyde. acetic acid. and MTBE (methyl tertiary butyl ether) that is used as an additive for cleaner burning gasoline. Methanol may also be used as a fuel source in fuel cells.

In addition to these uses. there are a number of innovative and industry specific uses of natural gas. Natural gas desiccant systems. which are used for dehumidification. are increasingly popular in the plastics. pharmaceutical. candy. and even recycling industries. In each of these industries. moisture filled air can lead to damage of the end product during its manufacture. For example. in the plastics industry. moisture can cause cracks and blemishes during the manufacture of certain types of plastics. Adding a natural gas desiccant system to the manufacturing or drying environment allows industrial users to regulate more closely the amount of moisture in the air. leading to a more consistent and high-quality product.Natural gas absorption systems are also being used extensively in industry to heat and cool water in an efficient. economical. and environmentally sound way. These industrial absorption systems are very similar to those used in commercial settings.

INFRARED HEATING UNITS

Infrared (IR) heating units provide an innovative and economic method of using natural gas to generate heat in an industrial setting. They are very useful in the metals industry. as they provide innovative ways to increase the efficiency of powder-coating manufacturing processes. Infrared heaters use natural gas to more efficiently and quickly heat materials used in this process. Natural gas is combined with a panel of ceramic fibers containing a platinum catalyst. causing a reaction with oxygen to dramatically increase temperature. without even producing a flame.

Using natural gas in this manner has allowed industry members to increase the speed of their manufacturing process. as well as providing a more economic alternative to electric heaters.

DIRECT CONTACT WATER HEATERS

Direct contact water heating is an application that works by having the energy from the combustion of natural gas transferred directly from the flame into the water. These systems are incredibly efficient at heating water. Normal industrial water heaters operate in the 60 – 70 percent energy efficiency range. However. direct contact water heaters can achieve efficiencies up to 99.7 percent! Obviously. this leads to tremendous cost savings in industries where hot water is essential.

INDUSTRIAL COMBINED HEAT AND POWER

Industrial consumers reap great benefits from operating natural gas Combined Heat and Power (CHP) and Combined Cooling. Heat. and Power (CCHP) systems. similar to those used commercial settings. For instance. natural gas may be used to generate electricity needed in a particular industrial setting. The excess heat and steam produced from this process can be harnessed to fulfill other industrial applications. including space heating. water heating. and powering industrial boilers. Since industry is such a heavy user of energy. and particularly electricity. providing increased efficiency can save a great deal of money. The industrial sector is also subject to regulations regarding harmful emissions. and the burning attributes of natural gas help industry to reduce its emissions.

INDUSTRIAL CO-FIRING

Natural gas co-firing technologies are also helping to increase industrial energy efficiency. and reduce harmful atmospheric emissions. Co-firing is the process in which natural gas is used as a supplemental fuel in the combustion of other fuels. such as coal. wood. and biomass energy. For example. a traditional industrial wood boiler would simply burn wood to generate energy. However. in this type of boiler. a significant amount of energy is lost. and harmful emissions are very high. Adding natural gas to the combustion mix can have a two-fold effect. Natural gas emits fewer harmful substances into the air than a fuel such as wood. Since the energy needed to power the natural gas boiler remains constant. adding natural gas to the combustion mix can reduce harmful emissions.

OIL AND NATURAL GAS SECTOR

The oil industry can be divided into three major components: upstream. midstream and downstream. The upstream industry includes exploration and production activities. hence is also referred as the exploration and production (E&P) sector. The midstream industry processes. stores. markets and transports commodities including crude oil. natural gas. natural gas liquids (NGLs) like ethane propane and butane and sulphur. The downstream industry includes oil refineries. petrochemical plants. petroleum products distributors. retail outlets and natural gas distribution companies. The downstream industry provides consumers thousands of products such as gasoline. diesel. jet fuel. heating oil. asphalt. lubricants. synthetic rubber. plastics. fertilizers. antifreeze. pesticides. pharmaceuticals. natural gas and propane. Both internationally and within India the oil and gas sector is characterized by existence of "integrated" companies. which are present in all these three sectors.

The Indian Oil and Gas sector is one of the six core industries in India and has very significant forward linkages with the entire economy. The oil and gas sector meets more than two third of the total primary energy needs in the country. The sector has been instrumental in putting India on the world map. At present India is the sixth largest crude oil consumer in the world and the ninth largest crude oil importer. The country is also increasing its share in the global refining market. At present Indian refining sector is the sixth largest in the world. At the end of 2005. India had 0.5 per cent of the Oil and Gas resources of the world and 15 per cent of the world?s population whereas the reserve to production ratio is 20.7. At the end of 1995 India had the 5.5 thousand million barrels of reserves. grown only 1% till the end of 2005 whereas crude oil consumption has grown more than 10% over the last 5 years.

Upstream sector: Exploration and production

Upstream sector. the first part of the oil and gas industry. deals with exploration and production of oil and gas. Oil exploration takes place at oil wells in four stages. The first stage is drilling. act of boring a hole through which oil or gas may be produced if encountered in commercial quantities. The second stage is completion. process in which the well is enabled to produce oil or gas. The third stage is production. production time of oil and gas and the final stage is abandonment. where the well no longer produces or produces so poorly that it is a liability to its owner and is abandoned. An oil field is a region with an abundance of oil wells extracting petroleum (oil) from below ground. Because the oil reservoirs typically extend over a large area. possibly several hundred kilometres across. full exploitation entails multiple wells scattered across the area. There are more than 40.000 oil and gas fields of all sizes in the world and the largest discovered conventional oil field is the Ghawar Field (75-83 billion) is Saudi Arabia. In tandem with the stagnated reserves. the production of oil has also been sluggish over the last decade. as a matter of fact in last ten years oil production has increased by only 1.6%.

Reserve to production ratio

Reserve to Production Ration (R/P Ratio) is the portion of the identified resource from which usable natural resources can be economically and legally extracted out of the ground. Production can be offshore as well as onshore. An offshore system of production is defined with a platform raised above the water to support a number of producing wells whereas onshore is a platform at the sea level. R/P ratio for the world at the end of 2005 is 40.6 implying that natural resources that has been identified subject to pull out till date is about 40 times the amount already taken out of the ground.

Downstream: Refining and marketing

Refining. the second part of the oil industry after exploration and production. is related with manufacturing petroleum products by a series of processes that separate crude oil into its major components and blend or convert these components into a wide range of finished products. such as gasoline or Aviation Turbine Fuel. Refining capacity depends on the technology used in refineries. capable of processing crude production into clean fuels. In the recent age of decreasing oil production refining capacity have to have well supportive technology. which meet increasingly more stringent environmental Standards.

With the increase in global oil demand and stagnant reserve. refining capacity deserves new capacity addition to meet demand. But the graph shows slightly increasing trend of refining capacity till date in last decade. Refinery throuput. as opposed to designed capacity. is computed by dividing the number of refined barrels of oil processed by the actual number of days the refinery was in operation.

Onshore and offshore oil and gas fields in India

In India crude oil is produced in Onshore and Offshore. Onshore fields are in Assam/Nagaland. Arunachal Pradesh. Gujarat. and Tamil Nadu/ Andhra Pradesh. Oil India Limited (OIL) and Oil and Natural Gas Commission (ONGC) have the onshore field for crude oil production. Offshore production occurs at Bombay High run by ONGC and Private/Joint Venture companies. For the natural gas onshore fields are the same for Crude oil in addition with Rajasthan as an onshore field. For the offshore Bombay high is the one for the production.

Exploration overseas

In keeping with the objectives of the Energy Security section of the National Common Minimum Programme. ONGC Videsh Ltd. (OVL). wholly owned subsidiary of ONGC. as well as other national oil companies such as IOC. OIL and GAIL. have been pursuing the acquisition of equity oil abroad. as well as the acquisition abroad of oil and gas exploration acreages and producing properties. These companies have participating interests in oil and gas projects located in Vietnam. Sudan. Russia. Iraq. Iran. Myanmar. Libya. Syria. Australia. Ivory Coast. Qatar and Egypt. OVL. in association with other oil sector PSUs. is aggressively scouting for E&P opportunities in countries such as Venezuela. Kazakhstan. Kuwait. Yemen. Chad. Niger. Nigeria. Angola. Cuba. Sierra Leone and Ecuador in addition to efforts to acquire more E&P assets in the countries where it is operating currently.

Production

Domestic production of crude oil has been a reason of worry for the Indian economy for some time now. For more than 16 years the total production of crude has stagnated around 32-33 MMT. This has been particularly disturbing given the crude oil consumption in the country implying an increasing dependence on imported crude. At present India?s crude dependence is around

78%. According to TERI estimates. by 2030 India?s import dependency may shoot up to a disturbing 93%. In the current year. the production of crude oil in the country during the first half was 16.14 MMT as against 17.00 MMT during the corresponding period of 2004-05. a shortfall of about 5%.

Refining

Oil refining is a continuous process and the cost of refining of individual petroleum products is not worked out separately because all products are produced together. The cost of refining crude oil depends upon a number of factors including the type of crude oil. size of refinery. refinery configuration. age of equipment. technology used. etc. The technology for producing the petroleum products from the crude oil differs from one refinery to another. The hydro cracker and catalytic hydro cracker technology are the two major technologies through which petroleum products are yielded. There are 18 refineries operating in the country. 17 in the Public Sector and'one in the Private Sector. with a total installed capacity of 127.37 million metric tonnes per annum (MMTPA).

Natural gas

Natural gas is a gaseous fossil fuel consisting primarily of methane. In India production of natural gas has increased over 3 times in the last two decades though the share of the production of natural gas with respect to world natural gas production wais only 0.6% at the end of 2005 and reserve to production ratio of 36.2. Petroleum and Natural Gas Regulatory Board (PNGRB) Act came into force on April 03. 2006 to protect the interest of consumers and entitles engaged in specified activities to ensure uninterrupted and adequate supply of petroleum. petroleum products and natural gas in all parts of the country and promote competitive markets in Oil and Gas sector of India.

BRIEFLY

- Agriculture sector grew by 4.5% in comparison of 2.6% projection.
- Transport and communication. trade and hotels grew by 12% with a projected 12.1% growth.
- Electricity and gas supply growth was 6.3% with a projection of 7.8%.
- Construction sector growth was registered at 9.8% with a 9.6% projection.
- Insurance. real estate recorded a marginally higher growth by 11.8% as compared to the earlier estimates of 11.7%

ECONOMIC PROSPECTS FOR 2010

The global economy seems to be recovering after the recent economic shock. The Indian economy. however. was hit in the latter part of the global recession and the real economic growth witnessed a sharp fall. followed by lower exports. lower capital outflow and corporate restructuring. It is expected that the global economies will continue to sustain in the short-term. as the effect of stimulus programmes is yet to bear fruit and tax cuts are working their way through the system in 2010. Due to the strong position of liquidity in the market. large corporations now have access to capital in the corporate credit markets.

RELATION BETWEEN IRAN AND INDIA. BROADENING TRADING OPPORTUNITIES

The government of India's largest crude oil import partner is Saudi Arabia. followed by Iran. Nearly three-fourths of India's crude oil imports come from the Middle East. The Indian government expects this geographical dependence to rise in light of limited prospects for domestic production.

India's oil sector is dominated In tune of the changing business environment of the world. Iran is exploring the new trading avenues in the world's 5th largest economy *i.e.* India. During the seminar hosted by the Confederation of Indian Industry(CII). delegation of the Iranian business leaders along with the senior officials from the iran. the Iran's government has reinforced in finding the new pathways of interacting with their counter parts from the Indian industrial market in relation to their new upcoming projects from the sectors of roads and railways. infrastructure. cement. power. shipping and maritime. pharmaceuticals. aluminum and steel. automotive and auto components etc. *Co-Chairman of the CII Gulf Council. Mr. A C Patankar said that "India and Iran share strong trade and cultural ties*. we can expand the trade amongst the two nations by acting as a facilitator in the exchange of expertise. CII is ready to take forth the issues faced by the corporate from either sides. and will be more then happy to address issues associated with the trade". Showing the optimistic Behaviour towards the Iran and India trading future. Mr. S Hossein Salimi. Senior office bearer of Iran Chambers of Commerce and Industry said"I being an entrepreneur in Iran. witnessed the ups and downs of the Iranian economy. At present the Iran trade and business sector has come of age. However we are yet to catch up with up with the world on various aspects of development. and we are confident to find Indian interest in sharing their technology and expertise with us. Iran is a promising option for India as it is just 3 hours air connectivity away. Iran at present seeks special expertise in the areas of automobiles. cement. steel among others".

Presenting the government's view point. Mr M.K. Anand. Director of the West Asia North Africa (WANA). Department of Commerce. Ministry of Commerce and Industry. Government of India. emphasized on the need of building strong trading relations between India and Iran. He said. "We praise the efforts made by the CII for streamlining the existing areas and developing new areas for trade. Iran is a radiant and vibrant market and we look forward to greater engagement by the Indian cooperates in sectors apart from Oil and Chemicals. We should look forward at the possibility of creating a Indian trade hub in Iran for further expansion in the region. We will be hosting a Joint Commission Meeting in Tehran. Iran on the 1-2nd November 2008. for facilitating stronger trade ties". Further hosting the trade perspective of the Micro. Small and Medium Enterprises (MSMEs). Mr. G C Narang. Managing Director. Progressive Thermal Controls stated."Indian small scale sector brings tremendous options for trade engagement.

A major chunk of business in the fields of automobile. food processing. pharmaceuticals. biotechnology. textile. electronics. telecom. retail and light engineering is being held by small sector. Iran's business fraternity should try to capitalize from the vast scope offered by the small scale sector". He reinstated on the need of diverting the India's industrial growth towards the Iran's business potential. Mr. Mahmood Ali Abadi. Director General. Foreign Investment Office. Organization for Investment. Economic and Technical Assistance of Iran. has candidly added. "Iran offers investment opportunities in different varieties. In a Joint venture. it is possible for a foreign country to hold 100% shares. We welcome Indians to invest in Iranian Stock market. which is not affect by the global financial crackdown. We ensure that the foreign investments will be protected here and good returns are generated for the investors". Bilateral trade between Iran and India has touched the mark of $9.53 billion in 2006-07 from $6.1 billion of 2005-06.

ENERGY SECURITY IN NORTHEAST ASIA

NUCLEAR POWER AS A LYNCHPIN OF THE ALLIANCE

Given rapid changes in the international energy landscape. Tokyo can not waste any more time in clarifying its post-Fukushima energy strategy. Japan is the world's third biggest oil consumer and tops the list of LNG importers; it depends almost completely on imports to meet its hydrocarbon consumption needs. The rapid increase of LNG imports following the post-Fukushima nuclear reactor shutdowns led to dramatic increases in natural gas prices in Asia. LNG import prices in Asia are indexed to oil prices. but do not benefit from the trend of decreasing prices elsewhere¯including North America¯that is a feature of the shale gas revolution. Therefore. in Asia imported gas prices basically hover at high rates in accordance with high oil prices while in North America gas prices are set competitively as supplies come from numerous domestic sources.

Therefore. the energy policy choices Tokyo makes will have major consequences not just for the domestic economy. but also for international energy markets. Given its extremely low energy self-sufficiency rate of four percent (without nuclear power). Japan's policy options for ensuring its future energy security are limited.

Simply put. Japan must restart nuclear reactors. and it must also introduce and enforce stricter safety regulations. In order to do so. the government must make a clear political decision to end the endless ideological and emotional debate about nuclear power. The "mythification" of nuclear safety before Fukushima was an important lesson the whole population obviously learned from the tragedy; people will and should now be more skeptical. Some activists argue that nuclear reactors should restart only after their "perfect safety" can be assured; obviously. it is an illusion to think that humankind could ever create perfect safely in its literal sense. However cautious we may be; complete mastery over nature. science. and the future is not possible. Only strong political leadership can put an end to this pointless debate; the government should identify. at the earliest stage and in light of international experience. a set of yardsticks to satisfy legal requirements for nuclear restarts even if we must recognize that it will be a learn-by-doing process. This is Japan's inescapable responsibility for its own economic life. the U.S.-Japan alliance. and the international community.

Postponing nuclear reactor restarts have drained Japan's national wealth considerably. It became a trade-deficit nation for the first time in more than three decades. A major factor in this development is the jump in LNG imports due to replacement of nuclear power generation by gas-fired thermal plants. Imports grew from 70 million tons from 2010 to 78.5 million tons in 2011 and 87.3 million tons in 2012 – an increase of almost 25 percent in two years. However. during the same period. the total value of LNG purchases increased by more than 70 percent from about 3.5 trillion yen in 2010 to 6 trillion yen in 2012 due to the sharp increases in LNG prices per million Btu (British thermal unit) destined for Japan: the average LNG import prices for Japan increased by about 55 percent from approximately $11 per million Btu in 2010 to approximately $17 per million Btu in 2012.

The increase in Japan's LNG imports accounted for the predominant chunk of its trade deficit of about 6.9 trillion yen in 2012. Nuclear restarts would result in huge savings in domestic fuel costs. Moreover. it would help stabilize the global LNG markets; the Northeast Asian natural gas market is most seriously affected with Japan consuming about one-thirds of the world's LNG demand.

It also must be emphasized that Japan's nuclear future will directly affect the range of U.S.-Japan cooperation which goes by far beyond mere energy issues. The Japanese and U.S. nuclear industries have developed as "twin brothers" for more than a half century.

Today. Hitachi and GE. as well as Toshiba and Westinghouse. have nuclear power joint ventures. Japanese nuclear vendors have made significant contributions to make up for the declining of the nuclear industry in the United States after the Three Mile Island accident in 1979. by developing high-tech nuclear products for civilian use and producing a large number of the world's top-class engineers.

A phase-out of nuclear power in Japan would also have an adverse impact on the global non-proliferation regime. While shale gas causes natural gas prices to remain low. there is increased uncertainty in the United States about introducing new nuclear power plants. Ironically. this has increased the importance of sustaining high standards for nuclear technologies against the background of diffusion of nuclear power for civilian use in the world. This diffusion is irreversible. regardless of U.S. and Japanese domestic nuclear policies. in order to meet drastic rises in energy demand in emerging economies. The loss of Japanese nuclear vendors' international competitiveness would jeopardize the bilateral alliance's presence in global nuclear markets. which would in turn weaken Washington's and Tokyo's voices in the future non-proliferation regime. Japan needs to rediscover its role as one of the most serious advocates for reinforcement of global efforts on non-proliferation.

Maintaining a certain amount of nuclear power in the energy mix is also important from a climate change perspective. Tokyo must realistically readjust the over-ambitious target of cutting greenhouse gas (GHG) emissions by 25 percent below 1990 levels that was announced by then-DPJ Prime Minister Hatoyama at the United Nations Summit on Climate Change in September 2009. which received little support from the domestic business community. But Japan should continue to play its own roles to combat climate change as long as a principle of fairness of international burden-sharing is guaranteed. A nuclear restart is an indispensable way to reduce a certain amount of GHG emissions. given that too many uncertainties await dramatic expansion of renewable sources in the energy mix at least in the foreseeable future. due in part to high costs.

LNG AS A FUEL TO INCREASE JAPAN'S BURDEN-SHARING

Increases of LNG exports from the United States to Japan will become a new way to strengthen the alliance. and the impacts extend beyond energy. Undoubtedly. Japan would benefit from prospective participation in the TPP. and co-designing the future framework of economic rules in the Asia-Pacific region would also reinforce the bilateral alliance. TPP membership for Japan would remove a potential obstacle to increase LNG exports from the lower 48 states. According to the U.S. Natural Gas Law. LNG exports to non-FTA trade partners must be authorized by the Department of Energy on a case-by-case basis (Japan has imported LNG from Alaska since 1969.) However. the meaning of increasing LNG supplies to Japan should be emphasized in a wider context. entailing geostrategic importance besides the economic benefits of improving the U.S. international balance of payments. LNG imports from the United States will beef up Japan's economic muscle. better allowing it to play the role of the main "bridgehead" of the U.S. strategy Towards the Asia-Pacific region. With sound economic growth. Japan can be expected to contribute more to burden-sharing as it will be able to increase its budgets for Defence. economic aid to developing countries. and many other issues that benefit the U.S.-Japan alliance.

Even if Tokyo decides in principle to restart nuclear reactors. both the political and technical processes will take some time. Public support will have to be nurtured in a step-by-step manner. This means that increased access to economically competitive LNG supplies remains urgent. As late as February 2013. Japan paid approximately five times more than the U.S. Henry Hub price per million Btu (British thermal unit). on average. for LNG purchases. Although of the price of future imports of LNG from North America remains uncertain. it is generally estimated that the final cost of LNG from the lower 48 states¯including liquefaction costs. transportation fees. and other costs¯are still lower than the average price of Japan's current LNG imports.

Aside from the price issue. securing new LNG supply routes from North America is also important to ensure the safety of Japan's seaborne hydrocarbon transportation. Currently. approximately 80 percent of crude oil and 30 percent of LNG destined for Japan cut across the East China Sea. where Sino-Japanese tension is simmering.

TOWARDS A JOINT ARCHITECTURE FOR ASIAN-PACIFIC ENERGY SECURITY

Against the background of the shale revolution. there are rising expectations about "energy independence" in the United States. which is thought not only to boost the domestic economy with cheap energy prices and reduce vulnerability to international oil prices. but also to increase policy options for U.S. diplomacy. The ongoing debate about diplomatic implications of U.S. energy independence within the next decade by and large tends to focus on the question of how it would affect the U.S. military presence in the Middle East. However. a blueprint for placing energy independence in the context of the so-called U.S. "pivot to Asia" has yet to emerge. New roles and functions for the U.S.-Japan alliance should be designed in the context of U.S. energy independence. Today in Northeast Asia. the energy security environment is rapidly changing with impending new challenges for the U.S.-Japan alliance to tackle.

First. the rise of China with its surging energy demand has raised concerns about its impact on the global energy market. According to estimates published by the International Energy Agency in its November 2012 World Energy Outlook 2012. China is forecasted to account for more than half of increases in global oil demand by 2030; its dependence on imported oil will increase from 54 percent in 2011 to 77 percent in 2030. Likewise. China is projected to account for about 28 percent of increases in global demand for natural gas with its import dependence to rise from 14 percent in 2010 to 44 percent in 2030. Its impact on global oil prices and thus on the growth of the world economy would be considerable. Furthermore. Beijing's anxiety about ensuring stable access to energy resources may stimulate the expansion of Peoples' Liberation Army Navy's power projection capabilities. as a means to increase and secure access to overseas oil and natural gas supplies.

The deepening of China's economic interdependence with both the United States and Japan is unstoppable in the foreseeable future. Steady growth of the Chinese economy. which requires finding a solution to the upsurge in China's energy demand. is of great significance to the United States and Japan. In this regard. the two allies should explore possibilities for strengthening cooperation with China in a number of areas. especially energy efficiency. clean energy. and nuclear power generation. Outside (or uninformed) observers of Sino-Japanese relations tend to be overwhelmed by the contemporary geopolitical dispute and rising nationalism that fill the headlines. and overlook the fact that Beijing and Tokyo have developed extensive cooperation in the energy sector. including on energy conservation and clean energy technologies. for more than three decades. Japan can share its rich experiences in energy and environmental projects in China with the United States to capitalize on the recent success of Sino-U.S. clean energy cooperation. Beyond the business benefits. such collaboration could have invaluable political implications. If the three biggest energy consumers in the world could find a joint flagship project it could help create a new international framework for engaging China.

From the standpoint of reducing hydrocarbon consumption and carbon dioxide emissions. the U.S.-Japan "nuclear twins" should pursue nuclear cooperation with China. which has 18 nuclear power plants currently in operation. The nuclear stakes in China are about to get much bigger: there are about 30 reactors under construction and more than 50 in the planning stage. This expansion is of global importance. Successful growth in nuclear power generation would reduce China's hydrocarbon consumption and GHG emissions. and operational safety of the plants amidst such a rush of construction is an obvious concern.

Secondly. Russia has devoted every effort to enhance its presence in the Asia-Pacific region. taking advantage of hosting the 2012 APEC Summit in Vladivostok last September. Moscow is anxious to accelerate the development of untapped hydrocarbon resources in the eastern regions of the country as a way to gain new business opportunities while enhancing its geopolitical influence in Northeast Asia. The 4700 km crude oil pipeline from Eastern Siberia to the Pacific Ocean (ESPO) was completed in December 2012. Russia currently exports about 0.6 million barrels per day by the ESPO pipeline. but aims to increase the volume as much as possible.

The U.S. shale gas revolution came as a harsh blow to Moscow. given that Russia is frustrated by the gradual decreases of its natural gas exports to Europe as consumption there declines and the EU seeks diversification of natural gas supply routes. The Sakhalin-2 is the only LNG project in Russia. as of today. with a maximum capacity of exporting 9.6 million tons per year; a new LNG plant in Vladivostok is in the planning stages. In recent months Russia has aggressively approached Japan. China. and the Republic of Korea to strengthen partnerships in oil and gas sectors.

Meanwhile. the United States already has a bastion in the energy landscape of Northeast Asia. with ExxonMobil as the operator of the Sakhalin-1 project. The destination of natural gas exports from the project has remained undecided due to conflicts of interest between ExxonMobil and Russia's state-owned gas company. Gazprom. which has monopolized Russia's natural gas exports to date. Yet. while President Putin has recently disclosed a plan to liberalize the natural gas export market. the state-owned oil company. Rosneft. has galvanized itself to find new foreign partners. It has expanded agreements with ExxonMobil. addressing new oil and gas projects in Russia's Far Eastern and Arctic regions. and has acquired a stake in Exxon's gas project in Alaska.

However. Russia does not yet seem to have emerged as a factor in the U.S. pivot to Asia. Especially since the collapse of the former Soviet Union and the demise of the Soviet military threat in the Asia-Pacific. Washington's approach to Russia has been overwhelmingly Euro-centric. Russia's aggressive move to the Asia-Pacific region in the energy sector should be taken into account. when we imagine diplomatic implications of U.S. energy independence for this region. Obviously. one of the impetuses of Russia's rapid move to the east is Moscow's concern about the rise of China.

Notwithstanding the economic benefit of the drastic increase in oil trade volumes with China. voices among the Russian power elite are gradually emerging to alarm that Russia might become a "resource appendage" to its neighboring geopolitical rival. It should be noted. however. that increasing hydrocarbon exports from Russia's eastern regions would also be one of the ways in which the impact of China's explosive energy needs upon the global energy market can be reduced peacefully. U.S. and Japanese policymakers should consider this point when they discuss Russia's role as a big energy supplier in the context of energy security in the Asia-Pacific region.

Energy security in the Asia-Pacific region entails numerous uncertainties in both energy markets and geopolitical dynamism. The robust U.S.-Japan alliance must be anchored in solving energy challenges. but this requires clarification of Tokyo's post-Fukushima energy policies including an internationally responsible political decision on restarting Japan's nuclear power plants. Wisdom and long-term perspectives are needed to reduce the economic and security costs of ensuring regional stability in the years to come. It is high time for the United States and Japan to begin to design a roadmap for an international framework of energy security in which other regional key players such as China and Russia are effectively engaged.

8

Energy and Water Security in India

ENERGY POLICY OF INDIA

The energy policy of India is largely defined by the country's burgeoning energy deficit and increased focus on developing alternative sources of energy. particularlynuclear. solar and wind energy.

The energy consumption in India is the fourth biggest after China. USA and Russia. The total primary energy consumption from crude oil (29.45%). natural gas (7.7%). coal (54.5%). nuclear energy (1.26%). hydro electricity (5.0%). wind power. biomass electricity and solar power is 595 Mtoe in the year 2013. In the year 2013. India's net imports are nearly 144.3 million tons of crude oil. 16 Mtoe of LNG and 95 Mtoe coal totalling to 255.3 Mtoe of primary energy which is equal to 42.9% of total primary energy consumption.About 70% of India's electricity generation capacity is from fossil fuels. with coal accounting for 40% of India's total energy consumption followed by crude oil and natural gas at 28% and 6% respectively. India is largely dependent on fossil fuel imports to meet its energy demands — by 2030. India's dependence on energy imports is expected to exceed 53% of the country's total energy consumption. In 2009-10. the country imported 159.26 million tonnes of crude oil which amounts to 80% of its domestic crude oil consumption and 31% of the country's total imports are oil imports. The growth of electricity generation in India has been hindered by domestic coal shortages and as a consequence. India's coal imports for electricity generation increased by 18% in 2010.

Due to rapid economic expansion. India has one of the world's fastest growing energy markets and is expected to be the second-largest contributor to the increase in global energy demand by 2035. accounting for 18% of the rise in global energy consumption. Given India's growing energy demands and limited domestic fossil fuel reserves. the country has ambitious plans to expand its renewable and nuclear power industries. India has the world's fifth largest wind power market and plans to add about 20GW of solar power capacity by 2022. India also envisages to increase the contribution of nuclear power to overall electricity generation capacity from 4.2% to 9% within 25 years. The country has five nuclear reactors under construction (third highest in the world) and plans to construct 18 additional nuclear reactors (second highest in the world) by 2025.

POWER GENERATION CAPACITY IN INDIA

Total installed Power generation Capacity (June 2014)

Source	Total Capacity (MW)	Percentage
Coal	148.478.39	59.51
Hydroelectricity	40.730.09	16.33
Renewable energy source	31.692.14	12.70
Natural Gas	22.607.95	9.06
Nuclear	4780	1.92
Oil	1.199.75	0.48
Total	249.488.32	
Sector	Total Capacity (MW)	Percentage
State Sector	93.540.7	37.49
Central Sector	68.324.63	27.38
Private Sector	87.622.99	35.12
Total	249.488.32	

ENERGY CONSERVATION

Energy conservation has emerged as a major policy objective. and the Energy Conservation Act 2001. was passed by the Indian Parliament in September 2001. 35.5% of the population still live without access to electricity. This Act requires large energy consumers to adhere to energy consumption norms; new buildings to follow the Energy Conservation Building Code; and appliances to meet energy performance standards and to display energy consumption labels.

The Act also created the Bureau of Energy Efficiency to implement the provisions of the Act.

RURAL ELECTRIFICATION

1. The key development objectives of the power sector is supply of electricity to all areas including rural areas as mandated in section 6 of the Electricity Act. Both the central government and state governments would jointly endeavour to achieve this objective at the earliest. Consumers. particularly those who are ready to pay a tariff which reflects efficient costs have the right to get uninterrupted twenty four hours supply of quality power. About 56% of rural households have not yet been electrified even though many of these households are willing to pay for electricity. Determined efforts should be made to ensure that the task of rural electrification for securingelectricity access to all households and also ensuring that electricity reaches poor and marginal sections of the society at reasonable rates is completed within the next five years. India is using

Renewable Sources of Energy like Hydel Energy. Wind Energy. and Solar Energy to electrify villages.

2. Reliable rural electrification system will aim at creating the following:
    1. Rural Electrification Distribution Backbone (REDB) with at least one 33/11 kv (or 66/11 kv) substation in every Block and more if required as per load. networked and connected appropriately to the state transmission system
    2. Emanating from REDB would be supply feeders and one distribution transformer at least in every village settlement.
    3. Household Electrification from distribution transformer to connect every household on demand.
    4. Wherever above is not feasible (it is neither cost effective nor the optimal solution to provide grid connectivity) decentralised distributed generation facilities together with local distribution network would be provided so that every household gets access to electricity. This would be done either through conventional or non-conventional methods of electricity generation whichever is more suitable and economical. Non-conventional sources of energy could be utilised even where grid connectivity exists provided it is found to be cost effective.
    5. Development of infrastructure would also cater for requirement of agriculture and other economic activities including irrigation pump sets. small and medium industries. khadi and village industries. cold chain and social services like health and education.
3. Particular attention would be given in household electrification to dalit bastis. tribal areas and other weaker sections.
4. Rural Electrification Corporation of India. a Government of India enterprise will be the nodal agency at Central Government level to implement the programme for achieving the goal set by National Common Minimum Programme of giving access to electricity to all the households in next five years. Its role is being suitably enlarged to ensure timely implementation of rural electrification projects.
5. Targeted expansion in access to electricity for rural households in the desired timeframe can be achieved if the distribution licensees recover at least the cost of electricity and related O&M expenses from consumers. except for lifeline support to households below the poverty line who would need to be adequately subsidised. Subsidies should be properly targeted at the intended beneficiaries in the most efficient manner. Government recognises the need for providing necessary capital subsidy and soft long-term debt finances for investment in rural electrification as this would reduce the cost of supply in rural areas. Adequate funds would need to be made available

for the same through the Plan process. Also commensurate organisational support would need to be created for timely implementation. The Central Government would assist the State Governments in achieving this.

6. Necessary institutional framework would need to be put in place not only to ensure creation of rural electrification infrastructure but also to operate and maintain supply system for securing reliable power supply to consumers. Responsibility of operation and maintenance and cost recovery could be discharged by utilities through appropriate arrangements with Panchayats. local authorities. NGOs and other franchisees etc.
7. The gigantic task of rural electrification requires appropriate cooperation among various agencies of the State Governments. Central Government and participation of the community. Education and awareness programmes would be essential for creating demand for electricity and for achieving the objective of effective community participation.

The electricity industry was restructured by the Electricity Act 2003. which unbundled the vertically integrated electricity supply utilities in each state of India into a transmission utility. and a number of generating and distribution utilities. Electricity Regulatory Commissions in each state set tariffs for electricity sales.

The Act also enables open access on the transmission system. allowing any consumer (with a load of greater than 1 MW) to buy electricity from any generator. Significantly. it also requires each Regulatory Commission to specify the minimum percentage of electricity that each distribution utility must source from renewable energy sources. The introduction of Availability based tariff has brought about stability to a great extent in the Indian transmission grids. A report in 2005 suggested that there was room for improvement in terms of the efficiency of electricity generation in India. and suggested that two factors possibly responsible for the inefficiency were public ownership of utilities and low capacity utilisation.

RURAL ELECTRIFICATION STATUS

Rural Electrification rates	N.o of states and UTs	Remarks
100%	16	
99%	4	(electrification per cent. un-electrified villages): Maharashtra (99.9%. 36). Himachal Pradesh (99.92%. 2). Uttara Khand (99.3%. 107). West Bengal (99.99%. 2)
+95%	7	Assam (96.8%). Bihar (95.5%). Chhattisgarh (97.6%). Madhya Pradesh (97.1%). Jammu and Kashmir (98.2%). Uttar Pradesh (98.7%). Tripura (97.0%)
+90%	3	Nagaland (90.1%). Rajasthan (90.2%). Jharkhand (92.1%)

+80%	3	Orissa (81.6%). Mizoram (85.2%). Manipur (86.6%)
Under 80%	3	Andaman and Nicobar (77.8%). Meghalaya (79.8%). Arunachal Pradesh (68.7%)

OIL AND GAS

India imports nearly 75% of its 4.3 million barrels per day crude oil needs but exports nearly 1.25 million barrels per day of refined petroleum products which is nearly 30% of its total production of refined oil products. India has built surplus world class refining capacity using imported crude oil for exporting refined petroleum products. The net imports of crude oil is lesser by one fourth after accounting exports and imports of refined petroleum products.

During the financial year 2012-13. the production of crude oil is 37.86 million tons and 40.679 million standard cubic meters (nearly 26.85 million tons) natural gas. The net import of crude oil and petroleum products is 146.70 million tons worth of Rs 5611.40 billions. This includes 9.534 million tons of LNG imports worth of ₹ 282.15 billions. Internationally. LNG price (> 16 US$ per mmBtu) is fixed below crude oil price in terms of heating value. LNG is slowly gaining its role as direct use fuel in road and marine transport withoutregasification. In the year 2012-13. India consumed 15.744 million tons petrol and 69.179 million tons diesel which are mainly produced from imported crude oil at huge foreign exchange out go. Use of natural gas for heating. cooking and electricity generation is not economical as more and more locally produced natural gas will be converted in to LNG for use in transport sector to reduce crude oil imports. In addition to the conventional natural gas production. coal gasification. coal bed methane. coal mine methane and Biogas digesters/ Renewable natural gas will also become source of LNG forming decentralised base for production of LNG to cater to the widely distributed demand. There is possibility to convert most of the heavy duty vehicles (including diesel driven rail engines) in to LNG fuelled vehicles to reduce diesel consumption drastically with operational cost and least pollution benefits.

The state-owned Oil and Natural Gas Corporation (ONGC) acquired shares in oil fields in countries like Sudan. Syria. Iran. and Nigeria – investments that have led to diplomatic tensions with the United States. Because of political instability in the Middle East and increasing domestic demand for energy. India is keen on decreasing its dependency onOPEC to meet its oil demand. and increasing its energy security. Several Indian oil companies. primarily led by ONGC and Reliance Industries. have started a massive hunt for oil in several regions in India including Rajasthan. Krishna-Godavari and north-eastern Himalayas. The proposed Iran-Pakistan-India pipeline is a part of India's plan to meet its increasing energy demand.

COAL

India has the world's 4th largest coal reserves. In India. coal is the bulk of primary energy contributor with 54.5% share out of the total 595 Mtoe in the year 2013. India is the third top coal producer in 2013 with 7.6% production share of coal (including lignite) in the world. Top five hard and brown coal producing countries in 2013 (2012) are (million tons): China 3.680 (3.645). United States 893 (922). India 605 (607). Australia 478 (453) and Indonesia 421 (386). However. India ranks fifth in global coal production at 228 mtoe (5.9%) in the year 2013 when its inferior quality coal tonnage is converted in to tons of oil equivalent. Coal-fired power plants account for 59% of India's installed electricity capacity. After electricity production. coal is also used for cement production in substantial quantity. In the year 2013. India imported nearly 95 Mtoe of steam coal and coking coal which is 29% of total consumption to meet the demand in electricity. cement and steel production.

Gasification of coal or lignite produces syngas or coal gas or coke oven gas which is a mixture of hydrogen. carbon monoxide and carbon dioxide gases. Coal gas can be converted in to synthetic natural gas by using Fischer–Tropsch process at low pressure and high temperature. Coal gas can also be produced by underground coal gasification where the coal deposits are located deep in the ground or uneconomical to mine the coal. CNG and LNG are emerging as economical alternatives to diesel oil with the escalation in international crude oil prices. Synthetic natural gas production technologies have tremendous scope to meet the transport sector requirements fully using the locally available coal in India. Dankuni coal complex is producing syngas which is piped to the industrial users in Calcutta. Many coal based fertilizer plants which are shut down can also be retrofitted economically to produce synthetic natural gas as LNG and CNG fetch good price by substituting imports. Recently. Indian government fixed the natural gas price at producer end as 5.61 US$ per mmbtu on net calorific value (NCV) basis which is at par with the estimated SNG price from coal.

BIO-FUELS

Gasification of bio mass yields wood gas or syngas which can be converted in to substitute natural gas by Methanation. Nearly 750 million tons of non edible (by cattle) biomass is available annually in India which can be put to higher value addition use and substitute imported crude oil. coal. LNG. urea fertilizer. nuclear fuels. etc. It is estimated that renewable and carbon neutral biomass resources of India can replace present consumption of all fossil fuels when used productively.

Huge quantity of imported coal is being used in pulverised coal fired power stations. Raw biomass can not be used in the pulverised coal mills as they are difficult to grind in to fine powder due to caking property of raw biomass. However biomass can be used after Torrefaction in the pulverised coal mills for replacing imported coal. North west and southern regions can replace imported coal use with torrefied biomass where surplus agriculture/crop residual biomass is available. The former President of India. Dr. Abdul Kalam. is one of the strong advocaters of Jatropha cultivation for production of bio-diesel. In his recent speech. the Former President said that out of the 6.00.000 km^2 of waste land that is available in India over 3.00.000 km^2 is suitable for Jatropha cultivation.

Once this plant is grown. it has a useful lifespan of several decades. During its life Jatropha requires very little water when compared to other cash crops. A plan for supplying incentives to encourage the use of Jatropha has been coloured with green stripes.

HYDROGEN ENERGY

Hydrogen Energy programme started in India after joining the IPHE (International Partnership for Hydrogen Economy) in the year 2003. There are nineteen other countries including Australia. USA. UK. Japan. etc. This global partnership helps India to set up commercial use of Hydrogen gas as an energy source. This will implemented through Public Private Partnership.

NUCLEAR POWER

India boasts a quickly advancing and active nuclear power programme. It is expected to have 20 GW of nuclear capacity by 2020. though they currently stand as the 9th in the world in terms of nuclear capacity.

An achilles heel of the Indian nuclear power programme. however. is the fact that they are not signatories of the Nuclear Non-Proliferation Treaty. This has many times in their history prevented them from obtaining nuclear technology vital to expanding their use of nuclear industry. Another consequence of this is that much of their programme has been domestically developed. much like their nuclear weapons programme. United States-India Peaceful Atomic Energy Cooperation Act seems to be a way to get access to advanced nuclear technologies for India.

India has been using imported enriched uranium and are under International Atomic Energy Agency (IAEA) safeguards. but it has developed various aspects of the nuclear fuel cycle to support its reactors. Development of select technologies has been strongly affected by limited imports. Use of heavy water reactors has been particularly attractive for the nation because it allows Uranium to be burnt with little to no enrichment capabilities. India has also done a great amount of work in the development of a Thorium centred fuel cycle.

While Uranium deposits in the nation are extremely limited. there are much greater reserves of Thorium and it could provide hundreds of times the energy with the same mass of fuel. The fact that Thorium can theoretically be utilised in heavy water reactors has tied the development of the two. A prototype reactor that would burn Uranium-Plutonium fuel while irradiating a Thorium blanket is under construction at the Madras/Kalpakkam Atomic Power Station. Uranium used for the weapons programme has been separate from the power programme. using Uranium from scant indigenous reserves.

HYDRO ELECTRICITY

India is endowed with economically exploitable and viable hydro potential assessed to be about 84.000 MW at 60% capacity factor. In addition. 6.780 MW in terms of installed capacity from Small. Mini. and Micro Hydel schemes have been assessed. Also. 56 sites forpumped storage schemes with an aggregate installed capacity of 94.000 MW have been identified for catering to peak electricity demand and water pumping for irrigation needs. It is the most widely used form of renewable energy. The hydro-electric potential of India ranks 5th in terms of exploitable hydro-potential on global scenario.

The installed capacity of hydro power is 40.730 MW as of June. 2014. India ranks sixth in hydro electricity generation globally after China. Canada. Brazil. USA and Russia in the year 2013. During the year 2013. the total hydro electricity generation in India is 132 billion KWh which works out to 25.000 MW at 60% capacity factor.

Till now. hydroelectricity sector is dominated by the state and central government owned companies but this sector is going to grow faster with the participation of private sector for developing the hydro potential located in the Himalaya mountain ranges including north east of India. However the hydro power potential in central India forming part of Godavari. Mahanadi andNarmada river basins has not yet been developed on major scale due to potential opposition from the tribal population.

Pumped storage schemes are perfect centralised peaking power stations for the load management in the electricity grid. Pumped storage schemes would be in high demand for meeting peak load demand and storing the surplus electricity as India graduates from electricity deficit to electricity surplus.

They also produce secondary/seasonal power at no additional cost when rivers are flooding with excess water. Storing electricity by other alternative systems such as batteries. compressed air storage systems. etc. is more costlier than electricity production by standby generator. India has already established nearly 6800 MW pumped storage capacity which is part of its installed hydro power plants.

WIND POWER

India has the fifth largest installed wind power capacity in the world. As of 31 March 2014. the installed capacity of wind power was 21136.3 MW. Wind power accounts nearly 8.5% of India's total installed power generation capacity. and it generates 1.6% of the country's power. The Ministry of New and Renewable Energy (MNRE) of India has announced a revised estimation of the potential wind power resource from 49.130 MW assessed at 50m Hub heights to 102.788 MW assessed at 80m Hub height at 15% capacity factor.

SOLAR ENERGY

India's theoretical solar potential is about 5000 T kWh per year (*i.e.* ~ 600 TW). far more than its current total consumption. India's long-term solar potential could be unparalleled in the world because it has the ideal combination of both high solar insolation and a big potential consumer base density. With a major section of its citizens still surviving off-grid. India's grid system is considerably under-developed. Availability of cheap solar can bring electricity to people. and bypass the need of installation of expensive grid lines. Also a major factor influencing a region's energy intensity is the cost of energy consumed for temperature control. Since cooling load requirements are roughly in phase with the sun's intensity. cooling from intense solar radiation could make perfect energy-economic sense in the subcontinent. whenever the required technology becomes competitively cheaper.

Installation of solar power plants require nearly 2.4 hectares (6 acres) land per MW capacity which is similar to coal fired power plants when life cycle coal mining. consumptive water storage and ash disposal areas are also accounted and hydro power plants when submergence area of water reservoir is also accounted. 1.33 million MW capacity solar plants can be installed in India on its 1% land (32.000 square km). There are vast tracts of land suitable for solar power in all parts of India exceeding 8% of its total area which are unproductive barren and devoid of vegetation. Part of waste lands (32.000 square km) when installed with solar power plants can produce 2000 billion Kwh of electricity (two times the total generation in the year 2013-14) with land productivity/yield of 1.5 million Rs per acre (6 Rs/kwh price) which is at par with many industrial areas and many times more than the best productive irrigated agriculture lands. Moreover these solar power units are not dependent on supply of any raw material and are self productive. There is unlimited scope for solar electricity to replace all fossil fuel energy requirements (natural gas. coal. lignite and crude oil) if all the marginally productive lands are occupied by solar power plants in future. The solar power potential of India can meet perennially to cater per capita energy consumption at par with USA/Japan for the peak population in its demographic transition.

SYNERGY WITH IRRIGATION WATER PUMPING AND HYDRO POWER STATIONS

The major disadvantage of solar power (PV type) is that it can not produce electricity during the night time and cloudy day time also. In India. this disadvantage can be overcome by installing pumped-storage hydroelectricity stations. Ultimate electricity requirement for river water pumping (excluding ground water pumping) is 570 billion Kwh to pump one cubic meter of water for each square meter area by 125 m height on average for irrigating 140 million hectares of net sown area (42% of total land) for three crops in a year. This is achieved by utilising all the usable river waters by interlinking Indian rivers. These river water pumping stations would also be envisaged with pumped-storage hydroelectricity features to generate electricity during the night time. These pumped-storage stations would work at 200% water pumping requirement during the day time and generate electricity at 50% of total capacity during the night time. Also. all existing and future hydro power stations can be expanded with additional pumped-storage hydroelectricity units to cater night time electricity consumption. Most of the ground water pumping power can be met directly by solar power.

ELECTRICITY DRIVEN VEHICLES

The retail prices of petrol and diesel are high in India to make electricity driven vehicles more economical as more and more electricity is generated from solar energy in near future without appreciable environmental effects. During the year 2013. many IPPs offered to sell solar power below 6.50 Rs/Kwh to feed in to the low voltage (< 33 KV) grid. This price is below the affordable electricity retail tariff for the solar power to replace petrol and diesel use in transport sector.

The retail price of diesel is 53.00 Rs/litre in the year 2012-13. The affordable electricity retail price (860 Kcal/Kwh at 75% input electricity to shaft power efficiency) to replace diesel (lower heating value 8572 Kcal/litre at 40% fuel energy to crank shaft efficiency) is 9.97 Rs/Kwh. The retail price of petrol is 75.00 Rs/litre in the year 2012-13. The affordable electricity retail price (860 Kcal/Kwh at 75% input electricity to shaft power efficiency) to replace petrol (lower heating value 7693 Kcal/litre at 33% fuel energy to crank shaft efficiency) is 19.06 Rs/Kwh. In the year 2012-13. India consumed 15.744 million tons petrol and 69.179 million tons diesel which are mainly produced from imported crude oil at huge foreign exchange out go.

V2G is also feasible with electricity driven vehicles to contribute for catering to the peak load in the electricity grid. The electricity driven vehicles would become popular in future when its energy storage/ battery technology becomes more long lasting and maintenance free.

POLICY FRAMEWORK

In general. India's strategy is the encouragement of the development of renewable sources of energy by the use of incentives by the federal and state governments. Other examples of encouragement by incentive include the use of nuclear energy (India Nuclear Cooperation Promotion Act). promoting windfarms such as Muppandal. and solar energy (Ralegaon Siddhi).

A long-term energy policy perspective is provided by the Integrated Energy Policy Report 2006 which provides policy guidance on energy-sector growth. Increasing energy consumption associated primarily with activities in transport. mining. and manufacturing in India needs rethinking India's energy production.

ELECTRICITY TRADING WITH NEIGHBOURING COUNTRIES

The per capita electricity consumption is low compared to many countries despite cheaper electricity tariff in India. Despite low electricity per capita consumption in India. the country is going to achieve surplus electricity generation during the 12th plan (2012 to 2017) period provided its coal production and transport infrastructure is developed adequately. Surplus electricity can be exported to the neighbouring countries in return for natural gas supplies from Pakistan. Bangladesh and Myanmar.

Bangladesh. Myanmar and Pakistan are producing substantial natural gas and using for electricity generation purpose. Bangladesh. Myanmar and Pakistan produce 55 million cubic metres per day (mcmd). 9 mcmd and 118 mcmd out of which 20 mcmd. 1.4 mcmd and 34 mcmd are consumed for electricity generation respectively. Whereas the natural gas production in India is not even adequate to meet its non-electricity requirements.

Bangladesh. Myanmar and Pakistan have proven reserves of 184 billion cubic metres (bcm). 283 bcm and 754 bcm respectively. There is ample opportunity for mutually beneficial trading in energy resources with these countries. India can supply its surplus electricity to Pakistan and Bangladesh in return for the natural gas imports by gas pipe lines. Similarly India can develop on BOOT basis hydro power projects in Nepal. Myanmar and Bhutan. India can also enter into long term power purchase agreements withChina for developing the hydro power potential in Brahmaputra river basin of Tibet region. India can also supply its surplus electricity to Sri Lanka by undersea cable link. There is ample trading synergy for India with its neighbouring countries in securing its energy requirements.

ELECTRICITY AS SUBSTITUTE TO IMPORTED LPG AND KEROSENE

The net import of LPG is 6.093 million tons and the domestic consumption is 13.568 million tons with ₹ 41.546 crores subsidy to the domestic consumers in the year 2012-13. The LPG import content is nearly 40% of total consumption in India. The affordable electricity retail price (860 Kcal/Kwh at 90% heating efficiency) to replace LPG (lower heating value 11.000 Kcal/Kg at 75% heating efficiency) in domestic cooking is 6.47 Rs/Kwh when the retail price of LPG cylinder is Rs 1000 (without subsidy) with 14.2 kg LPG content. Replacing LPG consumption with electricity reduces its imports substantially. The domestic consumption of Kerosene is 7.349 million tons with ₹ 30.151 crores subsidy to the domestic consumers in the year 2012-13. The subsidised retail price of Kerosene is 13.69 Rs/litre whereas the export/import price is 48.00 Rs/litre. The affordable electricity retail price(860 Kcal/Kwh at 90% heating efficiency) to replace Kerosene (lower heating value 8240 Kcal/litre at 75% heating efficiency) in domestic cooking is 6.00 Rs/Kwh when Kerosene retail price is 48 Rs/litre (without subsidy).

During the year 2013-14. The plant load factor (PLF) of coal fired thermal power stations is only 65.43% whereas these stations can run above 85% PLF comfortably provided there is adequate electricity demand in the country. The additional electricity generation at 85% PLF is nearly 240 billion units which is adequate to replace all the LPG and Kerosene consumption in domestic sector. The incremental cost of generating additional electricity is only their coal fuel cost which is less than 3 Rs/Kwh. Enhancing the PLF of coal fired stations and encouraging domestic electricity consumers to substitute electricity in place of LPG and Kerosene in household cooking. would reduce the government subsidies and idle capacity of thermal power stations can be put to use economically. The domestic consumers who are willing to surrender the subsidised LPG/ Kerosene permits or eligible for subsidised LPG/ Kerosene permits. may be given free electricity connection and subsidised electricity tariff.

During the year 2014. IPPs are offering to sell solar power below 5.50 Rs/ Kwh to feed in to the high voltage grid. This price is below the affordable electricity tariff for the solar power to replace LPG and Kerosene use (after including subsidy on LPG and Kerosene) in domestic sector. Two wheelers and three wheelers consume 62% and 6% of petrol respectively in India. The saved LPG replaced by electricity in domestic sector can be used by two and three wheelers with operational cost and least pollution benefits. Solar electricity price is going to become the benchmark price for deciding the other fuel (Petroleum products. LNG. CNG. LPG. coal. lignite. biomass. etc.) prices based on their ultimate use and advantages.

WATER SCARCITY AND SECURITY IN INDIA

WATER SECURITY

India has an abundance of water within its borders. with 13 major and 46 minor basins. The Ganges-Brahmaputra is the largest basin. covering 34 per cent of India and contributing approximately 59 per cent of the country's water resources. The major sources of water in India are rainfall and glacial snowmelt contributing to river flows from the Himalayan region.

Water availability and rainfall in India are dependent on two monsoons. the south-west (summer) and north-east (winter). Most rainfall occurs between the months of June and September. with the average annual rainfall approximately 1170mm. There is. however. considerable variation between regions. In the desert region of Rajasthan annual rainfall is often lower than 150mm; while on the Khasi hills of the northeast more than 10.000mm of rain can fall in the space of a few months.

According to the FAO's Aquastat. 80 per cent of India has an annual rainfall of 750mm or more. A key challenge for India's water security. therefore. is not so much physical water scarcity. but mismanagement and limited storage facilities. India's per capita water storage capacity is 200m^3. well below the world average of 900m^3 per capita. Estimates suggest as much as 65 per cent of India's rainwater flows out to sea uncaptured; presenting a huge opportunity for improving the situation by capturing those water flows.

The current average per capita availability of water is 1.600m^3 per year. Population forecasts indicate that by 2050 this average will be reduced to approximately 1.000m^3 per year. According to the UN water scarcity occurs when per capita water availability is below 1.000m^3 per year. The overexploitation of groundwater. a lack of storage capacity and increasing levels of pollution in a business-as-usual scenario. will greatly increase the risk of severe water insecurity across India.

Rainwater harvesting and programmes to revitalise traditional tank systems present a considerable opportunity to capture and store water during periods of heavy rainfall. The reduced risk of floods. increased aquifer recharge and year round access to greater stores of fresh water are all desirable potential outcomes. Increasing traditional tank volumes and general water storage capacity in India could reduce the pressure on overexploited groundwater resources and provide safer water for human consumption. In Andhra Pradesh programmes to regenerate traditional water tanks have had a significant impact on water access for agriculture. particularly for those unable to afford extending the depth of their wells as groundwater continues to retreat.

INDIA'S GROUNDWATER

For those without access to canal or tank irrigation wells are a critical source of water for both agricultural and domestic use. Groundwater irrigation is responsible for approximately 60 per cent of total irrigation and two-thirds of total agricultural production. In recent decades water extraction via electric pumping has proliferated due. in no small part. to federal government policies providing free electricity to rural areas. Introduced in an attempt to close the gap on poverty. the policy has encouraged the over-extraction of groundwater. This has led to a significant depletion in the water table. with open wells and shallow tube wells drying up. As the levels in aquifers continue to fall. the technology and capital required to dig deeper wells limits access to wealthier farmers. According to the World Bank crop failure due to drought and an inability to repay loans for well upgrades. have led to an increase in suicide rates amongst smallholder farmers.

The World Bank estimates that 85 per cent of India's drinking water supply is dependent on groundwater. Further. current groundwater use is between 70 and 100 per cent of the estimated annual recharge in some basins. In the city of Gurgaon groundwater is all but exhausted. creating severe water insecurity for the population. There have been suggestions the city will cease to exist if water availability is not addressed. By 2020 the city could have as little as 48 litres of water available per person per day (the world standard is 130L). Some predictions suggest that approximately 60 per cent of India's aquifers will be in a critical condition by 2035.

The development and availability of groundwater resources varies considerably from state to state. In India's eastern states groundwater is underexploited. Elsewhere. however. including the states of Punjab. Haryana. Rajasthan. Gujrat and Tamil Nadu. the FAO has reported that groundwater exploitation significantly exceeds recharge rates. The variability of water supply highlights the need for flexible water management practices adaptable to suit the various basins or sub-basins in India. A one-size-fits-all approach to water management is unsustainable; it will fail to recognise unique ecological and water resource influences at the basin level.

IRRIGATION

Irrigation for food production has reportedly been used in India for over 5.000 years. In 2010. irrigation accounted for 91 per cent of the total 761km^3 of water withdrawn (FAO 2010). Irrigation use predominately occurs in India's northern states along the Indus and Ganges Rivers. The FAO estimates that 97 per cent of India's 63 million hectares of irrigated land was serviced by surface irrigation in 2004. Two per cent of land was sprinkler irrigated and the last one per cent used localised irrigation. While the use of sprinkler and localised irrigation methods are increasing. there is considerable room for increased efficiency. There is currently a 40 per cent efficiency gap with groundwater irrigation. As water demand grows across all industry sectors it is crucial that the agricultural sector adopts more productive water practices. reducing waste and limiting potential deficits.

WATER POLLUTION

Water pollution will create further challenges for India in both food and water security. India's water quality is amongst the worst in the world. The UN has ranked the country 120th out of 122 countries for water quality estimating that 70 per cent of the supply is contaminated. At present 21 per cent of the country's communicable diseases are transferred by unclean water. Pollution is worst in the middle and lower reaches of rivers; underdeveloped wastewater treatment facilities. industry effluent and agricultural Run-off are all significant contributors to this pollution. The Ganges River supports over

450 million people and suffers from significant pollution. The newly elected government has promised to clean the Ganges. but it will require significant investment and long-term management to increase wastewater treatment facilities and change human behaviour.

HYDRO-POTENTIAL AND DEVELOPMENT

India is ranked 5th in the world in hydro-potential with an estimated 150.000MW generation. At present the hydro-generating capacity of India is over 40.000 MW according to the Central Electric Authority. As many as 300 hydropower projects are planned or under construction in India's five Himalayan states despite considerable risks to downstream communities. waterways and critical infrastructure. The region is one of the most active earthquake zones in the world and is still forming. Landslides and flash flooding are common during the summer monsoon and casualties are high. News Security Beat reports that India's plan to develop five or six new dams on the most turbulent stretches of the Himalayan Rivers will result in a dam development approximately every 10km.

In June 2013. an unusually heavy monsoon season caused significant floods in the state of Uttarakhand. killing approximately 6000 people. wiping out villages. destroying highways and infrastructure; they also destroyed a number of hydropower sites. Some reports suggest the total death toll was as high as 30.000 people. Following this disaster two Supreme Court judges issued an order indefinitely halting the provision of permits for hydropower projects in Uttarakhand. In addition. a commission to study the safety and benefits of dam development in the state was formed. with its conclusions likely to be announced later this year.

Experts suggest that an increase in similar disaster events in the region is likely under climate change impacts and ongoing heavy monsoon periods. Increasing climate variability and the geographic instability of the region. bring into sharp focus the risks that dam construction brings for downstream communities and critical infrastructure.

CLIMATE CHANGE IMPACTS

India is likely to face increased rainfall variability and longer drought periods under a changing climate. Agricultural production and water availability are dependent on the monsoons; increased variability in precipitation. prolonged drought and more intense weather events will significantly affect the long-term situation. The incidence of natural disasters is also expected to increase in India. affecting agriculture. the health of the population and water security.

The occurrence of the El Niño effect is of particular concern this year; warmer waters in the Pacific Ocean are expected to negatively impact this year's summer monsoon. reducing water availability and potentially reducing yields.

In 2009 El Niño was the cause of the worst drought in India for decades. reducing rice production by 10 million tonnes. Seeding is occurring earlier in some areas this year and stockpiled grains (15 million tonnes more globally than 2009) are on hand to reduce the likelihood of price increases and stock deficits should production fall short.

GLOBAL WATER CRISIS

Water is life because plants and animals cannot live without water. Water is needed to ensure food security. feed livestock. maintain organic life. take up industrial production and to conserve the biodiversity and environment. Hence. there is no life without water. Earth is the only plant. so far known to have water and this makes it fit for human living. However. with reckless abuse and increasing demand. due to growing population and unsustainable lifestyle. many countries are facing severe water crisis. In the absence of suitable corrective measures. many developing countries including India. will have to face crisis of food and water security in the near future.

Although. India is not a water poor country. due to growing human population. severe neglect and over-exploitation of this resource. water is becoming a scarce commodity. India is more vulnerable because of the growing population and in-disciplined lifestyle. This calls for immediate attention by the stakeholders to make sustainable use of the available water resources.

70% of the earth surface is covered with water. which amounts to 1400 million cubic kilometres (m km^3). However. 97.5% of this water being sea water. it is salty. Fresh water availability is only 35 m km^3 and only 40% of this can be used by human beings. Out of the total fresh water. 68.7% is frozen in ice caps. 30% is stored underground and only 0.3% water is available on the surface of the earth. Out of the surface water. 87% is stored in lakes. 11% in swamp and 2% in rivers (Anon. 2006).

Long before. when the population was low and lifestyle was simple. water was available in plenty and was considered as a free resource. However. with growing demand for water and depletion of the available water. assured supply of good quality water is becoming a growing concern. As the water resources are not evenly distributed. across different continents. some countries have surplus water while many other countries are already facing scarcity of water. Skewed growth of population in different continents is further adding to this crisis. Among various continents. Asia has 36% of the available fresh water reserves. with over 60% of the world population where water is a scarce commodity. Compared to Asia. Africa is in a better situation. where 13% of the population has access to 11% of the fresh water reserves. Australia and Oceana have plenty of water with 1% population owning 5% of the fresh water reserves. followed by North and Central America. with 8% population and 15% water reserves and South America with 6% global population and 26% fresh water reserves. Since generations. the pattern of water use in different countries is mostly dependent on their culture. lifestyle and industrial development. as availability of water was not a serious concern. The per capita water use in different continents. The data highlights a close correlation between economic prosperity and water use.

Table. Per Capita Water Use

Continents	Per Capita Water Use (m^3/yr)
Africa	245
Asia	519
North and C. America	1861
South America	478
Europe	1280
USSR (Former)	713

Major consumption of water is for agriculture. industrial production and domestic purposes. apart from being used for fishery. hydro-power generation. transportation and maintaining biodiversity and ecological balance. The proportion of water used for agriculture and industries varies from country to country depending on the lifestyle. extent of industrial development and water use efficiency. Developing countries are using comparatively less water for agriculture and more for industrial and domestic purposes. while the developing countries in Asia and Africa use 80-90% of the water for agriculture and only 5-12% of the water for industrial use. This is reflecting on inefficient use of water in agriculture and poor investments in industrial development. With the urbanisation and industrial development. the usage of water is likely to increase in the coming years. While the per capita water use in India will increase from the current level of 99 litres per day to 167 litres per day in 2050. the per capita consumption in USA will reduce from 587 litres to 484 litres per day in 2050. By then. India will be the highest water demanding country. needing 2413 litres/day. while China and USA would require 2192 billion litres and 1167 billion litres respectively.

Table. Current Water Usage

Usage (per cent)	World	Europe	Africa	India
Agriculture	69	33	88	83
Industry	23	54	5	12
Domestic	8	13	7	5

Table. Future Water Usage

Year	Agriculture	Industry	Domestic	Total	Per Capita
India Billion Lit/Day			Lit/Day		
2000	1658	115	93	1866	88.9
2050	1745	441	227	2413	167.0
China					
2000	1024	392	105	1521\	82.7
2050	1151	822	219	2192	155.4
USA					

2000	542	605	166	1313	582.7
2050	315	665	187	1167	484.6

WATER RESOURCES IN INDIA

India is blessed with good rainfall well distributed over 5-6 months in the year. The average annual rainfall in the country is 1170 mm with a wide range between 100 mm in desert areas of Rajasthan to 10000 mm in Cherapunji. The total available sweet water in the country is 4000 billion m^3 per annum. Out of this. over 1047 billion m^3 water is lost due to evaporation. transpiration and Run-off. reducing the available water to 1953 billion m^3 and the usable water to 1123 billion m^3. It is disturbing to note that only 18% of the rainwater is used effectively while 48% enters the river and most of which reaches the ocean. Out of the total usable water. 728 billion m^3 is contributed from surface water and 395 billion m^3 is contributed by replenishable ground water. Against the above supply. the water consumed during the year 2006 in India was 829 billion m^3 which is likely to increase to 1093 billion m^3 in 2025 and 1047 billion m^3 in 2050. as estimated by the Government of India (2009). As the potential for increasing the volume of utilisation of water is hardly 5-10%. India is bound to face severe scarcity of water in the near future.

While water for consumption is most crucial. it is equally important to provide water for irrigation to increase the food production and livestock husbandry. to ensure food security for the increasing population. Growing population. as everyone is aware. is a serious concern as it will create further burden on the per capita water availability in the future. The per capita water availability in 1951 was 5177 m^3 per year when the total population was only 361 million. In 2001. as the population increased to 1027 million. the per capita water availability reduced drastically to 1820 m^3 per year. By 2025. the per capita water availability will further drop down to 1341 m^3 and to 1140 m^3 in 2050. Based on the average requirement of water for various purposes. the situation is considered as water stress condition when the per capita water availability ranges from 1000 to 1700 m^3 per year and it is considered water scarcity when the availability reduces to 1000 m^3 per year. As the water available within the country varies widely as a result of rainfall. ground water reserve and proximity to river basins. most of the Indian States will have reached the water stress condition by 2020 and water scarcity condition by 2025. This would further hamper the food security. as the scarcity of water will directly suppress agricultural production.

Table. Per capita water availability in India

Year	Population (Million)	Per capita water availability (m3/year)
1951	361	5177
1955	395	4732
1991	846	2209

2001	1027	1820
2025	1394	1341
2050	1640	1140

Source: Government of India. 2009.

Presently. inspite of good rainfall distribution. the country is unable to make good use of rain water. because of lack of awareness and poor infrastructure to construct dams and reservoirs. As a result. only about 35-40% of the cropping area receives irrigation to take 1-2 crops in a year. Out of the total cultivable area of 182 m ha. only 140 m ha are under net cultivation and of this. 62 m ha are under irrigation. There is further potential to increase the area under irrigation to 140 m ha. 76 m ha through surface water and 64 m ha by using ground water. So far. the irrigation potentials have already been created to cover 107 m ha. although they are not utilised effectively. It is estimated that effective area under irrigation by 2025 will be 76 million ha. although the Government of India is estimating to cover 104 million ha. Ground water is the major source of irrigation and this trend will continue. By 2025. 60 million ha will be irrigated by using ground water and by 2050. the area under ground water will increase to 70 million ha. In 2000. the area under canal irrigation was 17 million ha. which will increase to 27 million ha by 2050. There is further scope to increase the potential by 35 million ha. by inter-linking the rivers and harnessing 36 billion m^3 through artificial recharging of ground water (Government of India. 2009).

Apart from irrigation. many rivers in India are also used for generating hydro power. Out of the estimated hydro power potential of 1.50.000 mw. only 21% has been developed so far and additional 10% power generation projects are under implementation. Presently. the country is facing many difficulties in further tapping the potential. due to difficult sites. forest conservation concerns. inter State issues. poor implementation and lack of commitment. It is also possible to develop multipurpose projects for power generation and irrigation which can improve the project viability. while increasing water supply.

Pollution of water resources is another major concern which is affecting the water supply as well as human health conditions. Although. 5% of the total water is used for domestic use. 27% of the villages and 4 to 6% urban population in India do not have access to drinking water. Apart from inadequate supply of water. there is a serious concern about the quality of water. which is severely affecting the health. It is reported that over 70% of the water consumed by rural population in India does not meet the WHO standards. It has been reported that 80% of rural illnesses. 21% of transmissible diseases and 20% of deaths among children in the age group of 5 years. are directly linked to consumption of unsafe water.

The major causes of water pollution are discharge of untreated sewage and industrial effluent into rivers. excessive use of fertilisers in agriculture and contamination of ground water with salts and minerals present in the lower soil profiles. It is estimated that in New Delhi alone. 36 million tons of sewage is generated everyday of which only 50% is treated and the rest is let out into the Yamuna river directly. Same is the situation in other cities. Only 31% of the sewage water generated in 23 major cities is treated and the rest is polluting 18 major rivers in the country. Most of the rivers in the country are also contaminated by fluorides. nitrites and several toxic metals. Presently. over 66 million people are suffering from fluorosis after consuming water containing more than 1.5 ppm fluoride. Poor sanitation both in rural and urban areas. is another reason for pollution of drinking water sources. Only 30% rural population has access to toilet facilities while 65% urban people use toilcts. Nitrates and harmful germs from human excreta flow and percolate down to contaminate the water tanks and open wells.

There is no precise estimate available about the extent of ground water polluted by excessive application of chemical fertilisers and pesticides. The problem is not only that of application of higher doses of fertilisers but also excessive use of water for irrigation. As a result. most of the well water used for drinking in irrigated areas is polluted. Excessive irrigation has also been causing further damage to soil productivity. as the water reaching lower layers of soil and the salts present in this region are dissolved in water. Subsequently. these salts come to the top soil through capillary action. Such soils with high concentrations turn into sodic wastelands. unfit for agricultural production. Presently. over 9 million ha fertile irrigated lands have turned into sodic wastelands and the water in these areas will have high salt concentration. unfit for human consumption as well as for agricultural production. As the people living in these villages are helplessly consuming such hard water. the incidences of illnesses are high.

DRIVERS OF WATER USAGE

The demand for water in India is steeply increasing because of the following reasons (Amarasinghe. et al. 2007):

- The primary reason is population as India's population which was 1.3 billion in 2005 is expected to rise to 1.66 billion in 2050.
- There is also going to be a major impact on development in the form of urbanisation. In 2007. 28.2% of the Indian population was living in urban areas and the urban population is expected to increase to 55.2% by 2050.
- The per capita income of Indians will increase from $468 in 2007 to $6735 in 2050.
- Increased industrialisation will demand more water as its contribution to GDP will increase from 29.1% in 2000 to 40% by 2050. Thus. the demand for water will increase from 30 billion m^3 in 2000 to 161 billion m^3 in 2050.

- The agriculture development will be more on water intensive cash crops and there will be 80% increase in the demand for water by 2050.

It is therefore necessary to address the bottlenecks affecting the water supply in India.

CHALLENGES IN WATER SECTOR

The water supply in India is going to be a serious challenge due to various reasons. The most serious concern is the growing population which is likely to increase to 1.66 billion by 2050. With the increasing population. the annual food requirement in the country will exceed 250 million tons. The total demand for grains will increase to 375 million tons including grain for feeding livestock. With the growth in the National GDP. at 6.8% per annum. during the period from 2000 to 2025 and 6.0% per annum. during the years 2025 to 2050. the per capita income is bound to increase by 5.5% per annum.

This will increase the demand for food. While the per capita consumption of cereals will decrease by 9%. 47% and 60%. with respect to rice. coarse cereals and maize. the per capita consumption of sugar. fruits and vegetables will increase by 32%. 65% and 78% respectively. during the period from 2000 to 2050. This will create an additional demand for water. The requirement of water for livestock will rise from 2.3 billion m^3 in 2000 to 2.8 billion m^3 in 2025 and 3.2 billion m^3 in 2050.

Over-exploitation of ground water is another concern. Presently. there are over 20 m wells pumping water with free power supply. provided by the Government. This has been depleting ground water. while encouraging wastage of water in many states. As a result. the water table in the country is dipping every year by 0.4 m. In many coastal areas. there has been heavy intrusion of sea water. making fertile agricultural lands unfit for cultivation. By and large. the infrastructure development in the water sector has been extremely slow and investment has not been optimum. Furthermore. the utilisation of created water facilities has been sub-optimal because of poor catchment area development resulting in heavy soil erosion and siltation and inefficient use of water because of distribution of water in open canals. flood irrigation and charging for water on the basis of area irrigated instead of quantity of water supplied.

It has been estimated that over 70% of the irrigation water is wasted by depriving irrigation to other dry areas. Farmers in India have been traditionally practicing flow irrigation which is resulting in huge wastage of water. while causing severe soil erosion. leaching of fertilisers. increasing the infestation of pests. diseases and weeds and suppressing the crop yields. Nevertheless. farmers as well as policy makers are not serious about the discontinuation of this unscientific practice. Immediate attention is needed to shift from flood irrigation to micro irrigation and to increase the water use efficiency. which can ease the water scarcity to a great extent. With regard to the water use efficiency in agriculture. India is far below most of the developed countries. This is not only due to flood irrigation and over-watering. but also because of improper water conservation measures and crop varieties which demand more water. However. farmers are not motivated to conserve water as there is no incentive for them to do so. Global warming is posing further challenge. as the water requirement for crops will increase due to higher evapo-transpiration. The rivers emerging from the Himalayas. are prone to heavy floods and subsequently face severe water shortage. thereby suppressing agricultural production.

Over 60-80 million ha of denuded forestlands and wastelands across the country are unable to retain rainwater which in turn would have ensured recharging of ground water and conservation of biodiversity. As a result. the rivers emerging from these mountains are unable to sustain the flow of water throughout the year. Heavy soil erosion has not only been causing floods but also forcing the rivers to change their courses. Such rivers will not be able to support agricultural production in the future.

Table. Water Use Efficiency in Agriculture

Water foot print (Lit/kg)		
Crops	India	World
Wheat	1654	1334
Rice	2850	2291
Sugarcane	159	175
Cotton	18694	8242
Milk	1369	990
Eggs	7531	3340
Chicken	7736	3918

It is therefore necessary to address these burning issues which are affecting the water availability. although India has adequate water resources to meet the growing needs.

THE NATIONAL WATER POLICY (NWP)

India had revised the NWP in 2002 with the following salient features (Government of India. 2009):

- Establishment of National and State level data banks to monitor the demand and supply;
- Facilitation for transformation of available water resources into utilisable water;
- Non-conventional methods for efficient water use;
- Supply of water from water surplus areas to water shortage areas;
- Judicious allocation of water for different uses and pricing of water to ensure sustainable development;

- Regulation on ground water exploitation and close monitoring of water table using modern scientific techniques;
- Sustainability of existing water bodies. involving all the stakeholders and local communities;
- PPP for water resource development and distribution;
- Master plan for flood control. by linking different rivers and promoting soil conservation measures;
- Development of drought prone areas through watershed development. afforestation and sustainable farming practices;
- Interstate water sharing policy and timely addressing of disputes.

Over the last 10 years. the situation has changed drastically and the progress in the water sector has not been keeping up with the expected target. It was therefore felt necessary to bring further changes in the policy. particularly in the following areas:

CHANGES PROPOSED IN THE NATIONAL WATER POLICY:

Agriculture Sector

- Improvement in water usage efficiency;
- Adoption of rainwater harvesting and watershed management techniques;
- Reduction of subsidies on power supply particularly for pumping water;
- Prevention of ground water exploitation by introducing differential pricing. rewards and punishments;
- Implementation of National River Link project which aims to connect 30 rivers and canals to generates 175 trillion litres of water.

Industrial Sector

- Encourage recycling and treatment of industrial wastewater through regulations and subsidies;
- Encourage introduction of new technologies which consume less water.

Domestic Sector

- Introduction of a policy for mandatory rainwater harvesting in cities;
- Propagation of efficient water usage;
- Creation of awareness about water conservation among common public.

AUGMENTATION OF WATER RESOURCES

While the consumption of water in India will increase by over 50%. the supply will increase only by 5-10% during the next 12-15 years. This will lead to water scarcity situation and most of the people. particularly those who are dependent on agriculture and living in poverty will suffer the most. Water scarcity will affect the food production. biodiversity and the environment. Environmental degradation will accelerate global warming. which in turn will accelerate water crisis. This is a vicious cycle. The only solution is to tap all the possible water resources and make them available for sustainable use. while improving the water use efficiency. This can be done by addressing various concerns and initiating suitable actions for development of new water resources. augmentation of available resources. prevention of water pollution and improving the efficiency of water use in all the sectors. For creating additional water resources. the following activities should be initiated:

Increasing Water Storage Capacity

Activities such as farm ponds. percolation tanks. water reservoirs and construction of small and medium size dams and rivers can retain more surface water. while increasing the ground water recharge. Series of contour bounds particularly in undulating areas will facilitate percolation of water in the soil and improve the ground water table. while reducing soil erosion. Gully plugging. construction of series of small dams on rivulets will help in storing water in reservoirs.

In the absence of harnessing rainwater in the forests and denuded hilly terrains. inadequate soil and water conservation measures are leading to severe soil erosion. silting of rivers beds and reservoirs and frequent flooding across the country. Presently. over 40 million ha are prone to floods in the country. Invariably. 8-10 million ha are affected by floods over year. During the year 2007-08. floods in India have caused 3689 deaths. loss of 1.14 lakh livestock and damaged 3.5 million houses. causing huge losses to the people. society and the Government. One of the major reasons for soil erosion and silting of rivers is severe deforestation. As a result of soil erosion. many of the rivers have been changing their courses almost every year damaging fertile agricultural lands. Brahmaputra is a good example where the width of the river during summer is 3-4 km which increases to 10-12 km during the rainy season. This highlights the extent of flooding of the river and harassment to the people living along the river. Due to poor management of this river. only 22 billion m^3 of water is utilisable while over 607 billion m^3 water is wasted. Similar situation is prevailing with respect to other rivers such as Ganga. Godavari. Mahanadi. Narmada. etc.

Interlinking of rivers will help in preventing floods while improving water distribution in the country. Control of water flow and floods will prevent soil erosion. Presently. billions of tons of fertile soils along with precious nutrients are washed out of our fertile agricultural lands and forests. In fact. the amount of nutrients lost due to soil erosion is almost equivalent to the chemical fertilisers produced in the country. This highlights the impact of soil erosion control on the food production. Reforestation of degraded forests and development of wastelands through afforestation will help in soil and water conservation (IDSA. 2010).

Judicious distribution of water for different uses can help in preventing water scarcity. The water distribution for different purposes is influenced by powerful lobbies and vested interests. Many sectors receive more water than what is needed at the cost of others. Even within the same sector. like irrigation for agriculture. the locations for infrastructure development are often influenced by those who are politically powerful. with vested interests. while depriving others in needy regions. To overcome such inefficiency and wastage of resources. a suitable investment mechanism should be developed based on the needs and return on investments. A transparent programme implementation mechanism and regular monitoring for quality can improve the speed and quality of the projects.

Efficient Irrigation Practices

Efficiency in irrigation is most essential. if the country wants to face the challenge of water crisis. As most of the crops are watered through flood irrigation. over 70% of the water used for irrigation is wasted. Furthermore. as the water supplied is not measured. farmers have a tendency to flood the field with excessive water without any additional cost. Such a practice has been creating a negative impact by way of increased cost of leached nutrients. pollution of ground water. increase in soil salinity and increase of pests and diseases. It is high time that India compels the farmers to adopt micro-irrigation systems. which will not only reduce the water requirement but also bring down the cost of production. while increasing the area under irrigation. The Government of India should consider enforcing a ban on flood irrigation in the country. Simultaneously. metered supply of irrigation water. recovery of water cost. promotion of micro-irrigation systems and involvement of water users' group for water distribution would significantly help in improving the water use efficiency and reducing the cost of agricultural production.

Watershed Development

Development of watersheds is an important programme to make best use of the rainwater for agricultural production while improving soil conservation and biodiversity. Fortunately. the Government of India has given top priority for watershed development to provide assured water supply of agriculture in rain fed areas. Under the watershed development programme. the catchment area of a basin is considered as a unit and efforts are made to harness rainwater by treating the land from the ridge to the valley. It is estimated that over 63%

of the cultivated lands in the rain fed areas need to be brought under watershed development to conserve soil and water. which in turn would improve the crop yields as well as ground water table. Watershed development programme introduced almost about three decades ago. had covered over 51 million ha by the end of the Tenth Five Year Plan. Additional 36 million ha were being developed under the watershed development programme during the Eleventh Five Year Plan. However. a large number of watersheds are still subjected to heavy soil erosion. due to poor quality soil conservation work undertaken in the past and lack of convergence with other agricultural development activities. Therefore. there is scope for developing over 125 m ha under the watershed. Out of these areas. 85 m ha are rain fed agricultural lands and 40 m ha are wastelands. The watershed development programme is presently focussing on contour bunding and gully plugging. as the budget provided by the Government of India is just adequate to carry out these activities. Additional funds are required to support the farmers to adopt improved agricultural practices.

Control of Water Pollution

Excessive use of water for agriculture. industries and domestic uses is leading to water pollution. because such excess water is transformed into saline water. sewage or effluent. Thus. rewards and punishments should be introduced for persuading people to make optimum use of the precious water. Discharge of sewage and affluent into water bodies and rivers must be banned and recycling of waste water must be pursued and enforced. This will help in keeping the water sources clean and reducing the future demand for water. Treated sewage and effluent can be used for agriculture and industrial production.

Desalination of Sea Water

Over 70% of the global water resources being saline. economic desalination of sea water is an excellent option to meet the future shortage of sweet water particularly to meet the human consumption. Presently. desalination of sea water is expensive and non-popular. However. with solar power. desalination can be a viable alternative to meet the water needs in coastal areas.

Research and Development

There is a need for investing in research related to ground water monitoring. weather forecasting. breeding water efficient and drought resistant crops and varieties which can cope up with the changing climatic conditions. arising due to global warming.

PRIORITY AREAS FOR ACTION

As the time is running out. it is necessary to act on priority in the following areas:

- The irrigation projects should be well planned and different activities such as relief and rehabilitation of project affected population. micro level land use planning and capacity building of farmers. should be initiated simultaneously;
- Afforestation on degraded forests. wastelands as well as river banks should be promoted on priority to facilitate soil conservation. recharging of ground water and preventing flooding of rivers and siltation of water reservoirs.
- Increasing irrigation efficiency from the current level of 35% to 50% in surface irrigation systems and 65% to 75% in ground water irrigation systems. can be easily achieved if careful planning and distribution of water through water meters. judicious pricing of water to recover the investment and investment in micro irrigation facilities are carried out. while improving the capabilities of the farmers. Farmers should be enlightened about the importance of water conservation and judicious uses. which are needed for achieving sustainability.
- Development of wastelands which are spread over 80 million ha and accelerating soil erosion and run off surface water. as improving the productivity of these barren lands. will help in conserving water while contributing to food production and biodiversity enrichment.
- Development of local capabilities by grooming new generation water management technicians and managers to implement various innovative projects with greater efficiency. There is also a need for promoting multidisciplinary researchers to study various aspects of water resources. conservation. efficient storage. reduction of losses and sustainable utilisation.
- Public Private Partnership. including civil society organisations and stakeholders in water resources development and conservation. So far. the State Governments were responsible for developing necessary infrastructure and managing water distribution. which lacked people's cooperation. It is also necessary to organise small farms to enable them to get their due share of water. as the poor are excluded from most of the development projects due to their ignorance and inability to make necessary investments. Civil Society Organisations as well as Farmers' Organisations can help small farmers in adopting modern technologies and for establishing forward and backward linkage. required for increasing their income.
- Convergence of various developmental programmes can help in increasing the outputs. There are many development programmes implemented by the Ministries of Water Resources Development. Agriculture and Rural Development. which are coordinated by a single

agency at the grassroot level to ensure effective utilisation of the resources while creating better impact.

- Review of the National Water Policy to enforce a ban on flood irrigation. discontinuation of free power supply to pump underground water and prevention of untreated sewage and effluent into rivers should be taken up immediately. as these practices do more harm than help the community. Realistic pricing of water based on the investment. followed by awareness and education for farmers. introducing reward and punishments for maintaining discipline in water management. would help in ensuring sustainable development.

REPLICATION OF SUCCESS STORIES

Impact of Watershed Development

Several watershed development projects have demonstrated positive impacts such as enhanced soil productivity through soil and water conservation. increase in the ground water table. improvement in biodiversity and micro-climate and improved eco-system. Integration of watershed development with other related agriculture development activities such as efficient water use. organic farming and improved agriculture practices have enhanced agricultural production without depleting soil fertility and water resources. In several projects implemented by BAIF Development Research Foundation. farmers could increase their cropping intensity by 31-63% while enhancing the crop yields by 40-80%. As a result of soil conservation and percolation of rainwater. there has been a significant increase in the ground water table by 1.5 m to 4 m. within a short span of 2-3 years. which eased the problem of clean potable water supply for local villagers. Improvement in soil moisture facilitated vigorous growth of shrubs and grasses. which improved the green cover. while easing the fodder supply. With a well planned watershed development programme and required investment both by the development agencies and the farmers. it should be possible to bring all the wastelands and degraded lands under agricultural production and enhance the income by several folds within a period of 5-6 years.

Establishment of farm ponds of 8 x 8 m or 10 x 10 m size with 2-3 m depth. is a unique concept for decentralised storage of surface run off water. Farm ponds are very effective for reducing the soil erosion and recharging of ground water. In areas where the rainfall is over 750-800 mm per year. these farm ponds fill up and over flow at least 4-5 times during the rainy season and retain water for over 4-8 months. which can be used for cultivation of high value crops as well as establishing fruit orchards.

Networking of farm ponds. 1-2 ponds per ha. has been successful in increasing the water table. thereby reviving the dried bore wells in the programmes implemented by BAIF in Karnataka. Andhra Pradesh and Maharashtra. There are several locations where with efficient network of farm ponds. the rivulets which were retaining water for 4-5 months in the year are now able to retain water throughout the year. Introduction of efficient irrigation systems has significantly enhanced agricultural production. There are many micro irrigation techniques adopted by small farmers without even depending on the power supply. There are several success stories across the country where farmers and field practitioners have innovated different methods for efficient and low cost water harvesting. Such sustainable practices should be recognised and widely replicated across the country.

Tree-based Farming System

Tree-based farming has great promise in the areas covered under the watersheds as well as for developing denuded and wastelands. This is because trees demand less water and withstand water stress to a great extent. While taking up this programme. there are many options to select useful tree species particularly on private lands. based on the soil productivity. moisture availability and local needs.

While shallow drylands con be covered with shrubs and grasses. deep. fertile lands can be used for growing high value fruit crops. BAIF has demonstrated the feasibility of cultivating various dryland horticultural crops instead of timber and fuelwood species where farmers are able to generate income every year without destroying the trees. This programme of agri-horti-forestry has become very successful in rehabilitation of over two lakh tribal families across the country.

Under the tree-based farming programme. the critical factor which needs to be considered. is to provide livelihood to the participant families during the gestation period of 4-5 years. till the fruit trees start bearing. To address this concern.

BAIF has promoted food crops in the inter space between fruit plants. Efficient use of available water resources and effective soil water conservation could enhance the crop yields. while ensuring food security. The orchard owners are able to come out of poverty. when the fruit trees start yielding. Trees in the field and farm bunds serve as wind breaks to reduce evaporation loss and to improve the soil fertility. Agroforestry is a viable option to mitigate global warming and to face the crisis of water scarcity.

Development of Wastelands

Reclamation of sodic lands is another important programme which needs to be pursued as over 9 m ha of good fertile lands are lying idle because of high salt content. Efficient reclamation of these lands and recognition of the water use will bring this area under multiple cropping while making surplus water available to bring additional 8-10 ha under irrigation. Reclamation of sodic lands for agriculture can enhance food production by 50 million tons per year. India also has 2 million ha of ravine lands particularly in the states of Uttar Pradesh. Madhya Pradesh and Rajasthan. where excessive soil erosion is damaging good agricultural lands. while flooding the rivers. Public Private Partnership for development of ravine lands owned by the farmers and community. can prevent soil erosion and formation of ravine lands. while helping the farmers to grow 1-2 crops every year. BAIF has demonstrated the process of soil and water conservation. resulting in increased ground water table. which could enable small farmers to drill tube wells at cost and water sharing basis to grow multiple crops.

Livestock Development

Animal Husbandry is another important sector requiring water for feeding 500 million heads of livestock and to produce fodder for them. However. as over 75% of these animals are of inferior quality. farmers let them loose in the field for free grazing. This has been causing denudation of vegetation and heavy soil erosion.

BAIF has demonstrated a new approach of improving the productivity of these animals which will motivate the farmers to take up stall feeding for reducing the herd size. Such a practice will reduce the pressure on natural resources. particularly water stress. while enhancing their income. Dairy husbandry is one of the most reliable sources of livelihood for small farmers. as the families maintaining 2-3 good quality cows or buffaloes are able to come out of poverty.

There are many voluntary organisations as well as National and International research and development organisations. who have implemented several successful projects with active participation of farmers. These success stories need to be widely publicised and replicated across the country with the financial support from the on-going Government schemes. Showcasing of successful holistic water-resource management projects can motivate the water users. particularly the farmers to adopt new practices and change their lifestyle to make efficient use of precious water.

CONCLUSION

India is not a water deficit country. but due to severe neglect and lack of monitoring of water resources development projects. several regions in the country experience water stress from time to time. Further neglect in this sector will lead to water scarcity during the next 1-2 decades.

It is therefore necessary to prevent this crisis by making best use of the available technologies and resources to conserve the existing water resources. convert them into utilisable form and make efficient use of them for agriculture.

industrial production and human consumption. Imposing regulatory measures to prevent the misuse of water and introducing rewards and punishment to encourage judicious use of water. will be helpful to conserve water. Finally. awareness and orientation of all the water users to change their lifestyle to conserve water. can help the country to tide over the water crisis in the future. The challenge is manageable provided we have favourable policies and mechanisms to persuade our people to change their lifestyle.

Bibliography

Abhijit Chakrabarti and Sunita Halder: *Power System Analysis : Operation And Control*, PHI Learning, Delhi, 2001.

Akhtar Kalamm and D P Kothari: *Power System Protection And Communications*, New Age International, Delhi, 2010.

B. R. Gupta: *Power System Analysis And Design*, S. Chand Publisher, Delhi, 2007.

Bala Bhaskar: *Energy Security and Economic Development in India: A Holistic Approach*, Teri Book Store, Delhi, 2012.

Bhupendra Kumar Singh: *India's Energy Security : The Changing Dynamics*, Pentagon Energy Press an Imprint of Pentagon Press, 2010.

Digumarti Bhaskara Rao and Digumarthi Harshitha: *Energy Security*, Discovery Publishing House, Delhi, 2001.

Er. Mrinal Kant Singh: *Power System : Operations and Control*, Globus Press, Delhi, 2012.

Gopi Nath Saha: *Water Security and Management of Water Resources*, National Atlas and Thematic, Delhi, 2004.

Hooman Peimani: *The Challenge of Energy Security in the 21st Century : Trends of Significance*, Bookwell Publications, Delhi, 2013.

Javed Ahmad Khan: *India's Energy Security and the Arabian Gulf : Oil and Gas Market in Decontrolled Regimes*, Arise Publication, Delhi, 2005.

K.R. Padiyar: *Power System Dynamics : Stability and Control*, BS Publication, Delhi, 2008.

KUNDUR: *Power System Stability and Control*, Tata McGraw-Hill, Delhi, 2006.

MILLER: *Power System Operation, Third Edition*, Tata McGraw-Hill, Delhi, 2009.

Natarajan: *Power System Capacitors*, Taylor and Francis, New York, 2010.

P S R Murty: *Power System Analysis*, BS Publication, Delhi, 2007.

RAO: *Power System Protection: Static Relays, Second Edition*, Tata McGraw-Hill, Delhi, 2004.

Rashmi Doraiswarmy: *Energy Security : India Central Asia and the Neighbourhood*, Manak Publications, Delhi, 2013.

Razia Parvez: *Energy Security and Conservation in India*, New Century Publications, Delhi, 2013.

Ruchita Beri and Uttam Kumar Sinha: *Africa and Energy Security : Global Issues, Local Responses*, Academic Foundation, Delhi, 2009.

S.D. Muni: *India's Energy Security : Prospects for Cooperation with Extended Neighbourhood*, Rupa Publication, Delhi, 2002.

S.N. Malakar: *India's Energy Security and the Gulf*, Academic Excellence, Delhi, 2006.

Surya Narain Yadav: *Energy Security and Environmental Sustainability*, Global Vision Publication, Delhi, 2010.

Surya Narain Yadav: *India, China and Africa : New Partnership in Energy Security*, Jnanada Prakashan, Delhi, 2008.

T.K. Nagsarkar and M.S. Sukhija: *Power System Analysis*, Oxford University Press, Delhi, 2007.

V. Guruprasada Rau: *Power System Dynamics*, New Age Publication, Delhi, 2010.

V. Ratna Reddy: *Water Security and Management : Ecological Imperatives and Policy Options*, Academic Foundation, Delhi, 2009.

Virendra Gupta and Chong Guan Kwa: *Energy Security : Asia Pacific Perspectives*, Manas Publication, Delhi, 2010.

Index

J

L

M

O

P

R

S

T

V

W

X